SHAKING HANDS ON THE FRINGE

Also published by
University of Western Australia Press
for the Charles and Joy Staples
South West Region Publications Fund:

A Tribute to the Group Settlers
Philip E. M. Blond

For Their Own Good
Anna Haebich

Dearest Isabella
Prue Joske

Portraits of the South West
B. K. de Garis

*A Guide to Sources for the History of South
Western Australia*
compiled by Ronald Richards

Jardee: The Mill That Cheated Time
Doreen Owens

Blacklegs: The Scottish Colliery Strike of 1911
Bill Latter

Barefoot in the Creek
L. C. Burton

*Ritualist on a Tricycle: Frederick Goldsmith,
Church, Nationalism and Society in Western
Australia*
Colin Holden

Western Australia as it is Today, 1906
Leopoldo Zunini,
Royal Consul of Italy
edited and translated by
Richard Bosworth and Margot Melia

The South West from Dawn till Dusk
Rob Olver

Contested Country
Patricia Crawford and Ian Crawford

*Orchard and Mill: The Story of Bill Lee,
South-West Pioneer*
Lyn Adams

*Richard Spencer: Napoleonic War Naval
Hero and Australian Pioneer*
Gwen Chessell

A Story to Tell
Laurel Nannup

*Alexander Collie: Colonial Surgeon,
Naturalist and Explorer*
Gwen Chessell

*The Zealous Conservator: A Life of
Charles Lane Poole*
John Dargavel

 The Charles and Joy Staples South West Region Publications Fund was
established in 1984 on the basis of a generous donation to The University
of Western Australia by Charles and Joy Staples.

The purpose of the Fund was to make the results of research on the South West
region of Western Australia widely available so as to assist the people of the South West
region and those in government and private organisations concerned with South West
projects to appreciate the needs and possibilities of the region in the widest possible
historical perspective.

The Fund is administered by a committee whose aims are to make possible the
publication (either by full or part funding), by University of Western Australia Press, of
research in any discipline relevant to the South West region.

TIFFANY
SHELLAM

SHAKING

Negotiating the Aboriginal World at King George's Sound

HANDS
ON THE
FRINGE

University of Western Australia Press

The Charles and Joy Staples
South West Region Publications Fund

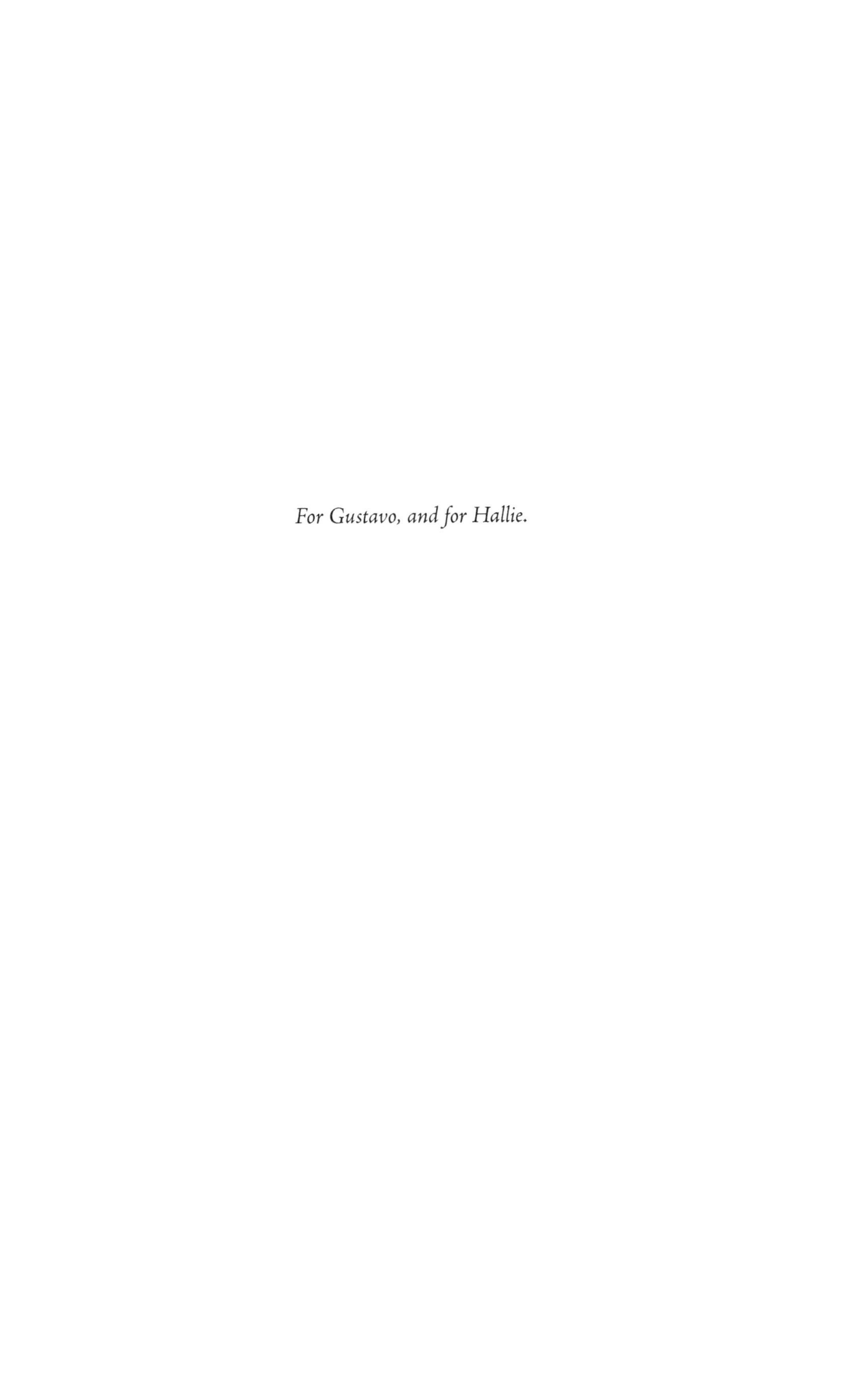

For Gustavo, and for Hallie.

First published in 2009 by
University of Western Australia Press
Crawley, Western Australia, 6009
www.uwapress.uwa.edu.au

National Library of Australia
Cataloguing-in-Publication entry:

Shellam, Tiffany Sophie Bryden, 1979–

Shaking hands on the fringe : negotiating the Aboriginal world at King George's Sound / Tiffany Shellam.

ISBN 978 1921401 26 8 (pbk.)

Includes index.
Bibliography.

First contact of aboriginal peoples with Westerners–Western Australia–King George Sound.
Aboriginal Australians, Treatment of–Western Australia–King George Sound.
Aboriginal Australians–Western Australia–King George Sound–Social conditions.
King George Sound (W.A.)–Colonies–Race relations.
King George Sound (W.A.)–History.

994.120049915

Typeset in 11/14.5 pt Adobe Jenson Pro by Midland Typesetters, Australia
Printed by Lightning Source

Contents

Contents

This book began its life in a different form, as a PhD thesis which I completed in the History Program in the Research School of Social Sciences at the Australian National University. Tom Griffiths, a dedicated and inspiring teacher and storyteller, encouraged me to think of this project as a creative piece of writing as well as a scholarly history from the beginning. Tom's gentle guidance gave me the confidence to narrate this history with a close attention to episodes of everyday life. Through the support of Bronwen Douglas I was constantly challenged to be more critical of the way I think about history and the past; about the way in which historians need to interrogate their historical sources in order to piece together the fragmentary traces they hold and conceal. Ann McGrath's interest in Indigenous history-making has influenced the way in which I have told the stories in this book. It was exciting and intellectually rewarding to be guided by such rigorous historians who think about the method of history as much as the topic.

I thank Geoffrey Bolton for his wisdom and generous feedback on a draft at a crucial stage. Paul Turnbull's supportive suggestions were likewise generous, useful and welcome. Jay Gitlin supported me through my research and writing, and suggested strong North American comparisons for my work. The Australian Centre for Indigenous History offered strong and exciting networks and I would like to acknowledge Frances Peters-Little and Gordon Briscoe for their encouragement and ideas. From the History Program at the Australian National University I thank Nicolas Brown, Desley Deacon, Barry Higman, Pat Jalland, Tim Rowse, Karen Smith and Kay Nante for their personal care and guidance. I have also been inspired from valuable discussions with Chris Ballard, John Cashmere, Greg Dening, Bill Gammage,

Sylvia Hallam, John Hirst, Stephen Hopper, Ken Inglis, Donna Merwick, Stephen Muecke, John Mulvaney, Barry Smith, Tom Stannage, Margaret Stevens and Carolyn Strange.

I received ongoing strength from my PhD colleagues in the History Program. Discussions in workshops, seminars and at the pub have been exciting, fun and passionate, and I really enjoyed their company along the way: Kylie Carmen-Brown, Abby Cooper, Kirsty Douglas, Janet Doust, Georgina Fitzpatrick, Karen Fox, Christine Hansen, Rani Kerin, Darryl Lewis, Ingereth MacFarlane, Joy McCann, Lawrence Nievojt, Chris O'Brian, Emily O'Gorman, Frances Steel, Barbara Thompson, John Thompson, Jo Weinman and Susan-Mary Withycombe. Other friends who have inspired and encouraged me include: Clare Carlin, Nick Coghlan, Charles Douglas, Allie Douglas, Khrob Edmonds, Mandy Edmonds, Sally Edmonds, Donald Edmonds, Jo Fitzhardinge, Chris Francis, Georgie Hardy, Declan Kelly, Maurice Le Guen, Brooke Potter, Rosa Salzberg and Terri-ann White. Kim Scott gave much needed advice from a south-west Indigenous perspective. He shared his Nyungar networks with me which paved the way for essential conversations.

Thanks also go to Beverly McGuinness, Ian Conochie and Gordon Harris from the Denmark Historical Society; Kerry Stokes, Erica Persak and staff at Australian Capital Equity for their kindness in allowing me to reproduce the images in the Kerry Stokes Collection; and staff at the following institutions who willingly guided me through their archives: The Albany Historical Society, Battye Library, State Records Office of Western Australia, National Library of Australia, Mitchell Library, Archives Office of New South Wales, Art Gallery of Western Australia, National Archives in Kew, UK, George Miles at the Beinecke Library, Yale University and The Howard Lamar Centre for the Study of Frontiers and Borders at Yale University.

I have felt very confident in the abilities of my editor, Olivier Breton, and other hard working staff at UWA Press, in particular Kate McLeod, Emma Smith, Jade Knight and the wonderful Terri-ann White. They have helped the book realise its potential in a very supportive way. This publication was aided by a generous subsidy from the Australian National University and I would like to acknowledge that support here. I would also like to thank the Charles and Joy Staples Fund for its generosity in the financial assistance in the publication of this book.

One friend in particular has had unrelenting confidence in me and my abilities as a historian for a long time. Travis Cutler has been the person who has challenged me the most in my work. His work on the colonial world in Victoria sets a standard for history that I always aspire to. I thank Travis for the hundreds of hours he has spent reading my work with a microscopic level of critical attention and sensitivity.

The practical support of Vilma, Pedro and Serge Geuna, along with Silvi San Juan, who kept me well-fed and looked after over the past few years, needs to be acknowledged here.

My parents, Fiona and Geoff, have been ceaseless enthusiasts of my studies and I have benefited immensely in unpredictable ways from our ongoing conversations and stories which began long ago about history and culture. I want to thank them for all of those holidays in the south-west of Western Australia. My grandmother Muriel Stanley, who read some of my earliest (and worst) writing, encouraged me to keep going. My sister Hallie's intensely creative thinking and imagination often inspires ideas in my own work. She has supported me every day through this book and given me confidence to be more imaginative in the way I narrate the histories I tell. And finally, this book could not have been completed without the daily enthusiasm and compassion from Gus who lovingly and patiently looks after me beyond any reasonable expectation.

The city of Albany is situated on the most southern tip of Western Australia. It is a large regional centre today, known as the 'gateway' to the Great Southern region, and hosts a population of around 25,000 people. The centre of the city lies on a slope between two rocky, granite hills, Mt Clarence and Mt Melville, and looks across at the vast, circular basin of Princess Royal Harbour. This harbour connects to King George Sound, a large open waterway which protects the town like a sentinel from the rough swells of the cold and wild Southern Ocean. A third inlet, Oyster Harbour, opens along King George Sound's northern shoreline.

I know these three harbours and the surrounding landscape intimately. My family built their 'tree house' in a small town called Denmark, 55 kilometres to the west of Albany on the top of Weedon Hill. The hill is dotted with tall, skinny, pale-grey karri trees and lumpy granite boulders. I have holidayed in Denmark and Albany since I was a child and I have strong memories of the majestic karri and jarrah forests, the wild beaches and the distant but foreboding mountain ranges to the north, the Porongurup and Stirling Range. My family are avid bushwalkers and we have spent many holidays walking along sections of the Bibbulmun Track – a track which honours the Aboriginal people of the south-west and recognises their ancient practice of walking long distances for ceremonies. The Bibbulmun icon is the head of a serpent and the track snakes its way around the southern coastal region, between Perth and Albany.

Although I have had an attachment to this place for many years, I have only recently discovered something of Albany's deeper human past. In 2003, during a rare walk through the main street (I usually stick to the beaches or the bush) I came upon a statue in a park next to the city library. This statue was the first material contact I had with this community's past. It is a life-size bronze figure of an Aboriginal man. The figure has an athletic physique and stands tall on two granite rocks, a spear grasped with one hand. It honours an Aboriginal man called Mokaré. He is remembered here as the 'Man of Peace'. The plaque beneath it reads 'in recognition of the role that Mokaré played in the peaceful co-existence between *Nyungar* people and the first European settlers'. The date 1826 is inscribed at the figure's feet. The statue was erected in 1997 as part of a Reconciliation project by local residents of the Albany community and funded by the Aboriginal Affairs department and the Albany City Council. It was a symbolic gesture, part of a movement of positive acts by non-indigenous Australians to reconcile with Aboriginal communities across Australia.

I was fascinated by this 'man of peace' and the supposedly peaceful past he represented. The term 'peaceful' is not commonly used in narratives depicting the relationships between Aborigines and newcomers in Australia. Historian E.P. Thompson has taught me to be wary of such simple terms. In his essay on the moral economy of the English working class in the eighteenth century, he wrote about the use of the term 'riot' in relation to the so-called food riots in England. He explained how this word is too exclusive to encompass all the people and all their actions in eighteenth-century English peasant life. He accused historians who use such broad brush terms in their histories of 'reductionism, obliterating the complexities of motive, behaviour, and function'.[1] The term 'peaceful', like Thompson's 'riot', conceals more about this past than it reveals.

Don Watson has written that 'monuments honour deeds and end questions'.[2] However, after encountering the statue I was eager to uncover more about Mokaré the person and his countrymen and women who lived where Albany now stands; to discover what they made of the newcomers who came and set up a British camp on the northern shore of Princess Royal Harbour. I wanted to get to know the man who lived and experienced that long ago present rather than let the language on the statue explain away the complexity of human experiences. The telling of this history emerges from my first encounter with Mokaré's statue that day in the main street of Albany.

The British garrison settlement party arrived from New South Wales on Christmas Day in 1826. It included a troop of soldiers of the 57th Regiment of Foot and a hand-picked group of skilled crown prisoners, and was overseen by Major Edmund Lockyer. In March 1831, the garrison was transferred from the authority of New South Wales to the colony of Western Australia, the headquarters of which was based at the Swan River settlement, the modern site of Perth. The date inscribed at the foot of Mokaré's statue, 1826, denotes the beginning of this British world, referred to as 'King George's Sound' by the newcomers.[3] The act of marking the statue '1826' instantly incorporates Mokaré into the British foundational narrative. This rendering of an Aboriginal man and his world into a British one recurs in Australian historiography and public histories around the country, and it serves to cloak the ways in which Aboriginal people like Mokaré also appropriated and understood the British within their own worlds and narratives.

This history depicts a series of events during the first few years of the British settlement at King George's Sound, from when it was established as a military garrison in 1826 until after its conversion to a free settlement within the colony of Western Australia. Several narrative episodes focus on the relationships between the Aborigines who lived beyond the shores of King George's Sound and the newcomers who stepped ashore and stayed. Some of these relationships confounded my expectations of nineteenth-century British military men and illuminated strategic Aboriginal behaviour. My intention is to offer explanations for these relationships and the behaviour of these people by scrutinising what their decisions to act might have actually meant to them; to understand their motivations and intentions as best I can in their own cultural contexts. In particular I want to investigate how individuals like Mokaré understood and used the British presence. This book is also an attempt to unravel the varied processes of world-rendering that the statue and other histories have forged. Several key episodes have been selected as entry points into the world at King George's Sound between 1826 and the early 1830s. They are stories which provide a context for interpreting the actions and motivations of the people who experienced them. This structure has drawbacks that I am aware of. I have not covered everything that happened in those years (which is impossible to achieve in any structure), focusing instead on a solid and close reading of particular episodes. The episodes have smaller reflections which explain some of the decisions of my narrative and offer a deeper analysis, separate from the tension of the narrative episodes.

My major questions while reading the British texts have focused on deducing what the Aboriginal men and women might have been up to. I wanted to understand the nature of the changes in the Aboriginal world with the arrival of these strangers and, most importantly, how particular individuals experienced change. How were the newcomers and their material culture understood and how were they incorporated into the Aboriginal world? How did Aboriginal people use the British presence to advantage through strategic actions and how did these Aboriginal people improvise to appropriate aspects of the British world into their own? The episodes considered make up a larger story about how a functioning Aboriginal world incorporated a new presence. It was not a simple takeover. In these first few years, a fusion of cultural expectations and material culture took place, with an unexpected Aboriginal use of, and varying interests in, the activities of the British who were setting up their own world on the fringes of an Aboriginal one.

I have encountered a very different Mokaré from the bronze statue, frozen in time and spoken for by a plaque in the town of Albany today. The statue appropriates Mokaré in the colonial British and postcolonial Australian worlds but, as the following history shows, the newcomers to King George's Sound were constantly being situated in the Aboriginal world too, in a wide variety of interesting ways. This history is an attempt to go beyond that Reconciliation statue and unearth some of the stories that Mokaré and his countrymen and women told and took part in.

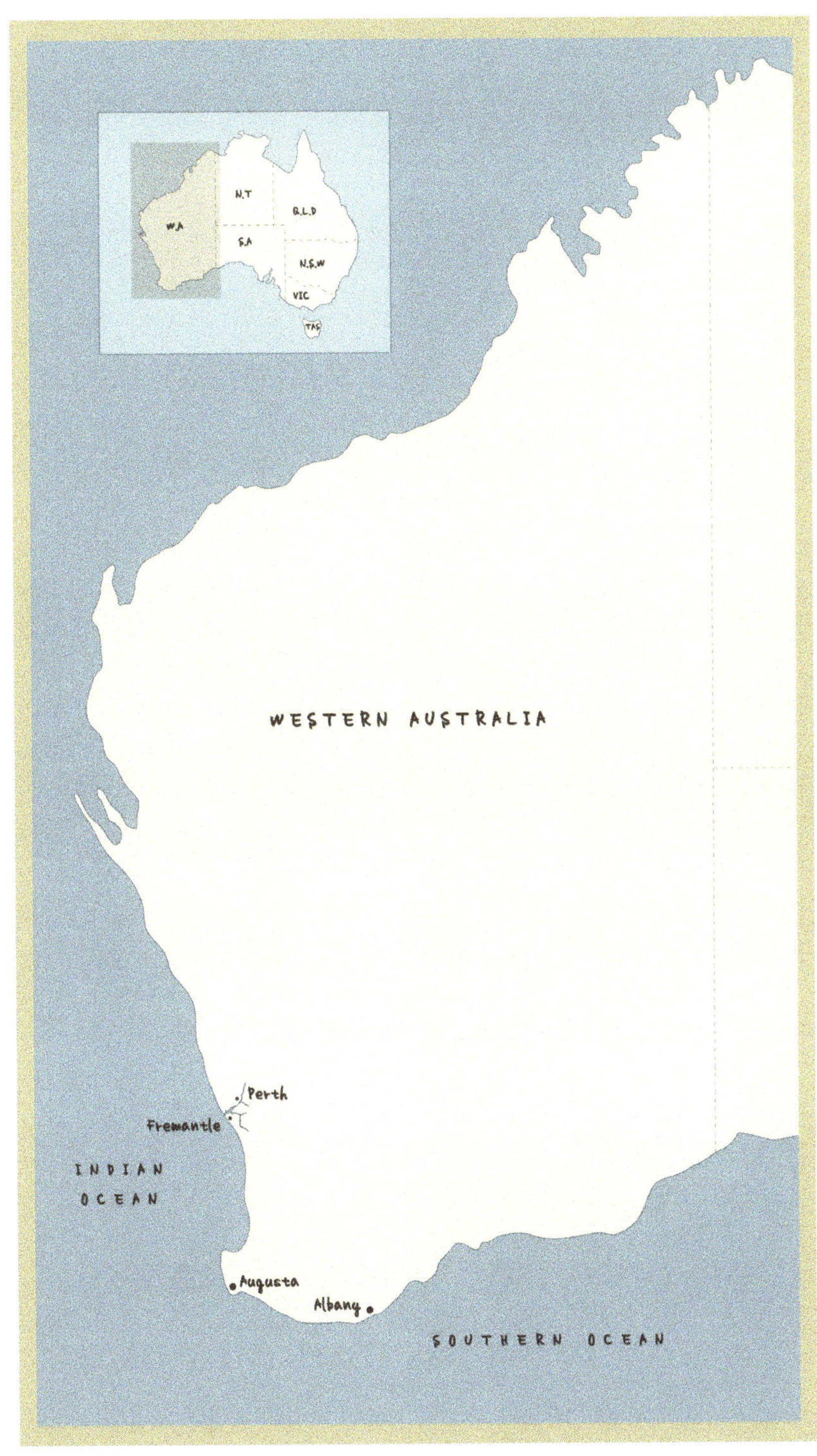

1: Map of Western Australia showing Perth, Fremantle and Albany. *Map Tiffany Shellam and Genevieve Giambazi.*

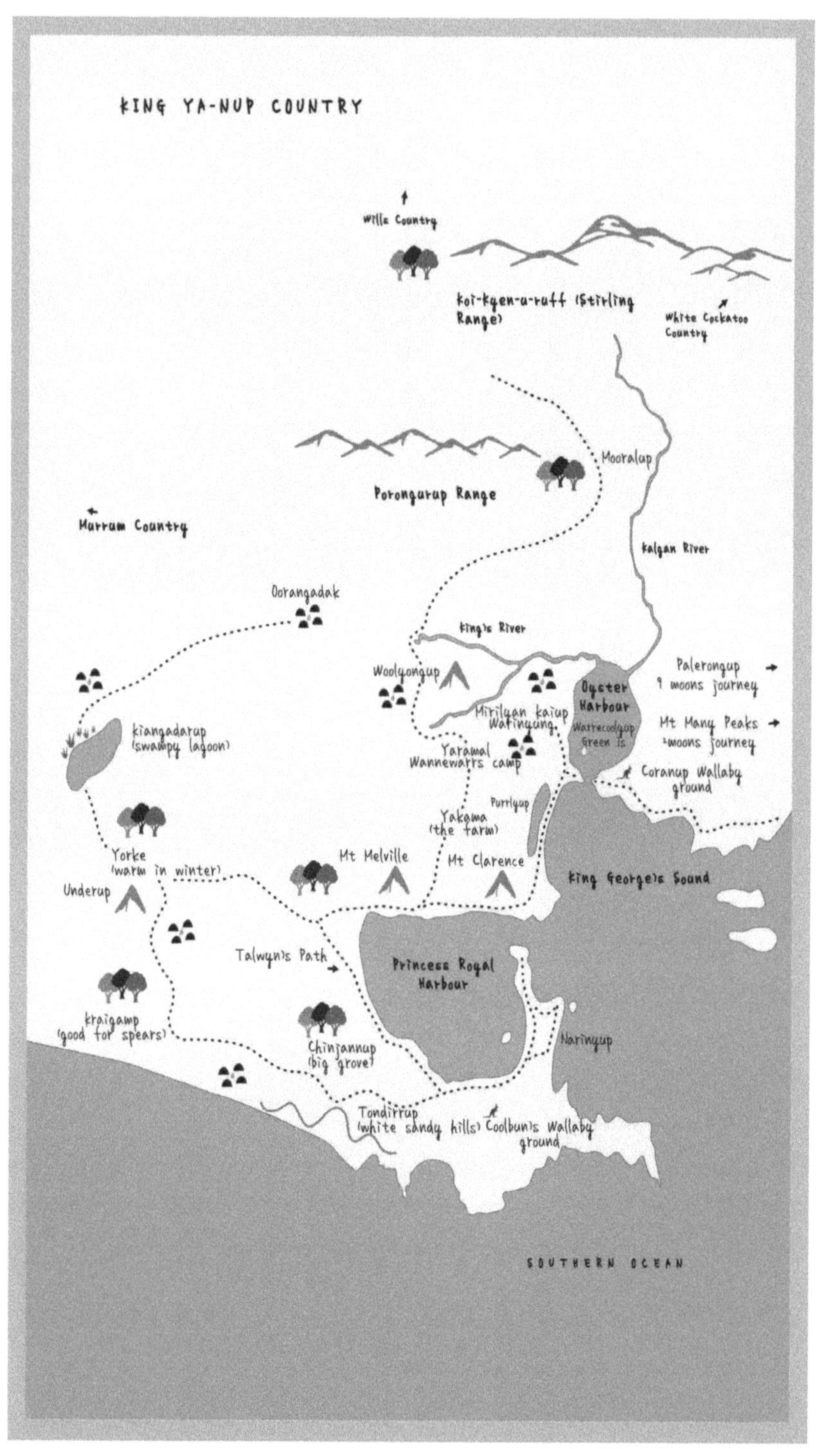

2: Map of King Ya-nup country, showing campsites, paths and significant places. *Map Tiffany Shellam and Genevieve Giambazi*

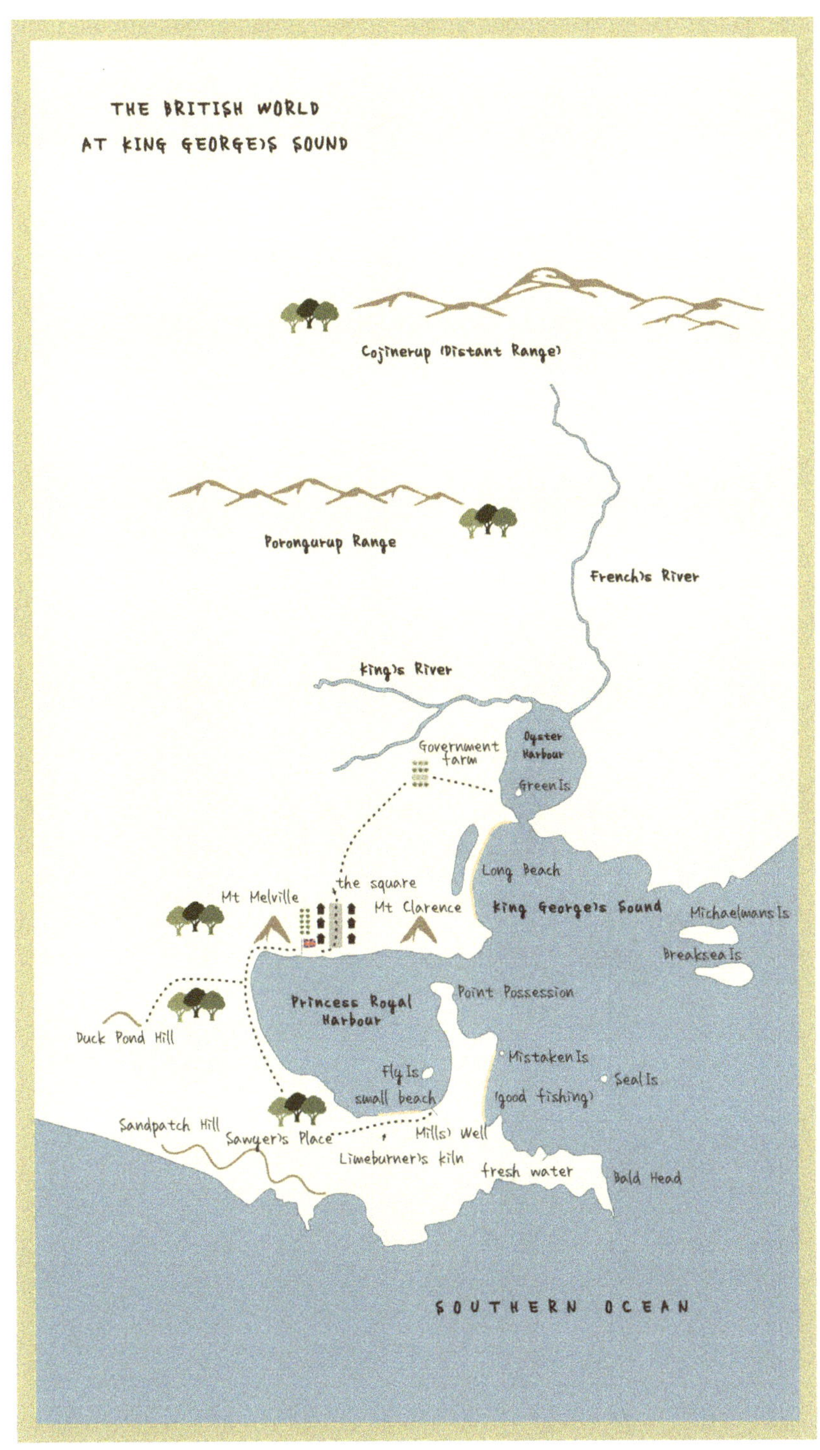

3: Map of the British world at King George's Sound, showing their camp between Mt Melville and Mt Clarence, the flagpole, government farm, Sawyer's Place and other sites of significance. *Map Tiffany Shellam and Genevieve Giambazi*

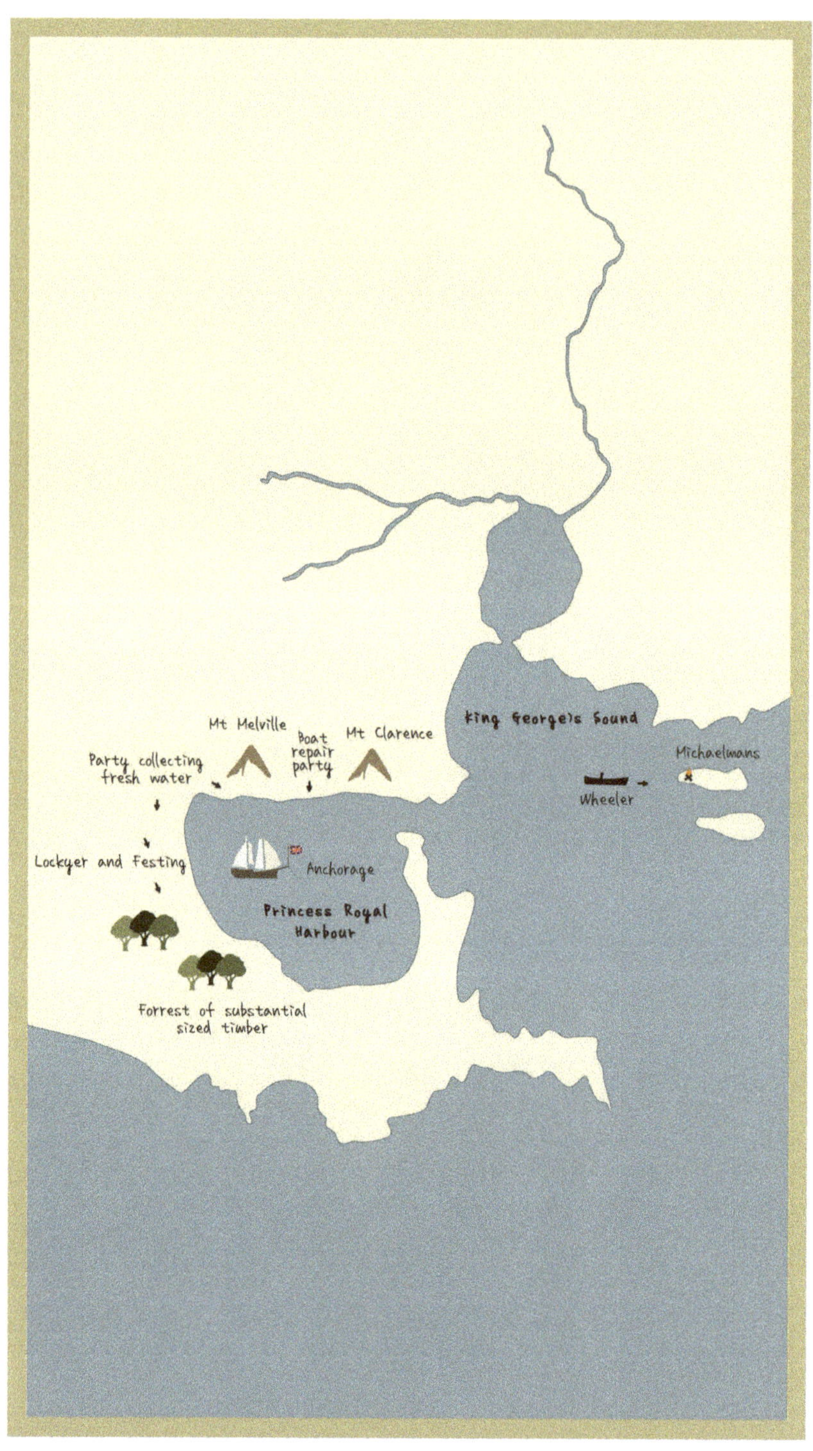

4: Map showing the relative location of the anchorage of the *Amity*, watering party, boat repair party and the direction that Lockyer and Festing were heading in. *Map Tiffany Shellam and Genevieve Giambazi*

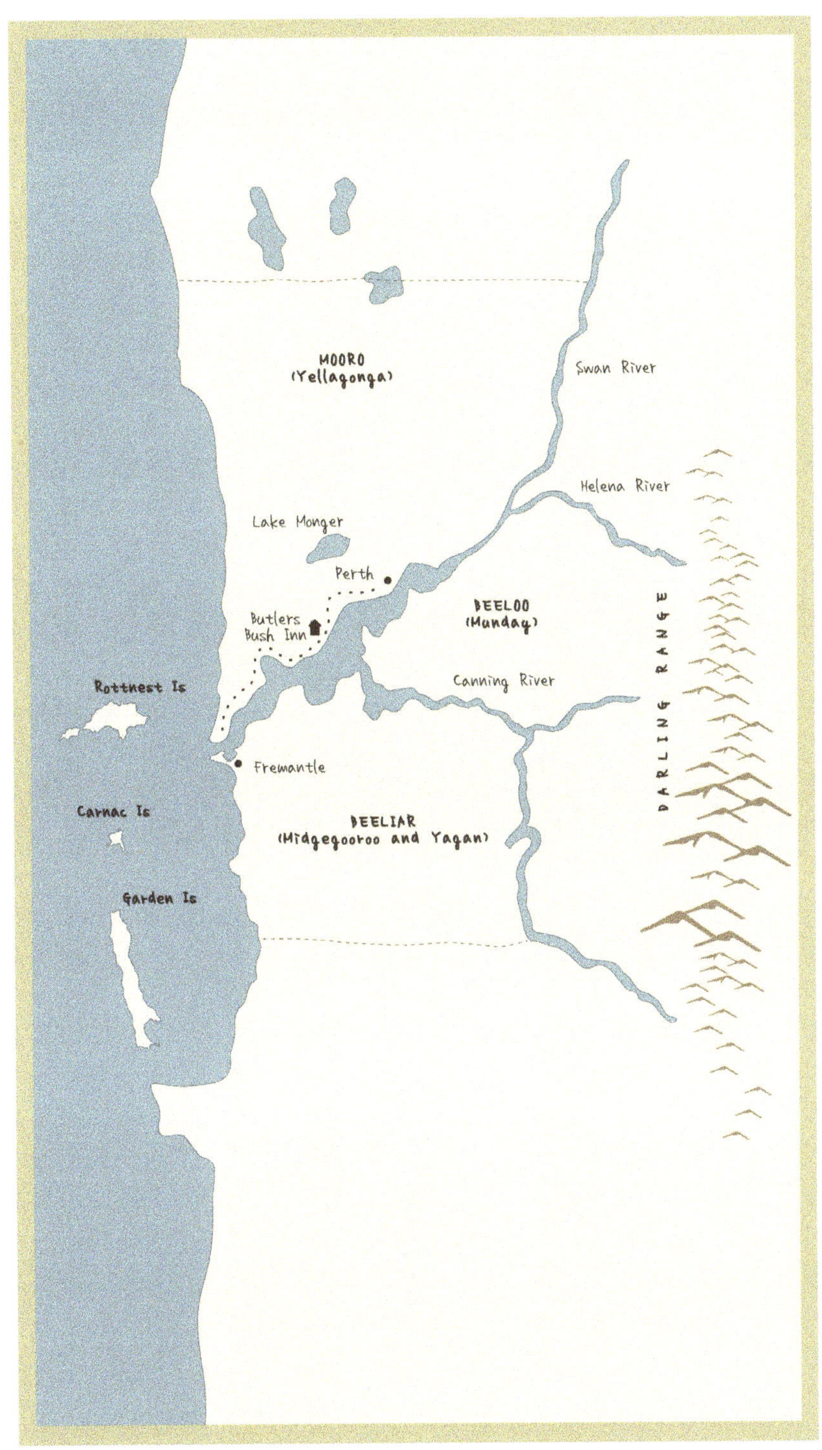

5: Map showing Aboriginal countries across the Swan River colony, including the prominent figures in each group. *Map Tiffany Shellam and Genevieve Giambazi.*

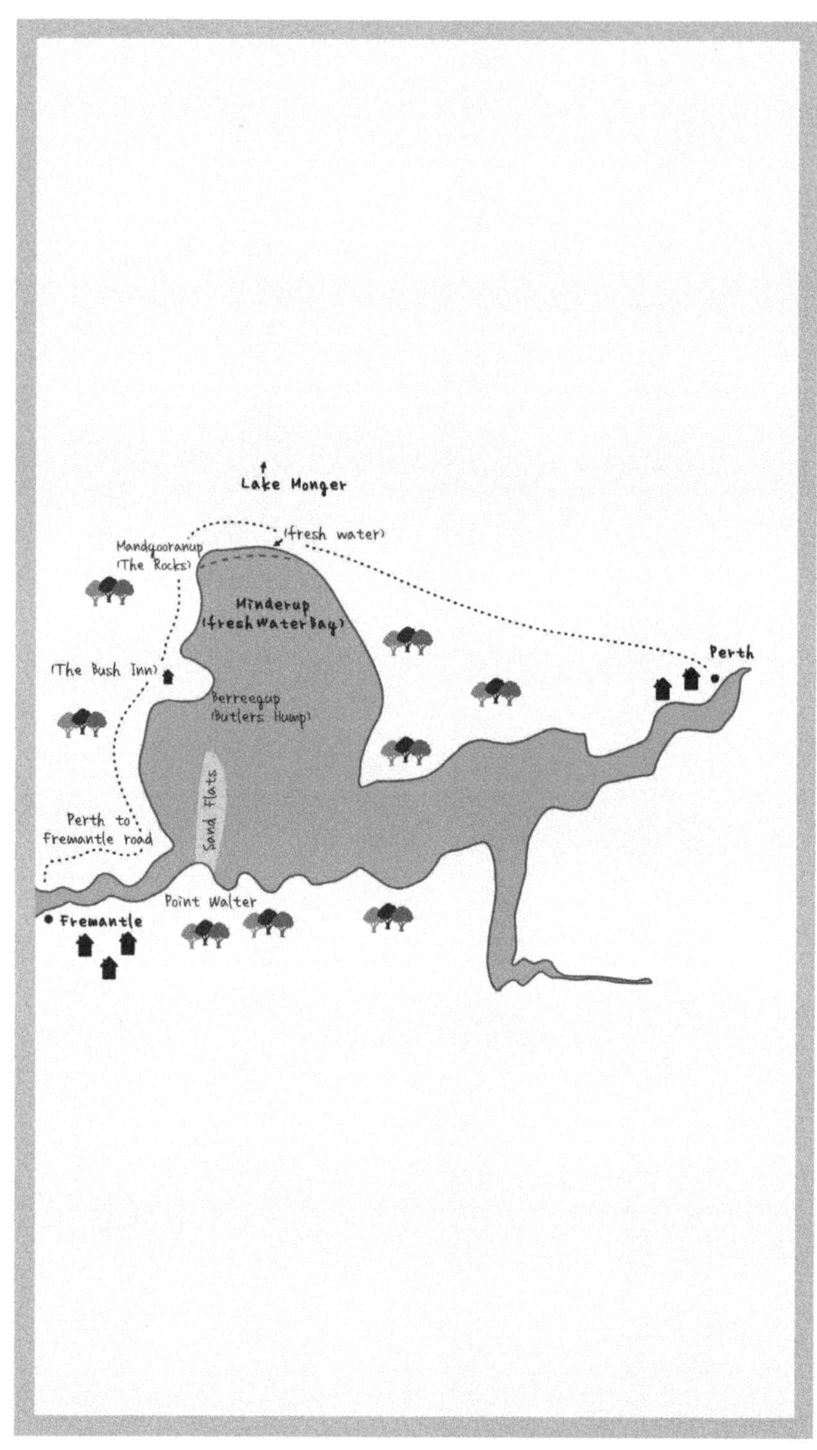

6: Map of Freshwater Bay showing Butler's Bush Inn, the road to Fremantle and the extensive sand flats where the *Mooro* would cross the river. *Map Tiffany Shellam and Genevieve Giambazi*

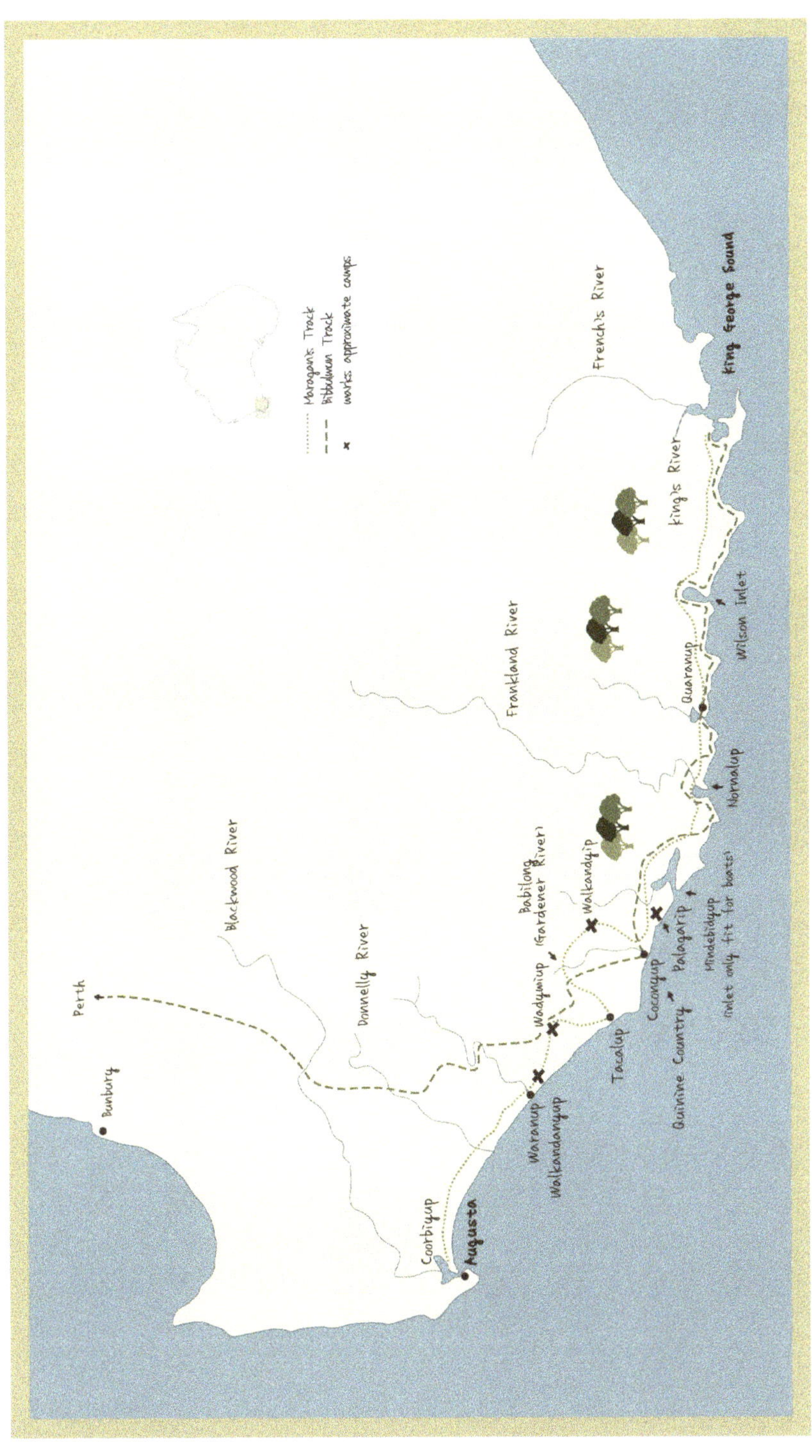

7: Map of paths: this map shows Maragnan (and possibly Gyallipert's) sleeping sites along a path that lead them from Albany to Augusta and perhaps even further north. I have placed the Aboriginal path next to today's Bibbulmun Track. Pilgrims and nature lovers continue this tradition of travelling today along this similar coastal track. *Map Tiffany Shellam and Genevieve Giambazi*

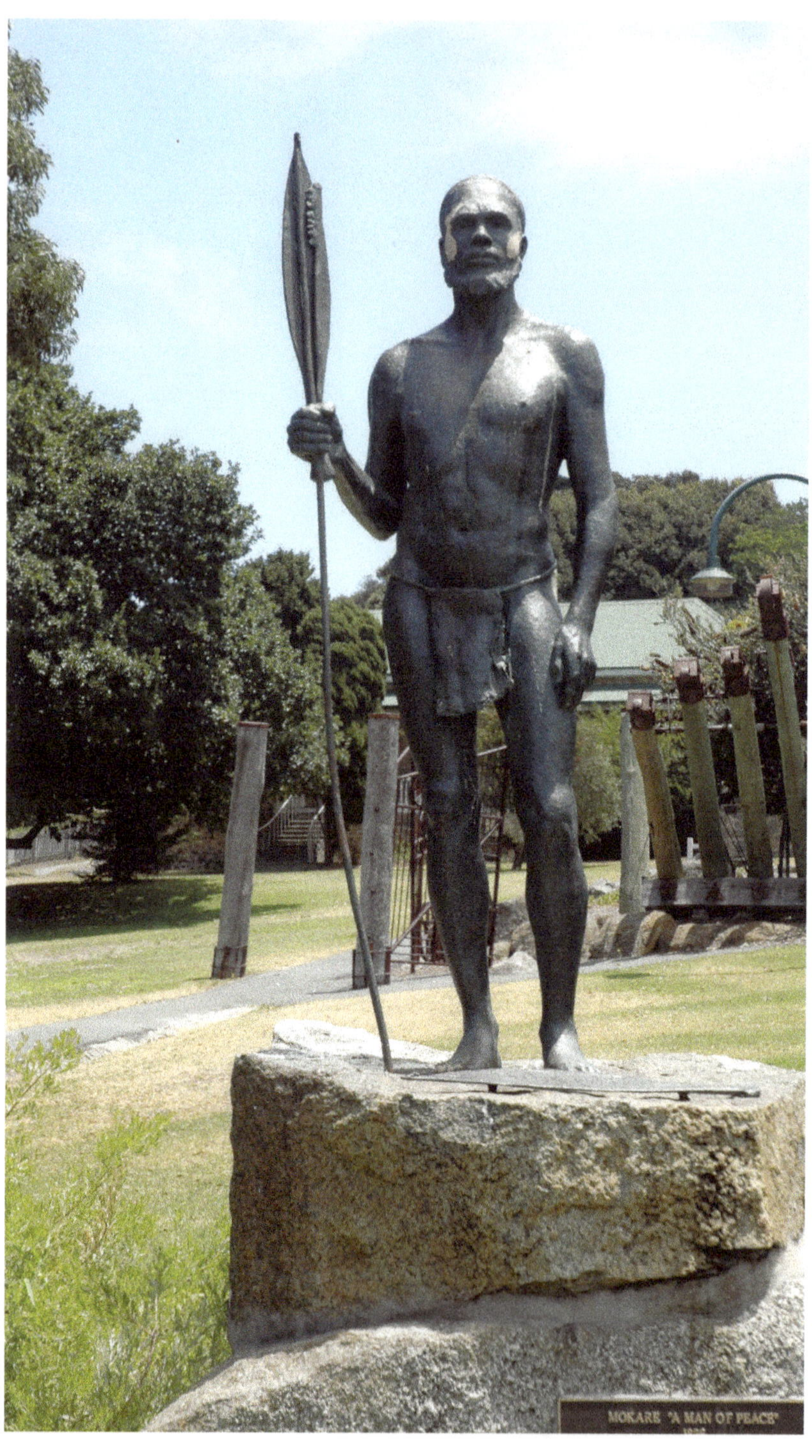

8: Mokaré's memorial. *Photo Tiffany Shellam*

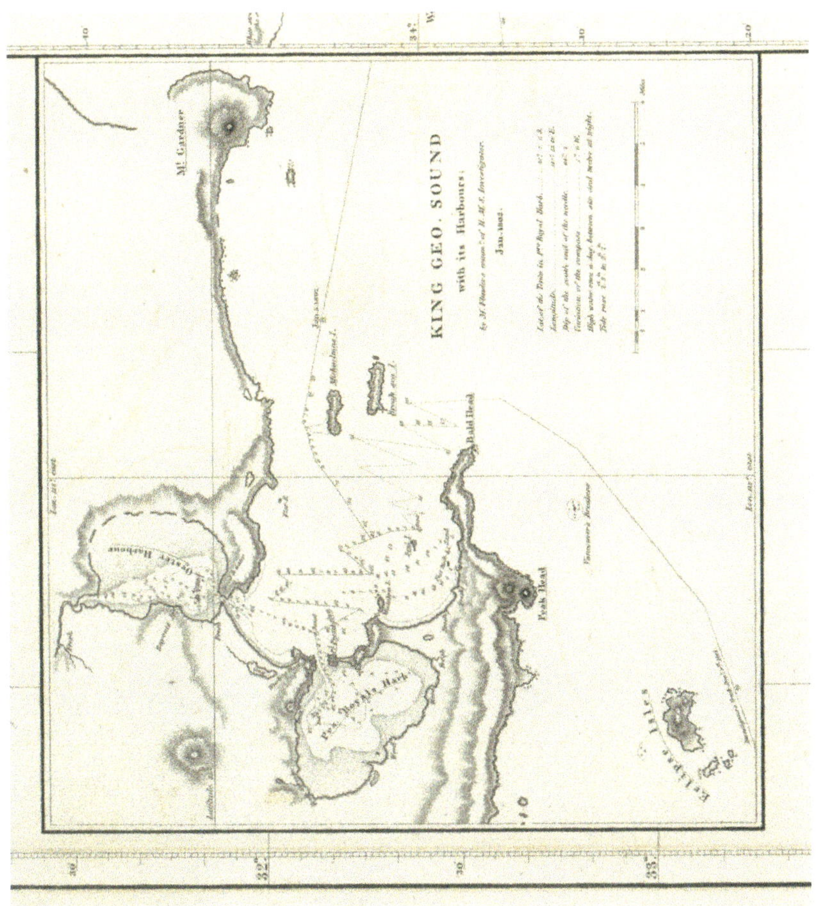

9: *Chart of Terra Australis, South Coast, Sheet One, January 1802,* by Matthew Flinders, showing detail of King George's Sound and its three harbours. *Courtesy National Library of Australia, map T571.*

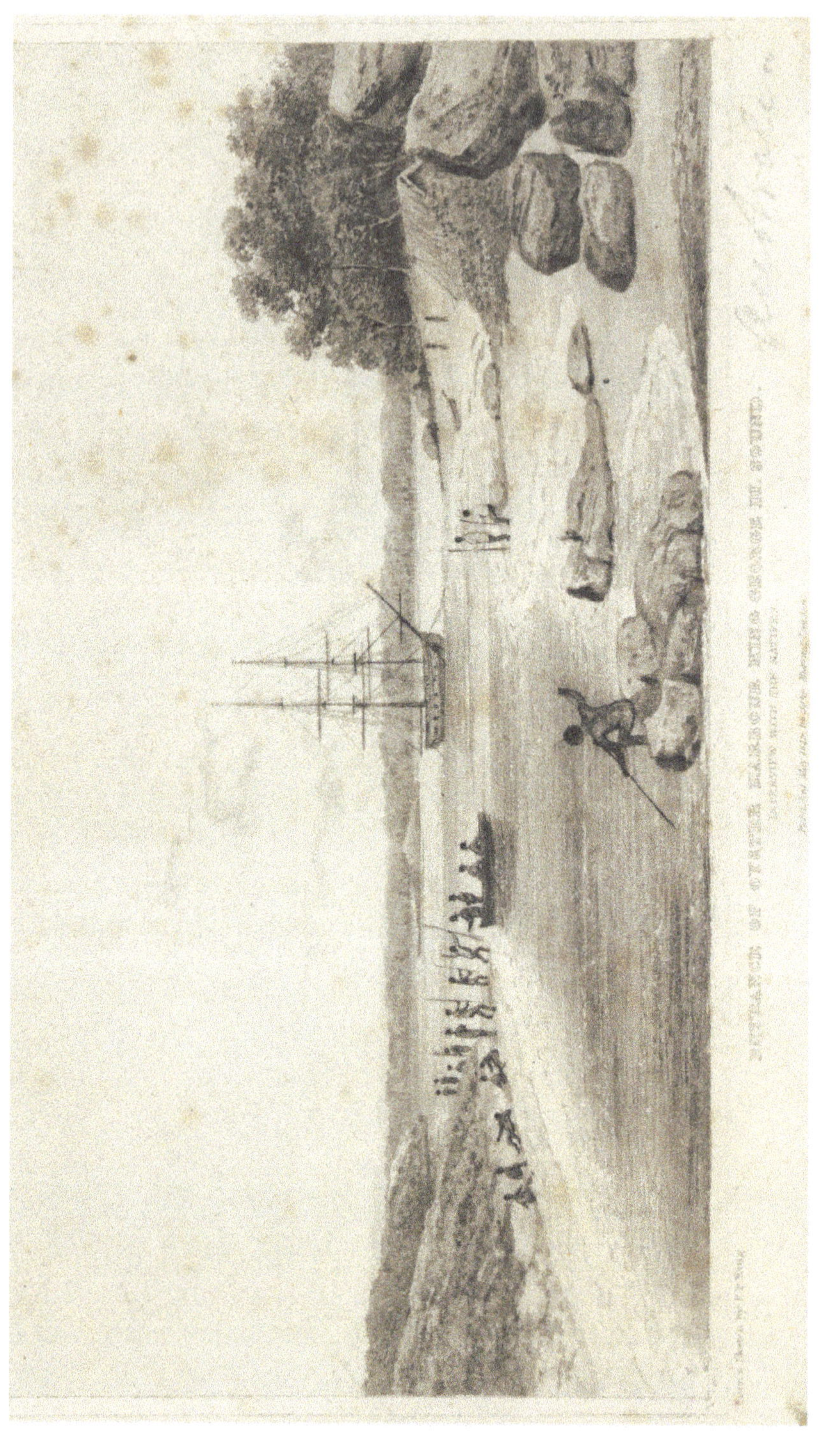

10: *Entrance of Oyster Harbour, King George III Sound, Interview with the Natives,* sketch by Phillip Parker King, John Murray, London, 1825. *Courtesy National Library of Australia, nla-pic-an* 7748236

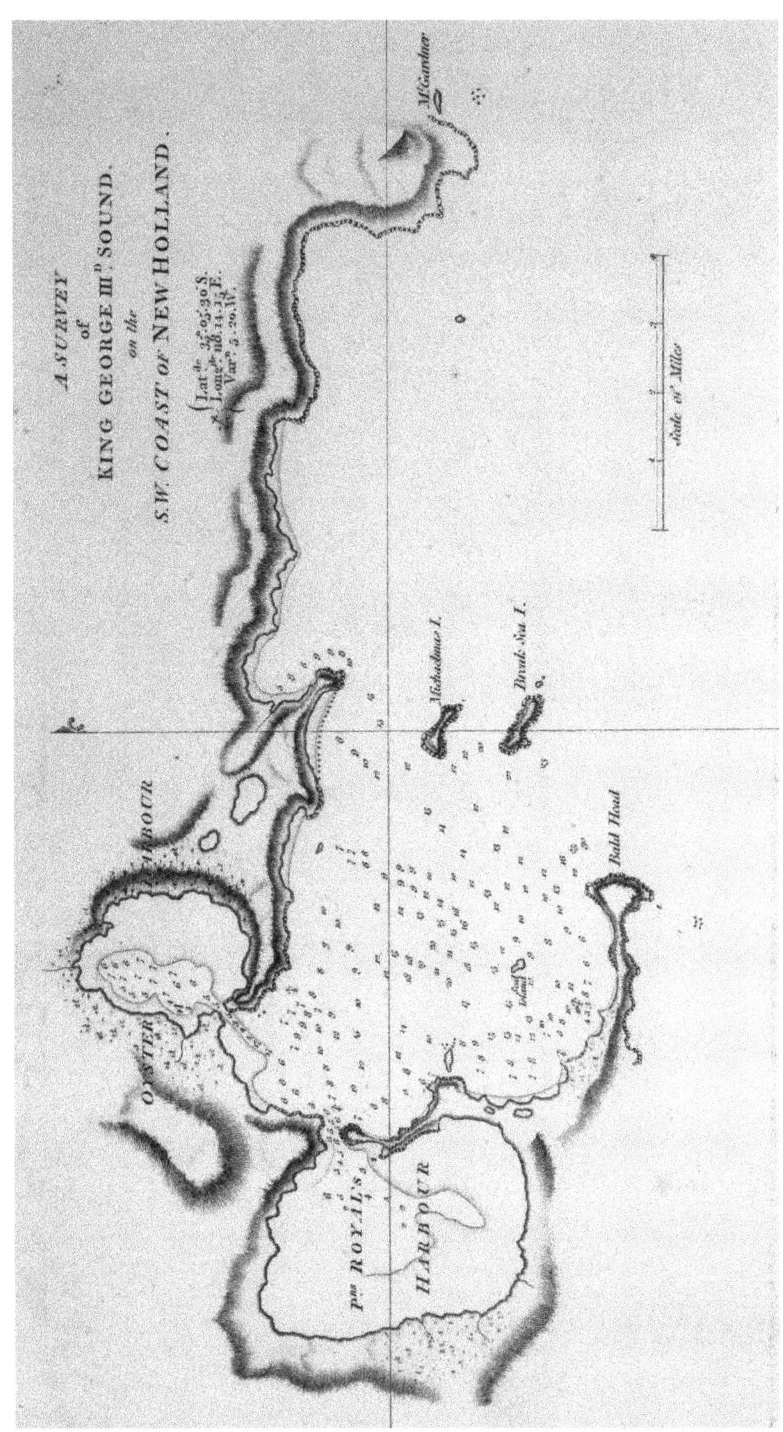

11: *Chart Shewing Part of the SW coast of New Holland 1791*, by Captain George Vancouver, engraved by T. Foot, 1793. *Courtesy National Library of Australia, MapT 1277.*

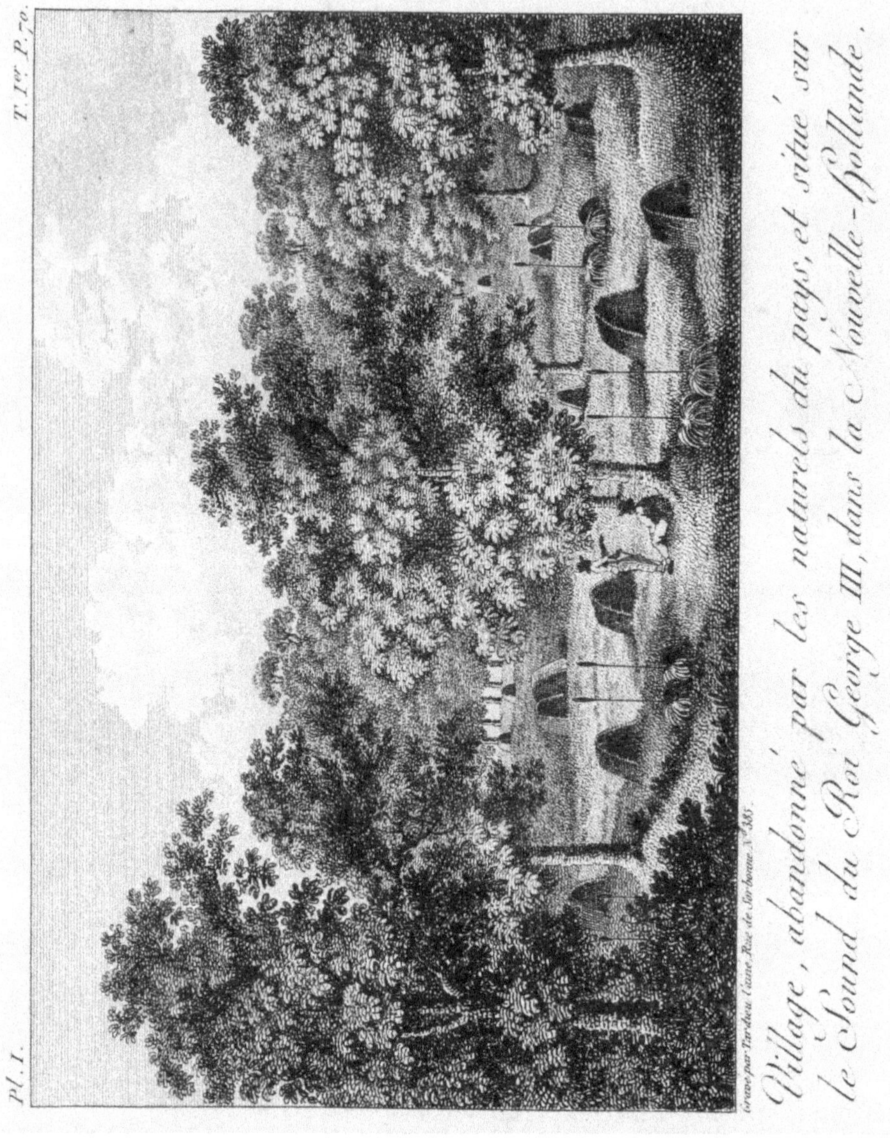

12: This engraving by Tardieu is taken from Vancouver's sketch of an abandoned village at King George's Sound during his expedition in 1791. *Village, abandonné par les naturels du pays, et situé sur le Sound due Roi George 111, dans la Nouvelle Hollande.* After J. Sykes Jr., Jean-Baptiste Tardieu engraver. *Courtesy Kerry Stokes Collection, Perth.*

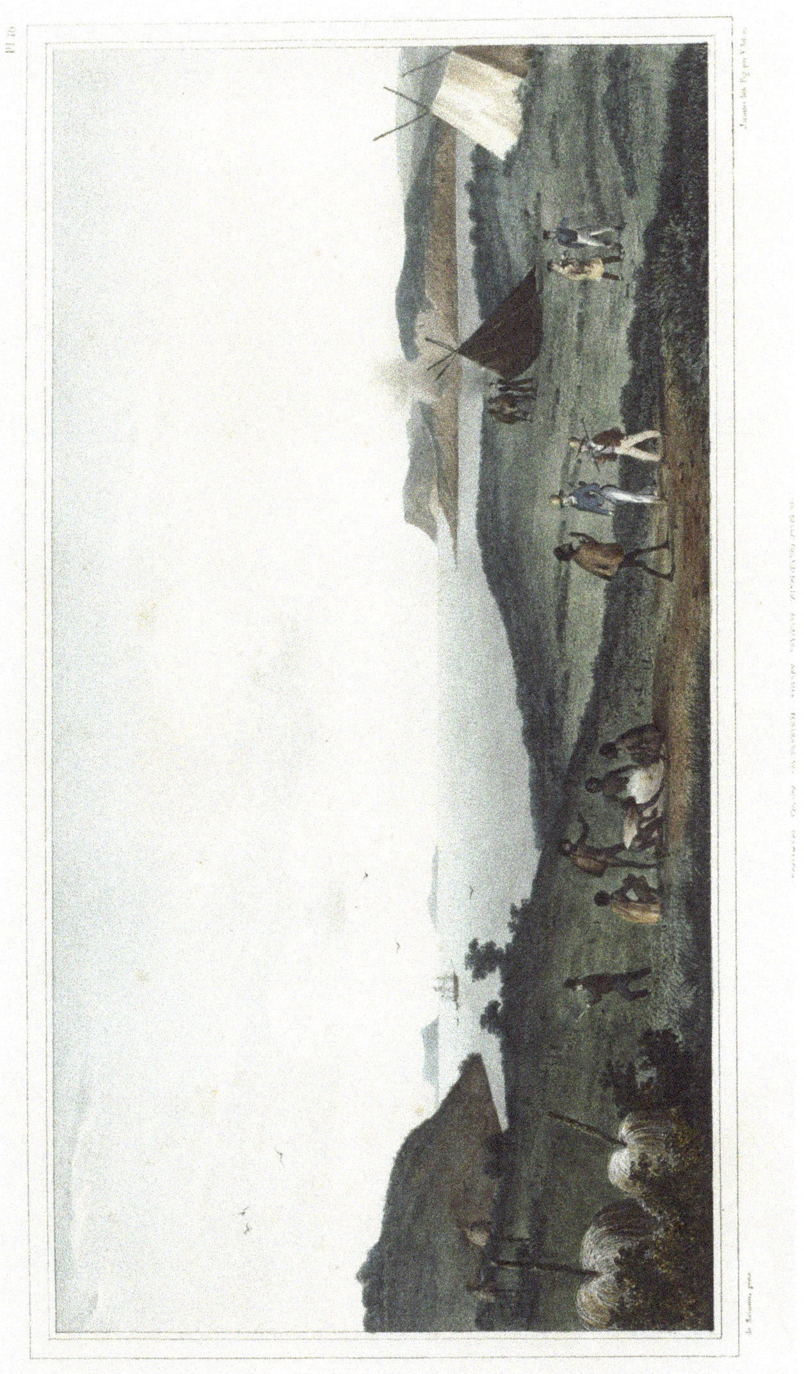

13: *View of King George's Sound, New Holland, 1833*, after Louis Auguste de Sainson, hand-coloured lithograph. *Courtesy Kerry Stokes Collection, Perth.*

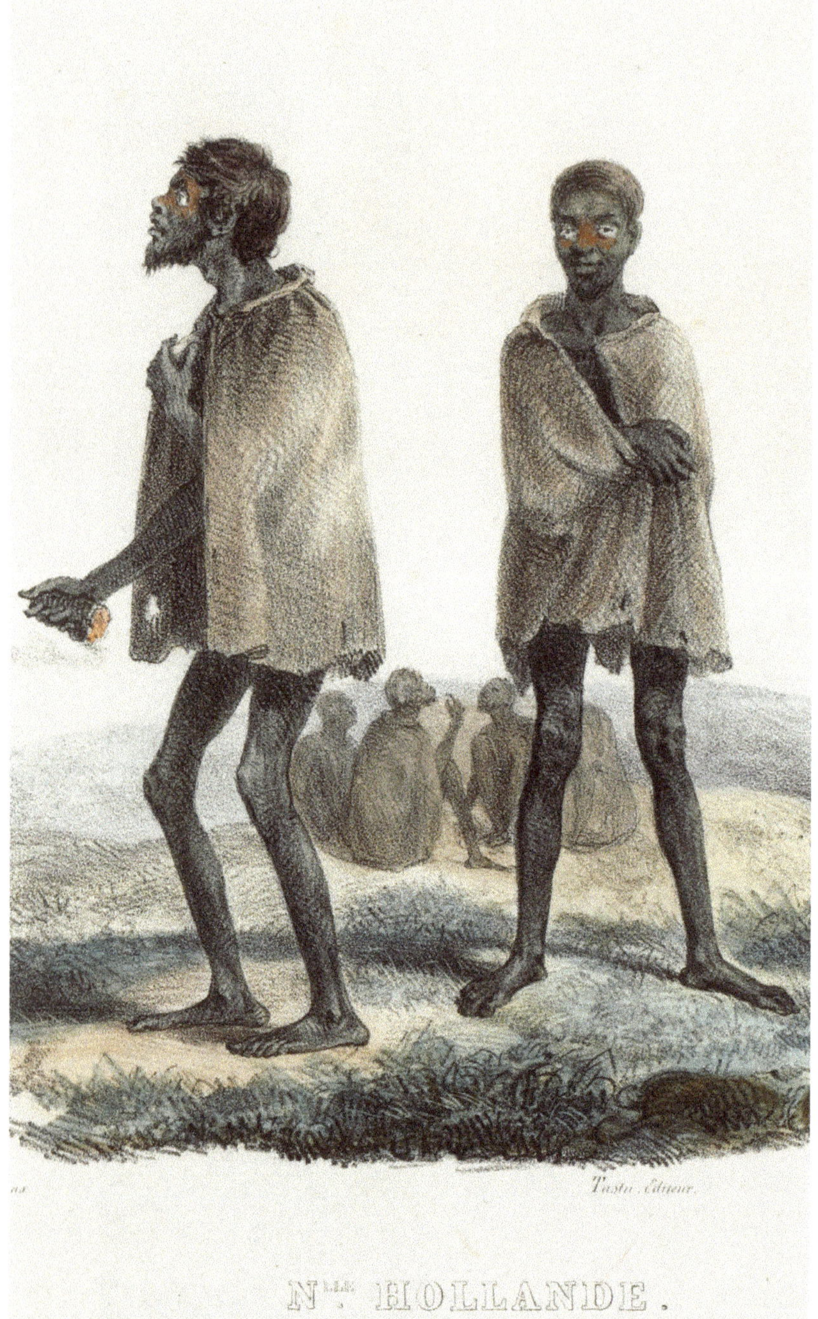

14: *Naturels du port du Roi Georges, N.Ille Hollande*, 1833. After Louis Auguste de Sainson, P. Langlumé, lithographer. *Courtesy Kerry Stokes Collection, Perth.*

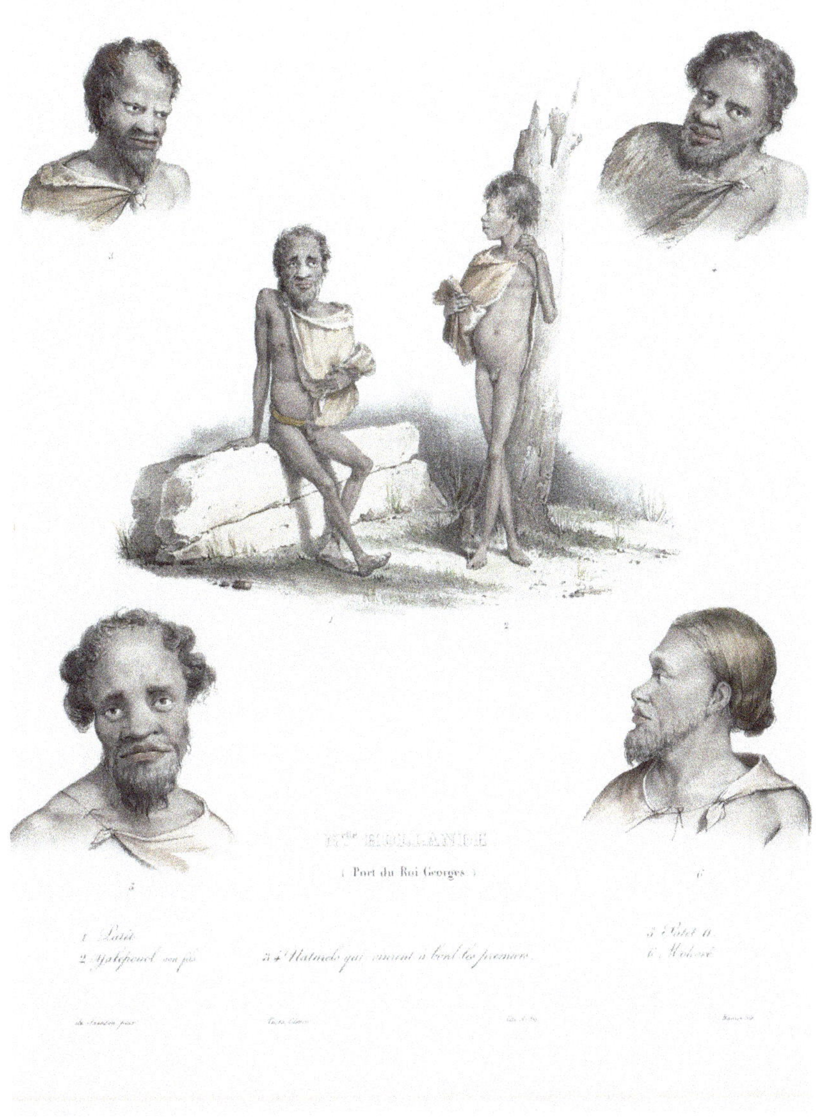

15: *Patet, Yalepoul and Mokaré, natives of King George's Sound, New Holland,* hand-coloured lithograph, after Louis Auguste de Sainson. *Courtesy Kerry Stokes Collection, Perth.*

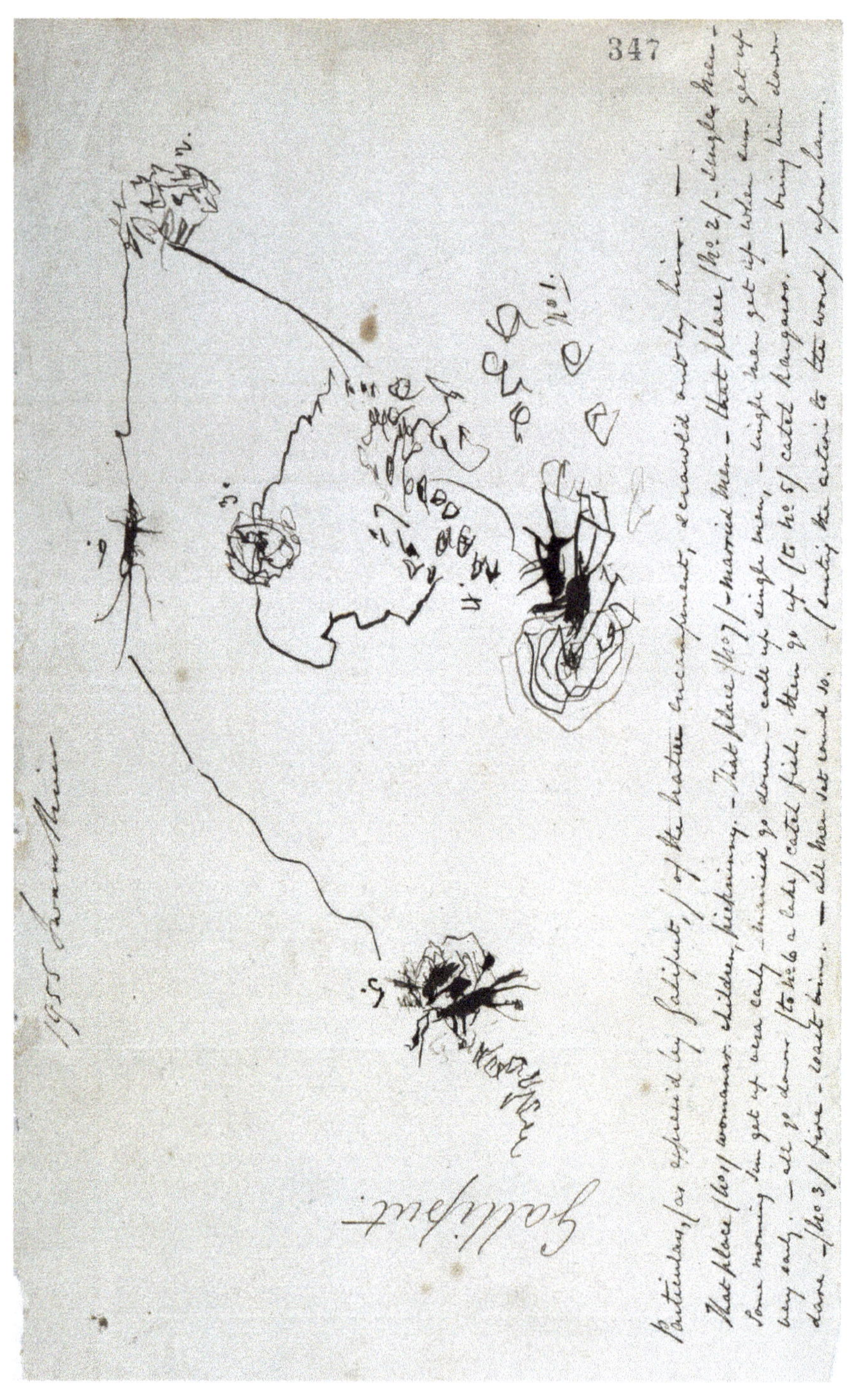

16: Gyallipert's Sketch in John Morgan's letter to Colonial Secretary Hay. *Courtesy National Archives, Kew, UK. CO18/13 f347.*

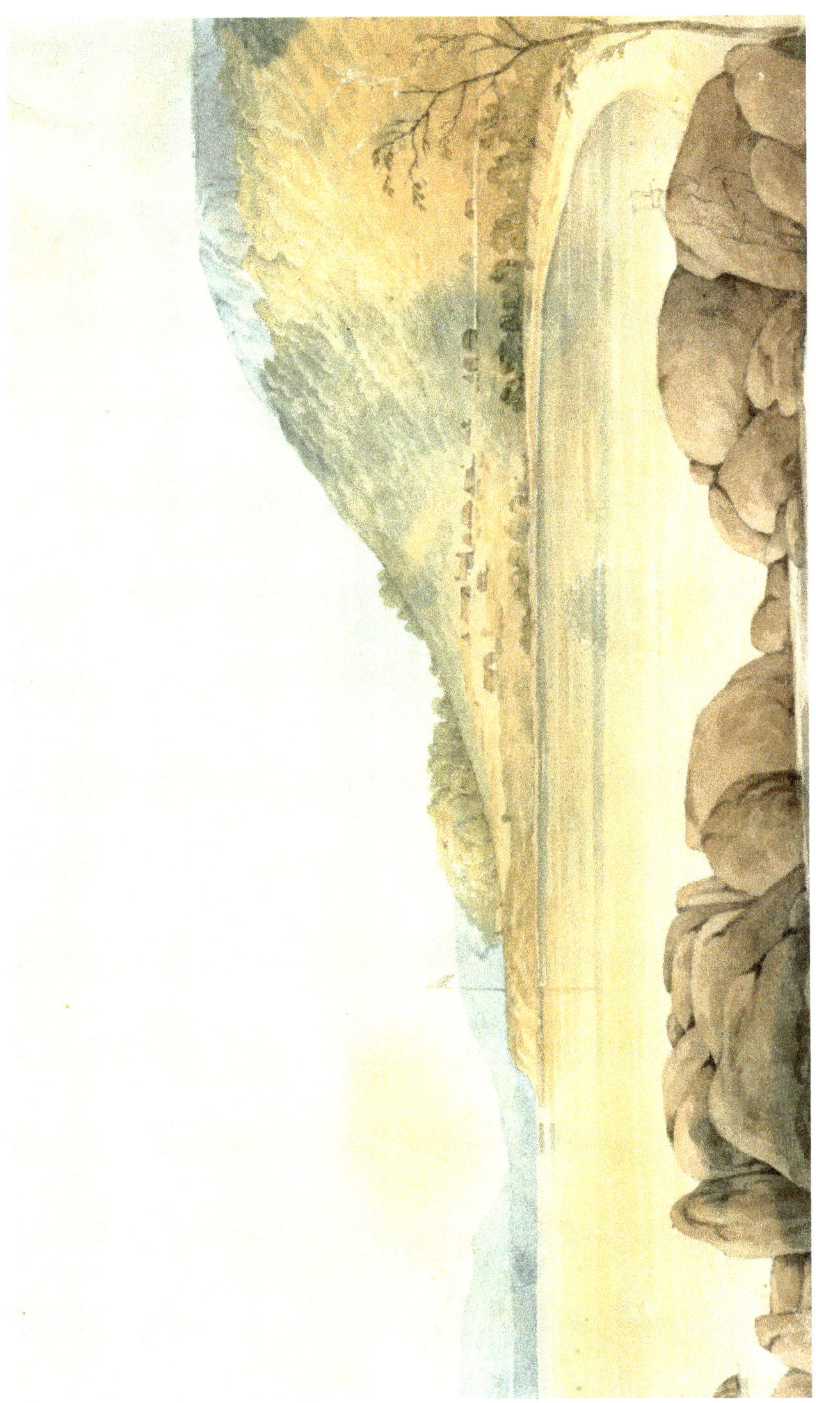

17: *Settlement at King George Sound, WA, taken 3 April 1827.* This sketch is generally credited to Isaac Nind. *Courtesy National Library of Australia, nla-pic-an5862932.*

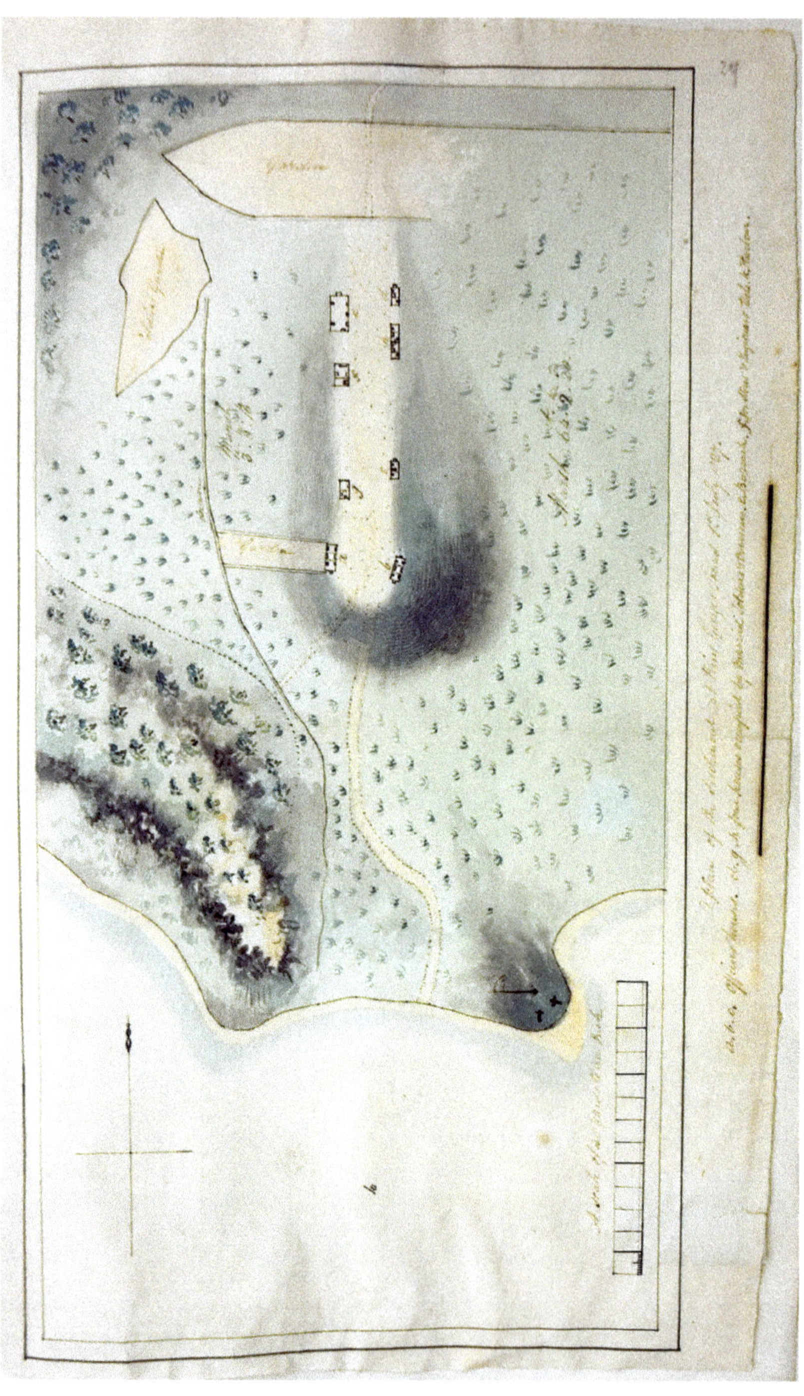

18: 'Wakefield's Plan', July 1827, AO NSW, CSO relating to King George's Sound (4/2092). *Photo Gustavo Geuna.*

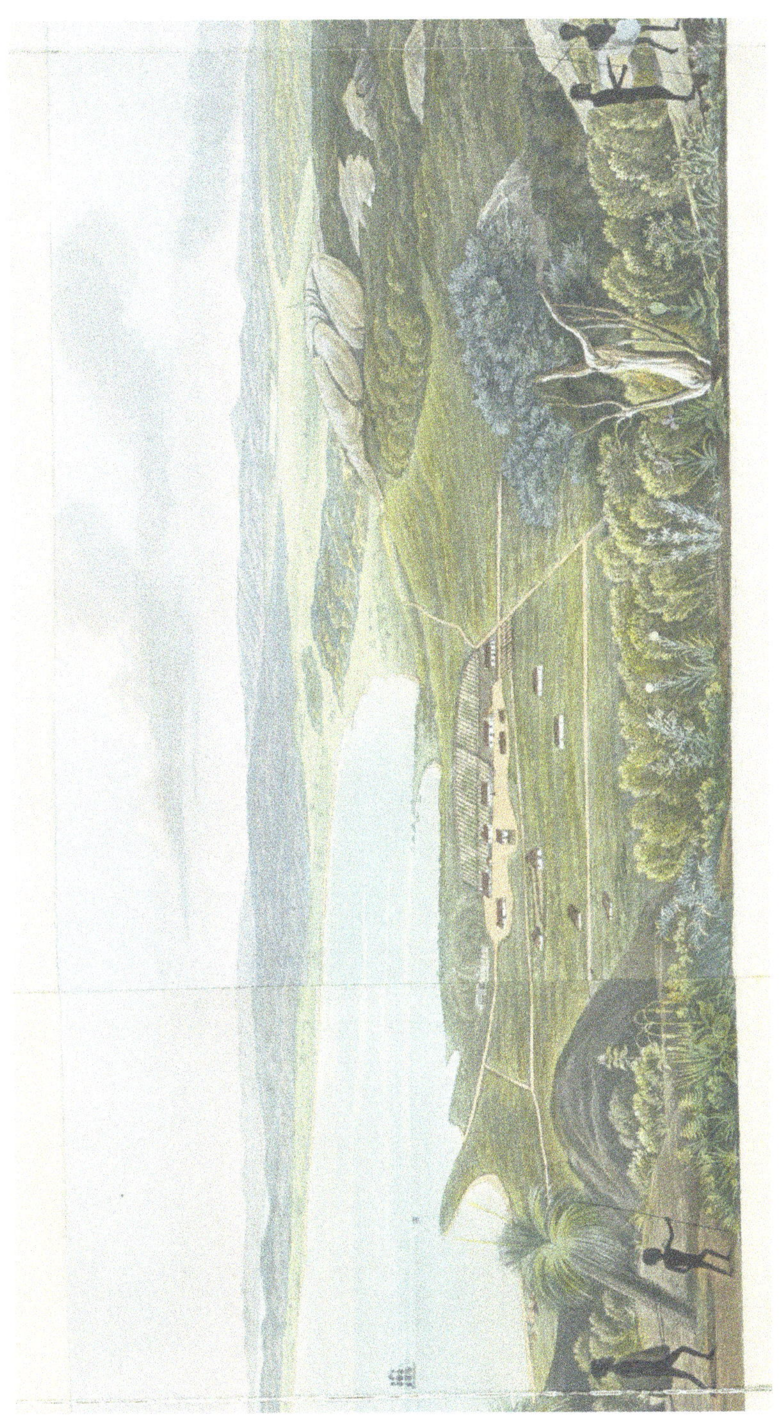

19: *Panoramic View of King George's Sound, part of the colony of Swan River* (detail), by Lt Robert Dale, 1834. *Courtesy National Library of Australia, nla-pic-an7404363-6.*

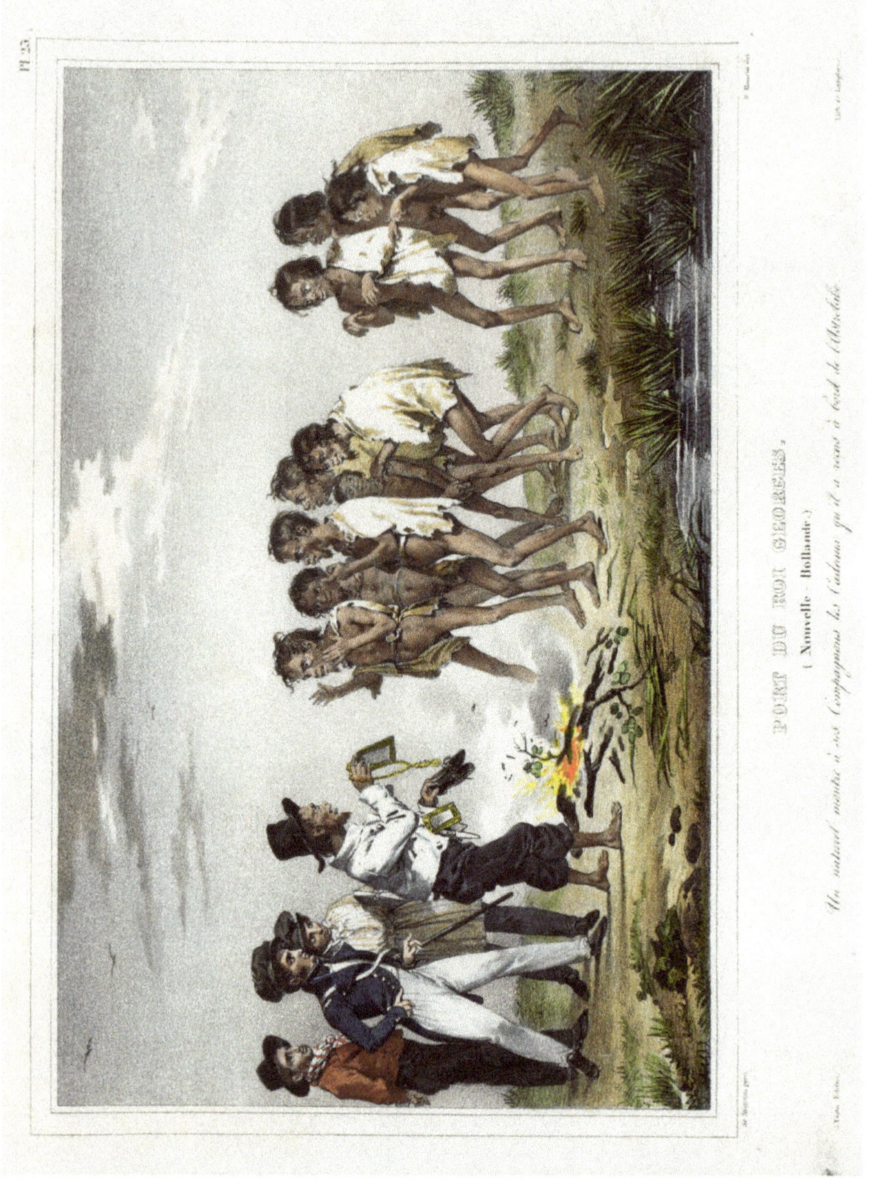

20: This sketch portrays a King Ya-nup showing his friends the bounty of his barter with the French visitors in 1826. *Port du Roi Georges. (Nouvelle Hollande) Un naturel montre à ses Compagnons les cadeaux qu'il a reçus à bord de l'Astrolabe, 1833.* After Louis Auguste de Sainson, P. Langlumé, lithographer. *Courtesy Kerry Stokes Collection, Perth.*

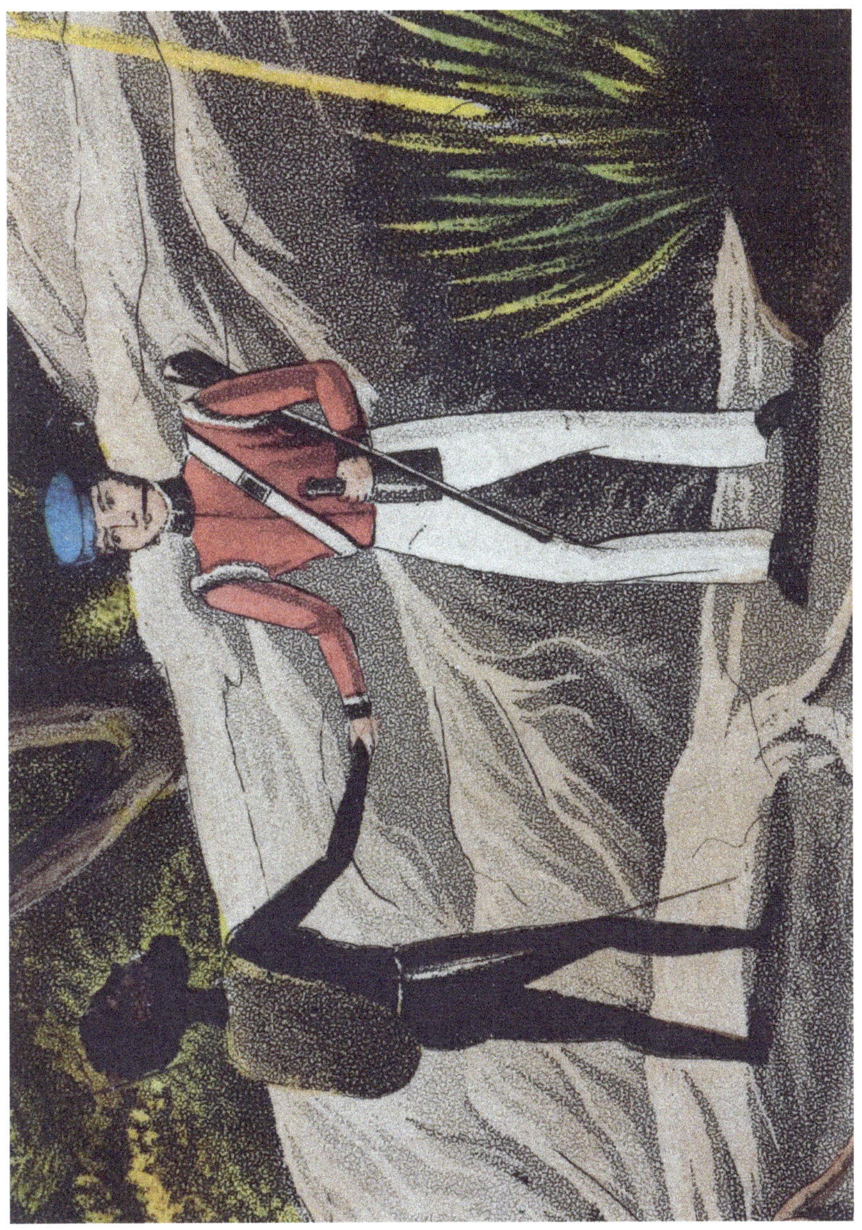

21: A section of Dale's panorama, showing a King Ya-nup man shaking hands with one of the newcomers after a kangaroo hunt. *Courtesy National Library of Australia, nla-pic-an S1118LOC1637.*

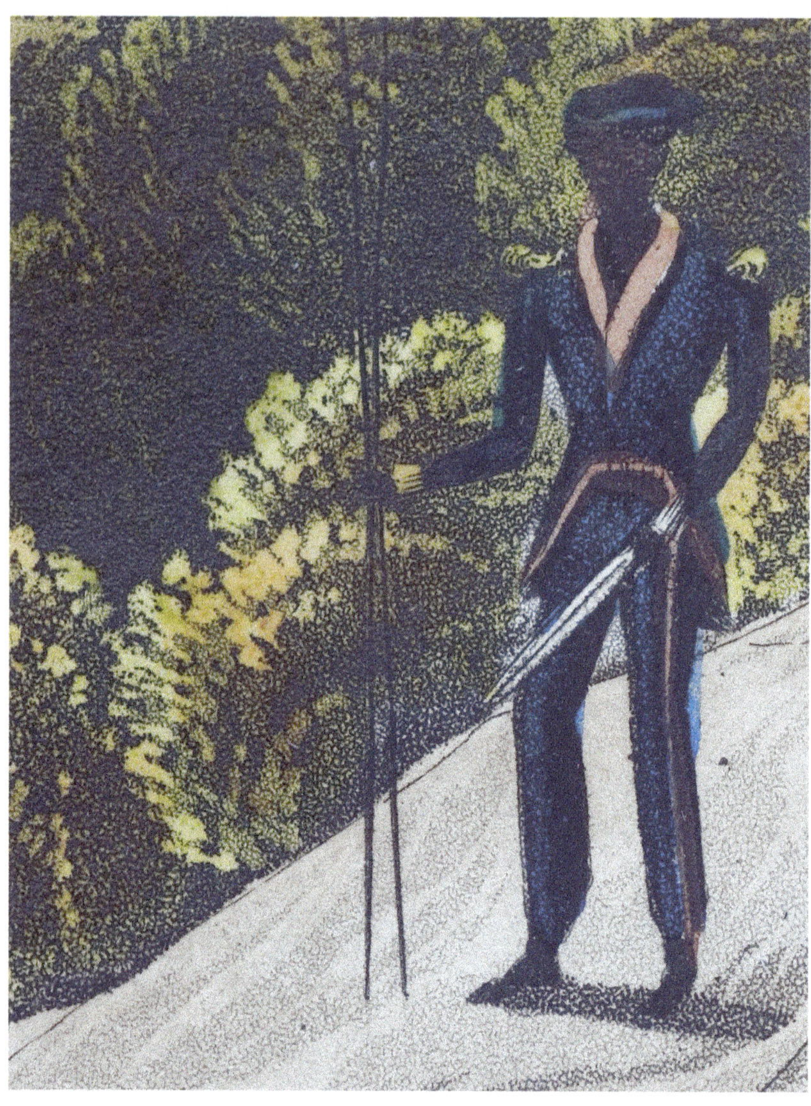

22: Nakinah in his makeshift naval captain's uniform – the bounty of his bargaining powers. Detail from *Panoramic View of King George's Sound*.

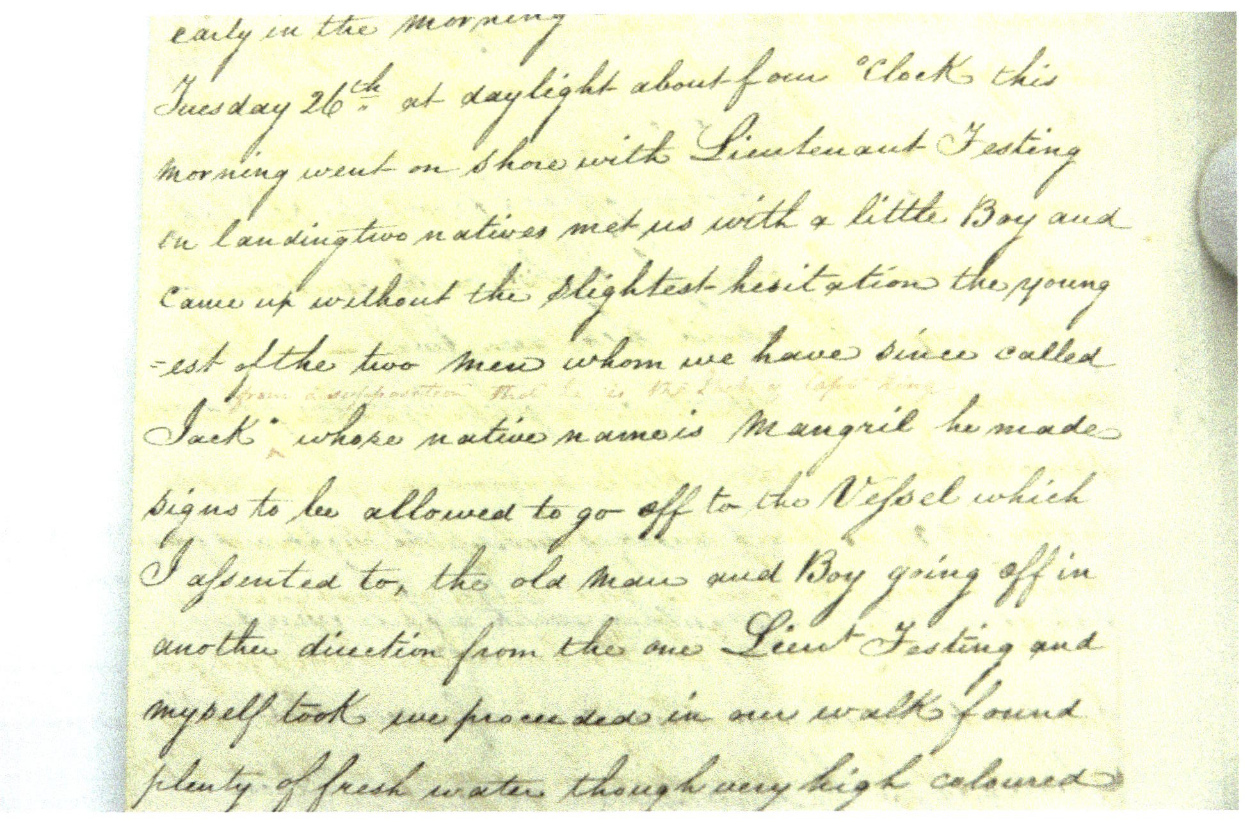

23: A section of Major Edmund Lockyer's 'Fair Copy' Journal, showing his acknowledgement that his thoughts about Jack came from Phillip Parker King. Original 'Fair Copy' journal held at AO NSW, 'CSO relating to King George's Sound'. 4/2092. *Photo Gustavo Geuna.*

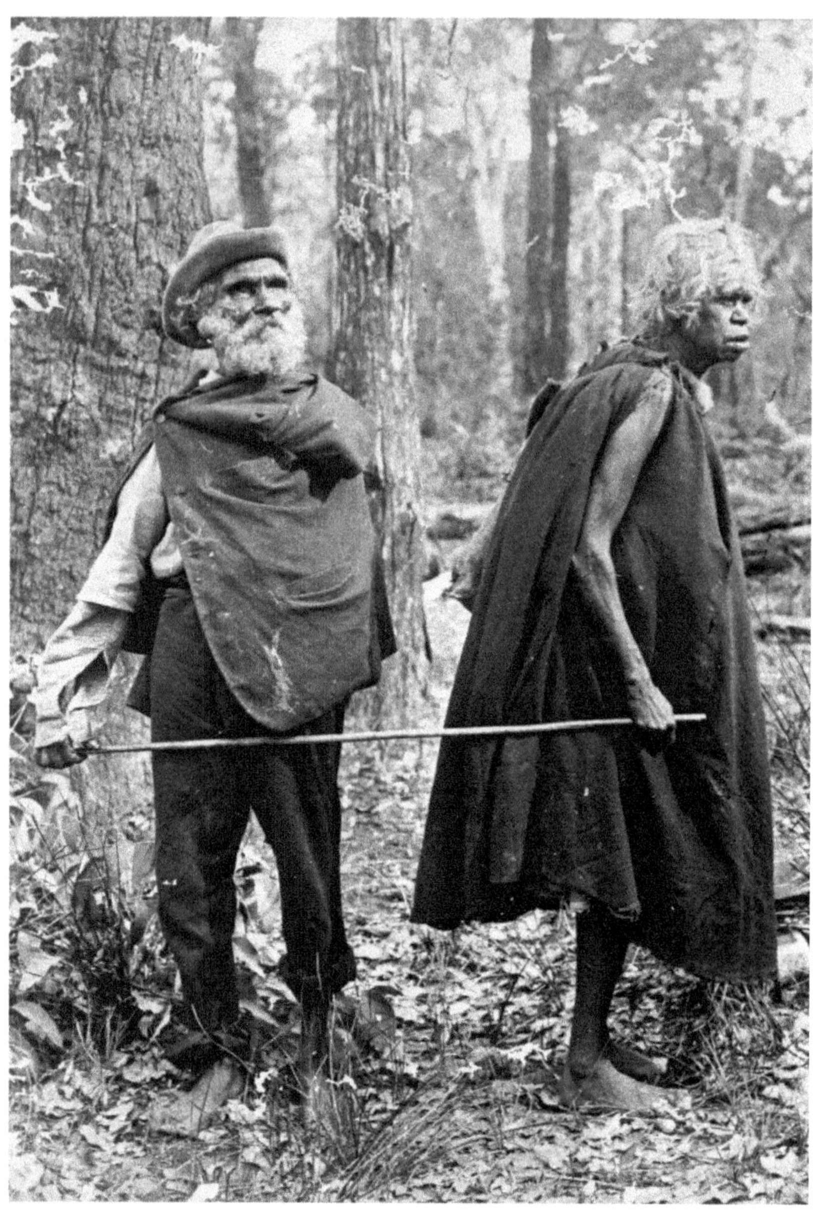

24: *Bobby and Jimmy, Aborgines from the Denmark District,* photo taken by the Dawson brothers in Denmark, 1890s. Bobbie is wearing European clothes, but he has buttoned up his jacket to his shoulder, in the same way that kangaroo skin cloaks were fastened. Bobbie was blinded for breaking tribal law. *Courtesy Battye Library, 706P, vol. 192.*

FINDING A VOCABULARY
FOR ENCOUNTERS

I

Stepping Ashore, Stepping Aboard

Bo-kēn-yēn-nă: Shall I go on board?[1]

I begin this history with a meeting that occurred before the British settlement was established, in 1821 between Phillip Parker King of the British Royal Navy and two groups of Aborigines in Oyster Harbour at King George's Sound. King was an Australian-born maritime surveyor and son of the third Governor of New South Wales, Philip Gidley King. This meeting was jotted down by King in his log book and reworked in his published narrative.[2] It was his second visit to King George's Sound and its adjoining harbours. He had stepped ashore in 1818, but he had not met any local people then – he saw smoke from their fires and they probably saw him and his vessels from the bush. King's visit in 1821, when he met and exchanged with Aborigines, is a good beginning for this history. His narrative alludes to other stories of previous meetings and sightings from ashore. Through King's descriptions, it is possible to read how he and other European seafarers and particular Aborigines were reciprocally adding to their shared vocabularies for communication and extending an evolving repertoire of knowledge about each other. A close reading of the Aborigines' and strangers' employment of their own expectations in this meeting also suggests a vocabulary with which to talk about cross-cultural engagements at King George's Sound when the British newcomers set up their garrison in 1826. King's published narrative disseminated the knowledge he gained in this encounter. It formed part of the repertoire of knowledge later explorers carried back to the colony; an inventory expanded by Major Edmund Lockyer when he experienced his first encounters with this place and its people five years later. It is an episode that I will constantly return to.

It was mid-afternoon on 23 December 1821. A square-rigged vessel with two masts, weighing 170 tons, sailed from the east around Bald Head and into King George's Sound. This large schooner, the *Bathurst*, like a swan and its cygnets, carried three smaller open boats – two whaleboats and a smaller cutter called a jolly boat. On board and in charge was Captain Phillip Parker King. On his previous visit in 1818 he had anchored in Oyster Harbour, to the north of King George's Sound, but on this visit he wished to explore the area near where in 1801 Matthew Flinders had anchored his vessel, the *Investigator*, during his circumnavigation of Australia.[3] On his first visit King relied on Flinders's maps, charts and descriptions of King George's Sound and the surrounding area. Flinders's writing and charting gave clarity to an expectation in King's mind of what King George's Sound might have been like: the well-wooded land, the depth and shape of the waterways, the character and habits of these particular Aboriginal people.

The purpose of this visit was to replenish the brig's supplies of wood and water before undertaking an extensive voyage up the west coast. King dropped the *Bathurst's* anchor near the western shore of King George's Sound and one mile from the entrance to Princess Royal Harbour. He was eager to explore the northern shores of Princess Royal Harbour, but was unsure whether the location would be suitable for wooding and watering his brig. Suitability was determined by the proximity of the shore to where the vessel could anchor. It was a safety measure for King and his crew; his vessel was his only site of security. It also allowed King to control the space of a possible encounter with the Aborigines and he needed to hold the power in such a space. He waited until early the following morning to take a whaleboat into Princess Royal Harbour for this purpose, before the sea breeze came up.[4]

King, his crew and their vessels were being watched. As he was preparing one of the whaleboats to test the depth of the harbour, King heard distant shouts. He and his crew looked around the harbour and saw, perched on top of the north head, 'several Indians … hallooing and waiving to us'. King returned their shouts but did nothing more until he had prepared the whaleboat and then he and his botanist, Allan Cunningham, pulled towards them. The communication would happen when King was ready, when he could control the space and pace of the meeting. But the encounter had already begun. From where he was, King could make out the appearances of this group of men. They were each dressed in a kangaroo skin cloak slung over the left shoulder with their left breast and arm uncovered. The whaleboat drew close to the north shore and the group of Aborigines came down 'to receive' the strangers, as King put it. Cunningham noted that they laid aside their spears.[5] The gestures of these men, King thought, were an invitation to land, but after what he described as a 'little vociferation and gesture on both sides', King pulled the whaleboat back into the harbour going near to where Flinders had anchored in 1801, opposite a cleared piece of land between two hills on the northern shore. As the Aborigines followed the boat along the shore, King realised that the depth of the water close to the shore was too shallow to anchor the *Bathurst* without 'being impeded' by the group. He assumed, however, that they would be 'amicably disposed', thinking of the meeting between them and Captain Matthew Flinders.

He began turning the whaleboat around to head back to the *Bathurst* and sail into Oyster Harbour where he had anchored in 1818, knowing that he would be able to control the space on the shores of that harbour with the brig at a secure distance. But before the whaleboat had pulled away, the group of Aboriginal men (Cunningham said there were nine) who had followed and watched the strangers' every move were already wading out through the water towards the boat which was sitting in the shallows. King did not wish to engage with them intimately at this stage fearing that if he did they would want some sort of gift or trinket, remembering his previous encounters with Indigenous people around the continent. King had nothing with him in the whaleboat to give them besides a few scraps of ships' biscuit, which Cunningham threw to them as King pulled off into deeper water so he could hold a conversation with them without physical contact. He was doing what he could to engage in the encounter on his terms.[6]

Despite, or perhaps because, of the distance and deep water between them, these strangers and Aborigines managed to 'parley'. According to King, it went like this:

> Upon making signs for fresh water, which they instantly understood, they called out to us – 'ba-doo, ba-doo', and pointed to a part of the bay where Captain Flinders had marked a rivulet. Ba-doo, in the Port Jackson language, means water; it was therefore thought probable that they must have obtained it from some late visitors; and in this opinion we were confirmed, for the word kangaroo was also familiar to them.[7]

This first conversation that King had with this group of Aborigines hints at and was shaped by previous encounters. After their conversation about fresh water, King turned back towards the anchorage of the *Bathurst*. Every time King and his crew changed direction, the Aborigines mirrored them from shore. When he reached the *Bathurst* near the harbour's entrance, the men who had followed the boat went to the north head again, and stood in the position where they had first made themselves known to King and his crew. King pulled up the anchor and the *Bathurst*, with its smaller vessels tacked towards Oyster Harbour, to the north of King George's Sound.

The mouth of Oyster Harbour was very narrow with sections of sand flats and dips of deep water. King knew this from his previous visit and so he took his time in mastering the entrance. As soon as the *Bathurst* had navigated successfully through the sandbar King noticed the appearance of three new Aborigines on the eastern side of Oyster Harbour, opposite to the other group whom he had conversed with, and retreated from, in Princess Royal Harbour. This was a secure space for King; he sent a whaleboat to the eastern shore to lay out the *Bathurst's* kedges for anchor. When the boat reached the shallows the three new Aborigines 'took their seats in it as unceremoniously as a passenger would in a ferry-boat', as King put it.[8] Perhaps they had done this before. The whaleboat with its Aboriginal passengers went back to the brig and the three men went aboard the *Bathurst* for the afternoon. King recorded that these men were 'totally free from timidity or distrust', and so too was King who now felt he was able to control the theatrics of this meeting.

On board the three Aboriginal men shed their cloaks of kangaroo skin and donned clothes that were given to them by the strangers. King was prepared now with gifts. Throughout this exchange they were being watched by the men on the opposite shore with whom King had conversed earlier. King was sensitive to competition and favour, noting that the Aborigines on the western shore, 'seeing that their companions were admitted [on board], were loudly vociferous in their request to be sent for also …' But the western group was on the lee shore – the wind was blowing towards them – and King could not get a boat to that side, nor did he want too many visitors on the deck at once. Again, his decisions were based on securing his control over the encounter. When King had stabilised the anchor of the *Bathurst*, two of the three Aborigines who had been on board went back ashore, King believing that they were 'evidently charged with some message from the other' man who voluntarily remained on board.

King and his crew also went ashore on the eastern side and began digging wells for water. After a while the two Aborigines who had been on board the ship earlier returned to where the strangers were on the shore. Tellingly, King now calls them 'our friends'. This small comment sheds light on how King is framing this encounter in his narrative. Friends can betray and be betrayed, strangers cannot. These two 'friends' had taken their time to prepare themselves properly for their return. King wrote that they had evidently been at their 'toilette'. They had smeared their faces with red ochre and replaced the strangers' gifts with their old kangaroo skin cloaks. They also carried a lighted fire stick which King supposed was intended for kindling a fire, so that they might spend the night close to the vessel, in order to watch these visitors' movements and work out their intentions. King and his crew returned to the brig, persuading the man who had stayed on board all day to leave. He left 'reluctantly'. While this man had been on board he had participated in an intimate exchange. He was amply fed by the crew: biscuit, yams, pudding, tea and grog were handed around. There was skin contact too, for his beard had been shaved, while his nudity – confronting to such strangers – was remedied, he swapped his cloak for a pair of trousers. He was 'christened' Jack by the men, a name to which, King wrote, 'he readily answered'.[9] This naming, shaving and clothing of an Aboriginal man was a way for King and his crew to transform this man in his mind and his narrative from 'native' to 'friend'. Jack went ashore after this personal and multi-sensory engagement on board, pleased with his new acquisitions. His freshly painted countrymen came to meet him on the beach, but King reported that 'without deigning to reply to their questions' he detached himself from them, watched the strangers in their ship 'in silence for some time' and then walked 'quietly and slowly' away. The others followed him at a distance. King assumed that it was the grog which had made Jack act in this alienated manner.

At daylight the following morning, the two Aboriginal groups were again assembled on the opposite shores of Oyster Harbour. The distance over the water which separated the groups was relatively small; their words easily travelled and were received across the gap. The group on the western shore had now also covered themselves in the red ocherous earth that the other men had applied the day before.

King and his crew rowed to the eastern shore to examine the wells they had dug the previous day. As soon as the jolly boat had touched the sand and the crew stepped out, Jack climbed in and was rowed back to the brig again. The Aborigines on the western shore were loudly vocal, King believing that they also wanted to go on board the brig. Their interest was held with Jack and the brig for a while before two of the group on the western shore began fishing. They saw a small seal that had been beached by the outgoing tide. A spear was fixed in a throwing stick and thrown at the animal, hitting it neatly in the neck. The other man ran up and finished it off, piercing it again with his spear and hitting it about the head with a small hammer. The whole group then assembled around the seal and carried it to their nearby fire, eating part of it before it was dead. King and Cunningham were interested in this 'barbarous feast' and landed the jolly boat on the shore to get a closer look. Their curiosity must have been stronger than the wind, allowing them to go to the western shore for the first time since their arrival. Seeing the boat approaching their shore, the Aborigines – who had added seal oil to their body ochre – 'sprang up' from the seal, threw their spears into the bushes and had boarded the boat before it had properly landed. King believed they wished to be rowed out to the brig where Jack was, but he made them wait while he and Cunningham went to observe the animal. The feast was near finished as the Aborigines had all stepped aboard except for one old man and a boy who had not run to the boat. They were seated over the carcass eating the remains. King and Cunningham returned to the boat and ferried the group who had been waiting in the boat out to the *Bathurst*.

It was soon time for breakfast and so the visitors were put ashore by King. The Aborigines were never allowed to be on board while the strangers were eating their breakfast. King knew that they would want food; perhaps he was concerned about his crew's rations and these men seemed to only eat once a day. Three 'new faces' appeared on the eastern side and were brought on board after breakfast, staying the whole day. In the afternoon the expedition's surgeon, Andrew Montgomery took a boat out to Green Island, a small island lying in the deep water of Oyster Harbour. He shot some parakeets and water fowl that were nesting on the island, some of which he gave to the Aborigines, although King does not record which group was given the birds. After Montgomery explained to them, through both body and voice, how the birds had been killed, they produced what King described as a 'great applause.'[10] And that evening before sunset, the group from the opposite shore was admitted on board the *Bathurst*.

With groups from each shore given successive turns to go on board the *Bathurst*, this encounter had become something of a power play between them. While one group was on board, the other was standing on shore watching or conversing with those aboard. Jack was the only one who was allowed to stay on board the whole time.

◆

Throughout King's visit, both Aboriginal groups 'assisted' these strangers with whatever activities they were engaged in, mostly 'wooding' and 'watering' the vessels and each day new black faces showed up that they had not seen before. King wrote: 'They were not permitted to come on board until four o'clock in the afternoon, excepting Jack,' who came and went as he pleased.[11] King did not believe there was any jealousy over Jack's being allowed on board, while others had to wait their turn. This suited King well. He wanted to 'detain' Jack as a 'hostage' for the safety of Cunningham who was collecting botanical specimens for his collections close to the vessel. But King wrote that Jack was not kept 'by force.' His status as hostage allowed Jack to accompany Cunningham on a few of his botanical searches, not only assisting in carrying Cunningham's plants, but also adding 'to the specimens he was collecting.'[12] Like King, Cunningham was using the knowledge and experience of previous visitors to these shores, examining botanists' sketches and descriptions of the natural world to guide him towards particular species. He was principally concerned in finding the species that Robert Brown had discovered at King George's Sound in 1801 when he accompanied Flinders.[13]

During his time on board the *Bathurst* Jack showed off his tree-climbing skills to the strangers, who had brought two trees with them in their vessel: he climbed the rigging as 'high as the topmast-head.' Jack's performance caused enough of a stir for King to write that this dexterous Aborigine amused his companions on shore as well as mortifying Bundell of King's own crew, who had never dared to climb as high as Jack. This performance of skill, or statement of masculinity, was possibly as much of a show for the two Aboriginal groups on shore as it was for the strangers on board. Bundell was an Aboriginal man from Port Jackson. He had replaced King's previous 'native aid' Bungaree, always called 'Boongaree' by King, whom he had joined after having accompanied Flinders on several voyages around the Australian coast. Bundell, too, had become something of a voyager – travelling to Norfolk Island in 1791 and participating in other colonial, sealing and fishing voyages. He wore a shirt and trousers with pride, just like Jack, and he stood out physically: one eye had been lost to a spear wound.[14] King failed to note in his narrative the possible power play that Jack engaged in with Bundell. King did not even record that Bundell was also Aboriginal. To King, Bundell was a crew member who happened to be Aboriginal; he was a friend like Jack, not a 'native'.

Each afternoon when King was ready, the Aboriginal groups were admitted, in turns, on board the *Bathurst*. The numbers in the two groups increased a little each day. There were about forty in total, all male and ten of them boys, gathering on opposite sides of the harbour. Some of the people they had first met had only come once or twice and had been replaced with new people. It was not just 'curiosity' and 'excitement' that was the impetus to step aboard the *Bathurst*. Every time that the Aborigines visited these strangers they received a gift of some kind and King tells us that they considered a ship's biscuit to be the most valuable; each person was 'always presented one' on leaving the vessel.[15]

King observed that many of the men who came to visit him from the eastern side had been on the western shore earlier, but how they crossed over from one side to the other was a mystery to him. He commented in his journal that they were not a 'navigating tribe', as he saw no canoes, and nor did he observe 'any trees in the woods with the bark stripped, of which material they are usually made'. King also noticed that the Aborigines approached the water in a 'timid manner', concluding that they were not even 'accustomed to swimming'.[16] It did not occur to King that his presence with the brig had created the shifting groupings of these people – the presence of the brig on the water created a mirage of a division in the local populace.

King's arrival at King George's Sound, in the brig and with his two boats, had also encouraged the local inhabitants to enter into a vigorous program of trade with the visitors. Spears, knives, and hammers were bartered each time they went aboard, or when King's crew stepped ashore. And in the morning the Aboriginal men came at first light with a fresh supply of weapons to trade, suggesting that they were manufacturing almost the whole time that they were not engaged in trading. King believed that it was their women who were busy between the hours of trade, manufacturing the weapons. He could only assume that this was the women's job because he never saw them.

◆

On the evening of 29 December 1821, King and his crew were visited by twenty-four men, from both shores, including their 'friend', Jack. According to King, the Aborigines soon realised that he was preparing to depart Oyster Harbour. They 'expressed great sorrow' at this, especially Jack who kept 'as he always did' at a distance from his countrymen and treated them 'with the greatest disdain'. When it was time to send them back on shore that evening, after a jovial barter, Jack avoided his countrymen and 'as usual' was the last to leave the vessel. Rather than getting into the smaller whaleboat that they all sat in to be ferried back to shore, Jack hopped into the other whaleboat on the opposite side of the brig that was preparing to get fresh water from the wells, 'evidently expecting', King wrote, 'to be allowed to return in her'. King had become attached to this 'friendly Indian' who was 'allowed' to visit King 'whenever he chose and to do as he pleased; he always wore the shirt that had been given to him on the first day, and endeavoured to imitate everything' that King and his crew were doing, particularly mimicking the sail maker and the carpenter at their work.[17] King seemed pleased to believe that Jack was becoming civilised. He was also the only Aborigine that King met at Oyster Harbour who did not make spears for exchange, laughing heartily whenever a 'carelessly-made spear was offered' to the strangers for 'sale'. King also wrote that he and Jack were becoming more and more intelligible to each other every day and King considered him to be 'certainly' the most intelligent 'native of the whole tribe'.[18] King judged Aboriginal intelligence in egocentric and ethnocentric terms: on the basis of assumed communication, his belief in his own ability to understand particular Aboriginal interlocutors or what he characterised as 'friendly' behaviour.

On 30 December, the anchors of the *Bathurst* were weighed and King and his crew prepared to depart, taking their time in getting out of the shallows and eventually mooring in the stream of the tide to wait for it to come in and lift them off the bottom of the harbour. At 8 am the Aboriginal groups visited them, as usual, but were 'disappointed' to see the brig had moved locations. King sent the jolly boat for one last barter. He and his crew had also enjoyed the exchanges and engagements aboard and ashore. The jolly boat was sent to the eastern shore. When the boat came back to the *Bathurst*, Jack had come too and was brought on board. King thought that he appeared 'attached' to them and he talked with his crew about Jack coming with them for their voyage up the west coast, if Jack was inclined to go. With communication between them not an issue for King, he wrote that 'there was not much difficulty in making him understand by signs that he might go with us, to which he appeared to assent'.[19] To make absolutely certain that Jack did want to leave King thought it wise that Jack tell his companions on shore about his voyaging plans. So it was not certain that they had understood each other all that clearly after all. King had one of his men, Bedwell, put Jack back ashore presumably to talk to his countrymen about his imminent departure with the strangers.

His friends seemed so involved in the barter which had started again when the boat touched the shore that they did not seem to care, King thought, about Jack leaving. Jack was talking to his countrymen and pointing to the sea, perhaps to show where he was going. King thought that his countrymen showed 'careless indifference' at the news of their friend, their attention 'being entirely engrossed with the barter that was going on.'[20] Suddenly, Jack revealed a throwing stick which he had previously hidden behind a bush, trading it with Bedwell for a biscuit before he got back into the boat. This was the first time during King's visit that Jack had bartered. And then he staged a grand performance: as he was being rowed back out to the *Bathurst*, Jack threw the biscuit – the spoils of his barter – to his countrymen on shore. In bestowing a biscuit, perhaps Jack was acting in the ways of these strangers, adopting their currency as well as their ship. King read Jack's drama as 'proof' of the sincerity of his intentions to travel with them.

After an hour on board, King was preparing for departure. The 'breeze freshened' making the water swell and the brig gently sway. King thought that that was enough for Jack, who walked up to King touching his tongue with his fingers and pointing to the shore. King believed that this gesture meant that he was sick and wanted to talk to his friends. Jack was immediately landed; since the whaleboat's position offered a further opportunity for bartering, the Aborigines rushed up to it. When the whaleboat was ready to row back to the brig, Jack 'shook his head and hung back,' King wrote, and was left on shore with his countrymen. The boat went back to the brig and the Aborigines 'dispersed' from the beach, but Jack remained separate from his group and 'walked away without exchanging a word with them.'[21]

Unfavourable weather detained the *Bathurst* at anchor in Oyster Harbour for three days and King spent four more days after that around King George's Sound, on Seal Island and near Bald Head before his boats – big and small – sailed out of the Sound on 6 January 1822.

I have spent time in retelling this encounter in order to draw out some specifics of the interactions between King and his crew and the Aboriginal people living around King George's Sound in 1821. The episode discloses several repertoires of encounter that recur throughout this history. To understand how these repertoires emerge and how these encounters were experienced by those involved, historians need to focus on the minutiae of action and context in each description.

King was not the first stranger to step ashore at King George's Sound. This is implied through his descriptions and his reliance on previous explorers' journals, narratives and maps. The way he constructed his descriptions is evidence of a knowledge bank of interaction and expectation that both he and his crew had of meetings with Indigenous people before this encounter in 1821 began. It is impossible to know what the prior knowledge and expectation of his crew were; it is unlikely they had read previous explorers' journals, and it can be assumed that their knowledge and assumptions were being reinforced and challenged during their expedition with King. Bundell probably travelled with other bases of knowledge and expectation and also, no doubt, contributed to those of King and his crew.

King's narrative reveals too that the Aborigines he met with also had a growing reservoir of knowledge about strangers who came to their shores. It hints at previous visitors: references to Flinders and the names that King used for the harbours and surrounding land disclose that this was a place where European visitors had previously spent time. King's stay at the harbour in turn added significantly to the store of knowledge available to subsequent visitors, his narrative significantly informing Lockyer's knowledge and expectation of Aboriginal behaviour.

The first conversation that King held with the group on the northern shore of Princess Royal Harbour reveals a developing storehouse of Aboriginal knowledge to which strangers like King were adding and reinforcing. The Indigenous men's response to King's gesture for fresh water with the words *badoo, badoo* is a telling point. King recognised that *badoo* was the Port Jackson Aboriginal word for water. This word was offered by the inhabitants before King had spoken: it was not mimicry. Not only did the Aborigines on shore understand what King's gestures meant, they knew what language to speak to him in. They had been eyeing off these strangers and the size and shape of their vessels, and were drawing on their previous experiences with similar vessels – and the visitors they housed – to know which language to use. We can assume that many of the strangers they previously conversed with would have come from Port Jackson first and picked up some local vocabulary, passing it on to the King George's Sound people through gesture and reference. Water was the first need of every seafarer.

This episode suggests the negotiation and education of both Aborigines and Europeans. They were learning how to communicate. Not only did King take home hundreds of Aborigines' tools and weapons from King George's

Sound, but during a subsequent visit in January 1822 he collected items of vocabulary. Reading through the words he translated, it seems likely that he learned and collected the words during the exchanges: items that were bartered are listed and decoded. Tellingly, the only phrase he collected was *bo-ken-yen-na* meaning 'Shall I go on board?' This question referenced the incessant requests by the local men to be taken on board the *Bathurst* and engage in trade.

Why were vocabularies collected, compared and published in traveller's accounts in the late eighteenth and early nineteenth centuries? A vocabulary list, like the weapons that King received, was a treasure to collect – a prize to take home. It was necessary knowledge and proof of the success of the voyage and of cross-cultural encountering.[22] It also represented the Aboriginal speakers as intelligent. Moreover, desire to learn the alien language was not limited to Europeans. The inhabitants of King George's Sound were collecting King's language too. King wrote in his journal: 'The words "by and by" were so often used by us in answer to their cau-wah, or "come here," that their meaning was perfectly understood.'[23] Both groups were learning on their feet how to communicate more effectively.

Jack, and other Aboriginal people represented as similar in personality and motivation to Jack, keeps re-emerging in the history that follows. His naming and the description of his actions epitomise European hopes and expectations of 'friendly' native behaviour. However, he acted in a very idiosyncratic way, dissimilar to the actions of his countrymen. Local loyalties did not always control human actions. Jack's likely political motivations and strategies will be considered in more depth later on.

King's narrative, and the fragmentary traces of Aboriginal actions inscribed within it, are also useful in explaining how I have found my own vocabulary with which to write and think about cross-cultural encounters like this. By the time the British established a garrison in 1826, the inhabitants of King George's Sound had developed a store of information about what to expect from strangers in different sized vessels who came to their shores. Knowledge of strangers began accruing before actual encounters happened. I shall return to Phillip Parker King and Jack. However, in order to understand how the Aborigines were developing a reservoir of knowledge about strangers and creating a common vocabulary for communicating with them, and how Europeans were accumulating knowledge about the Aborigines and their language, it is necessary to explain who the previous visitors were.

◆

In the seventeenth century, Dutch voyagers en route to the East Indies made frequent sightings of and contact with the coast of what they called New Holland. Blown off course by blustery winds, Dutch vessels sometimes traversed further south than intended. Aborigines living around the harbours of what would later be named King George's Sound might have seen the Dutch ship *Gulden Zeepardt* sail past in 1627. Peter Nuyts who was on board surveyed the coast around King George's Sound, but it is not clear whether he entered the harbours.[24]

The first recorded strangers to disembark in the area were Captain George Vancouver and his crew in 1791. They were in the early stages of a long voyage of 'discovery' (1791–1795) which had the mission of surveying and seizing territories for Britain before they were possessed by their Spanish rivals. Vancouver, who had twice sailed round the world as a midshipman with James Cook, was particularly interested in Nootka Sound and the north-west coast of America, but he also aimed to visit 'The South West part of New Holland, and endeavour to acquire some information of that unknown, though interesting country'.[25] He was aiming for what was called on the map, *Land Van de Leeuwin*, a Dutch name denoting the south-west extremity of the continent.

On 28 September 1791, aboard HM sloop *Chatham* and accompanied by the armed tender *Discovery*, Vancouver sailed through the heads of the vast bay he would name 'King George III's Sound'. During his two-week visit, Vancouver was kept busy mapping and naming much of this place: the harbours, islands and headlands. His crew went ashore on a western beach. Close to the shore and near a small cluster of trees they found 'the most miserable human habitation' they had ever seen. This Aboriginal site had not been vacated for long. Vancouver saw a freshly skinned fish on top of one hut and fresh 'excrement' from a native dog near it. He was unimpressed. 'The reflections which naturally arose,' Vancouver wrote, 'were humiliating in the highest degree.' This 'miserable' hut, he thought, was evidence of the 'lowly condition of some of our fellow creatures, rendered yet more pitiable by the apparent solitude and the melancholy aspect of the surrounding country' which 'presented little less than famine and distress'.[26] The strangers walked along the beach, climbing a high rocky point which Vancouver named Point Possession. This summit gave them a commanding view of the three harbours and surrounding land. While there, Vancouver hoisted the British colours, drank to His Majesty's health, and took possession for Britain of the land around him, including 'north-westward of Cape Chatham, so far as we might explore its coasts'. This ritual was 'accompanied by the usual formalities on such occasions' which were so 'usual' that he did not further describe them.

Vancouver's naming principles combined description, commemoration and tribute. 'Seal Island' was thus called because of its inhabitants; 'Bald Head' from its smooth appearance and absence of verdure. He sowed some seeds on an island in Oyster Harbour and optimistically named it 'Green'. He set aside the most majestic places for the greatest naming honours: contemporary royalty and high-ranking naval figures. The grandest harbour was named after the reigning King of England, George III. In fact, Vancouver and subsequent visitors referred to the whole area, including the adjacent land, as 'King George's Sound', not just the vast harbour. The southern adjacent harbour was named in honour of King George's daughter, Princess Charlotte, whose birthday it was.[27] The ceremony of taking possession being over, Vancouver and his crew went towards the north-eastern harbour. They discovered the narrow entrance that King would cross several decades later, the immense sand bars and sections of shallow water. On the way out of this harbour the boat grounded itself on a sandbank which was covered with oysters 'of a most delicious flavour' on which the visitors 'sumptuously regaled'. They celebrated the find by naming the harbour 'Oyster'.[28]

Before he departed King George's Sound Vancouver returned to the Aboriginal site he had seen when he was collecting water and (in an act of conscience?) decided to leave beads, knives, looking glasses and 'other trinkets', as a 'compensation' to the huts' 'solitary owner' for the wood he had cut down from their land. Vancouver did not meet any Aborigines during his visit, but it is important to note that encounters may happen even when actual *meetings* do not. The local inhabitants were presumably watching, studying and discussing the strangers.

To commemorate his visit and as proof of his act of possession, Vancouver erected a cairn of stones at a tree stump, 'for the purpose of attracting the attention of any European' passing through, and a glass bottle was sealed with a parchment inside describing the act of possession and the people and ships involved.[29] This act of possession, however, was not recognised seriously by the British government, as there was no crew member left behind to 'occupy' and hold the claim of land.[30] Vancouver's visit of over two weeks to King George's Sound had a larger importance. In his log books, he often mentioned seals and whales 'playing about the ship' while he was in the southern region. Rod Dickson has noted that, even though Vancouver's six-volume chronicle of his voyage was not published until 1798, the information and knowledge it would contain about King George's Sound, together with Vancouver's detailed sailing coordinates, maps and charts, became known to ship owners and seafarers who had a commercial interest in his discoveries, well before the journals were made public.[31] In London, Daniel Bennett, a merchant who owned ships engaged in the South Seas whaling trade, 'made it his business', Dickson wrote, 'to acquaint himself with any reports, personal accounts, log books and diaries of persons travelling through the South Seas to discover new grounds for his fleet of whalers to exploit.'[32] Sealing and whaling expeditions were already working the coast around Van Diemen's Land and Vancouver gave them an incentive to travel further to the south-west to King George's Sound. They were regular visitors. When Vancouver's journals were published, they were also read by British and French explorers and scientific naturalists who were excited by his descriptions of these large harbours and of the natives whose encampments he had seen.

Vancouver introduced King George's Sound and the surrounding region to the map of the world. But, importantly, it was also added to the mind maps of British and French imperialists. Napoleon Bonaparte, the first consul of France, who was already showing signs of a considerable appetite for territorial conquest, agreed to despatch a scientific voyage of discovery to New Holland and surrounding waters in competition with Britain whose convict settlement at Port Jackson provided a tenuous toehold on a very large and hardly defendable continent.

In October 1800 and July 1801, respectively, the French expedition under Nicolas Baudin and a rival English enterprise under Matthew Flinders set sail from Europe for New Holland. Both, following Vancouver's lead, would anchor in King George's Sound for about three weeks. Flinders did so in December 1801 and January 1802, making King George's Sound the first landing place in his circumnavigation of the continent after a rapid passage from England. In contrast, Baudin did not land there until February 1803 and made King George's Sound almost his final anchorage in New Holland waters. Flinders used Vancouver's map and log books to select King George's Sound as the 'proper place in which to prepare ourselves for examination of the south coast of Terra Australis.'[33] Flinders discovered there had been a visit of a sealing crew in the vessel *Elligood* since Vancouver's visit. The sealers had cut down trees with an axe and saw and removed Vancouver's bottle with his statement of possession and sailing coordinates.

Flinders mapped the coast in great detail and ventured a short way inland, meeting several times with Aboriginal people. The first meeting – which was the first recorded encounter between Aborigines and Europeans in the region – included the botanist Robert Brown and several crew members. Seeing smoke at the head of the harbour, they walked towards it where they met several men 'who were shy but not afraid', Flinders reported. One of these men was admired for his 'manly behaviour' and given a freshly shot bird and a pocket handkerchief by the strangers.[34] Flinders believed that these Aborigines did not want to communicate with him and his crew, as they made signs which Flinders interpreted to mean to 'return from whence [we] came'.[35] On 30 December, Flinders ordered his marines onto the beach to be 'exercised' in the presence of a group of Aboriginal men who had become constant visitors 'and friends', at the tents of the strangers. Flinders noted the 'red coats and white crossed belts were greatly admired' by the men as he believed they resembled 'their own manner of ornamenting themselves'.[36] Several of the Aboriginal men 'moved their hands, involuntarily, according to the motions; and the old man', who had been admired for his manliness earlier, 'placed himself at the end of the rank, with a short staff in his hand, which he shouldered, presented, grounded, as did the marines with [their] musket ...'[37] Isobel White has discovered that a hundred years later anthropologist Daisy Bates interviewed an old Aboriginal man who claimed to be the grandson of the old 'manly' Aboriginal man who met Flinders. He explained to Bates how the military drill subsequently became part of an Aboriginal dance ceremony at King George's Sound.[38]

Flinders' encounters with the local inhabitants during his visit to King George's Sound were amicable and intimate enough for his surgeon, Mr Hugh Bell to measure the height and anatomy of one man and Flinders' was enabled to collect a small vocabulary list from the men he engaged with.[39] He concluded, however, that the area was unfit for a British settlement.

During Baudin's visit in early 1803, his crew members had only one brief meeting with the local inhabitants. François Péron's narrative of the expedition, tellingly, makes constant reference to Vancouver, but he ignored Flinders' visit and wrongly claimed that one of his own colleagues, Jacques-Joseph Ransonnet, was the first European to 'approach the native people of this region'.[40] Ransonnet went to examine the coast between Mt Gardner and

Bald Island to the east of King George's Sound. He sailed into a 'pretty bay' where 'to his great astonishment' he saw a ship at anchor. It was the Anglo-American brig *Union*, captained by James Pendleton from New York. His mission was to procure seal skins and sell them to China. Ransonnet named this bay 'Two People's' to commemorate this meeting. After leaving the American brig he engaged in a 'long and peaceful' meeting with a group of local Aborigines. A brief exchange took place and Ransonnet noted that the Aboriginal men discarded their French gifts, leaving them on nearby rocks.[41] No other members of Baudin's expedition engaged with local inhabitants, although they had seen 'two or three individuals' who fled 'headlong into the woods.'[42]

Another French expedition, led by the navigata-naturalist Jules-Sebastien-Cesar Dumont d'Urville visited the harbours in October 1826. Several members of his crew spent an intimate night on shore camping next to a group of the King George's Sound men, including the artist Louis Auguste de Sainson who provided the only known sketches of Mokaré and his family. d'Urville's visit will be explored in more detail later. These French and English visits – fuelled by the strong desire for exploration, discovery and possession of land, the collection of natural knowledge and history and encounters with Indigenous inhabitants – had important human contacts that had considerable local impact. They contributed significantly to the growing and varied experiences of interactions with different kinds of strangers being accumulated by local Aboriginal people decades before Lockyer's settlement party arrived on Christmas day in 1826.[43]

Reflection: Finding My Own Vocabulary for Encounters

At the time the garrison was established in 1826, the local Aborigines did not transcribe their experiences, thoughts or desires. The European visitors and the British newcomers who stayed did write things down, some much more than others. The great distance in time from the present and the subsequent dispossession, disruption and dispersion of Aboriginal communities in south-western Australia mean that modern Aboriginal memories of particular events during the period in question are fragmentary or non-existent. Indigenous histories are critical in the construction of present identities and in establishing linkages between people and with places.[1] I respect the validity and vitality of such histories, but have not attempted to do oral history and do not claim to write Indigenous history. Rather, I bring my training in documentary history to bear to illuminate a series of personal interactions between Aborigines and British people during a brief period in the past at a particular place, relying primarily on a detailed critical reading of British accounts.

A few of the British commanders and medical assistants who spent months or years in the King George's Sound garrison created useful ethnographies and action descriptions. Traces of Aboriginal doings and sayings abound in several of these texts and by reading such traces closely and critically I have pieced together narratives which suggest what the actions in question might have meant. Traces of strategic action by Indigenous people have been aptly called countersigns by Bronwen Douglas, who describes them as:

> oblique traces of the imprint of local or subaltern agency on foreign or elite perceptions, reactions, and representations. They are manifest syntactically in

word choice and arrangement; grammatically in tense, mood, and voice; and semantically in presence, emphasis, or absence.[2]

I consider all actions, British and Aboriginal, to be strategic. As Jerome Bruner reminds us, 'all behaviour is directed towards goals.'[3]

This history focuses on a few key British texts: notably, Major Edmund Lockyer's journals; Isaac Scott Nind's report on Aboriginal customs; Captain Collet Barker's journal and Alexander Collie's reports, letters and travel narratives.[4] These British men described a world they saw and participated in. They recorded what they observed or heard, what they thought was exciting, important or unusual. But they could not accurately transcribe the way the world was for others. They described Aboriginal actions, conversations and gestures, and they drew their conclusions quickly using their storehouse of ethnocentric knowledge and cultural expectations. In order to understand both the forming of a British world at King George's Sound and the changing of an Aboriginal one, and how Aborigines and Englishmen were understanding, interpreting and using each other, the texts need to be penetrated to draw out descriptions of people *doing things*.[5] And such descriptions need to be situated in context to clarify something about the how and the why of the actions described. How do we read these long ago meetings? Inga Clendinnen explains: 'The trick is to cultivate double vision: to retrieve from British descriptions clues as to autonomous Aboriginal action, not the simple reaction to British actions the British naturally assume occurred.'[6]

Actions and words are thought up, articulated, responded to and made sense of within a specific cultural world, within a shared system of daily life, within a particular vocabulary. Using European (observers') texts to re-construct the meaningful past actions of Aborigines (the observed) and their interactions with the newcomers can only be achieved by the meticulous scrutiny of such texts, by paying sharp attention to the authors' tone, emotion and rhetoric. I need to get to know the British too in order to exploit their writings to ethnohistorical ends.

To attempt to map past mentalities is a complicated activity requiring an ethnographically informed imagination.[7] As Clifford Geertz suggested, this pilgrimage is 'more like grasping a proverb, catching an illusion, seeing a joke – or … reading a poem – than it is like achieving communion.'[8] Greg Dening has written, 'It is hard, painstaking work to see what others saw in different times and circumstances. It requires an ecumenicity of disciplines to see it

– geology, botany, anthropology, linguistics to name just a few.'[9] Although I am firmly grounded in the discipline of history, in my method and ways of thinking about history and past people's worlds I have been influenced by other disciplines, most obviously cultural anthropology, which provides useful conceptual tools for grasping something of the ways in which past people made sense of their worlds: that is, their cosmology and its pragmatic enactment in actions and behaviours.[10] People in the past – British and Aboriginal – had different mentalities, different cultural systems, different motivations and therefore different behaviours – different from each other and different from present-day Australians, whether Indigenous or not. Nineteenth-century Englishmen and Aborigines are both foreign to me though not equally so, given that I share a degree of linguistic familiarity with the British. My goal is to understand both British and Aboriginal behaviour as far as possible in terms of their own past contexts rather than impose an unthinking presentist framework. Both the British and the Aboriginal worlds need to be made strange before they can be rendered familiar.

Many historians have stepped horizontally into the practice of anthropology fusing the methodology of understanding how people act within their cultural system with the praxis of history, which aims to understand past events in the present. This fusion is known as ethnographic history. Dening describes it in 'its broadest sense' as an 'attempt to return to the past the past's own present, a present with all the possibilities still in it, with all the consequences of actions still unknown.'[11] Unlike anthropologists, historians' field notes come from the archives – we do not choose what to record, but we retrieve important actions and necessary context from what was recorded. Ethnographies require different interpretive practices from historical manuscripts, such as the journals of explorers or British commanders. There were conscious processes and agendas by which the journals were created and, in some cases, edited for publication. Donna Merwick's work on Dutch–Amerindian encounters in New Netherland has been particularly influential in showing the necessity of focusing on micro-narratives as the best way to use the methods of these two disciplines.[12] Bronwen Douglas's ethnohistorical work on missionary encounters in colonial New Caledonia shows her remarkable ability and honesty for drawing out indigenous agency from colonial missionary records, without imposing her own contemporary assumptions on her analysis. Inga Clendinnen's histories of the Aztecs and Aboriginal encounters with the British at Port Jackson have taught me how to read and use colonial documents. She shows what things to look out for in such documents and demonstrates how much patience is needed to do justice to past people in our histories. The considered and poetic writing of both Tom Griffiths and Greg Dening reveals the importance of finding your own vocabulary for writing and talking about such delicate, long-ago meetings. Their histories and anthropologies show that it is important to find the right words – in meaning and in sound – in the construction of our narratives and to find the right structure and rhythm for our stories.

My vocabulary for writing this history also comes, perhaps less obviously, from the approaches of philosophy and psychology, in particular the work of Jerome Bruner, who seeks to understand how humans act, react and make sense of themselves in their world. His writings on the narrative construction in everyday life and how our daily stories – internal and collective – shape our history and ultimately our culture, are particularly pertinent when thinking and writing about a group of people whose culture circulated, and in some ways relied on, stories constructed and told.

Inga Clendinnen has written that, when doing history, 'Particular cases are where the action is, and only a close examination of particular cases can lead us beyond a most sketchy and superficial understanding of how individual men understood their particular situations; how they responded to them; how they explained their actions to themselves.'[13] I agree that the best way to read and understand how cross-cultural relationships began and developed is to discover and try to reconstruct close-up stories of a day-to-day nature. This history, therefore, does not have a conventional or straightforward structure. I have favoured synchronic, complex episodes over a chronological start-to-finish history. As Hayden White advises, 'the events should not pose as the tellers of a narrative.'[14]

This history is about drawing out understandings rather than forcing conclusions. To spend more time on imagining people's motivations is a worthwhile activity; we see possibilities and choices rather than inevitabilities, and promote consideration rather than judgement and tolerance rather than fear.

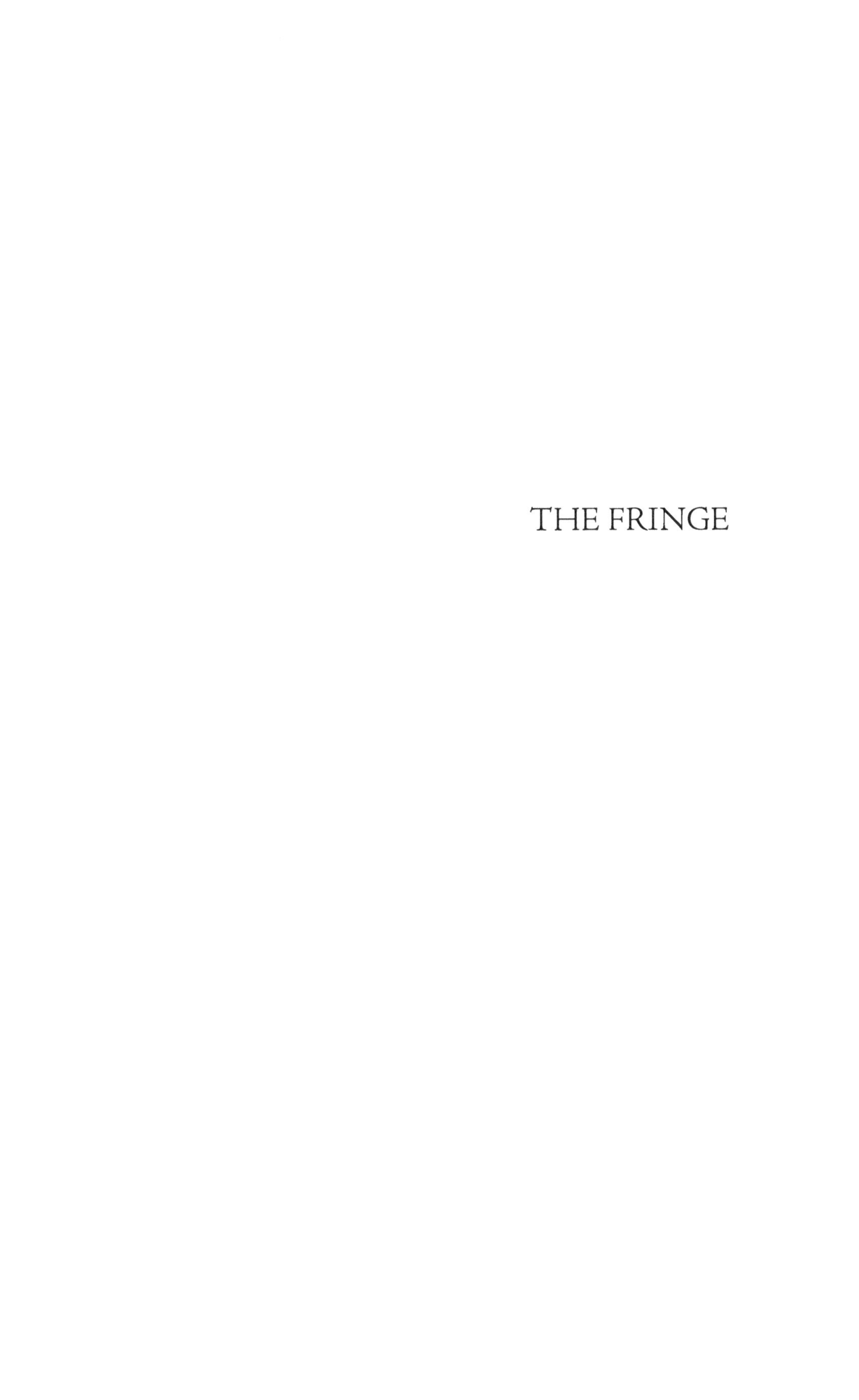

THE FRINGE

2

Beyond the Littoral: Reading the King Ya-nup World

I suspect no landscape … can be comprehended unless we perceive it as an organisation of space: unless we ask ourselves who owns it or uses the spaces, how they were created and how they change.[1]

Mokaré's mother gave birth to him in a birthing shelter away from their family's camp at the turn of the nineteenth century. His mother would have been away from her family and kin for eight days before the birth, but a few of the older women would have been there to nurse her.[2] She ate wallaby, kangaroo or fish, or whatever was to be had to give her strength for the labour. All the single men were dispatched to the bush during this time so that Mokaré's father would not get jealous. If the single men did intrude on a birth, and sometimes they did, they were sent away by the old nurses with 'a flea in their ear'.[3] It is most likely Mokaré was born in the season of *Moken* (or *Mokkar*), sometime between April and July.[4] The King Ya-nup knew when *Moken* had commenced by the presence of *whitepepoy*, the black magellanic cloud in the sky which looked like an emu laying its eggs.[5] *Moken* also marked the beginning of the rainy season and kangaroo hunting time.[6] Once he was born, Mokaré's placenta would have been securely placed in a tree, because the King Ya-nup believed that if a dog had come along and eaten it, the growth of the child would have been stopped.[7] Before he could walk, when he was just *peep-anger*, an infant, his mother carried him in a kangaroo skin bag, slung around her neck while she kept busy gathering plants, hunting small animals, building houses and hearths for her family.[8]

Mokaré had four brothers.[9] Nakinah was the eldest, represented by most of the newcomers as 'chief' or 'King of the King George tribe'. Dr Alexander

Collie, the first Government Resident after King George's Sound became a free settlement, wrote that Nakinah 'arrogates to himself the title of King of the tribe.'[10] Regardless of whether he considered himself to be holding the status of 'king', the newcomers believed him to be 'head of the family' whose ground the settlement occupied.[11] Barker and Nind described him as elusive, often standing apart from his countrymen. Nakinah ornamented his hair and his armband with a bunch of white cockatoo feathers, his chest and shoulders were distinctly marked with *umbin*, ceremonial scars made by a burning piece of wood or kangaroo claw. This signified his age and status.[12] It was not a man's wrinkles that signalled his age, it was the length of his beard. A youth was called *no beard*, a young man *beard growing* and a man of middle age was known as *full beard*.[13] It was forbidden at King George's Sound for young men to eat black eagles as this prevented them from growing a 'fine beard'. Nakinah was between forty and fifty years old in the early 1830s, was unmarried but had one child, a little boy called Wapere. Wapere's mother was never recorded by the British.

Mokaré had three other 'brothers': Waiter, younger than Mokaré and described by him as an honest man who would never steal, even 'if he were starving for 3 days'. He would not steal anything belonging to the black fellows, 'still less the whites'.[14] Taragon was another 'brother', and the youngest was Yallapoli whom the French artist on Dumont d'Urville's 1826 voyage, de Sainson, described as 'a child of twelve or thirteen years' whose 'shrill harsh voice dominated everyone else's in the gathering, he never stopped talking'.[15] Mokaré had one sister, Mullet, who was married to Nulloch, a King's River man. She slept at a camp near to where the first British farm was built.[16] Little is known of Mullet, possibly because she was married and her husband was seldom about the garrison, but also because during this period, women were very rarely in view of the newcomers. Unlike encounters with indigenous peoples in the eastern Pacific where women featured prominently and strategically, Aboriginal women at King George's Sound were rarely visible. The newcomers who wrote down what they saw were all men and many European visitors made mention in their journals that they were hurried away from where they assumed the women were camping. Some of the women's stories did, however, filter through into the British world and we shall discover them later.

Mokaré and his brothers inherited their mother's moiety and their father, Patyet's country.[17] Patyet had inherited the country from his father,

Mongheron, as had long been the way of life and most of their neighbours, most of the time, acknowledged their rights to it.[18] Mokaré never met his grandfather, Mongheron, but he had heard that he was a 'very large, tall, stout man', with ten wives, who even made Nakinah look like a child.[19]

The first encounter recorded in the archives with the man named Mokaré was reported by Dumont d'Urville in October 1826, when he visited King George's Sound while on his scientific voyage of discovery. It can be assumed that Mokaré had previous encounters with strangers like the French, possibly even with Phillip Parker King, but he is not specified until he met d'Urville. During that visit the artist de Sainson, the ethnographer Gaimard and the officer Guilbert spent a night on shore, camping next to Mokaré's family and kin. Mokaré was sketched by de Sainson during this encounter. He described Mokaré as being 'A man who was still young … he had an open face and was more lively than any of his comrades.'[20] When he met the French, Mokaré was probably in his mid to late twenties (*beard growing*). He was slim and tall, his hair was long, and he wound it tightly into a bun at the back of his head. He was *man-jah-lies*, an unmarried man, and therefore would have also had a dog's tail in his hair.[21] He was, however, by 1830, engaged to a 'little child'.[22]

The sketches by de Sainson (see images 13, 14, 15, 20) show the kangaroo skin cloaks that the King Ya-nup wore that were described by King in 1821. They were manufactured by the women out of several kangaroo skins and worn by all the men, women and children. First the women pegged the skins out on the ground to dry, then with a sharpened stone they were cut into the desired shape. With the stone, the inside layer was then scraped away until the material became soft and malleable. It was rubbed with grease and red ochre, called *paloil*, which they also used to rub on their faces, hair and bodies. The skins were stitched together with the sinews of the kangaroo tail. Mullet, Mokaré's sister wore a larger cloak than her brothers, made from the male kangaroo skins. The men wore the smaller and shorter cloaks and the children were scantily clad, their cloaks being 'but a mere strip of skin' according to Isaac Scott Nind, the garrison's first doctor.[23] These cloaks were fastened at the left shoulder with rushes from the *Xanthorrhoea* or grass tree, leaving their left arm free and mobile. Their cloaks were worn with the fur on the inside, except when it rained heavily and the winds squalled at which time they wore them with the fur on the outside.[24] The men also wore a *noodle-bul*, or waistband and armlets on their left arms. The *noodle-bul* was possum fur spun into a yarn and wrapped around the waist several times. The women did not have as many accessories as the men, and their hair was often worn short.

♦

I have begun with Mokaré and his family for a reason. He was the most written about Aboriginal person in the south-west during the period of this history, 1826 to the early 1830s. The British newcomers and explorers gave him a prominent position in their narratives of daily life in the region, and community historians give him the same status today in their narratives and public memorials. He was the informant, intermediary, guide and close friend of several of the newcomers, telling them stories about his people, their culture and history, describing some of their religious and cultural rituals, and illuminating personal relationships and family genealogies. He was a natural raconteur. Although many newcomers recognised Nakinah as 'chief' or 'king' of the group, Mokaré was the person who was constantly among them, living with them in their huts not long after they had set up camp. They awarded him a high status as an intelligent, friendly and, importantly, a trustworthy young man. He had a particularly close relationship with the doctor, Nind, and Alexander Collie, another medical man, who was Resident Magistrate from April 1831 to November 1832. But it seems that Mokaré's most intimate and fraternal-like friendship was with Captain Collet Barker, commandant at the settlement from December 1829 until March 1831. Mokaré, however, is not this history's only important Aboriginal character. Several other remarkable Aboriginal people and their experiences are revealed throughout this history.

By stitching together the traces of Mokaré's dialogue and actions recorded by the newcomers it is possible to imagine a functioning Aboriginal social world both before the British arrived and during the garrison period. This chapter will sketch that social world onto the canvas of King George's Sound to show that it was a world rich with meaning, not only geographically but in culture and structure too. As Jerome Bruner reminds us, 'Culture gives forms to the minds of those living under its sway.'[25] It will be possible to interpret the meanings implicit in Aboriginal actions if we understand something of their cultural world during this period. The symbolic systems that individuals used in constructing meaning need to be illuminated as they were systems that were already in place before the newcomers arrived 'deeply entrenched in culture and language.'[26] If this is understood, it will be easier to gauge the pace of the changes that were taking place during this period and how these changes happened, not just their outcomes, as well as adding depth to the understanding and analysis of the stories that follow. Rather than deploring the impurity of *true* Aboriginal action and culture which is necessarily contaminated through the descriptions of the newcomers, such 'contaminated' descriptions allow historians to read the strategic actions made by particular Aborigines in the presence of the newcomers. The cultural systems of the newcomers and their garrison will be studied for the same purpose. While I would like to introduce the Aboriginal characters of the region and the patterns organising the relationships between them, I do not intend to write a series of biographies.[27]

First and foremost, who am I writing about and what will I call them? Mokaré's family and the other Aborigines who lived around the region now known as Albany are often referred to as *Mineng* or *Minang*. This is a familiar term, featuring on Norman Tindale's map of Aboriginal Australia. The *Mineng* are considered a sub group of *Nyungar*. It is not easy to find the accurate origin and meaning of the name *Mineng* as there are several problematic spellings and vastly different meanings copied down by colonial ethnographers or later anthropologists. Nind was the first to record the term in 1831: 'The inhabitants of the Sound and its immediate vicinity are called Meananger, probably derived from mearn, the red root … and anger to eat.'[28] Collie recorded more about this root in May 1832. While travelling through country to the north of King George's Sound, his Aboriginal companion Manyat told him they had traversed into country where 'black fellow tă păluk (live upon the grubs which form on the decaying grass trees)'. Collie wrote: 'for by the word tă here he [Manyat] evidently meant that the natives gained a chief part of their Subsistence by this food, which he confirmed by comparing the King Georges Sound tribe eating Meen (the red root) to the tribe (Will?) of this part eating the grubs in question.'[29]

Another interpretation of the name *Mineng* is revealed in one of the stories Mokaré told to Barker. Late one night in Barker's hut, Barker persuaded Mokaré to tell him the story about the origin of his people. Mokaré gave this narrative about his distant ancestor *Moenang*: Barker wrote,

> He told me that a very long time ago the only person living was an old woman named Arregain who had a beard as large as the garden. She was delivered of a daughter and then died. The daughter called Moenang grew up in course of time to be a woman, when she had several children, (boys and girls), who were the fathers and mothers of all the black people.[30]

It is worth noting here that Mokaré's point of reference for the length of Arregain's beard is the garrison garden. Barker had one adjoined to his hut. With the altering of their landscape to include gardens, Aboriginal narratives about their world and their past were subtly and slowly changing. Before the newcomers arrived and established their gardens, Arregain's beard would have been measured up against something else. As stories like this changed shape, so too did their culture.

In the above story *Moenang* (or *Mineng*) was the name of the female creation spirit of the Aborigines around King George's Sound. *Mineng/ Moenang/Meananger* refers to many things – eaters of a specific food, a geographic location, an ancestral being and more recently a language group. Given the different meanings imposed on that name over time, I am not convinced it is the accurate term to use to identify the specific Aboriginal people I am writing about in the early 1830s. Mokaré did not refer to himself or his fellow countrymen as *Mineng*, nor did any of his contemporary Aboriginal neighbouring groups. The newcomers in the community did not refer to them as *Mineng*, opting for the more racialised terms, such as *blacks, natives, savages, Indians, blackfellows* or *Australians*. The names *Mineng* or *Nyungar* are more recent names evolving long after Mokaré and his contemporaries had gone. While I respect they are appropriate for other histories I am seeking other terms for this story.[31] Aboriginal people living in the Albany region today who claim ancestry to some of the individuals mentioned in this history now refer to themselves as *Mineng*. This history does not intend to redefine present-day Aboriginal identity, or conflict with any claims to Aboriginal ancestry. Rather, it looks at how daily narratives of a group of Aboriginal people were slowly and subtly changing. These changes included names that they used to refer to themselves and particular aspects of their country.

What then can this group of people living at this particular time in this particular place be called? What might they have seen themselves as? 'King Ya-nup' is the name that Mokaré and his family and other Aboriginals living in and around King George's Sound gave the area around the British settlement during this time period. The explorer and surgeon Thomas Braidwood Wilson first recorded the Aboriginal term 'King Ya-nup' in December 1829 as 'the name the natives give the Sound',[32] and subsequent variations were recorded by other newcomers. In 1831 assistant surveyor Raphael Clint called these Aborigines, 'natives of the King-gou-rup district'.[33] Barker refers to 'King Gannup' as a place where the Aborigines were planning to hold a battle with the neighbouring tribe somewhere near the garrison, but does not specify an exact location. James Browne who spent his boyhood among the Aborigines at King George's Sound wrote that 'Kincannup is the native name for that district upon which the town of Albany stands. The natives who generally stayed in and about that settlement, style themselves, therefore, kincannup men …'[34] By the late nineteenth century the name had changed several times again, therefore 'King Ya-nup' is only relevant to a very specific period of time and to a particular group of Aboriginal people and a particular selection of daily stories. It is the name chosen for this snapshot of a unique community.

It is impossible to know the origin of the name, but it sounds like a pidgination of 'King George', which is how most of the newcomers referred to the garrison, and a native name that the Aborigines might have given to their country before the newcomers arrived. 'Up' at the end of a word in the south-west means 'place of'. This fusion of new and native name is symbolic of what was happening during this time. It was not so much a changing of metaphors – Aboriginal to British – but a slow meeting and mixing of vocabularies and cultural reservoirs from both worlds.

For the purpose of this history I have identified a King Ya-nup to be any Aboriginal person who contributed to life around the settlement from 1826 to the early 1830s. It may sound erroneous to bunch groups of people together, but to me it is more accurate than trying (and probably failing) to determine particular language groups. Writing a cross-cultural history requires decisions regarding nomenclature and orthography. I have adopted the names of places and people as they appear in the sources that I am using. In the case of Aboriginal people's names, I have generally kept to Barker's orthography as he was the newcomer who became closest to the King Ya-nup and wrote down their names almost daily, changing the spelling as he got to know and understand them better.

◆

There have been a few thoroughly researched attempts to define and demarcate King Ya-nup country. W.C. Ferguson's paper, 'Mokaré's Domain', maps out approximate boundaries using the newcomer's observations of the 1820s and 1830s, and evidence from his own archaeological fieldwork. First to the newcomer's sources: Collie wrote that the 'natal ground' of Mokaré's family 'has always been understood to be on the shores of Princess Royal Harbour and towards Bald Head'.[35] Thomas Braidwood Wilson who visited the settlement in 1829 wrote that 'the land about the settlement belongs to Mokaré and his brethren.'[36] Ferguson agreed with these comments, stating that Mokaré's family 'always lived on the spot where Albany was built, it was the heart of their estate'.[37] These conclusions need careful consideration: they are culturally specific reasonings by outsiders. The newcomers did not venture beyond the vicinity of the settlement or the shores of the harbours very often – only when exploring parties set out. With a few exceptions they generally encountered the King Ya-nup within the vicinity of the garrison and so perhaps they concluded that this was where the King Ya-nup country was centred also. Naturally, the garrison was their reference point for everything else. While the ethnographic sources reveal a lot, they should be pushed beyond just what the British saw to include what they heard as well. Stories about country and camping sites can be incredibly revealing. If Barker's descriptions, in particular, are scrutinised, a denser picture of King Ya-nup country can be unearthed. Even though Barker also stayed in the settlement for much of the time, Mokaré's stories carry us beyond the British world and into the camps of the King Ya-nup, showing a larger more detailed scattering of camps inland.[38] There are also glimpses of who camped where. These precious hints need to be focused on as well as the overt outsider statements about country boundaries, in order to develop a deeper, more accurate frame for the King Ya-nup world.

The vegetation in this well-watered country is quite diverse, with karri and jarrah forests (eucalypts) to the west, peppermint woodland and patches of scrub and sandy dunes. It was also scattered with swamps, lakes and permanent rivers, generally fordable by the King Ya-nup at particular places. King Ya-nup country included several camp sites close to the settlement at *Purrlyup*, *Yaramal* and *Yakama* near the government farm. Different pathways took the King Ya-nup to different camps. The newcomers used these pathways too – exploring parties always set out via a 'native path'. Some of these paths led explorers for a long distance. In February 1830, when Barker and Mokaré were travelling to the west, Barker explained that the party 'crossed the river by a bridge formed by a tree that had fallen about fifteen years ago, still following the native path'.[39] Barker wrote about these paths as if they belonged to particular people, or perhaps they were the most used paths; well-trodden tracks that had been traversed for centuries.

During Phillip Parker King's visit in 1821, he wrote about the King Ya-nup *turloit* (huts) in the following terms: 'Their habitations were probably scattered about in different parts, for when the natives went away for the night, not more than three or four going together, and these generally returned in company the next morning by the same path which they had taken when they left us.'[40] Vancouver also noted the pathways. When he came across a camp on the southern side of Princess Royal Harbour in 1791 he was intrigued that it was 'intersected with several small streams of water'. One of the larger huts he thought must have belonged to a chief as it had several paths leading to it, coming from different directions.[41]

'Talwyn's path' was one named path that Barker mentioned.[42] It took the King Ya-nup around the edge of Princess Royal Harbour to *Chinjannup* a thickly wooded forest, *Narinyup* which was good wallaby ground and *Tondirrup*, or 'white sandy', known to the British as 'the sand patch'. The newcomers described this camping area as a 'continuation of a Ridge of tolerably high hills of white sand and Granite rocks' that gave the King Ya-nup an imperious view of the country to the west.[43] The ridge of hills acts as a barrier, breaking up the violence of the south and south-west winds as it slopes gradually down to the harbour shores. A few of the King Ya-nup camps were close to hills because a good view of their country was essential. They needed to watch for movement in the landscape. They looked out for smoke mostly, as this was a sign to tell them who was on the move and where intruders might be camping; there was someone constantly on watch for the stealthy approach of strangers. Mokaré often talked to Barker about a place called *Willyung* or *Woollyongup*, a large hill about 10 kilometres to the north of the settlement, near a creek. Barker described the hill as 'a kind of village near Woollyong…'[44] Named campsites suggest a permanency. Mokaré's stories do not describe a nomadic, wandering group but more of a family-defined spatiality. *Woollyongup* must have been a fairly large camp site as Barker mentioned several large gatherings there in his journal. It was also where the King Ya-nup seasonally collected *towan*, or parrots for eating. Further west of *Woollyongup* were the forests *Kraigarup*, *Undiup* and *Yorke*. These forests were generally uninhabited areas. Forests were thick with undergrowth which impeded mobility and curtailed visibility and they were not rich in plant resources. As Ferguson has written, there was a 'great variety of species concentrated at the forest edge, in the low-lying woodlands, and along the banks of the rivers, lakes and swamps.'[45] Forests were marginal to King Ya-nup life with the exception for the hunting of *towan* and the manufacture of their essential weapon: spears. Phillip Parker King who brought home one hundred Aboriginal spears in 1821 described them as being 'very slender'. They were made from a species of tree called '*leptospermum* that grows abundantly in swampy places.'[46]

Kraigarup, *Undiup* and *Yorke*, where the King Ya-nup used the forests to make their spears, were close to *Kiangadarup*, a small swampy lagoon where they hunted birds, ate the rich plant resources and came for water when drought had dried the smaller lagoons.[47] The King Ya-nup also camped on the south banks of King's River with visiting groups, close to where they crossed it, three quarters of a mile from the river mouth.[48] Further north-east near the Porongurup Range at *Moorillup*, they camped when they congregated in large numbers with some of their neighbours, dancing together and assembling for ceremonies, holding *toortunggur*, or corroborees, and battles.[49] Other camps more distant from the settlement included *Oorangadak* and to the east the King Ya-nup also camped at Mount Many Peaks and *Waychinicup* on the eastern side of Oyster Harbour.

The following history that Mokaré told Barker is a creation story about his country and people which gives deeper, spiritual importance to parts of King Ya-nup country, in particular Green Island in Oyster Harbour and the connected waterways:

A man and his wife a 'very long time ago' living there, the woman goes into the bush after food and sings out to the husband, who remains sitting at the fire, what she finds. He replies in the negative in recitative, varying the expression from time to time to a great number of things she mentions. At last she says 'Quohyt', a sort of snake said to exist in those days and to be still in the Eastern parts, the size of a man's body and esteemed a great delicacy. However, it appears she likes it as much as himself and eats it all up. He then becomes 'sulky', 'tabor', and striking her with the 'Pomnerum' breaks her leg and then leaves her. She becomes sick and dragging herself along in the line of where the King's river now runs, reaches Green island, where she dies. Whence the derivation of the name Warracoolyup from 'Warre', a female, and 'Cool', a walk. Her body became putrid and an easterly wind setting in is smelt by a dog at Whatami (a pretty good nose to scent 40 miles, but things were then on the grand scale). He follows her track and arrived at the place, commences scratching, which he continues so long that he digs a great hollow and the sea comes in and forms Oyster Harbour. Meantime the woman's son, 'a little boy', goes in search after her death, of his father, and meeting him near a mountain, spears him, hence the name of the Mount Yongernmere – 'man spear'. 'Mere' being the name of the stick from which the spear is thrown.[50]

Mt Yongernmere – a peak in the Stirling Range – was considered the northern boundary of King Ya-nup country. It is 70 kilometres to the north of King George's Sound. Oyster Harbour receives water from two rivers – the Kalgan River (known to the newcomers as French's River) drains the southern side of the Stirling Range and the King River and its tributaries drain the country south-west of the Porongurup.[51]

The King Ya-nup camps usually had about seven *turloit*, or huts except during the fishing and burning seasons when large parties would come together from other countries or when important ceremonies were taking place. The *turloit* were made out of a few small twigs stuck in the ground and bent over in an arch, about four feet high and six wide. They were thatched with the leaves of the *Xanthorrhoea*, also known as the 'grass tree'. When the weather was wet and windy they were roofed with pieces of bark, with stones securely placed on top. The *turloit* were built with their backs to the wind with a fire burning in front. The women were in charge of making the *turloit*, and as newcomers witnessed, a hut could be made quickly and on the spot.[52] Nind explained: 'One hut contained several people, covered in their mantles, huddled together, in a crowded state; the dogs are also admitted to a share of their bed.'[53] But this 'crowded state' had an order to it. The single men slept together in one *turloit*, the women slept with the children in a larger *turloit* near their husbands and they were positioned so they did not overlook each other. Their camps, Nind wrote, 'consist of near relatives and deserve the name of families rather than tribes.'[54] This hut structure was incredibly important as the King Ya-nup men jealously guarded their women from single men (*man-jah-lies*) and polygamous married men.

King Ya-nup men did not marry until they were at least thirty, and sometimes had as many as four wives (Mokaré's grandfather supposedly had ten). All these wives slept separate from each other. Women married much earlier than men, as soon as they reached puberty, and were often pledged to their future husbands from birth. Barker wrote of Trijolerriti, a man of about twenty-five who had 'two wives engaged for him', one of whom was Tiachabit, 'a fine little girl about seven years old'.[55] Marriage partners were generally sought outside the vicinity of King George's Sound: Mokaré's niece, Condalyan, was 'engaged to a man a long way off' and Talimamunde married a girl from the Porongurup.[56] This custom extended the men's geographic domain and hunting rights as he adopted his wife's family's place. As Nind recorded, 'It is considered best to procure a wife from the greatest distance possible. The sons will have a right to hunt in the country from whence the mother is brought.'[57] It possibly had benefits for the women too. Barker understood enough about King Ya-nup marriage customs to congratulate Talimamunde on his marriage in February 1831. Talimamunde came to Barker in his kitchen a few days after he had 'purchased' his wife from her father at Porongurup. The King Ya-nup who were in Barker's kitchen were highly amused at Barker saluting Talimamunde 'good morning Yokadack' (married man), and promising him plums in honour of his marriage.[58]

A remarkable sketch of a campsite with its gendered divisions was created by Gyallipert, a King Ya-nup man who travelled to Swan River in 1833. It tells several stories. Gyallipert was in the presence of John Morgan, colonial storekeeper at Swan River, when he sketched his camp. The story of their encounter will come later. After he sketched the plan using Morgan's quill and ink, Gyallipert explained to Morgan what the sketch meant. Morgan wrote: 'Particulars, / as expressed by Galiput, / of the native encampment, scrawled out by him'. These 'particulars' read like a poem. They give the pace of the day, the division of labour and gender, the order and structure of the family and kin. They show how important spatial structure was in King Ya-nup life. Morgan numbered the particulars as Gyallipert chanted them to him, transcribing the narrative in Gyallipert's voice. It reads like this:

> That place no.1 womanar, children, pickaninny. – That place (no.7) – married men – that place (no.2) – single men – some morning sun get up very early – married go down – wake up the single men, – single men get up when sun get up very early. – all go down (to no.6 a lake) catch fish, then go up (to no5) catch kangaroo. – bring him down dare (no.3) fire – roast him. – all men sit around so. (entering the action to the word) upon [him]. [see image 16]

It is telling that the fire (no.3) is in the centre of the camp in Gyallipert's sketch. Barker noted the essential nature of fire in King Ya-nup life. In June 1830 Barker saw Wannewar and his family when he passed them in a boat in Deane's Harbour. He wrote that 'they have taken a snug berth and made their fire under a large rock by a bush near the water side'. He noticed that there was no hut. 'Huts pretty general, I believe even for the single men', Barker wrote. 'The blacks however, do not talk of such a one's hut but, to express his home or resting place, they say such a one's fire.'[59] Gyallipert's chant does not mention a hut, but the hearth sits at the centre of his sketch, suggesting that Barker's understanding was accurate.

Gyallipert's map and accompanying narrative shows that it was not just geographical space that made up the King Ya-nup world. Country was important but the social spaces and stories that were recounted about daily life were also vital. Gyallipert's narrative is similar to Mokaré's daily story which he told to Barker in February 1830. He said: 'Now, now (about 9 pm), the married men are all gone to sleep but the single men will talk and laugh till 12 o'clock. Tomorrow morning single men "sleep plenty" married men obliged to call them to make them get up.'[60] The recounting of these two narratives by Gyallipert and Mokaré which tell of social daily order was an unconscious reinstating of these men's understanding of their social space, in compliance with their gender, age and status within their community. Mokaré's story was given in response to Barker's describing to him the country he was from, England. Mokaré wanted to know what countries were near it, making Barker tell him the names of all of the adjacent countries and how they were situated in relation to England.[61]

The term 'country' is often used for the tract of land which is home to a particular group of Aboriginal people, but it does not translate to simply mean the 'landscape'. Ian and Patricia Crawford explained that 'country implies not only the physical nature of the land — its rocks, soils, vegetation and animals — but also its particular history within the legendary accounts of creation and its spiritual links'.[62]

The King Ya-nup stories — ancient, spiritual and contemporary events — gave names and depth to their country. Some of their camp names related to the surrounding geography: *Tondirrup* translated as 'white sandy' but others told stories. One of their camps, called *Mirilyan Kaiup Warinyung*, was on the south side of King's River. The name represents the story of Wannewar's sister, little Mirilyan, told by Mokaré to Barker (who perhaps misinterpreted some of the story). Mirilyan was at the King's River camp with her mother. She asked her mother for some water and her mother replied, 'Ah Mirilyan Kaiup Warinyung?' meaning 'Ah Mirilyan sees water' and so that is what the camp was known as.[63] Different events like this were recounted as stories. The stories we tell, both internal daily narratives and public collective ones, create and recreate our cultural contexts. Events that became stories, like this one about little Mirilyan, changed the naming of places and in turn slowly changed the King Ya-nup culture. Ancient camp sites were known, told and retold through stories. Bruner has written that what creates culture is a 'local' capacity for accruing stories of past happenings, ordering the events to continue into the present as stories told.[64]

In addition to such stories, ceremonies, rituals, resources and seasons dictated the camping sites that the King Ya-nup would live at for a particular time. The camp site near King's River, for example, might have been a good site to accommodate large numbers of people as it was where ceremonies and corroborees were often held with large parties from the north and east. And in winter the King Ya-nup tended to live at their camps situated further from the coast, in the well-wooded areas which were generally warmer.

Within this country the King Ya-nup were the custodians of particular tracts of land: their named pathways were part of this. They inherited ongoing obligations for the land's proper management of which they were very protective. Permission was needed by the custodian of the country if someone wanted to hunt or fire that country. As Sylvia Hallam has pointed out, Indigenous use of fire in the south-west was strategic – it was used for control in farming the land, for hunting, cooking and communication. In regulating land use, large tracts of country were burnt. Fires were started with a lighted fire stick made of the dry leaves of the *Xanthorrhoea*, setting alight the under wood and dry grass.[65] King was amazed at how the country was controlled by the King Ya-nup. He wrote about it in 1818 on his first visit to King George's Sound. In regards to landscape transformation, 'a lapse of sixteen years will in this country create a complete revolution in vegetation; which is here so luxuriant and rapid that whole woods may have been burnt down by the natives, and grown again within that space of time …'[66]

Fire was used in a small scale way too. The women carried a smaller fire for their hunting and procuring tasks and used it to start their cooking fires. Nind noted that the women 'set fire to the ground by themselves.'[67] Fire was not always easy to generate. In August 1830, Barker wrote that Nakinah came into the settlement to light his fire stick from the newcomers' fire because 'they were unable to kindle it at this time of year and if the fire goes out, [he] must go without until they are lucky enough to meet with it from their friends.'[68] The newcomers helped the King Ya-nup with their firing requirements when it was difficult. In January 1831 several King Ya-nup were taken to Bald Head with an officer, Mr Kent. Kent returned to the settlement in the boat to get some fire which they had forgotten to take with them and which they were unable to kindle at Bald Head, being as its name suggests, bare of any verdure.[69]

Burning season began in the height of summer, in *Preoe* and finished in autumn, at the start of *Moken*.[70] Violators of the rules of firing country were dealt with according to the seriousness of offence and their relationship to the owner of the country. Barker recorded several occurrences of illegal burning of country. In January 1831 he wrote that 'Mokaré asked permission to go in Mr Kent's boat, as I understood him, to the ground opposite Narinyup to burn for Wallabi, which I gave provided it was not 'quipple' [stealing], which he said it would not be, as he should only make a little fire…'[71] Coolbun, who was in the settlement at the time, was the custodian of *Narinyup* country, near Bald Head. He saw the smoke and said Mokaré was 'quippling', but Barker thought that Coolbun did not seem too annoyed about it.[72] Mokaré and Coolbun were close friends and their families held neighbouring country, and so perhaps Coolbun shrugged off Mokaré's cheekiness. Barker understood some of these rules of burning on country and perhaps the King Ya-nup realised this, taking advantage of his knowledge. They came to him for information on who was firing where and which smoke belonged to whose fire.

The King Ya-nup world was one which was influenced by seasons. The seasons gave rhythms to their everyday life; the new season was announced, activities changed and hearths relocated. It dictated their daily doings. A few of the newcomers made attempts at recording the changing Aboriginal seasons, reported to them by Mokaré. Seasons were marked by arrivals: the salmon seen swimming in the shallows of King George's Sound, the croaking of the frogs and the appearance of particular stars and cloud formations. There were never distinct beginnings and endings of seasons, but a merging and slow crossing over. When the salmon stayed longer, or the frogs croaked earlier, the Aboriginal world would be living within two simultaneous seasons. The outgoing season would be dominant and the incoming would be peripheral: for example, *Pruhner* would be ending and *Metelok little* would be beginning.[73]

Seasons were also connected to King Ya-nup neighbours and their visiting 'rights'. Aboriginal groups neighbouring the King Ya-nup country were an essential part of their intricate social network of trade, rituals, marriage and law. To the west of the King Ya-nup were a group known as the *Murrum*. To the north were the group who were the most important and worrying of their neighbours – the *Will/Weill*, and to the north-east were a group called *White Cockatoo*. Barker interpreted Mokaré's descriptions of these groups in the following way:

> Will's people [to the north] gay & volatile like the French. Very early risers, up
> at cock crow, sleeping little. White cockatoo tribe great sleepers & of a grave
> disposition. To the westward [murrum] of a medium cast between the two. He
> has heard of people far off to the East or NE, all life & spirit, fond of laugh
> & joke from morning to night.[74]

Mokaré knew of several groups to the north of his country, telling Barker the names of some that were '1, 2, 3 and even 4 moons' journey'.[75] The King Ya-nup had never met any people from these distant groups, but Mokaré had heard of them from groups in-between his country and theirs.[76]

The King Ya-nup neighbouring group to the north, recorded by Barker as the *Wills* people were the most important presence in the King Ya-nup social world. Rather than the name for a particular group, it is probable that the term *Wills/Weal/Weill* was used to refer to anyone who lived north of King Ya-nup country. According to Ferguson, 'Will' could 'depending on the context', mean 'people on the adjoining estate, people far away about whom they had only heard, or anyone in between'.[77] James Browne reflected on these northern neighbours: 'the natives belonging to the weal tribe wander over the country to the northward of Albany'.[78] It is possible the term was a generic one, used throughout the south-west. Swan River migrant, George Fletcher Moore, commented on the Swan River Aboriginal geographic perspective when he wrote: 'Some of the northern tribes … appear to be indiscriminately referred to under the name of Waylo men or Weel men …'.[79] The *Wills* people were often enemies of the King Ya-nup, but they also formed an essential part of their close social network and shared a kinship system. Many *Wills* people visited the settlement throughout the year and were met without hostility. Browne wrote that the 'weal tribe', which were not as large as the Murray [or Murrum] tribe, were 'physically stronger, and of greater importance in the estimation of the Aborigines [in the region] generally'.[80] He also believed they were 'proportionally stronger and more robust' than the King Ya-nup.[81] Similarly, at Swan River the northern *Wailo* men were 'much dreaded, and … believed to possess supernatural powers'.[82]

In 1901 anthropologist Daisy Bates observed that between the Aboriginal groups in the south-west there was 'a remarkable homogeneity' in language, culture and ritual.[83] While there must have been some similarities in their cosmologies and regulations, Mokaré's stories paint a different picture from Bates's theory of homogeneity. Nind stated that the King Ya-nup language 'differs entirely from that of the natives of the eastern coast; and even tribes very nearly situated differ so considerably, that I do not think at two hundred miles they would at all understand each other'.[84] Not only were languages within the region dissimilar, cultural practices were distinct too. Whereas only male King Ya-nup had *umbin* – ceremonial scars from a burning piece of wood – at *Coconyup* to the west, some single women also participated in this ritual.[85] Anthropologist Michael C. Howard wrote that, 'Aborigines in the south did not form a well-integrated social group … and interaction beyond the level of the multiple band units was very limited'.[86] As evident in their engagements with King, the King Ya-nup were experts in learning new languages. Mokaré related to Barker that the *Murrum* to the west spoke a completely different language from the King Ya-nup. Mokaré told Barker that he did not speak the language at *Coconyup*, to the far west, but Maragnan, a knowledgeable well-travelled man, knew the language well. In recounting the story, Mokaré suddenly remembered the word that this distant group used for water, *canpie*.[87] This reminds us of King: perhaps it was universal that the local word for water was one of the first words learnt, for both European voyagers and Aboriginal travellers.

It is not easy to understand all the complexities of this larger social network as the newcomers understood only a small portion of what they were being told and even less of what they saw. When Barker was trying to understand a King Ya-nup genealogy, he poignantly wrote, 'There is always a puzzle in these things even when described in one's own language'.[88] Nind also wrote about the complex nature of the King Ya-nup social world in 1831: 'Their customs as regards their women are not only very curious, but also so intricate and involved in so many apparent contradictions and singularities that it is probable we have been mistaken in some of them'.[89] And again, when writing about their tribal divisions he recognised that there 'exists so much intricacy, that it will be long before it can be understood'.[90] This did not stop him from defining some of their inter-group customs. He believed that throughout the region, all Aborigines, except the *Murrum*, were divided into two classes: *Erniung* and *Tem* or *Taaman*. He wrote that the 'chief regulation is, that these classes must intermarry, that is an *Erniung* with a *Taaman*'. People who violated this rule were called *Yuredangers* and were punished severely.[91] All the children were affiliated with their mother's division. Another rule that Nind tried to grasp was *Moncalon* and *Torndirrup*. This related to territorial ground. 'Yet', he wrote, 'there are few who are neither'. Nind thought that they could 'scarcely be distinguished as tribes, and are very much intermingled. The *Moncalon*, however, is more prevalent to the eastward of our establishment, and the *Torndirrup* to the westward', he wrote.[92] Nind also observed that 'every individual' when approached 'would immediately announce to us his tribual [sic] name and country'.[93] Barker mentioned this group division once when he was told about a large group from the east and *Wills* country to the north coming to meet the King Ya-nup. He wrote 'they were all Mongalons and Tonderups'.[94] *Tondirrup* was also the name of the King Ya-nup camp to the west of the settlement. Collie mentioned that Talimamunde's natal ground was on the borders of the 'King George's Sound (Mongalan) Tribe', so it can be assumed that he lived towards the north-east.[95]

It was not only the British who found Aboriginal culture difficult to understand. Mokaré often quizzed Barker on aspects of his life and cultural practices: 'when did ships die?' he asked. And he laughed in bewilderment at Barker's earnest collection and labelling of native mosses.

♦

Aboriginal and Torres Strait Island coastal cultures around the north and east of Australia have country that incorporates kilometres of ocean into their worlds. They utilise the ocean and rivers daily by swimming in them or traversing them in their water craft. Noni Sharp has done a study of northern coastal groups, in particular the Mer Islanders whom she calls 'Saltwater people'. They are an 'intrepid sea people', she writes, 'who, up until the end of the 1800s, made sea journeys of over 150 kilometres for trade, for battle' and so on.[96] The islanders have a form of 'sea ownership' which comes from 'local custom and law'. This customary maritime tenure is as important to them as land ownership. When the anthropological expedition from Cambridge University visited the Torres Strait Islands in 1898 they observed that the islanders were competent navigators and geographers. 'All the islands, large and small, the sandbanks, coral reefs, capes, coves and prominent rocks had distinctive names too.'[97] The anthropologists also noted the Islander's immense 'mental store' of geographic knowledge, which Sharp writes was 'demonstrated by the readiness with which they drew maps'. These islanders were granted Native title rights to the sea in September 2001, by proving that their spiritual, economic and cultural heritage comes from the sea.[98]

The King Ya-nup boundaries, camps and resource usage tell a different story. They were on the edge of their country when they were up to their waists in water. While spiritually the ocean and harbours which bordered their country were a large part of their world as evidenced by Mokaré's creation stories, the King Ya-nup barely used the ocean and harbours for economic purposes even though they offered rich resources. The King Ya-nup caught fish in their intricate weirs in the rivers and Oyster Harbour, and speared fish in the shallows, but they did not venture into water that was *murtagh* (very deep). They ate seals if they were washed ashore, but did not attempt to utilise the large seal colonies on the islands close to the coast. Interestingly, their diet did not include the abundant shellfish on which Vancouver and subsequent explorers 'sumptuously regaled'.[99] According to Nind: 'Oysters, and other edible kinds of shellfish … None of [which] were eaten by the natives previous to the formation of the settlement, but since its establishment they eat them, after being cooked, and consider them very good food'.[100] The restriction of shell fish in the King Ya-nup diet may have been a ritualised proscription, or taboo. Explorer George Grey wrote of the south-west Aboriginal avoidance of the mollusc *unio*: 'the natives of south-west Australia would not eat [*unio*], because, according to a tradition, a long time ago some natives ate them, and died through the agency of certain sorcerers who looked upon that shell-fish as their peculiar property'.[101] It seems that the King Ya-nup lifestyle was almost entirely land-oriented.

When Vancouver took possession in 1791, he not only placed a glass bottle on a cairn on Point Possession, he placed a second bottle describing the ritual on Seal Island in King George's Sound. His reason for this second evidence of his claim of possession was, he wrote, a 'precaution…taken, on a presumption that Seal Island was entirely out of the reach of the inhabitants, which might not be the case where the first bottle was secured'.[102] The surgeon's mate who accompanied the expedition, who was often highly critical of Vancouver, poured scorn on this opinion in a note in the margin of his copy of the published *Voyage*. 'It is the greatest Absurdity to suppose this Island is out of the reach of the Natives when it is in the Sound where the Water is generally smooth and near the shore of the Main Land from which any one might Swim or float himself upon a Log of Wood'.[103] All subsequent European visitors however, either took Vancouver's insinuation as gospel and reproduced the assumption in their journals, or independently observed that the King Ya-nup did not swim. King for example commented on the timid way in which the Aboriginal men he met approached the water and observed their lack of canoes.[104]

The European observers in the 1820s and 1830s noted the King Ya-nup seeming fear of deep water and the absence of any form of water craft. Mokaré detested the deep water because it was cold. When the soldiers called out to Mokaré to help them with the hauling of the seine one evening: 'Come in Mokaré, there's plenty of fish,' he replied to them: 'Plenty fish, plenty cold.'[105] Barker commented that 'All the blacks here seem to dislike the water (deep) and none of them know how to swim, which is singular, as at sometimes in the year they gain their subsistence by spearing fish.'[106] When Barker and Mokaré went fishing together in March 1830, Barker had to swim after all of Mokaré's spears because Mokaré could not venture far into the water.[107]

The King Ya-nup were not the only coastal Aboriginal group in the west who allegedly did not have an ocean focus. Groups as far north as Shark Bay did not have canoes either. At Swan River, colonial newcomer Robert Menli Lyon noted that the Aborigines around the Swan 'have been seen to paddle themselves across deep water with their hands, where the distances from bank to bank was short; but of the art of swimming, they are entirely ignorant.'[108]

These comments that the King Ya-nup did not swim, have any water craft and did not utilise the resources of the surrounding harbours have puzzled me. They need to be critically questioned and thought about, precisely because the concept is difficult to grasp. Robert Darnton has written that in the praxis of cultural history – in his case the French peasantry – confusion about a particular action is a good point in which to enter a foreign world. He wrote, '… anthropologists have found that the best points of entry in an attempt to penetrate an alien culture can be those where it seems to be most opaque.'[109] As well as acknowledging that swimming is not necessarily a universally desired human action – many of the European observers, including sea-going voyagers, did not swim either – it is worth wondering whether there were particular reasons why the King Ya-nup did not swim, or extensively utilise the oceans and harbours. By trying to understand why they did not, we can perhaps come to terms with a 'basic ingredient' of their culture during this period. Darnton again: 'you can see where to grasp a foreign system of meaning in order to unravel it.'[110]

Archaeological research combined with ethnographic observations points to ways of understanding this aspect of the King Ya-nup world. The south-west coast is unique in its noticeable absence of archaeological shell middens. South-western archaeological sites of around 20,000 years BP are far from the shoreline, situated between 20 to 50 kilometres inland. Kalgan Hall, a site in the Albany region, is 19 kilometres from the present coastline, situated near the Kalgan or French's River. Other sites in the region are located in woodland and well away from the hilly southern coast, suggesting that this land resource focus was a long practiced tradition.[111]

The King Ya-nup inland focus, as opposed to a coastal one, has been analysed by prehistorian Sylvia Hallam. Hallam argues that the equation of all Australian Aboriginal coastal populations living and the using the littoral, or shoreline, and having a marine-dominant lifestyle has been largely based on the 'high archaeological visibility of shellfish' along the eastern coast. Both the earliest and some of the most influential archaeological studies have dealt with late Holocene middens on the eastern coast and in northern Tasmania, 'where the margin of the continent has the highest gradient, and least coastal plain intervenes between shore and steep forested mountain slopes.'[112] Western expectations of littoral usage by coastal peoples combined with the east coast studies have created generalisations about Aboriginal coastal economies and do not, according to Hallam, 'fully illustrate the variety of the continental periphery through space and time.'[113] Whereas the NSW coastline offers many visible archaeological shell middens and early ethnographic records show that there were 'more Aborigines around Sydney than in the ACT uplands', Hallam believes the eastern coastline was unusual among Australian coastlines in 'lying on a steep gradient from the uplands of the Dividing Range down onto the continental shelf, so that many Aboriginal people in many stretches lived off the narrow margin between forest and sea, with little or no coastal plain to balance the marine component in their resource base.'[114]

The Western Australian south-west corner is unique in Australia for the rich qualities in the immediate hinterland with an extensive coastal plain between the sea and the forested mountain range. This diversity meant that the King Ya-nup had a variety of resources available to them inland as they utilised the rivers, swamps, vegetation and small animals beyond the coastal strip. While staying clear of shellfish, their rich diet was varied, with a range of birdlife, plants, small animals and estuarine fish making up their meals. With the archaeological and rich ethnographic sources revealing a land centred world – both economically and socially – Hallam stresses, 'it does not follow that people were clinging to the beaches … coastal does not equal littoral.'[115]

A few of the King Ya-nup camps were near the coast but the majority of them were around hills, away from the coast at *Woollyongup*, *Tondirrup*, and further to the north at *Oorangadak* – where they conducted sometimes daily lookouts inland to their country and to the northern boundaries of their world where the formidable *Wills* people lived. They would look for the approach of foreigners and friends from neighbouring groups because it was there, looking inland, rather than towards the sea where the action and drama of their world unfolded. It is important to grasp that this was their focus, where their stories of encounter and exchange began, well before the newcomers arrived in different sized boats on the fringes of their world. Their social and economic world was anchored to the land, not the sea and this planetary focus is something to keep in mind as we look at how the King Ya-nup navigated through the shoals of permanent British presence.

3

Setting Up the Fringe

The sun sizzled its way into the sky on Sunday 21 January 1827, giving the troops of the 57th Regiment at King George's Sound the signal to display the British colours on the flagstaff. The flagstaff had been erected a few days before on the shores of Princess Royal Harbour on the point where the land juts out into the basin. It was here on the edges of land and sea that the flag was flown – not on a mountain inland – to show that the country was taken in the name of Britain. It was 'easily seen [by] a ship crossing the Sound'.[1] The Union Jack needed to be clearly visible to seafarers so that if the French arrived they would immediately see and read this sign; a *prise de possession*. Two guns had been mounted on the beach next to the flagstaff a few days earlier, pointing out into the harbour.[2]

At twelve o'clock on that Sunday a 'Royal Salute' was fired from the battery and a *feu de joie*, fire of joy, was enacted by the troops, the shots filling the land and occupying the waterways with a boom of sound and the smell of gunpowder. These celebrations were integral to the process of possessing country, a process that the British troops and commanders had come to know well by 1827. It was a performance that was enacted – with varying degrees of drama – every time a 'new land' was occupied for the British Empire. It was a highly structured ritual beginning precisely at sunrise, followed by a sober celebratory gunfire at noon before an extra allowance of 'Flour with Raisins and suet was ordered' for the eighteen soldiers and twenty-three prisoners. It would not have felt like a genuine act, would not have seemed as serious or official in this far distant place, a long way from imperial eyes and with such a small audience, if the ritual had been conducted without the structure and stoicism that it called for.

A 'number' of King Ya-nup had come into the settlement that morning. They had seen military parades before; some would remember the military drill that Matthew Flinders had conducted on the same shoreline in 1801. Major Edmund Lockyer decided that the King Ya-nup should be incorporated into this ritual too. He ordered the seine to be hauled in order 'to give them a feast' of fish: they too should celebrate the possession. At the end of the eventful day, Lockyer – who believed strongly in rules and order – felt satisfied and pleased as he sat down to write a reflection. 'The day proved fine,' he wrote, 'and the whole went off well.'[3] It was also his forty-third birthday.

Edmund Lockyer, a major in His Majesty's 57th Regiment, had been at King George's Sound for nearly three weeks by the time he performed this ritual of possession. He had been sent on a mission by the Governor of New South Wales, Ralph Darling, to establish a military garrison to be an outpost of the colony of New South Wales. Nothing more had been done to secure British ownership of the region since Vancouver's claim of 'possession in a bottle' in September 1791, which had been little recognised by the British government, let alone their rivals, the French. There had been several French expeditions cruising the south coast – those of Baudin, Freycinet, Duperrey and d'Urville – and they were perceived by the British to be a threat to Britain's tenuous claim of possession in the far distant and deserted south-west corner. Even though the Napoleonic Wars ended in 1815, both nations remained highly suspicious of the other's presence in the South Seas, particularly the unoccupied parts. Remnants of past enmities persisted in the minds of maritime men. Lockyer's garrison was to be a military defence post. A holding station. A symbol to show the French that Britain occupied the south-west and indeed the whole continent. Governor Darling told Lockyer that, if he encountered the French, he should be 'careful to regulate [his] language and communications [with them] so as to avoid any expression of doubt over the whole of New Holland being considered within this government…'[4] D'Urville was known to be exploring near King George's Sound in late 1826 and his presence there was enough to set off the government's imperial nerves. Governor Darling ordered Lockyer's immediate departure to form a settlement.[5] D'Urville arrived at Port Jackson a month after Lockyer's expedition left and for all of the British paranoia about French threats, all that d'Urville noted in his journal was that he was bewildered that Britain had not yet occupied King George's Sound as he perceived it the perfect place for a settlement.[6]

Lockyer's expedition arrived at King George's Sound on Christmas Day

1826. On board the brig *Amity* – a mobile micro-village – was a detachment of the 57th Regiment, consisting of one officer, Captain Joseph Wakefield, one sergeant, eighteen soldiers, twenty-three prisoners, an array of animals and six months' worth of 'fresh provisions'. They were all crammed into the 23 metre long, 6.8 metre wide and 3.5 metre deep brig. Isaac Scott Nind was responsible for the medical duties of the expedition and settlement, and Lieutenant Colson Festing, RN, from HMS *Fly*, assisted them in the passage to King George's Sound. Ensign Edmund Lockyer, the son of the major, was appointed assistant storekeeper, but the rest of Lockyer's family, his wife Sarah and his fifteen children from two marriages, stayed behind in Port Jackson. There was a convict gardener, John Brown, and two convict overseers who brought their wives, the only women of the entire expedition. The brig's six-week-long journey had been a 'boisterous and tedious passage' from Port Jackson, stopping for supplies and repairs in Hobart, before finally arriving at King George's Sound, a protective haven from the squally seas.[7]

The members of the garrison community are best referred to as *newcomers*. They were an ethnic, cultural and religious mix, with English, Scottish and Irish heritage, and therefore cannot go under the generalised and lazy term of 'British'. They were all, however, living within a *British* world at King George's Sound.

Lockyer was given precise instructions for this mission from Governor Darling and the Colonial Secretary Alexander Macleay. He was to set up the basics of the garrison: temporary accommodation, establish the gardens and settle the livestock. Then he was to go back to Port Jackson, leaving the settlement in the hands of Joseph Wakefield who had come with the settlement party. Lockyer carried the Governor's instructions with him to remind him of his duties which he would endeavour to uphold and then he would hand them on to Wakefield when he departed. The instructions not only meticulously listed what he was obliged to do, but also the order in which the instructions had to be carried out. Lockyer took these instructions very seriously, enacting each (as much as he could) in the order dictated. First he was to choose a 'site as may be most eligible for a Penal Settlement', close to a good supply of fresh water, where the soil was rich and close to a 'safe anchorage'.[8] And only after the site had been chosen and secured could the formal ritual of possession begin; it was three weeks before that vital ritual was enacted. When all the work was done Lockyer was to despatch the *Amity* back to Port Jackson with a report of the progress of the garrison, a sketch of the settlement and a description of the neighbourhood with a focus on its suitability for future settlers. Lockyer was also requested to keep a journal and deliver a copy to Colonial Secretary Macleay. He wrote a daily account of events – his 'rough copy' – and then rewrote the events in a 'fair copy' for the Colonial Secretary, which reveals his reflections a month later. The fair copy has an official tone and the ritual of possession is rehearsed in full, whereas it gets a brief mention in the rough copy. The last item on his instructions obliged Lockyer to 'use every exertion to conciliate' the Aborigines and he was supplied with 'Tomahawks and Blankets', standard colonial gifts in an adventure such as this, to give to them for this purpose. These instructions were intended to impose on the mission and garrison a strategic order and pace. As will be seen in Chapter Four, the King Ya-nup had a narrative that began before Lockyer and his settlement party arrived, ensuring that expectations of conciliation and rhythms of daily life took on their own order, re-organising the way his instructions were carried out.

This was a new adventure for Lockyer who was born in Plymouth, England, in 1784 into a large family. He was commissioned as ensign in the 19th Regiment of Foot at the age of nineteen and stationed in Sri Lanka. From there he quickly climbed the ranks from Lieutenant, to Captain and finally to a major in the 57th Regiment. Lockyer's other military posting was in Ireland. In November 1824, a Napoleonic war veteran, he left Ireland for the rapidly growing colony of New South Wales with his family. Prior to arriving at King George's Sound, Lockyer explored the Brisbane River in 1825 where he had his first experience with Aborigines beyond the bounds of Port Jackson.[9]

It was not until 29 December 1826, four days after their arrival at King George's Sound, that Lockyer, with the assistance of Lt Festing, decided on the site for the settlement. It was the same place that Matthew Flinders and his crew had camped in 1801. Lockyer described its position: 'it lays [sic] on a slope facing the anchorage … between two Hills forming nearly an amphitheatre.'[10] And it was in this 'amphitheatre' that the stage for the British world at King George's Sound would be set up. They turned their backs on the country, the hills sheltered their sides as they looked out to sea and to the world of naval rivalry. Unlike the King Ya-nup who set up their camps to minimise the effects of prevailing winds, the newcomers pitched their tents in a line from north to south, facing the breeze even though the strong westerly's were unpleasant, covering 'everything in the Tent with dust and sand' Lockyer wrote.[11] Naval strategy was often more important than comfort or practicality.

On 30 December Lockyer wrote, 'took possession of my Tent and slept on shore.'[12] It was at this stage just a camp and it would be some time before the title of Lockyer's letters to the Colonial Secretary changed from 'Camp, Princess Royal Harbour – King George's Sound', to *Frederickstown*. This was the name that Lockyer gave to the settlement, in honour of Frederick Augustus the Duke of York and Albany, Commander in Chief of Britain's Army and a son of King George III. The name *Frederickstown* was never taken up officially and Lockyer was the only person to use it – all successive commandants referred to the camp or settlement as King George's Sound, or simply, King George.[13]

Once the newcomers landed on shore the prisoners were quickly put to work erecting huts for their accommodation and protection for the stores. It was cold when they arrived, the wind blowing in squalls with heavy showers, and they needed shelter quickly. It seems likely that these prisoners were handpicked for this expedition according to their skills, as was common in the establishment of British garrisons. They were mostly young men, aged between fifteen and forty-eight, and included carpenters, blacksmiths, sawyers and a gardener.[14] At the camp they worked hard cutting down timber, hauling the seine for fish, working on the gardens and collecting fresh water. Supplies were not sufficient and would not last and so the ground needed to be dug up and seeds put down. Where they could they used local sources to supplement their supplies: shells were found on the south and western shores of Princess Royal Harbour and burnt for lime, and native plants were sampled.

Lockyer quickly ordered everybody into a rigid routine, forging a sense of community based around the small, sequestered world that they were establishing. The day began with a bell at sunrise and the prisoners were mustered and given their orders. In the middle of camp, between the huts, was a space which Lockyer called the Square.[15] It was as if this little camp was a village in England and needed an agora where the townspeople held their community meetings, a place to assemble together. Lockyer distributed the rations to the prisoners in the Square and it was where the (few) floggings took place; so, perhaps it meant less about community to the prisoners, symbolising punishment instead. It was also where Lockyer gave out the daily orders and read out prayers on Sundays.[16] It might have only been a small community, but this British camp at King George's Sound still had a centre, a focal point and it was here in the Square. Later on it would be transformed into a different space; it would be where a large fire was kindled, around which the King Ya-nup men would perform their dances for visitors from Swan River and Port Jackson.[17]

Lockyer's imposed schedule meant that each person from each division, prisoner, soldier and officer alike, knew his place in the community. However, the prisoners and soldiers took advantage of King George's Sound's distance from imperial eyes. They sometimes slept in, scoffed at their ration of beef and used bad language in front of Lockyer. On Sunday 28 January 1827 Lockyer had had enough of their cheek. He wrote, 'A disposition to disobey and set at defiance all authority on the Prisoners' arose from the idea that they would not be punished physically, for "want of a scourger".[18] However, the distance from Lockyer's superiors in New South Wales did not stop him from carrying out his job and all the formalities that it required of him. He had to be accountable for every event, reporting each happening within the garrison back to the authorities. His instructions obliged him to uphold the order. When the prisoners left their weekly ration of beef on the scales in the Square in January, Lockyer demanded to know what was going on. When he asked the prisoner John Ryan about it, Ryan declared that the ration was not their allowance and they 'would not take it'. Lockyer ordered Ryan to take it and he refused. Lockyer then ordered the guard to seize Ryan, who revealed that the prisoner William Gee had given them all a short allowance in weight. Lockyer did not believe him as Gee had to weigh the rations in the presence of the storekeeper – Lockyer's son – who would not let him get away with dealing out short rations, Lockyer thought. To make an example Lockyer ordered Ryan to be 'punished on the spot'. He was tied up in the Square but when ordered to flog him with the cat, the overseers (the soldiers) refused to deal out the punishment themselves as they said it was not their duty. Another prisoner was then asked to deal out the flogging, but he said he 'could not either'. Lockyer was angry: 'I saw not the slightest chance of enforcing my authority but by the most summary act,' he wrote, and so he 'determined to inflict the punishment' himself, instead of allowing a 'Ruffian to get the upper hand'.[19]

Lockyer inflicted sixteen lashes on prisoner Ryan, which seemed to 'have the effect', he wrote, 'of putting down the spirit'. His tone was angry as he wrote about this disrespect, not because the prisoners' precious rations were left on the scales, but for a much worse deed: his orders had been disobeyed, from prisoner to soldier and he was forced to deal out the punishment himself. Perhaps he was not used to the intimacy of it. The ordering of punishments had a distance from the performance; dealing it out was close and personal. The prisoners were standing up to their belief of what did and what did not constitute a decent ration.

It is not clear why both the prisoner and the soldier refused to inflict the lashes. It suggests that the institutional hold of the garrison was not strong. It was not the duty of a common soldier to flog prisoners. Tellingly, in his Fair Copy which the Colonial Secretary would read, all that Lockyer wrote for the day was: 'Ordered that the prisoners should have the afternoon to themselves for the purpose of washing their clothes etc, etc.'[20] Perhaps he did not want the colonial authorities to think that he was not in full control. With the flogging of Ryan, Lockyer enacted a performance to reinstate the colonial hierarchy that would still operate even in the isolated garrison of *Frederickstown*. He repeated this performance again on Sunday 11 February.[21]

Lockyer had limited time and much to do, but that did not stop him from feeling lonely in such an isolated place. There are glimpses of loneliness in his journal. The first is when Lt Festing left the camp, taking the *Amity* back to Port Jackson at the end of January 1827. It was not just the departure of the brig – their mobile village – that Lockyer felt, but the loss of a friend. He wrote, 'The loss to our society here is very great in the departure of Lieutenant Festing whose gentlemanly pleasant demeanour on all occasions will long be recollected and never forgotten by any one here, and we trust that the chances of service may bring us together again …'[22]

With the brig gone and a companion with it, Lockyer began looking out to sea for a vessel from Sydney each day. 'We now begin to think of expecting a vessel from Sydney,' he wrote, and a few days later a 'Vessel reported in sight; all in expectation that she must be from Sydney.'[23] And the disappointment rings loud in Lockyer's realisation when 'at last it reported that she has passed Bald Head and is a schooner consequently not coming here'. But the community's hopes were still up by the month's end, Lockyer optimistically writing 'any day now …'[24] Every member of this community could *read* a vessel. Cutter, schooner, brig or man-of-war. From a distance, the size, shape and number of masts and sails told the community who and what was on board. They knew what kind of vessel would be carrying their fresh supplies. This was also true during Captain Collet Barker's command in 1830. He wrote: '5pm barque in sight, coming round Bald Head. Is it the *Lucy Anna* to ship us, or a stranger from Swan River? Dr [Davis] says the *Sulphur* is a barque, if so it is most probably her.'[25] Lockyer put the community on tight rations while they waited for a supply ship, halving the prisoners' weekly food allowance, which was probably the cause of some of the unrest.

At *Frederickstown* all signs of hope and all lifelines came from the sea. It was from where vessels came carrying news, letters from home, instructions from the authorities and, importantly, fresh provisions. *Frederickstown* was isolated – the closest town was Hobart and then Western Port and Port Jackson on the east coast, and Melville Island way up in the north west. This isolated coastal settlement pattern was called an 'archipelago of islands' by explorer Captain Charles Sturt.[26] Settlements formed a chain of islands, scattered along the rim of the continent with a density in the south-east.

Not only were the British community's eyes towards the sea, searching for a vessel; at the garrison, the British were sitting on the fringe between land and sea, and their minds and thoughts drifted towards the sea rather than the land. They had come from Port Jackson, where maritime culture dominated the town and for many of them the ocean, rather than the land, was a world they understood. *Frederickstown* was a defence post, a naval base, not a settlement which would expand and rapidly colonise the country inland. All its qualities were seen from this space, from the edge looking out.

In Lockyer's 'Report on the progress of the settlement' to the colonial authorities he wrote about the importance of King George's Sound as a place that was fit for Britain 'to occupy'. Everybody who was 'acquainted with this Country', would agree, he wrote. However, it was not the 'country' that was its selling point for Lockyer, but the size and location of its harbours. It would make a fine port, a good place to form a depot, a trading station. King George's Sound was on the shipping route between Europe and Sydney: 'An Enemy holding it', he wrote, 'would with its cruisers completely cut off the trade, except by Convoys to Van Diemen's Land and Port Jackson, from Europe, the Cape, Isle of France and India.' The country offered little, but the ocean offered much. Lockyer did not promote the country as being fit for cultivation, colonisation or cattle (although he did not necessarily discourage this). Instead, his focus was on the penguins, seals and whales, sea sponge, mutton birds and even salt from the rocks in the harbours; these things he wrote about with enthusiasm.

This was a common notion in the history of Australian colonial outposts. Ross Gibson has written of the concept that Australia was conceived as an 'ocean settlement'. These colonial camps were essentially establishments that clung like limpets to the edges of land. Larger settlements, such as Swan River and Adelaide, had their centres inland with an additional port town facing the sea in an age where travel was mostly conducted on the ocean.[27] It was not only the newcomers' minds that were seaward, but their economies too. Gibson wrote that 'European attempts to treat seals and whales as cattle' was a 'blundering project that exhausted its resources within fifty years.'[28] Even though Lockyer saw the benefits in trade from the sea, he also predicted this blunder and suggested laws and licenses for the ruthless sealing trade.[29]

Lockyer was not at King George's Sound for very long. He left to go back to Port Jackson in April 1827. He set up the huts and chose the site for the garrison, got the gardens under way and did some minor explorations so that he could report on the 'neighbourhood' to the colonial authorities. Rather than exploring inland, which he did just once, these explorations consisted mostly of visits to the islands in King George's Sound and Oyster Harbour. On Sundays, the one day of rest for the community at *Frederickstown*, Lockyer went to Green Island, Seal Island and Breaksea Island. Being a military man his mind was often occupied with thoughts of law and order: Seal Island would be excellent, he thought for 'solitary confinement' – this island he visited straight after inflicting sixteen lashes on prisoner Ryan – and at Breaksea Island the isolation would be a good place to 'punish incorrigibles.'[30]

Captain James Stirling, who would later become the first Governor of Western Australia, had been exploring the country around Swan River with the aim of establishing a commercial settlement there. He stopped in at the garrison on his return to Port Jackson. Lockyer left his *Frederickstown* with Stirling in the *Success* on 3 April 1827, handing over the command to Wakefield. In a letter to the Colonial Secretary written on his arrival in Sydney, he wrote, 'I returned … to Head Quarters.'[31] For him, this small, isolated garrison was nothing more than a tentacle of the British Empire, a symbol for the French, sitting on the fringes between land and sea.

◆

Captain Joseph Wakefield inherited a makeshift, temporary looking camp and an unhealthy community that had numerous complaints of the bowel and a few cases of scurvy. One soldier, Private Banks, who had been unwell and 'weakly' when he left England, died on 8 March 1827.[32] Scurvy was fairly easily remedied with limes and doses of wild celery that had been pounded into a juice, administered by Nind. But Wakefield saw the bowel complaints as more sinister. He believed the issues of health and temporary accommodation were one and the same problem. It was also the 'swampy ground' that framed the camp that he thought was the 'chief cause of the bowel complaints', and so to 'remedy the evil' Wakefield decided to drain the marshy bog.[33] By 1 July he had put together a detailed plan – colour painted and labelled – to take this garrison from temporary camp to settlement. It was not just about making the buildings more permanent and weather protective, although this was part of it: the previous huts 'were so extremely temporary that they were unfit to be occupied'. This plan included a landscape transformation, albeit on a micro scale.

Wakefield's visionary plan was carried out at the end of 1827: a soldier's barrack was built with a six foot high mud wall, hammocks were strung up, the floors were boarded and there was a fire place. Two glass windows were put in and two glassless windows, a design that would create sufficient airflow for a culture who believed that fresh air determined good health. He had made the prisoners work hard too – they built a surgeon's house with an infirmary, a storehouse for the commissariat, four huts for the married soldiers and their wives and the overseer, and three huts for the officers. There is no mention of accommodation for the prisoners, so presumably they remained living under canvas tents. These buildings were mostly built with wattle and daub and thatched with leaves of the *Xanthorrhoea*, a local improvisation. The huts were built on the same spots as the temporary ones, remaining in a line from north to south, facing the sea.

Wakefield was dedicated to the success of the garrison. He worked hard on the gardens, was thrilled when they produced an edible crop and devastated when they perished. 'We have completely failed in every endeavour to raise vegetables,' he wrote in May.[34] Wakefield started another garden on Green Island in Oyster Harbour where Vancouver had unsuccessfully sown seeds in 1791. A hut was built on the island where a full-time gardener lived, sometimes supplying the settlement with vegetables. With the beginnings of a garden on an island called *Green*, this little camp started to look much more like other British settlements around the empire where maritime minds were often searching for an island on which to start a garden, rather than somewhere inland which was often seen as infertile.[35] Familiar names and shapes were imposed on the landscape to make it recognisable as something British. Besides his Plan and official letters, Wakefield's command of the settlement remained largely unrecorded. He did not keep a journal, even though his instructions, passed on by Lockyer, ordered him to do so, and no personal record of his life has been found.

Wakefield's Plan might have been improving the camp, but he was not expanding it. He might have predicted that the government was not interested in making King George's Sound a permanent settlement. By 10 July, only three acres of land in total had been cleared around the garrison. Colonial traveller Colonel Hanson observed after his visit to King George's Sound in the early 1830s that it was 'strange to find, that King George's Sound, though so long occupied as a penal settlement from Sydney, exhibits at this moment hardly a vestige of man's works – what the convicts can have been about, during the many years they have been stationed there, it is difficult to imagine.'[36] In early 1828, Wakefield received a copy of the letter from Governor Darling in Port Jackson to Viscount Goderich in London in which Darling proposed that the garrison be abandoned. Darling wrote, 'The Communication' between King George's Sound and Sydney, 'is always tedious, is often difficult and uncertain, and the place itself a barren Waste, totally unavailable for any purpose of Agriculture'. He advised that to retain it as a settlement would be 'entirely a question of policy', leaving the decision on its future in the distant hands of Goderich.[37] A shoulder shrug was given in return to Darling's letter by the British government on 30 January 1828, keeping the decision up in the air.[38] This temporary feeling probably had an effect on the garrison community: an isolated camp with an uncertain future and all the community's hard work in the shadow of abandonment. On 12 June 1828 Wakefield wrote to the Colonial Secretary requesting leave to return to Sydney.

♦

At around noon on Sunday 29 November 1829 a ship dropped its anchor in King George's Sound, about a mile from the entrance of Princess Royal Harbour. Early the following morning a boat came out from the settlement, carrying the commandant Lt Sleeman who was keen to 'welcome his successor', Captain Collet Barker, who had sailed from Raffles Bay via the newly established Swan River settlement. He had travelled with Scottish medical practitioner, explorer and good friend Thomas Braidwood Wilson. Barker and Sleeman had performed this exchange of power before. Officers of the 39th Regiment were commanding settlements around Australia via rotation in the early nineteenth century and Sleeman had served as commander before Barker at the equally isolated Raffles Bay settlement in the north. The three men went ashore to have breakfast together.[39]

After breakfast Barker was taken on a tour of the settlement by Sleeman, who had taken command after Wakefield returned to Port Jackson in

September 1828. Wilson was shown around by Nind's replacement, Dr Davis who had also been at Raffles Bay but had transferred to King George's Sound with Sleeman. They went to the Government farm where Wakefield had started a garden and Sleeman had enlarged it and built a gardener's hut. They walked there along the newly made six-foot wide road and walked back via Mt Melville so that Wilson could get an idea of what the surrounding country looked like. He was keen to explore. When all the men returned to the settlement, Sleeman offered Wilson whatever assistance he might need on his excursion: prisoners, provisions and 'an intelligent native, named Mokaré (who was now out shooting ducks for dinner) …' They later all dined together, 'wild ducks and green peas were highly relished'.[40] This sequestered little settlement had come a long way since its inauspicious beginnings on Christmas Day, 1826, although its future remained an uncertainty. The isolation was not as great as it had been as a new settlement had begun at Swan River in June 1829.

The British settlement at Swan River was to be different from King George's Sound. It was set up as a colony, not an outpost, with thousands of free settlers arriving in 1829 and 1830 who occupied large amounts of land along the coast and inland on the banks of the Swan and Canning rivers. This settlement was a colonising one; colonising both the country and the people. With the beginnings of a new settlement to the north of King George's Sound, the prisoners' focus shifted from the sea to the land and some began to entertain thoughts of escape.

There must have been lots of questions and answers volleyed between Barker and Sleeman over the wild duck and peas about the operation of the garrison, the surrounding land, supplies and rations, the conduct of the prisoners which had improved under Wakefield and Sleeman, and of course, the King Ya-nup, several of whom were now living among the newcomers.

Like Wakefield, Sleeman's time at King George's Sound is not recorded with a day-to-day (or even month to month) regularity. And he recorded almost nothing of the King Ya-nup world. Aboriginal doings pop up rarely and accidentally, such as in an enclosure about the procurement of seal skins. Whereas Lockyer had been concerned about the sealing trade's devastation on the seal colonies around the coast (particularly the attacks on the seal pups), Sleeman ordered a boat to go out to the islands and obtain furs and skins for use in the settlement. Mokaré received a jacket and trousers that had been made for him by the prisoners out of the skins they had procured from a number of seal pups.[41]

Sleeman's sparse, official letters instead show the effects of desolation caused by isolation, and the boredom of daily life at King George's Sound, in particular for Nind whose mental deterioration and unusual conduct dominated Sleeman's letters to the Colonial Secretary. Sleeman's dispatches, the only record of his time at the garrison, were filled with disputes and conflict between him and Nind. Sleeman issued many complaints to the Colonial Secretary, angry over Nind's antisocial behaviour which Sleeman felt insulted, perhaps even embarrassed by. Nind refused to obey Sleeman's orders on several occasions, sometimes in quite a public manner, the most important for Sleeman being when Nind did not show up to witness the flogging of a prisoner – which was always conducted in a public manner as a matter of cultural instruction and an obligation for Nind in his role as colonial surgeon – and therefore was seemingly not taking Sleeman's position of authority seriously.[42]

The penny dropped for Sleeman after months of complaining about Nind when one night Nind literally went mad – he became hysterical and suicidal. Sleeman finally understood that Nind's behaviour was caused by his suffering some kind of a nervous breakdown. Nind's reality shows how desolate King George's Sound must have felt for some of the newcomers. He had been at the garrison for three years and, as Sleeman wrote, his 'extreme dejection of spirits and … morbid state of mind bordering on derangement' was, 'probably increased by his long residence here, where he has had so little to amuse or to divert his attention from dwelling on Subjects and events connected with his past life of rather a painful nature'.[43] It is unknown what those painful events from his past were; Nind confided in Wakefield before Wakefield returned to Sydney, requesting a resignation, but Wakefield did not write anything on the subject. Sleeman eventually wrote to Colonial Secretary Macleay asking him to ignore his previous complaints about Nind. It should be noted that Sleeman raised complaints about Dr Davis at Raffles Bay also and so perhaps Sleeman was not coping with the reality of isolation in such sequestered settlements either, taking out his pain on the medical staff. Despite being unhappy and unwell, Nind managed to create a remarkable ethnographic account of the King Ya-nup world during his time at King George's Sound, informed by Mokaré who lived with him in his hut. This report, which was read to the Royal Geographical Society of London by botanist Robert Brown in 1831, does not give a day-to-day account of Nind's experiences, but is an overall reconstruction of King Ya-nup customs, albeit from a Eurocentric viewpoint. It is worth thinking about Nind's state of mind a bit further.

What does it mean that the author of such a major ethnographic resource was depressed and on the edge of madness? He was also on the edge of his world and perhaps closer and more sympathetic to the Aboriginal world.

Barker's daily journal also reveals the boredom felt by some of the community at 'King George' – his name for the settlement. Possibly none felt the feeling of desolation more than the soldiers' wives, although we know little of their experiences. The written records only mentioned them when they were unwell. Barker took Mrs Mills the first rose that bloomed at King George's Sound. He recorded that 'She liked to look at it as it put her in mind of home.'[44] Barker described some inventive and humorous ways in which the soldiers and prisoners survived the boredom. In April 1830 he wrote that, 'An espirit [had] risen among the soldiers for running to the top of Mt Clarence and back.' The race was timed and Michael Quin was the quickest, going up and down in 18¼ minutes. One week later the soldiers had found a new game: this time they were blindfolded in the settlement and had to try and walk in a straight line to the flagstaff on the point. Barker thought that at least this game was better than breaking their necks running down Mt Clarence.[45] And he was right. A prisoner, Thomas Noel, almost did break his neck from a severe fall while running down the mountain.[46] These games were mentioned sporadically throughout the year in Barker's journal and they collected the whole community to watch, including the King Ya-nup. Mokaré joined in one of the races against Quin to see who was the quickest. Bets were placed. Mokaré was the favourite, everyone expecting him to beat Quin's record time. Perhaps this was aligned to the expectation that Aborigines were more agile than whites. Mokaré told Barker his plan was to go up the hill 'systematically', sparing himself on the climb – it was 600ft – and reserving 'all his strength to come down'. However, in the race, Mokaré was almost half a minute slower than Quin, 'having lost nearly a minute' Barker wrote, 'by walking at first and then stopping a little.'[47] These races say a lot about this little community and the social dynamics in play. Not only were soldiers playing games with the prisoners, but Mokaré was participating too. The rigid class and racial divisions of Britain were played out differently at King George's Sound. It is hard to know if Mokaré's loss of the race was a diplomatic one or a genuine misjudgement. Perhaps he thought it an odd game to play, revealing different cultural measures of strength?

Barker might not have always felt isolated at King George's Sound, but he certainly had moments of frustration being so far from any other settlement. When he lost his quicksilver he was angry as he knew it was 'irreplaceable' in a 'place like this.'[48] He was excited to receive letters from his two sisters 'E and M' (Elizabeth and Mary) and had a constant companion in Mokaré. He got along well with Dr Davis, although he thought that Davis lacked 'tact', particularly in his dealings with Aborigines. He had a close friendship with his long-time private servant James Mills, his wife and their son George. Mills is described as a caring but clumsy person who strictly followed the formalities of British societal hierarchy in the remote outpost. When he ran out of bread, Barker thought it silly that Mills was too formal to breakfast with him. When Mills was bitten 'repeatedly' by a snake in early 1830, Barker seemed to find this humorous and wrote in his journal that it was 'too apt to make a good story.'[49] Mills was also attacked by sharks, but managed to escape. In January 1831 Mrs Mills became very unwell and Barker thought she was dying. He was very saddened by her illness but questioned his emotions, writing: 'Why is it I feel so much sorrow for her? It really seems as if I were losing a near relation.'[50]

Barker was a gifted storyteller and a keen-eyed ethnographer. This powerful combination makes his daily narratives informative, suspenseful and exciting to read. Barker's journal contains many anecdotes such as the races up the mountain that other commanders would have perceived as too trivial to write down. His journal is a unique source and it has been vastly underused by historians, probably because Barker's handwriting is at times illegible and always difficult. His journals at Raffles Bay and King George's Sound were archival strays from the Colonial Secretary for nearly a century and were transferred to the Archives Office of New South Wales from the Mitchell Library in Sydney in 1934.[51] Barker's writing is immediate and personal, revealing not only his actions, and those of others, but his thoughts, frustrations and desires. Unlike Lockyer, whose journal is guarded and in-house, Barker was reflective, asking questions when he was confused or uncertain and laying things bare for his readers. Barker had a zest for constructing intriguing narratives with careful attention to sequences of action and drama. This journal was a record for the colonial authorities, as the Instructions requested of him. He wrote in a code when he had to record issues to do with the crown prisoners, and wrote informative narratives about his excursions inland with Mokaré as promotions for the colonial authorities. But his journal was more than just an official record; it includes a torrent of stories about his experience at King George's Sound and it is probable that he had publication in mind. He saw the importance of publishing colonial experiences, persuading explorer Thomas

Bannister to publish his journal of his overland trip from Swan River to King George's Sound in 1831.

Barker's daily entries construct him as a sensitive and considerate man, calm in his manner. This entry about a baby possum given to him by one of the soldiers is a good example of his softness: Barker was really taken with this little creature and looked after it in his hut. It would not sleep in the blanket and flannel that he had prepared for it and so he took it into bed with him, where, he wrote, 'it lay very quietly nestled close to me'. After the King Ya-nup told him that it would eat flowers, Barker went and collected several varieties of flowers to feed it with. When it had finished eating it 'crept of its own accord' into the warm bosom of Barker's waistcoat, where he had put it the day before. And then the next day we feel his sadness when he wrote, 'Lost my opossum this evening'. Mills, his clumsy private servant, had nearly trodden on it and scared it off.[52]

Barker continued with the rigid routine that Lockyer, Wakefield and Sleeman had started when he arrived at the settlement, although he adapted it slightly. The King Ya-nup were allowed to disturb Barker first thing in the morning when they received biscuit and tea from him.[53] Some might visit again throughout the day, but not in a large group. Lockyer had read prayers in the Square, but Barker held a church service every Sunday, attended by the whole community, and Barker followed this with a walk to the farm and dinner with Davis who would read him various Presbyterian sermons. The bell was rung to start the order of the day, the prisoners were counted to make sure there had been no absconders during the night, and their duties were assigned. Just as the seasons dictated the King Ya-nup daily rhythm, the newcomers had a strict routine to their days and weeks too. Most of the soldiers and prisoners had been stationed at 'King George' since Lockyer established the garrison. A few, though, had been with Barker in Raffles Bay. Barker also brought an orphaned Aboriginal girl from Raffles Bay with him, named Mary Waterloo Raffles Bay.[54] Little is known of her experience of travelling to a distant and foreign country and how she was adopted into a new community. She lived in the soldiers' barracks where Nakinah's son, little Wapere, also slept.[55] When the garrison changed over to a free settlement in March 1831, Barker did not know what to do with Mary Waterloo: the government ordered that she be assimilated into the King Ya-nup population, but they rejected her. She left to go to Port Jackson in March 1831 in the schooner *Isabella*.

Barker kept settlement life busy with a variety of jobs assigned each day:

the hauling of the seine, collecting fresh water and repairing the garrison's leaky boat. Barker spent a lot of his time sorting out quarrels between the soldiers and between the prisoners who were often eating each other's rations or dobbing one another in for stealing potatoes from the gardens. Everybody in the community, including the King Ya-nup, came to Barker with their problems and questions and he felt bogged down by their disturbances. He detested attending to bureaucratic matters, often writing how the days escaped him because he was always on call for the whole community. In June 1830, he wrote that the day, 'as is often the case, was frittered away by constant interruptions.'[56]

Barker had a strong interest in geology and enjoyed examining the lumpy granite boulders that dominated the surrounding landscape and the islands in the harbours. He thought it was an 'interesting spot' for a geologist.[57] In his first few months at 'King George' he obsessively studied the ebb and flow of the tides, questioning his diary if they truly only ebbed once a day. Barker also kept busy collecting different plant species, trying to boil down the resin from the *Xanthorrhoea* that Talwyn and Mokaré brought him as gifts, and sealing the holes in the leaking long boat with it. He also experimented with other technologies and native agriculture, boiling seaweed to make manure, and trying plants and food that Mokaré suggested. What exhausted Barker endlessly was a roaming bull which taunted him often and always managed to avoid capture. He did see the humour in it though, writing, 'Bull paid us a little visit before noon.'[58]

Barker had an interest in music and he brought a flute with him from England. He played it once: 'Took out flute this evening,' he wrote, 'I fancy for the first time since I left Sydney.' The instrument had adhered to the case and the leather was stuck to the metal. He played it one night in his hut in January 1831. It sounded 'as much as usual' he thought, 'as well as I can recollect'. There are no clues to why he did not play it more often and why after so long of not playing, he took it out on that particular night.[59]

Throughout all these activities, the community still kept an ever-hopeful lookout for a ship with fresh supplies and news from home coming from Swan River or New South Wales. And when a sighting occurred excitement filled the small, quiet settlement at King George's Sound and jobs were momentarily put on hold. Even a rumour of a sighting was enough to set everyone on '*qui vive*' one evening in June 1830 after a report of a light near Possession Point. To everybody's disappointment this was just a false alarm.[60]

This French term *qui vive* is one of many examples of the French references that litter Barker's repertoire – remnants from his time in the Napoleonic War – and these remnants dominated his cultural assumptions. In 1830 a group of families who had emigrated from Britain to Swan River established a settlement in Augusta, on the coast between King George's Sound and Swan River, and so vessels were sailing past a little more frequently than before.

In September 1830, Barker received letters from New South Wales regarding the future of the settlement. He had been promised to be able to return to Port Jackson by June 1831, but the decision was being kept up in the air by the government. He wrote, 'looks like a waiting expectation of [the garrison's] abandonment.'[61] On 18 February 1831, the schooner *Isabella* stopped in at King George's Sound. She was on her way to Swan River from Hobart. On board were Lieutenant William Carew and twenty men of the 63rd Regiment who were to stop off to meet with Governor Stirling at Swan River before returning to King George's Sound to take over from Barker and the soldiers of the 39th Regiment. Carew carried orders from Governor Darling to transfer the administration of King George's Sound over to Swan River, which was now the headquarters of the colony of Western Australia. The troops and prisoners were to return to Sydney with Barker. Darling's instructions of 11 January 1831 ordered him to explore the region of the Murray River mouth before returning to Sydney with Captain Charles Sturt.[62]

◆

On 7 March 1831, control of King George's Sound was transferred from New South Wales to the government of the Swan River settlement and the military garrison was handed over to civil control in the changeover to a free settlement. Command of the settlement was briefly in the hands of Lieutenant William Carew before it was transferred to a Government Resident, Dr Alexander Collie, who arrived from Swan River in April 1831. Governor Stirling changed the name of King George's Sound to Albany, after Frederick George Augustus' title as Duke of Albany. However, even in official letters and reports, the settlement remained known as 'King George's Sound' for many years. Collie slowly changed the title of his letters from 'King George's Sound' to 'Albany'. Most of the soldiers left to go back to Port Jackson, but a few stayed behind to make their way as settlers in this new establishment.

Collie was a Scottish medical man and his interest in health and the natural sciences is evident in all of his writings from King George's Sound. His writing survives in four different forms: a report on the Aborigines at King George's

Sound published in the *Perth Gazette* in 1834, which takes the form of a reflective diary; his travel writing from his explorations into the interior; official reports to the government at Swan River; and personal letters to his brother George. He also kept a daily meteorological journal, which tabled the temperature in the shade, the barometer's record, the direction and force of the wind, description of the clouds and general weather outlook.[63] He also recorded the Aboriginal seasons, although not in such a methodical way. These different publications reveal him to be a learned man with a strong empathy for and interest in Aboriginal people and their welfare, but he was not without his quick judgements of their habits and at times he was critical of them in racial terms. Collie's experience at King George's Sound is most revealed in his letters to his brother. From these letters it is clear that he wanted to return to Scotland and that his posting at King George's Sound was mostly unpleasant. He wrote of this civil position: 'bye the bye civil authority has not a tenth part of the allurements of military (Naval is here included).'[64] With the shift of space and pace from military depot, with issues surrounding soldiers and prisoners, to free settlement, Collie's days were taken up in different ways from those of the previous garrison's commanders. In October 1831 he wrote: 'At such an out-of-the-way place as this, with about a population of 40 souls, comprising young and old of both sexes, one would readily suppose I could have but very little occupation, and consequently a superabundance of time for epistolary correspondence.'[65] There was still concern for the vegetable supplies in the two government gardens and he wrote to his brother George explaining that he was 'chiefly among cabbage, turnips, potato's and c'. By July 1832 Collie was writing increasingly of his boredom. He felt 'free from employment', and was busy doing the 'same thing, that is nothing, day after day'. He complained that there were 'no new faces unless by the arrival of a vessel once, twice or perhaps three times a year. No new books unless I should make one. Abundance of time undoubtedly.'[66] He wrote to Stirling in July 1832, describing the situation of the settlement. Collie wrote of the good soil, excellent grass and the crops doing well, but he complained of the lack of people migrating to Albany: 'The few adventurers here are timid at the present aspect. Numbers are wanted, to aid and assist each other, create a mutual demand and supply.'[67]

Perhaps because of this boredom, in 1831 and 1832 Collie undertook a series of expeditions into the country, travelling to the north of the settlement and taking different King Ya-nup with him as 'guides' and 'interpreters'. Collie had a close relationship with Mokaré – friend to all the commanders except Lockyer – and Nakinah.

In the change of authority from Barker's garrison to Collie's free settlement, Collie requested that 'the general principle so successfully pursued by the late and much lamented Captain Barker' be continued. It was a principle, Collie argued 'never to be lost sight of in the intercourse between foreigners and the natives; this was to observe an uniformly kind and steady demeanour towards the latter, with occasional and well-timed gratuities of provisions and other articles of essential benefit to them'.[68] Collie also requested that a public record be left with the 'chief authorities' of the district 'by their predecessors, in addition to the more essential personal information to be obtained, whenever it is possible, of the customs and manners, and as far as may be known, of the individual disposition of such natives as frequent the settlement'. He had a strong interest in and respect for the King Ya-nup and Barker's kindness, and interest in King Ya-nup life had become well known at Swan River.

In November 1831 work on a road had commenced at King George's Sound, with 16 miles in a 'straight line' having been already completed. Under Collie's command, although still looking out for a ship, the community's mind began to slowly shift its gaze inland, towards the country and the other settlements as the settlers arrived and began taking up land around Albany.

With the newcomer's minds seaward and the King Ya-nup with a planetary focus, a unique colonial situation developed. The garrison at King George's Sound was a British possession without an Aboriginal dispossession, and this allowed for some distinct relationships to develop between the newcomers and the King Ya-nup on the fringe that was being created.

This reconstruction of life at King George's Sound relies completely on the writings of the people who were there. Not everybody was interested in keeping a record of settlement life. Lockyer and Barker were the only two commanders who kept daily journals and they differ markedly in their style and level of detail. Reconstructing the newcomers' setting up their camp is only possible by stitching together what writings they left behind about their world. These accounts should not be thought of as mirror images of what really happened but rather, they need to be constantly read as particular persons' 'versions' or interpretations of the world they saw. They are their attempts to tell stories and these stories are told from the fringe settlement that they were creating and inhabiting. As a historian I try to stand with them at the fringe and read to understand their culture-laden descriptions of what they saw and how they felt.

<h1 style="text-align:center">Reflection: Shaking Hands</h1>

The newcomers at the Swan River settlement were amused and astonished to discover that the Aboriginal groups living around the Swan thought of the newcomers as *Djanga*: the ghosts of their dead ancestors returning from an island to the west where the spirits rested.[1] Such interpretations by newcomers of their presence in Aboriginal Australian cosmology were common, as some were greeted by Aboriginal people as the spirits of dead relatives.[2] The King Ya-nup, however, did not seem to interpret the presence of the newcomers in this way, although it has been concluded that they did, as when they were asked by Nind where their ancestors were, some King Ya-nup pointed to the west.[3] As some of the newcomers arrived at King George's Sound from the west, they assumed that the King Ya-nup believed they too were returned spirits. Lockyer's settlement party, however, came from the east.

The King Ya-nup had two names for the newcomers: *Torndiller* and *Maupern nerran nerran*.[4] These names were only recorded by one early observer and it seems that once the King Ya-nup knew the newcomers by name they addressed them with those names: Barker was called 'Commandan'. *Torndiller* may have referred to the location of the British camp as Aboriginal camps to the west near Princess Royal Harbour had a similar name: *Tondirrup*.

Barker wrote down a conversation that he had with Mokaré in June 1830 about the first arrival of white people at King George's Sound. Mokaré explained to him that 'blackfellows knew nothing about them or their reasons for coming and were suspicious of them. When they found they had no ill intentions, but on the contrary were kind and friendly, they readily became friends ('shook hands') with them and would always continue so.'[5] This simple explanation by Mokaré must have been a story, handed down from his family and countrymen because he was not born when his ancestors experienced their first encounters with whites.[6] The shaking of hands referred to by Mokaré in his story was a physical touching, a grasping of right hand to right hand and a moving of hands up and down. It was also a powerful metaphor for friendship and peace.

It is not clear how or when the practice of handshaking began at King George's Sound, but by the time Lockyer arrived in December 1826, it was an action that the King Ya-nup instigated in their first meeting with him. In Lockyer's rough copy of his journal he wrote that a group of men 'came and exchanged the usual salutation of shaking hands.'[7] Of this same first handshake Lockyer would later write in his Fair Copy that the Aborigines 'appear to understand [it] to be friendly'.[8] The gesture might have been usual and friendly to him, and he assumed the King Ya-nup used it with the same social meaning as he did, universalising the metaphors of bodily gestures.

When Barker arrived three years later the handshake was a clear and powerful symbol, used in the same symbolic fashion by both the King Ya-nup and the British. As a gesture understood by both, its meaning could be changed and altered, and its changing significance was followed and accepted by both newcomers and King Ya-nup. To the newcomers it had become something more than a polite greeting. It was a show of acceptance and friendship, and withholding it could denote disapproval. It was an act that could be easily read – and precarious relationships such as these needed clear signs. Barker refused to shake hands with certain King Ya-nup to show them his disappointment with their behaviour; Mokaré shook hands with many people in the settlement, always with Barker and Davis and sometimes with Mrs Mills. He also talked about shaking hands with other Aborigines – his countrymen and his neighbours – although it is not clear whether this was always a physical act involving skin contact (sometimes it was) or simply a figure of speech – a way of explaining to Barker that he was at peace with his neighbours, or had at least forgiven them. Nakinah, Mokaré's elder brother also used the handshaking in a symbolic fashion. After the death of his youngest brother, Taragon, he avoided shaking hands with Davis, the medical assistant whom he thought was in some way responsible for the death of Taragon.[9]

Shaking hands was an action that was easily transferred. When Barker travelled beyond the bounds of the British world he would sometimes encounter Aborigines who had never been into the garrison, yet these

Aborigines all came up to Barker and offered their hand in his.[10] It is impossible to know whether this handshake ritual was picked up by the King Ya-nup from observing the newcomers, or if it was an indigenous Aboriginal practice. The traditional British ritual was one that the newcomers knew how to take part in. It was an ancient and respected greeting in British culture, showing trust, equality and acceptance; it was also a gesture to show that the hand holds no weapon. On the fringe, however, it transformed into a new ritual, constructed jointly by both Aborigines and newcomers, and it signified different feelings and intentions.

Seeing the King Ya-nup participating in this familiar ritual, and perhaps believing that it was part of traditional Aboriginal culture too, European visitors to King George's Sound wrote and talked about these Aborigines and transferred to other colonies an image of 'friendly natives'.[11] This seductive image – Manichean in its categorisation – quickly became a recognised trope and has been encouraged and added to by recent histories. It is explicitly celebrated in the memorial of Mokaré as the 'Man of Peace'. Ferguson wrote admiringly of Mokaré whom he thought was a naturally friendly person. 'He was a peacemaker,' he wrote, 'and all Australians of the southwest, both white and black, owe him a debt. Without him, their history would have been a great deal bloodier.'[12] The history of the relationships that formed during the garrison period has entered the historical discourse under the theme of *friendly frontier*, guided by the scholarship of Neville Green who used the term in the title of an article.[13] This friendly frontier has been set against the more explicitly violent encounters in the settlements further north where notorious racial conflicts occurred around the Swan River settlements at York and in Perth.[14] Green concluded simply that, 'the violent frontier had been held in check [at King George's Sound] because the relationship between the Aborigines and Europeans was based on mutual respect and trust.'[15] But if it was based on mutual respect and trust, how did that come about? And does the term friendly frontier lead to understanding the complexities of these relationships? What else can we read in the simple yet powerful symbol of a friendly handshake?

◆

There is a familiar colonial narrative in Australian historiography in which the British arrive and stay on Aboriginal land. The Aborigines are at first elusive but soon either 'friendly' or 'violent' encounters take place. After these encounters the Aborigines stay away from the British camp for a period of time, before there is a general 'coming in' of the Aboriginal groups from beyond the settlement. Richard Baker has written that the Yanyuwa people of northern Australia used the expression 'coming in' to describe the move of their kin from bush to town.[16] While this narrative could be plotted out from the literature of King George's Sound, I desire a more complex understanding of this mobility. The King Ya-nup did not participate in the British camp just to 'satisfy their curiosity' and shake hands with these strangers, even though Mokaré's story about the first arrival of white people suggests that this is exactly what happened. His story should not be taken literally, but probed for the metaphorical meaning within it.

Inga Clendinnen has written about an Aboriginal man named Baneelon and his countrymen who engaged intimately with the British newcomers at Port Jackson. Of Baneelon's family and other *Eora* people coming in to the settlement, she wrote: 'we cannot know precisely what shifts of mind or circumstance persuaded particular Australian groups to "come in"', describing the pattern of Aboriginal participation in the settlement at Port Jackson as a 'frogs-in-a-pond process'. Different families 'came, saw and decided to stay for a while'.[17] Baker agrees that there was not one single reason for Aboriginal people coming in to the settlements, and he argues that 'to hold such a view glosses over the fact that different groups came in for different reasons, at different times and in different places'.[18] Baker lists a number of reasons for coming in: economic necessity due to environmental damage; curiosity about Europeans; following other groups that had already come in; disease and security and protection.[19]

In *Born in the Cattle*, Ann McGrath wrote about a 'super waterhole' idea which theorised one reason why Aboriginal groups migrated towards British settlements. The theory is a general one and it states that Aboriginal people usually gathered at places where the supply of food was ample, and therefore European settlements simply offered new, better and larger waterholes.[20] Baker adds to McGrath's theory the idea of a 'super ceremony', which stresses that Aboriginal people came together 'whenever possible for social reasons and European settlements provided a new means for (or cause of) such gatherings'.[21] Baker also argues that there was not just a simple 'coming in' to the British world by the Aborigines, but also a 'going back', or 'going bush'. This term 'going bush' was written down and commented on by Barker throughout 1830. It usually referred to King Ya-nup who had left the settlement for a prolonged period of time. Alexander Collie also mentioned the phrase in a letter to his brother George in 1832, explaining to him that 'going bush' was a 'colonial term'.[22] The phrase also inferred that whoever had 'gone bush' had also 'gone native'; they had left the fringe and gone back into the Aboriginal world, living by their 'native' ways. Barker commented when Mokaré was ill that it would do him good to 'go bush' to get better.[23] Aboriginal culture was not left in the bush, and British culture went beyond the fringe too.

What historians have seen as a 'coming in' was also part of a traditional Aboriginal group movement. King Ya-nup coastal comings and goings were generally seasonal, with the majority of people going inland to the forests for several months during *Mokkar*, or winter, and returning partly in *Maningull*, or spring. Barker noted in late November 1830 that the King Ya-nup had 'come [to King George] for the season and should be in daily'.[24] But within this seasonal system many individual King Ya-nup used the space of the garrison independently to the seasonal drives. Throughout 1830 and 1831 there were times when few King Ya-nup were in the garrison. Barker recorded in March 1830 that few Aborigines 'had come to the settlement latterly'.[25] And in January 1830 Barker wrote that: 'Little Wapere seems to have regularly taken to the bush again'.[26] Collie similarly recorded a sporadic and unpredictable presence of particular King Ya-nup in the settlement.

'Coming in' has been seen either as an 'inevitability' by historians, who consider Aboriginal groups to have been drawn into the world of the newcomers, attracted to all that it offered, or conversely as an act revealing Aboriginal agency – a strategic, decisive move. While it is impossible to know with any certainty why different individuals started spending more time in the British world at King George's Sound, it is clear that not every King Ya-nup used the space regularly, only a certain few, and there were deliberate and meditated reasons for these particular individuals to be among the newcomers more than others. There was a tense relationship between some of the prisoners and the Aboriginal men, who jealously guarded their women. There is only one suggestion in the records, however, that the prisoners were anything more than a threat and Barker kept a watchful eye on them.[27] Single women were never in the settlement and the presence of the prisoners is possibly one reason why. Married women rarely came in without their husbands and children, and when they did it was an autonomous decision: their presence was for a specific reason. It is interesting to question why people like Jack in King's encounter, and Mokaré a few years later, spent time away from their groups, and opted to live closer to the newcomers.

Victor Turner pointed to the emergence of the concept of personality in the study of cultures that was promoted by Edward Sapir in 1934. Sapir wrote that the 'vast reaches of culture, far from being "carried" by a community or group … are discoverable only as the peculiar property of certain individuals, who cannot but give these cultural goods the impress of their own personality'.[28] Turner added to this that individuals will 'desire, and feel, as well as think, and their desires and feelings impregnate their thoughts and influence their intentions'.[29] Within one Aboriginal group, as Ronald and Catherine Berndt pointed out, no two personalities would be exactly alike. 'Everyone would have his (her) individual peculiarities, moulded and shaped by his own personal experience'.[30]

While possible answers to the questions about individual motivation will be raised in the narratives that follow, it is necessary here to look at how King Ya-nup people related to the newcomers and in what ways they 'came in' and used the newly occupied British space on the fringes of their world; and also which individual King Ya-nup spent increasing amounts of time in the British camp and why. Were different personalities attracted more than others? I have to rely on the different observers' accounts for our information and each commander at King George's Sound had different experiences and wildly different levels of interest in the King Ya-nup. Without pushing beyond British perceptions and descriptions, it is easy to conclude that Aboriginal people were 'coming in' to a British world, without seeing that some people were continuing ancient customs and others were utilising the new presence in particular ways.

♦

Lockyer's exchanges with the King Ya-nup varied from day-to-day meetings to scarce sightings of men in the scrub beyond the settlement (the first of these exchanges will be explored in detail in Chapter Five). As the weeks went by, Lockyer wrote of the King Ya-nup increasing 'confidence' with the newcomers. In January 1827, he wrote, 'The natives visit us every day,' but their 'increasing familiarity' was inconvenient and unwelcome from the 'disagreeable smell' which was produced by their 'rubbing their hair with fish and seal oil of a rancid quality'.[31] In March he wrote about Aboriginal 'strangers' walking into the camp with the expectation of receiving tomahawks: 'from the fame of the Tomahawks having spread abroad the subject of their visit [into the camp] was to solicit that they might be furnished with one each'.[32] These Aborigines were 'coming in' to receive the new technology of the British tomahawk, the news of these items having infiltrated the Aboriginal currency.

After a few months, Lockyer had begun to recognise familiar faces, but he did not write down any names, suggesting that communication with the King Ya-nup was still limited, or that he was not interested in the Aborigines on such an intimate level. Lockyer was not actively seeking out the King Ya-nup, spending much of his time on the coast and exploring islands in the harbours. He did, however, begin to see the way that the King Ya-nup occupied the spaces and he began to categorise them into different 'tribes': those who lived about the settlement (he thought) and those who lived on the opposite side of Oyster Harbour, reiterating King's false division of groups over the water. Tellingly, he refers to the latter group as the 'Oyster Bay Tribe', rather than Oyster Harbour, giving them a name that was familiar to him from his knowledge of Aboriginal Van Diemen's Landers.[33]

During 'Wakefield's Time' (as the King Ya-nup called it), some of the King Ya-nup were in the settlement on a daily basis.[34] Wakefield wrote in May 1827, 'The Natives continue to visit us daily.'[35] Their increasing familiarity however, was something of a mixed blessing. Some of them were 'becoming troublesome'. Instead of friendly engagements, Wakefield wrote that a few of the King Ya-nup had become thieves. It was not all of the King Ya-nup who were 'stealing' British materials; to prove this Wakefield told this story to Colonial Secretary Macleay as an example of the honesty and trustfulness of the few King Ya-nup who had begun to sleep the night in the garrison, one of whom was identified as Mokaré.[36] It is a rare example of Wakefield's interest in the Aboriginal world and perhaps this story was told more for its audience – the Colonial Secretary – than its subject, to show the success of Wakefield as commander of this isolated station and 'friend' to what he thought of as the conciliated Aborigines. 'A short time ago,' he wrote, 'two Natives expressed a wish to sleep at the cooking fire, which was allowed; early in the morning they went away each taking an Axe.' When the 'trusty' Aboriginals (as Wakefield called them) who sometimes slept in the newcomers' huts, arrived at the settlement Wakefield tried to explain the theft to them. He wrote that 'they appeared very angry and promised immediately to restore [the axes]'. Several of these 'trusty' King Ya-nup left the settlement for a few days. When they returned they made 'signs' that they had speared one of the thieves. Communication between the newcomers and King Ya-nup was still achieved with the language of the body. Shortly after this communication, 'the other Native who had slept by the fire, brought in the Axe he had stolen'. Wakefield explained that 'several attempts' were made by the trusty King Ya-nup to 'spear him also', but this was stopped 'by the interference of some of [Wakefield's] party'. This last 'thief' was allowed to escape, Wakefield wrote, 'tho' not until a severe wound had been inflicted in his leg'.[37] The Aboriginal actions within this story show the attempt by a few individuals – Mokaré and possibly Nakinah – to forge a political alliance with Wakefield and the newcomers. Spearing the two 'thieves' was a signal to Wakefield; a strategic action directed to this powerful new presence. Even though Wakefield tried to stop the second spearing, the 'trusty' King Ya-nup made sure that he received a 'severe wound' in his leg.

It is interesting that Wakefield constructed the above story of himself as peacemaker in his letter to the Colonial Secretary, and did not mention the incident that follows. This is the only other recorded incident involving the King Ya-nup during Wakefield's command at the settlement (although there would have been more that were not written down). It was Barker rather than Wakefield who dug up and wrote this buried story in January 1830. Barker was on his way to examine the new ground that had been broken up by the prisoners near the farm. On his way there he came across a 'small enclosed place' which he had not seen before. The overseer who had accompanied him explained that it was the grave of one of Mokaré's younger brothers, Yallapoli who had been buried a year and a half before. Yallapoli had come into the settlement one day during Wakefield's command and lay down on one of the prisoners' beds. A few of the prisoners examined him and discovered that he was dead. The King Ya-nup were 'furious about it and collected in great numbers about the place with their spears shipped, threatening vengeance'. To explain the seriousness of their anger, the overseer who was recounting the event to Barker, added to his story that even 'peacemaker' Mokaré was violent, 'tearing off his clothes with his teeth, and shewing many symptoms of rage'. Coolbun threw his spear at Wakefield but it must have missed him, otherwise this event would have surely made it into Wakefield's reports or letters. Wakefield did not allow anyone to retaliate and 'managed to pacify them by degrees', keeping a close watch on the King Ya-nup movements for three weeks.[38] This story has a story within it. Coolbun's spear missed. Knowledge of Aboriginal dexterity with spears suggests that it was thrown by him with the intention of missing. This possibly signifies that for the King Ya-nup, the newcomers' presence on their country had already come to hold powerful political possibilities that they could not risk by the actual spilling of British blood. The overseer told Barker that the King Ya-nup still became angry in 1830 if anyone mentioned Yallapoli's name. Barker discovered from

Mokaré later that day that he now referred to Yallapoli with a different name: *Mollian*. Mokaré said that Wakefield had 'cried' for his brother Mollian, but he said nothing about his own grief or violence or Coolbun's spear.[39]

These moments of danger, witnessed through stories such as these, cannot be narrated out of this 'friendly frontier'. They define the slippery side of such unpredictable exchanges for both the newcomers and the King Ya-nup as they were negotiating the new occupation of shared space on the fringe. Stories such as these assist understanding how particular King Ya-nup were experiencing and dealing with the British camp's permanency. They also show some of the practicalities of communication between these unlike people.

Wakefield mentioned that several 'trusty' Aborigines had been living about the settlement in May 1827. Mokaré lived with Nind from at least the first few months of 1828 and possibly earlier. In a letter to Sleeman, Nind requested an extra pound of flour to help him 'provide for Mawcurrie,' who had resided with him for 'many months.'[40] In November 1829 Wilson noted that 'several of them [Aborigines] reside constantly in the camp, where they are treated with kindness' and he added that Mokaré had 'always slept in the Commandant's apartment.'[41] Barker, however, gives much more detail about who was sleeping where and the subtle shifting of people through the spaces. Mokaré was almost always in his hut and a few other King Ya-nup slept at the soldiers' barracks, or wherever they could get a bed. Talwyn was also a frequent house guest of Barker's. It is telling that the King Ya-nup who came in to sleep at the settlement were always the younger, single men; the married men continued to sleep with their families. The huts where the King Ya-nup got a bed were all single men's huts; soldiers or officers who were not accompanied by a woman. This living arrangement was not a radically new situation, but fitted into the newcomers' and the King Ya-nup daily narratives about their lives.

It is worth mentioning that Mokaré, a single man, only shared huts with other single men – Nind, Barker and Collie. He did not share the hut of Lockyer, who was married, or Dr Davis, whom Mokaré noticed wore two wedding rings on his fingers. Observant to this British cultural rite, Mokaré asked him if he had two wives. 'Are your wives dead? – You give them physic?'[42]

Mokaré and Nakinah were still sharing the quarters of the chief of the British world in 1831 when Collie was the Government Resident. In December that year when Stephen Henty visited the settlement, he wrote in his travel diary that he 'Slept at Dr Collie's by the side of a native named King

Knackana, chief of the King George tribe.'[43] Collie wrote about the use of the settlement by the King Ya-nup in the following way: 'The male part of the Natives extended their stay in the Settlement often till after dark, especially if biscuits and tea were held out to them … The women almost invariably left before night-fall, and, with the old men, and young children, chiefly occupied the more distant bivouac; whilst the young men … betook themselves only to the adjoining grove.'[44]

◆

European interactions with Aborigines in contact scenarios are often described as destructive. The devastation of colonial situations remains strongly felt today in Aboriginal communities across Australia and should never be downplayed in our histories. However, it is important to realise the constructive aspects of these colonial interactions too, as such narratives help to encourage intercultural acts of construction rather than destruction today. Creating a language with which to communicate on the fringe at King George's Sound was a mutual undertaking by a few of the newcomers and the King Ya-nup, and was a necessary link for an ongoing relationship. Linguists call these new languages 'pidgin'. At King George's Sound during the period of this history the development of this language was not a switching from mother tongue to new language, but is best described as the creation of an additional Aboriginal language.[45] The King Ya-nup were already multilingual before the arrival of the newcomers and adept in learning new languages. This new language was not the primary language of either the newcomers or the King Ya-nup, but, like much in their relationship, a meeting halfway between, with many of the words from the King Ya-nup repertoire making up the vocabulary.[46] The British saying of waking up at 'cock's crow' was localised to 'cockatoo's crow'.[47]

Barker stands out among these commanders as being unusually enlightened and curious about Aborigines. And what is most striking about Barker's narrative of his time at King George's Sound is that he had an ear for spoken detail. He transcribed 'he said, she said' conversations between him and the soldiers and prisoners, and between him and the King Ya-nup. No other text from this period and place includes the same depth in its descriptions of people not only *doing things* but *saying things* too.[48] One brief story shows the innovative language and linguistic obstacles between Mokaré and Barker as they struggled through the slow process of finding a new vocabulary. In January 1830, Barker and Mokaré were in Barker's hut and the commandant was endeavouring to learn what the King Ya-nup belief was of a future state:

his most passionate Aboriginal interest was religion and he often questioned the King Ya-nup about their ideas on creation and spirituality, consulting his encyclopaedia for further answers.[49] But Barker could not clearly make out if the King Ya-nup believed in an afterlife.[50] Mokaré replied to his interrogations on the subject, saying 'something about "Quaylite", when black fellow die,' repeating in a shrill voice "Cuylite, cuylite, cuylite", which Barker described as similar to 'the way I have witnessed children imitate the speaking of a ghost'. Mokaré laughed 'heartily' at Barker not being able to understand what he meant. He finished a long attempt at explanation, Barker wrote, by saying 'Captain Twang-poit', which Barker translated as 'does not hear' (*twang* being their word for ears or to hear) and therefore, 'does not understand'. Mokaré continued, 'Captain-Sunday-Book-Paper' – 'alluding', Barker wrote, 'to our church service on Sundays', Mokaré continued, 'Black fellow twang poit. Now – Cuylite Cuylite – white fellow twangpoit.'[51] This humorous conversation between Mokaré and Barker shows that not only were different religions hard to comprehend, but there were also difficulties in communication between the newcomers and the King Ya-nup that existed four years after the settlement had begun – Barker, or Captain *Twang-poit*, was the one newcomer who took the time and had a patient interest in understanding the King Ya-nup. During his command at King George's Sound, Barker often wrote that he could only understand parts of what Mokaré was trying to tell him. Communication between them certainly got better the more time they spent together, and Barker spoke to Mokaré often using King Ya-nup words or the pidgin language they were developing. Later that year, in April, after perhaps more practice and steady listening, Barker discovered what Mokaré had meant. He wrote: 'Women after death become little birds; men larger birds. Quaylite.'[52]

A lot had happened since Jack and King's heavily gestured pantomime on board the *Bathurst* in Oyster Harbour in 1821. The King Ya-nup linguistic abilities meant that many of them developed and learnt a new language to communicate with the newcomers. Not all King Ya-nup spoke the new language and it was only used when they conversed with the newcomers, not with each other. Therefore, during this period they were not losing their mother tongue, but adding to it. It seems that Mokaré was still needed as interlocutor between Barker and the other King Ya-nup, Barker writing occasionally, 'Mokaré much needed as interpreter.'[53] Nind also commented on the language barrier in the first few years of the garrison, writing, 'Of their language we have, as yet, little knowledge.'[54]

When Wilson took Mokaré as a guide on his exploration to the west of King George's Sound, they encountered one of Mokaré's acquaintances from the north, a Wills man. Wilson wrote of Mokaré's change in language as he began to converse with this Wills man: 'He and Mokaré entered into an animated conversation. The stranger, in relating [a] story, did it in a sort of recitative, far from being disagreeable. Mokaré, who, at first, talked in the tone that he had acquired from us, soon relapsed into the same recitativo, which, it would appear, is their natural way of communicating with each other.'[55] Mokaré's quick change back to mother tongue with all its particular styles and accompanying gestures shows his fluidity at moving between the British world and the King Ya-nup one, and the enlarging of his traditional communicative and cultural repertoire.

Mokaré also surprised Barker with his linguistic skills and his quick movement from pidgin to his recitative mother tongue. In April 1830 Mokaré brought in the tea to Barker's hut, as Mills was out and Mrs Mills was sick. Mokaré brought the tea tray in 'rather awkwardly', Barker wrote, but he was anxious to be of use. Talwyn joined them later and Barker wrote that 'Mokaré surprised me by addressing him, with "Where have you been a' the [day]", attempting at the same time the air of the Scotch song'. Mills was a Scot, and it is possible that Mokaré was performing as Mills, in his role in bringing in the tea. Barker was amazed that Mokaré then instantly slipped into a recitative style to talk to Talwyn, which the King Ya-nup 'seem to adopt whenever they have anything interesting to relate' to each other.[56]

◆

The British and historical narrative construction of 'coming in' operates in a similar fashion to Mokaré's statue: it renders the Aborigines in the British world. The British narrative always sets the tone and tells the story. It is essential to remember that the British also participated in an Aboriginal world, living on the edges of their country. The 'coming in' narrative is a good example of how the way in which we write about the past changes the way we tell the stories. In narrating the Aborigines 'coming in' to the British world they are represented as being enveloped by a dominant culture, as 'reacting', not acting with their own intentions. In order to show the King Ya-nup acting we need to change the way we tell this past.

The following episodes complicate this coherent narrative of the friendly Aborigines 'coming in' to the British world and shaking hands. The phrase 'coming in' can, in some contexts, be an unhelpful one as it cloaks the experiences and motivations that were part of an independent, individual and gradual development of relationships. And while some of the King Ya-nup actions could be read simply as 'friendly', this term misrepresents the hard work of negotiations, slippery moments of misunderstandings, hostility, laughter and storytelling, and does not allow us to see individual people's strategic decisions, or what advantages such people – like Jack and Mokaré – might have gained from such alliances.

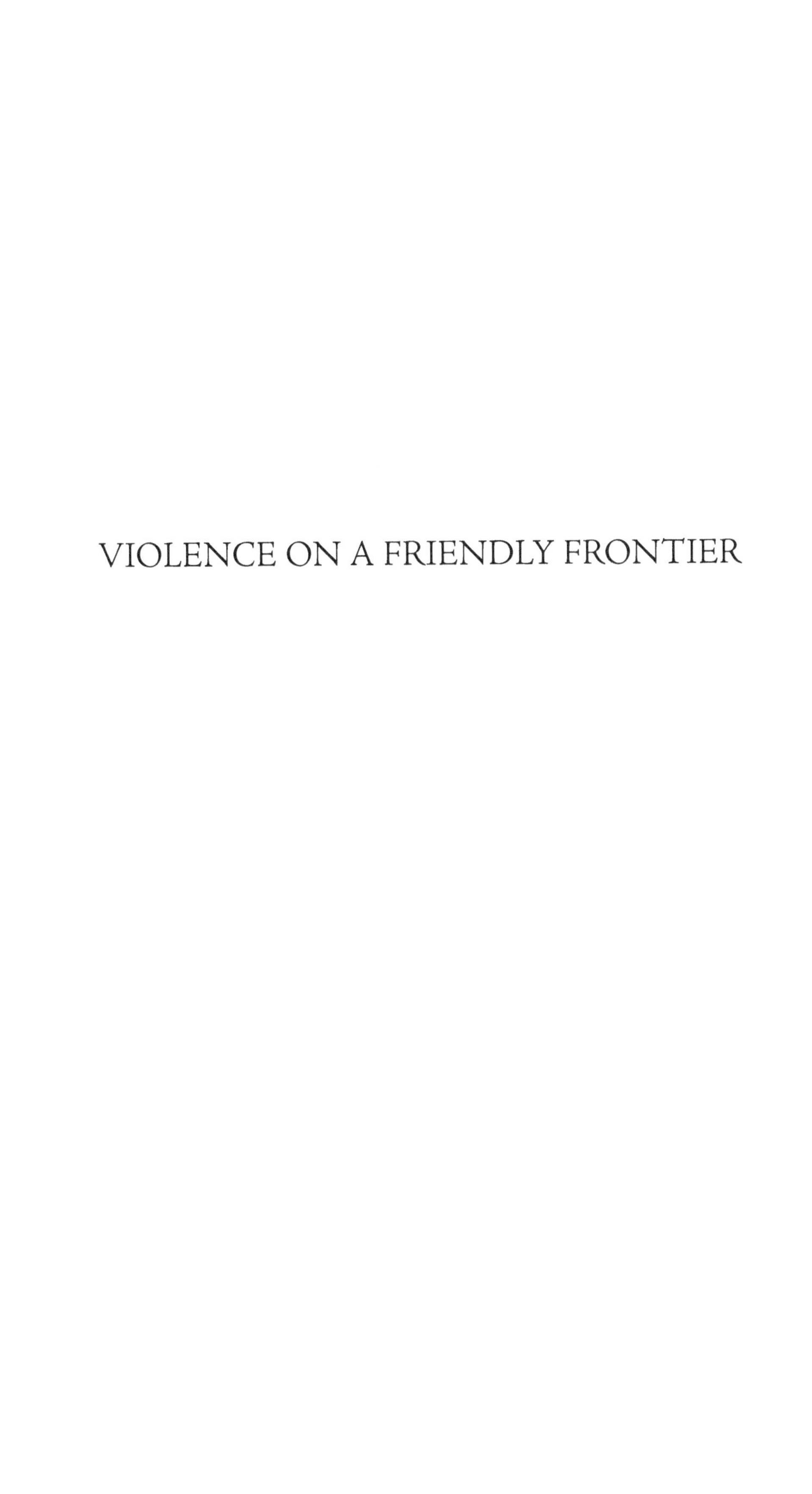

VIOLENCE ON A FRIENDLY FRONTIER

4

Violence Performed

From the *Amity*'s deck, Major Edmund Lockyer saw the islands and landmarks of King George's Sound noting the entry to the two harbours and then the nearby land. Like King, he had read about this place in the journals of earlier European visitors to the south-west coast and probably developed a distinct picture of the landscape in his mind's eye through the vivid descriptions these explorers left in their detailed travel accounts.[1] He recognised their descriptions: 'At 12 O'clock noon made Bald Island. Weather very hazy. Well it may be called Bald Island. Not the least sign of verdure on it or vegetation or anything ...'.[2] He understood Vancouver's barefaced naming of that barefaced island. As the *Amity* sailed past Michaelmas Island, Lockyer observed a fire burning on it at the end facing the mainland, 'made as if by some persons who required assistance'. He looked out for Aborigines on shore but saw none and no smoke to indicate their presence.[3] The brig anchored half a mile off shore in Princess Royal Harbour and the passengers and crew enjoyed the rest of their Christmas evening on board.

Even though conciliation with the Aborigines was the last order given to Lockyer in his official instructions, it had to come first. Colonial adventures to remote places often meant that relationships with native inhabitants had to be 'sorted out' before any imperial work could be done on shore. King George's Sound was no exception and getting along with the locals quickly became Lockyer's first priority.

Written histories remember Lockyer as a pioneering founder of the town of Albany.[4] The town honours Lockyer in its place names, monuments and historical re-enactments, and a replica of his brig dominates the foreshore. Honours aside, I wanted to know more about this man, about what it was like for him and his crew when they arrived in 1826 on the isolated shores of Princess Royal Harbour and – most importantly – how their first encounter with the Aborigines was played out. This episode is a reconstruction of that first encounter through the pen of Lockyer, using both his immediate 'rough copy' journal and his retrospective 'fair copy' which he transcribed for the Colonial Secretary on 20–22 January 1827.

Aboard the *Amity*, Lockyer awoke at daylight to hazy, windy weather. He went on shore with Lieutenant Festing in search of a suitable site for the British garrison. On landing, Lockyer had his first meeting with the King Ya-nup. He had presumably met Aborigines previously at Port Jackson and certainly experienced brief encounters on his exploration along the Brisbane River.[5] These previous meetings must have in some way shaped his ideas and expectations of the King Ya-nup. And again those previous explorers' journals came to his mind, allowing him to draw on his knowledge storehouse of 'native' expectations. Lockyer described what this meeting meant to him and his men. I will also look at his conclusions and try to understand what the Aborigines made of it.

Two men and a little boy approached Lockyer, when he called to them. The younger man signalled that he was keen to go on board the brig, which Lockyer allowed. In his retrospective journal Lockyer wrote that this young man was later named Jack. An addition to this sentence is in a red ink and it reveals that Jack's naming was from a 'supposition that he is the Jack of Capt King'; a later thought acknowledging that Lockyer's expectation came from the reports of a previous visitor. King's 'Jack' had also been keen to board the brig.[6] Lockyer recorded in his Rough Copy that Jack answered to the 'native name of Monga' – a name Lockyer found in King's vocabulary. One of his friends also answered to that name. His retrospective journal, however, shows that Lockyer finally settled that his 'native name is Mangril'. Lockyer, however, continued to call this young man Jack in his Fair Copy.

The other Aborigine with Jack, an old man, walked off with the little boy. Jack spent most of the morning on board the *Amity* and went back on shore to join his countrymen wearing a pair of white trousers given to him as a present by the men on board the boat. Lockyer remarked that Jack's curiosity had been 'satisfied'.[7]

It is interesting that Lockyer regarded this brief meeting with Jack and the two other King Ya-nup as one in which they were 'presenting themselves' to him. Of this encounter he concluded, honestly, that Jack was curious and friendly. This is a reasonable assumption for Lockyer given that the King Ya-nup had only just entered his story. This was his first encounter. But it is important to remember that Lockyer had now entered their story too, and, as has been seen with King, their story began well before Lockyer arrived. Lockyer fits into a broader frame for the King Ya-nup – he entered their story mid-plot. What, I wonder, did Jack and the other King Ya-nup make of Lockyer, his men, their boat and the white trousers? Jack is a character who is constantly in view in this episode. He needs to be watched closely.

At dawn the following day, Lockyer ordered a boat to be sent to Michaelmas Island in King George's Sound as the fire that he had seen there on his arrival was still burning. And during the night a 'light on the west end facing the harbour' was seen, cementing his thought that they were 'persons in distress.'[8] Mr Wheeler, the convict overseer, set out in a boat for the island to see if someone had been marooned out there that might need help. After breakfast all hands were put to work: Lockyer and Festing landed on the northern shore to examine the 'upperpart' of Princess Royal Harbour where they had spotted forests of 'substantial sized timber'. Meanwhile, ten prisoners with an overseer were ordered to repair one of the boats of the brig which had been damaged during the journey from New South Wales and another party were instructed to fill casks with fresh water from a stream close to shore at the base of Mt Melville, opposite to where the *Amity* was at anchor. This was where Flinders had marked a rivulet on his map. Captain Wakefield and Isaac Scott Nind were also on shore.

Lockyer lists who were carrying weapons. Nind and Wakefield were armed with double barrel guns, as were Lockyer and Festing, and a ship's musket was sent with the party collecting fresh water. Lockyer noted that from the 'contiguity' of the brig to the shore, he thought the weapon was unnecessary. Was he thinking about King's security measures? It should be noted that the one person who might have been expected to carry a weapon – Wheeler who had gone out to Michaelmas Island to face the unknown – was empty handed.

Festing and Lockyer decided to walk along the beach until they got to the forests while Nind and Wakefield walked above them in the scrub on the rising ground. After Lockyer had walked for about 2 miles (near to where the watering party had gone to collect fresh water), an Aboriginal man came out of the thick scrub. When he saw them he spoke to someone in the scrub who came out, and then immediately two more men joined them. Lockyer made signs for them to approach, which they did. Lockyer noted that even though he and Festing were both armed, the four men left their spears in the scrub where Lockyer was certain there were more Aborigines. Why did they come out to meet these strangers without their spears? Lockyer seems to know that this was significant; he wrote in his journal that they were rarely without them.

Lockyer's classification of these men was in terms of friend or foe, a common polarisation constructed in the first moments of a meeting such as this. The four King Ya-nup shook hands with Lockyer, cementing their friendly characterisation in Lockyer's mind. He thought they were 'fine young men' and noted that they were 'all painted and their hair Clubbed and daubed all over with a red ochre and fish or seal oil as described by Captain King'.[9] Lockyer was unsure whether their painted bodies signalled a preparatory sign for war, although he might have only thought this later, reflecting on the events of the whole day. Whatever the occasion meant to these King Ya-nup men, we can conclude here that they were painted for a particular reason.

Soon after the Aborigines had come out of the scrub and exchanged a 'mutual salutation', Lockyer spotted a large fire burning at the head of the Harbour, and a short time later he saw a very large smoke about 10 miles away on the hills to the south-west, possibly near the camp *Tondirrup*. Lockyer was starting to place the presence of these men in a wider theatre of activity. Two of these 'friendly' King Ya-nup remained with Lockyer to show him kangaroos, the other two 'made signification' that they would go to where the brig *Amity* was anchored. Of this 'friendly encounter' Lockyer wrote: 'accompanied by these two natives who showed great good nature and tractability, carrying birds, that we shot, going up trees, satisfied us and particularly myself that these people were friendly, and [they were] satisfied we were equally so, I flattered myself that matters would go well as regarded our intercourse with them'.[10]

The two men who remained with Festing and Lockyer walked with them into the forest, and on being asked where kangaroos were to be found, they pointed. Perhaps to show that he was not to be outdone, Lockyer saw a black cockatoo and shot it. The King Ya-nup saw this and showed 'admiration' as it fell to the ground. Of all this 'friendly business', Lockyer wrote that he still took the precaution not to discharge more than one barrel from his gun as he was 'well aware that these people have always spears at hand', although Lockyer had previously noted that they were not carrying them this time.[11]

By this stage it was near 1 pm and Lockyer was anxious to know what had happened on Michaelmas Island. He told Festing he would go down to the harbour shore and then return by the beach 'to the place where the Boat would come' for him and Festing, near the watering party. One of the Aborigines went with Lockyer, leaving Festing with the other man. Lockyer and his new companion returned nearly to the place where he saw the four King Ya-nup come out of the scrub, but decided to rejoin Festing who had walked at least a mile closer to the vessel on the beach from where Lockyer was. (see map, image 4)

Festing was close to the base of Mt Melville, on the beach near a rock at a point which 'projected' into the harbour. This would later be the place where the flagstaff was erected. Lockyer was on his way to where Festing and his Aboriginal companion were, when Festing stopped to look towards Lockyer. Just above Festing, coming out of the scrub at the bottom of Mt Melville were six or seven King Ya-nup men.[12] Four of these 'very tall men' were 'strangers' he had not met with earlier.[13] They passed Festing and headed straight towards Lockyer and his Aboriginal companion on the beach, who, Lockyer later wrote was 'laughing and appearing quite delighted at meeting his friends.'[14] As they approached, the man who was with Lockyer called out to the group who answered him in what Lockyer interpreted as an 'authoritative manner' to come away. He joined the group of men 'without saying a word' to Lockyer. As they all passed Lockyer, in the direction of the watering party, about 50 yards away up from the beach, he tried to stop them but failed. Their looks convinced him that something was wrong. Festing had also tried to speak to them when they passed him, but they would not stop. Festing had been ahead of Lockyer and could see the beach opposite to where the *Amity* was anchored. He told Lockyer that four of these eight Aborigines had been brought back from Michaelmas Island by Wheeler.

Festing and Lockyer then headed to the boat that was being repaired on the beach about 150 yards east of the watering party, and found Jack, who Lockyer now referred to as 'our friend', helping the carpenter with the repairs. Lockyer fired off two rounds as a signal for a boat from the brig to come and collect them. Suddenly a prisoner came running up to them saying that the Aborigines had attacked the watering party and were 'spearing the people.' Friendly Jack instantly, sensibly, took off. Lockyer turned around and at a distance of 60 yards he saw the prisoner, Dennis Dineen standing in the water with three spears sticking in him. 'Spearing the people' turned out to be the spearing of one man.

The group of Aboriginal men had 'crept down' through the bush near Mt Melville and onto the banks of the stream to throw their spears. Lockyer wrote that they 'would probably have speared every Man, had not one of them [Dineen] got up to go into the [fresh] water to bathe, and saw the natives on the bank above fixing their spears, they [the Aborigines] all ran away except one man who picked up his spear and threw it twice; four of them were those brought from the Island'.[15]

The eight Aboriginal men (four of whom had come from the island) who approached Lockyer and his companion had come to 'collect' the two 'friendly' Aborigines who were with Lockyer and Festing. They must have been crucial participants in the imminent spearing.

One spear was deep in Dineen's high thigh, penetrating behind the hip bone and coming through the fleshy part of the thigh near his groin; another about two and a half inches in the muscle close to his spine, and the third through the fleshy part of his arm above his right elbow. Look at the blows closely. Thigh, back, arm. None of the spears were thrown near vital organs. Perhaps the King Ya-nup were targeting ritualised areas of the body. What can be known is that Aboriginal skill with spears reveals that if the King Ya-nup had wanted to kill Dineen, they would have. The desired outcome for a spearing such as this was not always death, but often just the spilling of blood.

Nind had gone back on board the *Amity* before the spearing took place, so Lockyer ordered the three spears to be cut off Dineen 'within four inches of the body' while they waited for a boat to come back to shore to take them to Nind who then removed the spears. Lockyer was very doubtful of Dineen's recovery.[16]

◆

In some ways this is not a typical Australian violent encounter that historians might construct: its key elements are the speed with which the violence escalates and Lockyer's steady consideration of its meaning. He did not reach for his gun when he saw Dineen speared, as might be expected, but surprisingly, gave orders that no retaliation should take place from the British 'side except in absolute self defence'. With a man speared, one might have considered this was a case for self-defence. I wonder why Lockyer described all those weapons if he did not intend to use them. Perhaps he would have reached for his weapon if a soldier or an officer had been speared in the place of this mere prisoner?

Lockyer did not have the full account of events until he got back on board the safety of the brig (it was after all called *Amity*) and was told what happened when the overseer Mr Wheeler with the rescue boat had reached Michaelmas Island. As Wheeler rowed up to the island, he saw four Aborigines crouching under a rock. They 'did not speak until pointed to'. When they stood up Wheeler was hesitant to approach these desperate men without having a firearm and so decided to go back to the vessel (recall how many weapons were on shore). As Wheeler was pulling away from the island he saw the King Ya-nup men fall on their knees, making 'sad lamentations' – it was clear that they wanted to get off the island – he felt sympathy for them and took a chance, allowing them into the boat. He ferried them back to the vessel and then to shore. From this description I think it is clear that neither Lockyer nor Wheeler thought that the people who had lit the fire on Michaelmas Island were Aborigines until Wheeler saw them. Why else would Wheeler have so confidently rowed out to the island without a weapon when everybody on shore was carrying at least one?

The four marooned Aborigines had been very anxious to meet up with their countrymen and women. On getting to the shore from the island, one of them showed his neck to his countrymen who had come to greet them, which 'had four or five deep scars as if from a sharp instrument a Sword or Cutlass.'[17] Lockyer wished that these four men had been 'detained' on board the brig until he had met with them. He wrote, 'it would be extremely desirable to have endeavoured to have learnt their story and how they got on the Island and if any inhuman wretches had placed them there ...'[18] He knew from reading King that the Aborigines at this place did not have any canoes.

Why was Dineen, a prisoner, targeted? It is difficult to know what offence, if any, he represented. Perhaps he was a symbolic figure. As Nind would later record, the Aborigines 'are not particular whether they kill the principle offender or any other of his tribe.'[19] Often in a spearing such as this, the target was an individual who represented the 'tribe', rather than a particular person.

Looking back now to Lockyer's first brief meeting with the King Ya-nup, when he met Jack, it can now be conceived that these three men were not coming to 'present themselves' to him. They knew about their four countrymen on Michaelmas Island – their intentions for meeting Lockyer ran deeper than 'curiosity'.

◆

At six o'clock the following morning, 28 December, in another attempt to carry out the Governor's instructions and find a site for the settlement, Lockyer set out with Festing for Green Island in Oyster Harbour. Here Lockyer found the corpse of an Aboriginal man. He predicted the man had been dead about two months and described in quite unusual detail its decomposing state. Near the body they found a raft made with some dead wood fastened together with grass which had been woven into a rope. As discussed earlier, the King Ya-nup did not have any form of canoe when Europeans began arriving on their shores and did not swim. In that context, this improvised raft is particularly remarkable. Lockyer pondered that the man had made it for the purpose of leaving the island but could not get it into the water, perishing from want.[20] Could a desperate situation like this have called for an improvised technology? Finding the dead body made Lockyer think that 'bad work' must have been going on before he arrived and he blamed a sealing gang, who were known around the south coast for their 'treacherous ways' of treating the locals. For Lockyer, the plot of this encounter was thickening.

◆

Eight days had passed since the spearing of Dennis Dineen, who was recovering, and the British had not sighted any King Ya-nup. Then, on the morning of Friday, 5 January, Lockyer's 'friend' Jack walked into the British camp – now a few makeshift tents between Mt Melville and Mt Clarence on the shores of Princess Royal Harbour – and was brought to Lockyer's tent. Lockyer tried to explain to him in 'the best way' he could that he was 'very angry' that the Aborigines had thrown their spears. Jack may have misread Lockyer's pantomime of the spearing and thought that Lockyer was going to spear him. Lockyer wrote that Jack was at first 'frightened' at his tone 'apprehending some retaliation was intended him', but he 'calmed down' after Lockyer, who was keen to have a peaceful reconciliation with his countrymen, gave him a tomahawk and something to eat. After staying an hour with Lockyer he made signs that he wanted to leave. Jack went off up the hill at the back of the camp, cutting trees with his new tomahawk as he went.[21] Jack's presence and his interplay are interesting. He was the first Aborigine that the newcomers met, he played a distinctive part in the event of the spearing and he was the first to visit the British camp after it. Lockyer was still puzzled by the eventful first week at this new outpost. It is easier to understand why it took so long for him to determine a site to camp and to enact his ritual of possession.

◆

Five days after the visit by Jack, a schooner, the *Governor Hunter*, belonging to a Mr Robinson of Hobart, pulled into Princess Royal Harbour. This boat contained a rag-tag mix of voyagers, including several tough sealers, Robert Williams (described as 'a Black man'), Pidgeon, an Aborigine from Sydney and several members of the sealing vessel *Brisbane*. From this second vessel was William Hook a Maori man from Kerikeri on the North Island. The master of the *Brisbane*, Mr Kemp of Hobart, had allegedly taken off, leaving part of his crew on the islands around the south coast.

These men claimed to be 'destitute of provisions'. Lockyer was suspicious of them immediately. He suspected that they were guilty of the atrocities committed against the King Ya-nup and sanctioned them to be detained on board the brig. He considered it his duty to investigate the crimes against the four Aboriginal men on Michaelmas Island and the murder of the man on Green Island to determine who the perpetrators were.[22]

The following day Lockyer's suspicions of the sealers were realised when he ascertained from William Hook – the Maori man who spoke good English – that the dead Aboriginal man on Green Island had been killed by a gang of the sealers. Lockyer asked Hook to repeat his statement and swear to it under oath and sign his name in the presence of Lockyer's son, Ensign Lockyer.[23] The second part of this story is informed by Hook and retold by Lockyer.

Hook recounted the events as follows: the sealing crew of the schooner *Brisbane* was visiting Oyster Harbour about eight weeks prior to Lockyer's arrival, in late October 1826. Another sealing vessel, the *Governor Hunter*, was docked in Princess Royal Harbour. During their visit, the crew from both vessels had been 'frequently visited' by the local Aborigines 'who were friendly'. They escorted the sealers on fishing expeditions in the sealing vessels; perhaps the Aborigines in hope of trading opportunities and the sealers in need of a good fishing area. During this time the sealers did not see any Aboriginal women, but they were looking out for them.

During the sealers' visit, the French navy corvette *l'Astrolabe* captained by Dumont d'Urville sailed into King George's Sound and anchored in Princess Royal Harbour. The journals of the French officers, while interesting, do not offer further insight into this episode. After the French expedition left the Sound five King Ya-nup men approached the sealers and asked to be rowed out to Green Island in Oyster Harbour to catch birds. It is worth deliberating here. As I have already mentioned, Green Island is close to the shores of Oyster Harbour, approximately 1,600 metres away, but it sits in *murtagh*, deep water. It is possible that the King Ya-nup might have wanted to go out to Green Island for some time to catch birds. Recall that when King visited King

George's Sound in December 1821, one of his men went to Green Island and 'shot a few parakeets and water birds, some of which he gave to the natives after explaining how they had been killed, which … produced great applause.'[24] They also witnessed d'Urville's crew who killed 'several sea birds on the islet.'[25] Seeing them from the mainland the King Ya-nup wanted to hunt the birds; the sealers with their boats provided the means of getting to the island.

Green Island meant more to the King Ya-nup than a place to hunt birds. The creation story that Mokaré told Barker in 1830 was about a woman who dragged her body in a line to Green Island where she died, creating Oyster Harbour and King's River. This story represents Green Island, or *Warrecoolyup*, meaning female walk, as a burial mound for a female ancestral being. It is worth raising the question of what sort of impact this ancestral story might have had on the death of the man on Green Island for the King Ya-nup.

Back to Hook's account: Hook was ordered with another deckhand, Ned (also from the *Hunter*), by Randall and Everitt, the boat steerers, to take five Aboriginal men to Green Island, under the auspices of 'bird hunting', and abandon them there. Hook and Ned complied with this order – rough sealers were not to be reckoned with – and rowed the men out in a boat to the island. When the Aboriginal men saw the boat leaving the island without them they called out and made signs to be taken back to the mainland. But they were left there. This is probably when they began building the raft: a desperate attempt to get back to shore. It suggests too that the sealers knew the King Ya-nup were not sea people. And perhaps this was not their first visit to the area: sealers and whalers had been frequently working the southern coast since Vancouver's journal became known.

The following morning four sealers set out into the country armed with guns and cutlasses. They returned to their camp at four or five that evening with four King Ya-nup women. The women, who must have been terrified, were tied together in pairs by their arms. During the night two of them managed to escape (there is no more information on their manhandling). The following morning both boats' crews set off together again, armed, probably in search of the two women. They were gone all day and returned alone.

Hook and several of the sealers were sent in a boat to Green Island the next day to take a keg of water to the marooned, and no doubt distressed, Aborigines. When the boat approached the island the Aboriginal men 'made a rush' to get into it, but the men in the boat stopped them by pushing away from the island and rowed back to the shore. Four 'fresh hands', including

Lockyer's informant Hook, took the boat out again to the island, this time taking with them guns and swords. One man got out taking the keg of water on shore and the Aborigines again ran to get into the boat. The sealers struck them with oars and swords, but the Aborigines persisted in climbing into the boat. Kirby fired shots 'over their heads to frighten them', but this did not deter these desperate men's attempts to get into the boat. When a second round was fired Hook saw one of the Aborigines fall forwards on his face in the water, 'Blood spouting out from both his sides.'

One of the sealers, John Randall, went out to the island alone the following morning. He took the four remaining men in his boat, leaving the dead body on Green Island, and rowed out to Michaelmas Island. Here the King Ya-nup men were again abandoned. Randall then rowed to Breaksea Island (next to Michaelmas Island), where he was joined by another boat that carried the two King Ya-nup women who had not been lucky enough to escape. One of these women, with a seven-year-old girl named Fanny who had been abducted earlier from Middle Island to the East, was sent to Eclipse Island (in the Southern Ocean beyond Princess Royal Harbour) with Samuel Bailey. The other woman was taken 'Eastward' by George Magennis.

Once Lockyer had ascertained from Hook who was responsible for abducting the Aborigines, he ordered Lt Festing to send a boat the next morning to Eclipse Island to bring Samuel Bailey, the chief perpetrator, to be detained at the British camp and to return the woman and child.

No further antagonisms had taken place between any of the Aborigines and the British since the spearing, but Lockyer still considered them 'mistrustful'. It seems that he needed a 'formal' reconciliation, a law and order ritual for him to feel satisfied.[26] On 11 January 1827, Pidgeon the Aboriginal voyager from Sydney was put on rations and employed by Lockyer to help bring about a 'reconciliation' and 'communication' with the King Ya-nup. On 13 January Pigeon reported to Lockyer that he saw some King Ya-nup 'coming down the side of the high hill'.[27] He was ordered to call to them, but they were already on their way into the camp. Lockyer's 'friend' Jack arrived first and then shortly afterwards two more men. Presents of tomahawks and blankets were given: they threw off their kangaroo cloaks and put on the blankets 'as they wear their mantles'. Watching them closely Lockyer thought that he 'frequently heard' in their conversation with each other the word 'Woman' distinctly mentioned.[28] Had he been studying the vocabulary lists of King and Flinders? He told Pidgeon to communicate to them that a boat had been sent to bring back one of the women who had been abducted and another boat would be despatched for the other woman shortly, who was thought to be a long way away to the east. Pidgeon did not speak the King Ya-nup language (although they knew some of his Port Jackson words) and his employment as communicator and conciliator was probably quite a useless one. He pointed to the sun and then to the west, Lockyer happy in believing that they all understood that this meant a boat would return at sunset. Jack and the other two King Ya-nup sat down and the boat soon pulled into the harbour with an Aboriginal woman who was 'put off to shore' with the young girl, Fanny.

Lockyer once more performed a ritual in a very particular manner – enacting it with symbols that he assumed, or hoped, the King Ya-nup would read, making clear the British intentions of conciliation and showing them that they were of a different 'tribe' to the ruffian sealers. Lockyer described his motivations: 'I desired that the [three] Natives would remain at my Tent and gave orders for a File of the Guard to go down and march up the Prisoner and went down myself to meet the Party and returned with them up again having the Poor Woman and the little native Girl in front with the prisoner following handcuffed in charge of the Escort…the Prisoner Bailey was to be kept in confinement and their [King Ya-nup] seeing him handcuffed it is hoped that they will be convinced and understood that the Persons who have acted so outrageously towards them will meet due punishment …'[29]

The three King Ya-nup men, one of them Jack, who had been waiting, began 'shouting' and 'expressed great pleasure' on recognising their woman, Lockyer wrote. One King Ya-nup was 'either the father or some relative of the woman', Lockyer assumed. She cried when she stepped back ashore. Not much is recorded of her ordeal, but we know it was violent: 'her right arm was much injured by a blow', and Nind examined her arm and bound it up with a bandage. The woman was given a biscuit and blanket. Sadly, the little girl called Fanny who was also retrieved did not 'belong' to King George's Sound. The King Ya-nup men looked at her when she stepped off the boat and shook their heads, Lockyer interpreting this action to mean 'she did not belong to them'. They then pointed to Pidgeon and then at the girl, which Lockyer again understood to mean 'that he [Pidgeon] must take care of her'. The reunited group went off up the hill at the back of the British camp towards Oyster Harbour.

The stories of King Ya-nup women in the archives are few and this episode points to the reasons why. Aboriginal women at King George's Sound were always kept out of view of the newcomers by their men.

Samuel Bailey did not admit to the murder of the man on Green Island, but told Lockyer that he 'drew cuts' for the woman. Lockyer detained him. Even though he felt there had been a reconciliation of sorts, he gave orders to the prisoners not to go further than half a mile from camp and their names were called every four hours on Sundays, their one day off.[30]

It was not until 10 March that two more sealing boats arrived at King George's Sound, bringing the sealers James Everett and John Randall. On board with them were three Aboriginal women – Dinah, Sally and Mooney – all of whom had been abducted from Cape Jervis in South Australia and had been living with the sealers on Kangaroo Island for some time.[31] When Captain James Stirling arrived at the garrison in April, Lockyer was eager that the sealers be taken on board and sent to Sydney to face trial. However, Stirling did not allow them on board, only taking Lockyer. These sealers were eventually released from custody by Wakefield who seemed at a loss to know what to do with them. He wrote about his doubts as to the extension of the law to men who committed 'lawless acts' in a place which, at the time, had not had the ritual of possession enacted. Such 'lawless acts' slipped through loopholes in the liminal space between unoccupied land and possession. The twelve sealers and the three Aboriginal women from Cape Jervis eventually left King George's Sound in the *Mary Ann* in May 1827.[32]

Lockyer's sketch of this episode comes from my close reading and comparing of his journals. I would like to go back and sketch in another dimension by re-reading what was going on with a more critical eye, interrogating the King Ya-nup actions further and suggesting some possible motives for their behaviour. While Lockyer's reaction to the spearing was non-retaliatory he saw quick, random violence in the Aboriginal actions and interpreted the spearing as 'revenge' against the white sealers who had committed the crimes against them. He wrote: 'With them in their minds it was white men who had ill used them and on white men they would seek their revenge.'[33] By reading the King Ya-nup actions as revenge, Lockyer misread the intent and significance of the spearing and missed the pace and consideration with which the violence was taken up.

The rules governing relationships and meetings in King Ya-nup society were highly structured. Strict obligations were placed on both the host and the visitors. John Mulvaney has written about particular Aboriginal groups across Australia and the meetings they held, explaining that, 'there were behavioural codes for appropriate relations…between strangers; codes governing the settlement of disputes, and responses to the approach of potential enemies; or of known foes.'[34] All the King Ya-nup actions were premeditated and performed with a specific outcome in mind.

In attempting to decipher the King Ya-nup intentions in this meeting and spearing at King George's Sound, the techniques from the discourse of anthropology are the most helpful, in combination with history, in pushing the sources to the limits of what we can know and intelligently imagine. Actions are as important to us as language. Codes of cultural significance are conveyed as much in gesture and costume as they are in words. As Rhys Isaac has written, actions in texts must be viewed as statements and these action statements are what we have to work with if we want to get close to understanding what the King Ya-nup were up to.[35] The task is to search for the meanings invested and conveyed in these actions.[36] It is interesting to read the different signs that were transmitted by the newcomers and the King Ya-nup and how they were interpreted. Some of the meanings of these signs were understood, others were misread entirely.

When Lockyer first sailed into King George's Sound and saw a fire burning on Michaelmas Island he thought it was made by a person in distress. This fire might have been a different kind of distress signal; a tool of communication between the four Aboriginal men stranded on the island and their countrymen on shore; a sign to let them know that a boat was coming in. When Lockyer met with the painted Aborigines just moments before the spearing he also spotted a 'large fire at the head of the harbour' and then shortly after that a very large smoke 10 miles away to the south west. From these descriptions it is conceivable that the King Ya-nup on the mainland were also communicating with the other King Ya-nup around the area and possibly with the four men on the island. Sylvia Hallam's work is particularly helpful here. In her study of Aboriginal fire usage in Western Australia she explains the multiple uses of fire. It was a vital tool of communication in the region.[37]

By returning to the moments before the spearing, it is possible to understand certain signals that the King Ya-nup conveyed to Lockyer and Festing. The four men who came out of the scrub were painted with ochre. Lockyer wrote that their hair was 'clubbed and daubed' and they only approached the strangers once they had conferred with some of the other Aborigines in the scrub. In his 1831 report, Nind remarked that unlike the Aborigines of Port Jackson, painting their bodies was not a sign of war for the King Ya-nup:

'It is considered by them merely as an ornament, and is never neglected at their dances, or when they visit neighbouring tribes.'[38] Nind's statement needs to be interrogated further as reports from subsequent explorers (and indeed this very encounter) suggest otherwise.

While exploring country to the north of the Swan River, George Grey noted the importance of Aboriginal men painting their bodies before they met with a group of strangers: 'The natives here saw the recent signs of strange blacks,' he wrote, and 'insisted upon my coming to a halt, whilst they painted themselves, and made sundry additions to their toilette…Their weighty affair having been completed, we again moved on, the natives keeping a careful look out for the friends they expected to see.'[39] Painting themselves with ochre was an integral part of the ritual process of Aboriginal meetings in the south-west, particularly meetings with strangers – white and black. Recall the Aborigines who met King in 1821. They took the time to prepare themselves for the meeting with him by covering themselves with 'ocherous earth'.[40] Barker also recorded the specific use of *paloil*, or ochre, when visitors were expected. He wrote about Mokaré preparing it to paint on his body, roasting it in a fire all day, knowing that visitors were coming from the north in a few days time.[41]

When the painted King Ya-nup came out of the scrub to meet Lockyer, they deliberately put down their spears before they approached. This was an intentional sign: they were giving Lockyer a message. Examples of this symbolic action of putting aside, and sometimes actually hiding, spears is prevalent in the journals of the newcomers and explorers at King George's Sound and indeed Australia in general.

By this time the King Ya-nup would have seen the boat on its way back from Michaelmas Island with their countrymen in it. They were painted in preparation for a spearing, but when they saw Lockyer, the timing was wrong. Concerned about giving the wrong signs to Lockyer, they deliberately put their spears down – their spears were not for him, or not yet anyway – and walked straight up to Lockyer and Festing to shake their hands. Just as Lockyer was trying to understand the actions of the King Ya-nup, they were trying to gauge the meaning in his actions too: Lockyer and Festing were carrying rifles. In the King Ya-nup minds, Lockyer too was preparing for hostilities and so throwing away their spears signalled that this meeting would be in peace. Initially.

The spearing was imminent, but the timing was crucial, the Aborigines were not back from the island yet, they knew there was a boat on its way and the King Ya-nup on the mainland had to wait. So the 'friendly' Aborigines that

Lockyer and Festing hunted kangaroo with and shot birds for were waiting for the signal from the other King Ya-nup. Hallam has noted that in Aboriginal meetings in the south-west, often after the 'initial joyous ceremony of greeting, came a time to undertake responsibilities of retribution'.[42] When the eight King Ya-nup approached and called for Lockyer's companion to come away in an 'authoritative manner', he left Lockyer immediately and joined them for the spearing on the beach. He had received a signal from them. At this stage Jack was helping repair the boat, but as soon as he knew about the spearing he also left.

Jack's movement between the British camp and Aboriginal life is interesting as it reveals some of the behind-the-scenes negotiations that were taking place during this encounter. Just like his namesake from King's encounter, Jack had a very particular position. His motivation and actions were important and strategic, but are not simple to decode. First, he initiated contact with the strangers. Lockyer's first meeting with the King Ya-nup, when he met Jack, was a meeting initiated by Jack and his group. They knew that four of their men were marooned on Michaelmas Island and probably also knew that one of them was dead as they could see Green Island from the shore of Oyster Harbour. They also knew that two of their women were held captive by the sealers. It is possible that Jack was sent by the group to meet with the new visitors.

Approaches or exchanges between Aboriginal groups were often made by an intermediary known to both groups.[43] What can be seen from Jack's to-ing and fro-ing between the Aboriginal camps and the British is a lot of information gathering across this space. Lockyer wrote that Jack went on board the boat to 'satisfy his Curiosity', but probably not in the way Lockyer assumed; he was not necessarily there to observe the peculiarities of 'British culture', but to work out these men and their motivations and possibly to become known to them in his status as an intermediary. Perhaps the Aborigines also saw the newcomers as potentially useful in retrieving their compatriots from the island.

The second point to make about Jack is that he was the first King Ya-nup to come back into the British camp after the spearing. Jack's returning alone is significant. It could be read as a signal that Aboriginal law had been carried out and Jack returned to neutralise the situation with the newcomers. He had held previous meetings with the strangers. He had been on board the brig and helped the carpenter repair their other boat. He probably was an obvious choice for the group to send into the camp after the spearing.

Jerome Bruner has written about individual motivations within particular cultural groups, arguing that in one sense, 'cultures are stable groups working together, but cultures are [also] made up of individuals and so we are autonomous agents as well'. And individuals stand as guardians 'of permanence and as a barometer responding to the local cultural weather'. Bruner argued that culture also 'provides us with guides and stratagems for finding a niche between stability and change: it exhorts, forbids, lures, denies, rewards the commitments that the self undertakes.'[44] This idea of individual political players within a cultural group is useful when thinking about the way Jack was participating in this encounter. Like King's Jack, he kept at a distance from his group and participated in the visitor's activities, staying on board the brig and helping with the boat's repairs. It is probable that by getting to know the newcomers he was seeking political gain within his community. Individual tactics are important to keep in mind. In her analysis of the spearing of Arthur Phillip at Manly Cove, Inga Clendinnen illuminated the role of Baneelon in the event, likening his position to that of 'a master of ceremonies.'[45] In many of these first encounter scenes it was not simply group against group, but different individual characters participating in particular, politically charged ways, looking out for opportunities from which they could benefit within their communities.

It is hard to know what the spearing signified for the King Ya-nup. In what context can we presume to make sense of the spearing as an act in a functioning Aboriginal society? Lockyer's understanding can more easily be interpreted, but his action statements still need careful attention. He was a man of law and order. He treated these injustices with a dour seriousness. And justice, in the British sense would be upheld, even in the remote outpost of King George's Sound, far away from the imperial eye. The significance of these events for Lockyer was focused on impressing the King Ya-nup with the decency and majesty of British law. He would gain their trust and live together in amity.

Three years after this event, in early December 1829 when Thomas Braidwood Wilson was visiting King George's Sound, he found a 'Judicious Order' in an old order book in the Commander's hut, written by Lockyer in early January 1827. This order shows more clearly Lockyer's conclusions about the actions of the King Ya-nup. He re-narrated his thoughts in a reflective, clear and dichotomous form: reasons for actions are always rendered simpler in retrospect. He wrote, 'Without any offence [having] been offered to them by any individual of the expedition,' the King Ya-nup 'committed an act of hostility, by watching an opportunity, and throwing their spears on a party employed filling water casks …' He was certain these vengeful men were 'driven to it' by gangs of sealers who had committed 'acts of cruelty'. Their motives and complex actions were quickly reduced to reasons of savage mentalities: as it was 'white men' who committed atrocities against them, 'it is not to be wondered at', Lockyer wrote, 'that they should, as people in a state of nature, seek revenge'.[46] In a situation such as this it was easy and perhaps necessary to cast the Aborigines as knee-jerk reactors. Lockyer saw the Aboriginal men as victims and aggressors, but ultimately viewed them reacting to white man's acts, rather than acting consciously, with precise and deliberate motivations within their own cultural, political and individual contexts.[47] But as Clendinnen has pointed out, spearings were generally not performed on a whim, but were considered, deliberated acts performed for precise reasons.

Lockyer's response to the spearing was to impose British law and order on an already ordered situation for the King Ya-nup. It did not occur to Lockyer that with the spearing, justice for the King Ya-nup had been served on their own terms. They were not only trying to inflict damage in the spearing but it was also, more importantly, about putting their social world back in order. Three spears in Dineen and honour was satisfied.

5

Violence Told

This story starts in late January 1830. The season of *Metelok* had begun and plentiful schools of salmon were seen swimming around the warm waters of King George's Sound. Mokaré told Barker that there was a 'great assemblage' of Aboriginal people at King's River, 10 kilometres to the north of the settlement. People had come from vast distances to the north and east, corroborees had been danced and there were feasts of kangaroo. There were plenty of 'blackfellows and plenty of women', but no single women, who, Mokaré said, were a 'long way off'.[1] Taragon, Mokaré's younger brother came in to the settlement and informed Mokaré, who then told Barker that three men had been speared. The reason: a consequence of the death of some others. Barker expressed his disapproval of the spearings and Mokaré 'seemed to have learnt it was wrong', Barker wrote. Mokaré told Barker that he often spoke to the King Ya-nup about the spearings, telling them that the newcomers did not 'do so' when someone died, but they would not listen to him. He reassured Barker that they would stop doing it, in time.[2]

A month later, in early March, Taragon had been bitten by a snake on the finger while hunting bandicoots and was dying. Barker and Dr Davis and several King Ya-nup walked about three and a half miles to the west of the settlement to where Taragon lay. He was wrapped in his kangaroo skin and sheltered by a bough of trees that had been made for him by some of the soldiers a few days earlier. They heard several people crying as they approached Taragon's resting place. The young man then breathed his last. Mokaré sat down at his head and gently drawing aside the kangaroo skin cloak took a melancholy look at his face. Dr Uredale, the *mulgarradock*, or medicine man, had been with him for some time. He lay down next to Taragon with his powerful left hand hovering over the body and his right hand under the head. A scene of lamentation began which, Barker wrote, 'was loud and under little control'. To show his sympathy, Barker 'mingled' his tears with theirs. He felt sincerely for Taragon whom he thought was 'a most amiable character'.[3]

The women who had been at a nearby fire, then came up crying with blood on their cheeks and foreheads. They had been scratching their skin with their finger nails to help them produce tears. Before Barker left Taragon's grave he went to shake hands with a few of the King Ya-nup men. He overheard something being said about their spearing one of their enemies before they returned to the settlement. Coolbun had got up two or three times for his spear, 'but was quieted by the others and persuaded to relinquish it', Barker wrote. After Taragon's burial his *meara*, spearthrower, was placed in a tree above the grave. The bush all around the tree had been cut down so that if the ground was fired, the *meara* would not get burnt.

As part of their mourning rituals the King Ya-nup were to leave King George's Sound for a period of time. Some would be gone for three months. Mokaré however, was to only go away for three days and then return to 'King George'. Before Mokaré left he heard the croaking of the *cyrye* (the frogs) which announced the simultaneous season of *Pruhner* and *Metelok little*.[4]

◆

The King Ya-nup were a warrior culture. During Barker's recorded experience at the garrison, from January 1830 to March 1831, the King Ya-nup were often involved in retributive and ritual spearings. These spearings – mostly one spear, through the thigh – were for violations of country, from jealousy regarding their women, and to avenge the death of one of their kin. Even natural deaths needed to be avenged. Spearing was a way of settling scores; it was a justice system and was an essential way of re-ordering their world after rules had been broken. There were also strict rules governing the spearings and most of the time fair play had to be observed by witnesses. When somebody died there was a particular way of understanding and dealing with that death. The deceased's *meara*, or throwing stick, was erected on top of the grave, or secured in a tree, and had to be carefully guarded by kin for some time. The nearest relatives of the deceased expressed their grief in less violent and more controlled ways than others. Close kin were, however, always involved in the retaliation that accompanied the death. *Mulgarradock* played a distinct part in deaths and retaliatory spearing. As well as being an esteemed medical man, a *mulgarradock* held power in both the spirit and natural world, and was influential in the group's political affairs. Their right hand was thought to be the source of much of their power. Dr Uredale (*full beard*) was a *mulgarradock*. He was Coolbun's elder brother and the father of young Talwyn.

Barker made frequent references to such spearings and associated violence in the Aboriginal world, between the King Ya-nup and their feared enemies who Barker recorded as the 'Wills people'. The Wills people were not perpetual enemies of the King Ya-nup. They also formed an essential part of their close social network and shared a kinship system. Many Wills people visited the settlement throughout the year and were met without hostility. Barker knew some of them who had come in and shaken hands with him. Not all Wills people were seen as enemies during the periods of violence, as Nind explained in his report: 'their wars appear to be more between individuals and families, than between tribes or districts.'[5] Several observers recorded that the northern neighbours were more formidable than any other neighbouring group in the south-west and were believed by the coastal southerners to possess supernatural powers.[6]

This violence between the Wills people and the King Ya-nup has been sidelined or ignored altogether in histories of King George's Sound and in colonial and cross-cultural histories of Australia. The 'friendly' relationships with the newcomers at King George's Sound have received most attention, and collective Aboriginal violence is seen as something separate to the King Ya-nup relationship with the newcomers. In addition, there is a fear today when discussing Aboriginal violence of recasting Indigenous people of the past as violent 'savages'. Strong tropes express the discourse on Indigenous violence, and a warrior culture does not sit easily next to the powerful myth of 'friendly Aborigines'. So why is violence and people talking about violence important? This becomes obvious quickly when reading the British texts. Every commander at King George's Sound (apart from Sleeman) recorded traces of Aboriginal *inter se*, or 'collective' violence. Lockyer observed old spear wounds on a few of the men's legs when he arrived in 1826. Nind wrote that the King Ya-nup were 'so constantly at war that their numbers must be considerably diminished by it.'[7] And Wakefield and Collie described spearings that can be interpreted as a performance to redress some sort of an upheaval. Collie did not understand the nature of the violence, writing that 'the origin of their own quarrels was difficult to be ascertained, but it was clearly seen they were *quick* and *violent* in resenting conceived insults from one another.'[8]

Retaliatory spearings were a vital regulation of the King Ya-nup world, but this system remains largely mysterious and very much misunderstood today. Outside observers at the garrison, particularly Lockyer, misread the meaning and intent of the violence. Such times of violence provoked the richest descriptions of action, but also the least understanding.

Neville Green is one historian who has written on the topic of Aboriginal violence in the south-west. In his book *Broken Spears*, Green included a table as an appendix, listing every Aboriginal *inter se* conflict recorded by Europeans from first settlement until 1841 in the south-west. He included location, description of the incident and number of dead or wounded.[9] This table further clouds a reading of Aboriginal collective violence. Listing facts does little for understanding. Green concluded, simply, that the violence represented a breakdown in Aboriginal culture and the arrival of Europeans must have increased the numbers of 'vendetta killing.'[10] John Cashmere has written persuasively about historian's misconception of violence, arguing that 'we tend to perceive violence, wherever it is practised, as signalling the degeneration and disintegration of lawful order.'[11] Understanding requires episodes and micro-stories that enable the drama and law associated with violence to be conceived.

Mokaré's stories and conversations with Barker signal the reverse of Green's conclusions. Rather than the violence increasing with the permanency of the British, Mokaré told Barker that the violence was previously more frequent. There was a spot near the camp *Woollyongup*, he told Barker, where a 'bad black' called Walyagopp who had killed a 'great number' of people in his time was buried 'very deep' in the ground. He reassured Barker that the King Ya-nup were becoming 'less ferocious' with 'fewer murders being committed now than in the time of yore.'[12] He pointed out and named several stars that were formerly 'blackfellows.' There used to be other stars which represented the women, but they were no longer visible, suggesting that this was an ancient belief and that the violence happened long ago.[13]

This episode, which began in early 1830 with the death of Taragon is a complicated story which reveals aspects of the King Ya-nup warrior culture. The meaning within it is largely concealed to outsiders, but it seems likely that the King Ya-nup interpreted Taragon's death in reference to sorcery because of the presence of *mulgarradock* and *wirago* (doctors and witches), the stories of ghosts and stars that were involved in the death and the months of retribution that followed. There is an assumption in some Australian Aboriginal communities that by using special techniques, humans can manipulate or control forces which are otherwise inaccessible.[14] Nind wrote on this supernatural belief in his report: 'if a man be killed by accident, by falling from a tree, drowned in the sea, or any other way, the friends of the deceased will impute his death to some *mulgarradock* of an adverse tribe, and kill an individual belonging to it in retaliation'.[15] Taragon's death needed to be avenged by spearing an enemy: one of the Wills people. The spearing of certain individuals of the Wills people initiated a spiral of retaliation, which in turn increased the King Ya-nup fear of their enemies.

Barker's stories are again the ones that take us beyond the British camp and into the Aboriginal social dramas. Nobody else during this period wrote down anything like the stories that Barker did. Perhaps other observers thought such stories of ghosts, medicine men and sorcery to be childish fantasy. Or perhaps they were not revealed to them. Barker was very interested in the spiritual and sacred phenomena of the Aboriginal world and all was included in his diary, even though not much of it made sense to him. He would write down a query in his journal and then consult his encyclopaedia on indigenous religion. Barker did not actually witness with his own eyes any of the spearings between the King Ya-nup and the Wills people. But he was given, mostly by Mokaré, daily stories, reports, dramatisations and exaggerated gossip about the events surrounding the spearings. He provided descriptions of actions. And when closely studied, these action-statements reveal some extraordinary and unpredictable goings on in the Aboriginal world at King George's Sound. What makes this particular episode interesting is that the stories bring us full circle: we read from the fringe, we are taken into the Aboriginal world and catch (confusing) glimpses of spearings and violence and then we are whisked back to the fringe where the utility of the newcomers for some of the King Ya-nup during this violent period becomes apparent. These stories are not only a valuable way into the Aboriginal world; importantly, they show us how the King Ya-nup world was relating to and dealing with the newcomers. They show how some of the relationships were operating. And it is this process, rather than just the *acts* of violence themselves that I am interested in.

The actions and stories relating to the collective violence reveal the autonomy of some of the King Ya-nup: the choices they made to act strategically in the context and circumstances they were living in. It is also possible to observe both the hierarchy of concerns of the King Ya-nup and the changing priorities of the newcomers. It is important to keep in mind that these are stories told and retold and much reshaped in their retelling.

◆

A few days after Taragon's burial on 12 March, Barker sensed a fear intensify among a few of the King Ya-nup. They were anxious about the Wills people approaching their camps. Mokaré told Barker that several spearings had already taken place. Tulicatwale, Coolbun and Nakinah had speared a King's River man named Wallangoli while he was asleep and Barker noticed that when Nakinah came in to shake hands with Barker after Taragon's funeral, he had a slight spear wound in his thigh, which Nakinah explained that he 'got by accident'.[16] Nakinah was to leave the settlement to 'go bush' for a while and Mokaré followed him because, as he told Barker, it would 'not do for one black' to remain in the settlement alone. He also told Barker that he could no longer go shooting on his own which he did using Barker's gun – he could only go if he was accompanied by a soldier or by Barker. Mokaré seemed unwilling to go into the bush and put on a dramatic show before he left. He told Barker that he would return in a few days, but he had an 'apparent fear that he could not return alone without safety on account of the tribe, one of whom had been speared'. Mokaré asked Barker if he would come to collect him in a boat from *Coranup*, on the eastern shore of the entrance to Oyster Harbour, if he did not return soon. Mokaré also talked about Barker 'crying for him if he died in the bush' and never saw him again. He went to the little wood next to the settlement to fetch some spears and then left with Nakinah, 'very sorrowful'.[17]

Barker thought that the King Ya-nup 'system' of wandering a long way into the bush on the death of a loved one was 'not a bad one'. He wrote, 'The hunger and fatigue they endure and the change of scene is probably a relief to the mind'.[18] But Barker was concerned about Mokaré going bush and always endeavoured to stop him from leaving the settlement. After five days' absence, Barker started looking out for Mokaré. He took the boat to *Coranup* on two occasions and talked to a few men who had neither seen nor heard of him. The following day Mokaré and Nakinah returned to the settlement in good spirits. Mokaré said he had 'dreamt about King George' while away and that he would not again 'leave the settlement'.[19]

Over the next month the fear of Wills people approaching King Ya-nup country grew within the community. Reports of imminent spearings were brought to Barker in his hut almost daily by Mokaré. Rumours of who would next be speared circulated within the King Ya-nup world and Mokaré kept Barker informed. Barker described how the fear of being speared was dominating King Ya-nup life. Mokaré stopped fishing for salmon at night

– which he had previously done by torchlight – because he was worried this would attract them. Coolbun was at *Tondirrup*, near the sand hills to the west acting as a *mialopen*, someone who watches – Barker called him a 'sentry'– and he sent notice if there was danger.[20] Smoke from fires was the telling sign, a sign of the Wills people's movement. During this time of fear, the King Ya-nup daily life was organised differently, accommodating to the drama associated with the Wills people. Dr Uredale procured food for his brother Coolbun who was too busy on lookout to fetch his own food. All hands worked together.

Mokaré came in one morning in early April with a mouthful of stories about spearings, and Barker wrote that, 'The barbarous custom of spearing has been in full activity.'[21] The Wills people were said to be 'sweeping the country' to look for King Ya-nup men to spear. This was probably to avenge the spear Wallangoli received from Coolbun. Mokaré's sister, Mullet, who was married to a King's River man, had been speared by Wannewar and Patyet (two brothers), and a 'child and a man' had been killed. Barker listed several others who were speared to death and one man from Mt Many Peaks who had been paralysed from an earlier spearing also died. These spearings and deaths had to be avenged by particular King Ya-nup, according to invariable custom. Barker found the spearing and retaliatory violence deplorable. However, he could only show his disapproval through symbolic actions. Words were not effective. He stopped serving tea and biscuit to Wannewar, Patyet and Coolbun and any others whom he suspected were involved in the violence.[22] He wrote with a forceful tone: 'I expressed strong disapprobation of this [spearing] to all of them and would not allow Coolbun into my room with the others, though he often attempted it and I was generally obliged to put him out which I did decidedly but gently, always expressing to him my abhorrence of what he had done.'[23]

This fear of the Wills people was documented many times during the year by Barker. It was a recurring theme: the King Ya-nup running into the settlement and telling him their stories, explaining their 'fear' that the Wills people were approaching. In April, Nakinah's son, little Wapere came in one morning and reported to Barker his alarm about some Wills people looking for King Ya-nup to spear. He feared that his father would be targeted as there was allegedly 'great expected spearings with Nakinah'. He told Barker that he had seen some Wills people but they had not seen him: he was terrified of them and so he pulled his trousers off and left them behind to enable him to run faster back to the settlement.[24] Many of the stories of fear, Barker thought, were nothing more than exaggerated gossip. Barker discredited Wapere's story, calling it 'imagination or invention' because Dr Uredale had told Mokaré that all was 'quiet'. Mokaré suggested that Wapere, who had been left alone at the Sawyers' place across the harbour, found there to be a greater 'scarcity' of tea and sugar there than at the settlement, inducing him to return. Walking alone may have made him uneasy and created the story in his mind of seeing Wills people, Barker thought. The stories went round and round.

In the afternoon of 2 April a group of King Ya-nup came in to Barker's hut with a story that a party of Wills people was approaching. All the King Ya-nup who were near the garrison (it is not clear how many) immediately assembled with their spears. Only two remained in the settlement – to be on guard, Barker wrote – and everyone else left at about 5.30 pm to 'reconnoiter'. But interestingly, Barker reported that before they left, the King Ya-nup put the settlement's soldiers – the 39th Regiment of Foot – on their guard, at the same time as cautioning them not to interfere in any battle that might take place between them and their enemy. Barker followed the King Ya-nup, not to join them in battle, but he wrote, to 'pacify the parties should there be an opportunity'. But after the rush of drama, it turned out to be another false story. He reported that he saw nothing that looked hostile, only 'our own blacks looking out from among the rocks on the North of Mt Clarence'. Four hours later Mokaré returned to the settlement saying no Wills people had been seen.[25]

This request to be militarily guarded by the soldiers is a highly suggestive Aboriginal action. It is also something that happened several times throughout the year. Mokaré was the most eager to be escorted by a soldier and often remarked to Barker (without telling him anything specific) that he would not be able to go anywhere unless accompanied by a soldier or by Barker himself.

Coolbun's wife, Neerwenga, gave birth to a boy not far from the settlement a few days before the soldiers were asked to 'guard' the King Ya-nup. The alarm of the Wills people had made her move earlier than expected. She came in to see Barker on 3 April with her new-born, and the strategic purpose of the visit became clear when she begged Barker for some rice to give her husband Coolbun. She managed to get food for herself and her children from Barker, but he kept a 'prohibition' on Coolbun.[26] This rare appearance of a King Ya-nup woman unaccompanied by her husband in the settlement is significant. She wanted to get food for her husband from Barker, which was part of her traditional duty of procurement. She most likely understood the reasons and meaning of the violence and perhaps her presence was also an attempt to reassure Barker.

During April, Wannewar and Patyet, the two brothers involved in the spearings, were camped at Wannewar's *turloit*, on the eastern side of Mt Clarence near the government farm. Ever the diplomat, Mokaré went to see them and shook hands with them and forgave them for their spearings against the women. Mokaré's sister who had been speared earlier by these two men was now recovering and had 'walked bush' and Talimamunde's sister who had been speared earlier was also recovering, as was the child that Wannewar had speared.[27] Wannewar and Patyet had been speared a few days earlier by Talimamunde and Copran and 'a few others'. The brothers had come across their enemies unexpectedly. They stood on the spot for a certain amount of time to try and dodge the spears before the air became too thick with them. They ran away to Wannewar's camp. Wannewar however, was 'doomed' to die, Mokaré said. And if Wannewar did not die, then it would be Patyet and if not Patyet, Numal their other brother. Coolbun was also to die for spearing Wallangoli and if not Coolbun, then his older brother, Dr Uredale, as the inheritance of grievances went from brother to brother. It is important to note that although the women were mostly not visible to Barker, it is suggested from the stories that the spearings were largely about them. Their context was an important part of the retributive cycle.

Within all this confusing detail and stories upon stories of spearings, some telling scenarios begin to emerge. The following night on 16 April, Mokaré and Talwyn came to Barker's hut and proposed to him that Wannewar should come in to the garrison 'for security' and sleep at the soldiers' barrack. Barker wrote, 'They had previously wanted me to keep him at Green Island', in Oyster Harbour. The King Ya-nup saw the advantage in the offshore seclusion of Green Island, just as Lockyer had envisioned the same isolated island as a place to punish 'incorrigibles' in early 1827. The King Ya-nup imagined the island as a place of security, but perhaps if Wannewar was taken to the island and the Wills people could not get to him, the access they had to this island would have also been seen as a powerful political advantage that the King Ya-nup had over them. Barker did not agree to their proposal. He wrote, 'I would not consent to protect a man who had speared a woman and child. Shall not protect him if he comes in of himself, but then I should not be bound to protect him if the blacks [Wills people] take offence at his being here.'[28] He did not want to interfere with the King Ya-nup rituals, no matter how much he detested their violent ways. He wrote: 'In our present weak state it is desirable to interfere by acts as little as possible with their customs, however much one may wish them abolished … As we have not the power to rule them [the British being outnumbered] we must at present be content with endeavouring to reform them by persuasion.'[29] Wannewar and Patyet came in to Barker's hut the following afternoon, 17 April. They were brought in by Mokaré who had been on lookout at Mt Clarence. They denied having speared anyone but Barker still refused to shake hands with them.[30] Even though he had refused to protect the two brothers from their enemies, this did not deter them from seeking further aid from the newcomers.

In May the idea of security and protection was upgraded to the pro-position of an alliance. 'A great number' of King Ya-nup came up to Barker in his garden and 'quickly turned the conversation' to the expected attack from Wills men, which was 'the great subject of interest', Barker wrote. The King Ya-nup proposed to Barker that he should join them against the Wills men, with a party of soldiers, 'which', Barker wrote, 'no doubt appeared to them a very capital scheme'. Barker did not agree to their proposition and put an 'end to it at once', saying he would never consent to support the bad acts of the likes of Tulicatwale and Coolbun, whom he believed to be two of the chief perpetrators in starting the conflict by spearing Wallangoli. He thought they deserved to be hanged.[31] Coolbun and Tulicatwale pleaded innocence and were very annoyed at Barker's accusations and his refusal to give biscuit. Coolbun said his spear had passed Wallangoli but not 'materially injured him'. They were possibly also annoyed that an 'alliance' had fallen through. To defuse the situation, Mokaré, always the comedian, went and collected all the *meara* and when he had collected everyone's, he put them in a bundle on his shoulder and pretended to walk away saying he would steal 'all the black fellows' *meara* and carry them off and hide them, and they would be forced to leave off spearing each other. Everyone, except Tulicatwale and Coolbun 'laughed heartily', and as a race up the mountain by the soldiers was just beginning, Barker wrote that all walked off to watch.[32] Mokaré's comedic performance hints that he too was eager for the spearings to end. Or perhaps it was more of a diplomatic act, wanting to please Barker and smooth over the tensions between Barker and some of the King Ya-nup.

This proposition for Barker and a group of soldiers with their flintlocks to join the King Ya-nup in their intergroup grievances is striking. But it was not the first time that such an alliance or coalition had been suggested by the King Ya-nup to the newcomers. There are subtle suggestions of it elsewhere. In his report Nind also described how he was approached by Mokaré to align with the King Ya-nup. He wrote, 'It once occurred to me to be out shooting, accompanied by Mawcurrie … and five or six of his tribe, when we heard the cry *coo-whie, coo-whie-ca-ca*, upon which my companion stopped short, and said that strange black men were coming, and were "no good", and wished me to accompany him to attack them.'[33] Nind did not record what his response was to this military request, but we know that Barker saw the proposal of an alliance as conniving, calling it a 'capital scheme,' and he refused to comply with the King Ya-nup demands.

Alexander Collie recorded a similar incident in 1832 when Talimamunde was killed and buried far to the north of the settlement. His 'natal ground', Collie described, bordered King Ya-nup country, which caused the neighbouring tribe to visit the settlement and 'revenge' his death. This threat of revenge from the Wills people put the King Ya-nup into what Collie described as the 'greatest terror of their lives'. They either 'dispersed into the bush, kept close in the settlement, or sought the protection of some white person at no great distance, until the dreaded visitors had retired', Collie wrote.[34]

These statements of desire for an alliance with the newcomers are not unique in Oceania. Bronwen Douglas has looked at traces of indigenous actions in missionary and colonial records on New Caledonia, sketching Melanesian political and military actions during the colonial period. Intertribal grievances between coastal and inland groups and rumours of a 'hostile inland tribe' alarmed the European settlers in New Caledonia who were eager to take up land. In several instances, the indigenous coastal group aligned with the French settlers to attack the inland group. Douglas argues that this alliance of the coastal group with the French against their traditional enemies inland was one factor, amid other military and political reasons, for the coast dwellers to view the French as 'a meaningful element in their present political realities.'[35] Of most significance to the coastal Melanesians was the 'potential value of the French in their relationships with other Melanesians, as useful allies in the event of attack and as political tools for conquest or for vengeance.'[36]

Based on extensive linguistic and historical research, Carl Georg Von Brandenstein has argued that prior to European settlement in Western Australia an alliance was formed by groups to the east of Albany with their formidable northern neighbours. Von Brandenstein wrote:

as elsewhere in Australia, frequent clashes occurred between aggressive 'law' factions of the interior tribes and the more defensive and conservative non-circumcising tribes along the coast. During one of these clashes, most likely just prior to the outgoing eighteenth century, the circumcising northern Ngadjumaya succeeded in converting substantial numbers of young shell people [coastal people] to the law of the Western Desert people. Those who 'joined' were called 'allies' by the Ngadjumaya and accepted the new name Nyungurra.[37]

Perhaps the newcomers and their garrison were viewed in similar terms by the King Ya-nup: as 'useful allies' and 'political tools' for vengeance against the Wills people. As Douglas shows in New Caledonia, coalitions were also formed between different indigenous Melanesian groups in conniving attacks on the French. Similarly, throughout 1830 at King George's Sound, there is evidence in Barker's journal that the King Ya-nup were merging with other Aboriginal groups along the coast to the east – not to fight against the newcomers, but against the Wills people. As James Browne's comment suggested, the Wills people were seen as a 'formidable' group by all other neighbouring groups.[38] Their attempted alliance with the British was not a new tactic but part of a traditional strategy of gaining political strength and self-protection.

In a similar way, although under different circumstances, Marie Fels, in *Good Men and True*, told the story of the choices made by Aboriginal men in the Port Phillip district to join the Europeans in a native police corps as an attempt to share in the power and authority of the colonisers. Fels wrote of the way that Aboriginal men of the corps used the prestige and influence they derived from corps membership and the material things they acquired to extend their influence within Aboriginal social relationships. The Aboriginal men of the corps had little difficulty in recruiting Aboriginal men from a vast range of different countries.[39]

In early May 1830, Barker wrote that a 'great battle' was expected between Wills people and several groups on the coast to the east. He noted that these groups were assembling to protect the King Ya-nup. They were coming from *Palerongup*, Mount Many Peaks and as far away as *Pepedyup* and *Corrandyup*. Either the Wills people had many enemies at this time, or the King Ya-nup were good at convincing groups to join an alliance with them. Perhaps the allied groups saw the benefits in trade, food and materials that the King Ya-nup gained from the presence of the newcomers and regarded an alliance with them as worthwhile. This intergroup conflict was due to take place where a patch of new ground had been broken up by the prisoners, near the farm at about noon. This place was called *Yaramal*, and was close to where Wannewar – who had done much of the spearing – had his camp. The 'battle' was to continue until a man on each side was dead. These fights often needed an even score. Barker mentioned the vital participation of the women in these battles: they would be focused on picking up the spears that had fallen onto the ground and handing them to the men, whose attention would be fixed on their opponents. The wounded who fell into the enemies' hands would be killed.[40]

Explorer George Grey witnessed a similar battle at Moore River, north of Swan River in Western Australia in the late 1830s. His description reflects his knowledge of Roman and medieval sparring contests. He had this to say about the fairness of play:

> The combats, one of which was now about to take place, much resemble ancient tournaments. They are conducted with perfect fairness. The combatants fight in an open space, their friends all standing by to see fair play, and all the preliminaries, as to what blows are to be considered foul or fair, are arranged beforehand, sometimes with much ceremony.[41]

In addition, Nind also reported that in their fights the King Ya-nup often did 'not attempt to kill each other; and the moment one of the party is wounded, the engagement ceases.'[42] Barker noted that a 'kind of council' was held before some spearings took place in which it was decided whether the person was to be speared in the limbs or the body.[43]

Barker was anxious about this expected battle at *Yaramal* and expressed his frustration at his inability to control it: 'I could say little against it except to point out and condemn its probable causes,' he wrote. 'I spoke strongly, however, against the practice of putting the wounded to death, describing very different treatment they received from us when we were at war.'[44] Barker often told Mokaré about his disapprobation of the spearings. However, he was not in a position where he could coerce the King Ya-nup to stop the violence. He had command over the functions of the garrison, but not the Aboriginal world, and the only way he could air his disapproval in an effective way was through symbolic gestures – he refused biscuits and tea to the perpetrators and stopped shaking hands with them. These symbolic acts were simple, yet clever and effective. Coolbun with his wife and children came to the garrison from the other side of Princess Royal Harbour early one morning, *urelap*, or 'very hungry'. Coolbun begged very hard for biscuit with the others, and Barker wrote that he 'seemed to think it strange he should be debarred' until Barker mentioned the name 'Wallangoli'– the man whom he had speared – after which he begged no more.[45]

Barker regarded the violence as senseless and referred to it as 'barbarous'. He also viewed it with reference to his own experiences in the Napoleonic Wars against the French – his constant use of British war language, such as 'reconnoitre', 'battle', 'enemy bivouac in home territory', 'sentry' and 'war wounded' shows his interpretation of the violence in military rather than criminal terms, as an ongoing war rather than a series of redress for past and ongoing actions. Barker's interpretation of Mokaré's description of the Wills people is also telling of the way he viewed this violence. In a list of the Aboriginal groups that neighboured the King Ya-nup, he wrote that the Wills people were 'gay and volatile like the French'.[46] It is unlikely that these were Mokaré's words (even though he had spent a night on shore with d'Urville's crew in 1826), it is more probable that it was Barker's description, which reveals where Barker's mind was directed. His reference to 'enemies' was still associated with the French. His mind remained partly in the world of naval rivalry and he was reminded of his time in service during the Napoleonic Wars.

Barker was not the only newcomer to show his disapproval or shock at Aboriginal violence. When Mokaré accompanied Wilson on his excursion in 1829 to the west of King George's Sound, Wilson tried to explain 'white man's religion' in order to get Mokaré's response to the subject. Wilson told him that bad men go to the 'Devil', to which, Mokaré asked: 'who were bad men?' Wilson replied, 'those who killed others without just cause'. Mokaré agreed saying, 'Very good, bad man go to the Debil.' Wilson seemed taken aback when Mokaré admitted 'it was all right, so far as regarded killing a white man,' but Wilson could not persuade him, 'that there was any harm in one black fellow spearing another; which, on the contrary, he considered in some cases, meritorious.'[47]

The stories of action surrounding this time of violence tell of the choices and strategies employed by the King Ya-nup in their interactions with the newcomers and also Barker's choices or limits of control. These stories also point to the priorities of the King Ya-nup: the spearings and the movement of the Wills people were of highest importance in the King Ya-nup world during this period. And, as the garrison wanted (needed) to stay on friendly terms with the King Ya-nup, Barker was obliged to be on call to their many demands. These episodes show that the King Ya-nup were finding a meaningful and advantageous place for the newcomers in their world, they found innovative ways to utilise their presence within their existing political tensions. In April Barker wrote: 'Hindered by the natives. They were not aware of how much they torment me so that I could not find in my heart to drive them away.'[48] He tried to continue with the rigid daily rituals of settlement life which had been set up by prior commanders, but the King Ya-nup business was starting to come first.[49]

On 23 April 1830 the King's birthday was celebrated with a *feu de joie*, and a holiday was given to the prisoners.[50] This was perhaps the most important day to celebrate on the colonial calendar, the other being St Patrick's Day.[51] Barker was preparing for the King's birthday parade when a group of King Ya-nup, who had come into the settlement in the morning, heard a report that 'some blacks' had appeared on the farm road. It was assumed that they were Wills people and they all grabbed their spears quickly. But, as usual, the fuss turned out to be a false alarm – it was Tulicatwale, Tringoli and their brother Mongway who were approaching. These visitors were also accompanied by Wallangoli, the man Coolbun was said to have speared after Taragon's death, but he was not dead after all. Rather than preparing for the King's birthday parade Barker had to give up his time to hold counsel with these King Ya-nup, to shake hands with all of them and listen to the latest stories about spearings. He was told that the women who had been speared were recovering well. Patyet was to be speared at *King Gannup* the following day by Talimamunde and Wallangoli, who were waiting on the arrival of Copran. Patyet was to be speared 'a little', six spears by each thrower. Wannewar would die if he did not 'go bush'. Metyalpin, a King Ya-nup man was also to be speared 'and to die, reason not known' and if he did die, Mokaré would be given one of his two wives.

The violence between the King Ya-nup and the Wills people was not only taking priority in the King Ya-nup life – from incidents such as this, it is clear that it had started to become a priority in the settlement's daily structure too. We can sense frustration by Barker in his lack of control. Again in May Barker wrote, 'Had a great number in my room whom fed, I could not easily get rid of. Obliged in good humour to give myself up to them and the greatest part of the morning was gone before I could set to anything.'[52] The focus of Barker's mind was changing slightly, as these stories show that although his mind was still seaward, his daily narratives, driven by Mokaré, were also of the inland. He was more aware than others of the depth and focus of the Aboriginal world.

It was of paramount importance for Barker that he kept the peace between the prisoners and the King Ya-nup as well. In November Mokaré complained to Barker that two of the prisoners, Fitzgerald and Marsden, named his dead brother, Taragon, too much. Barker had told Marsden not to speak Taragon's name, telling him that 'the blacks did not like it'. He spoke to the prisoners about the custom and then issued a station order to ban the practise of naming any Aboriginal deceased person.[53] This unusual order is telling of Barker's strong desire for an amiable relationship within the settlement and shows how seriously he took the King Ya-nup complaints. It is also an index of his remarkable familiarity with Aboriginal customs as well as his own respect.

Each day, with each fresh piece of gossip that Barker was given, he pieced together a little bit more of the complex structure of these spearings. There was no hiding his interest in the activities as he wrote down every piece of information he received, no matter how confusing or improbable. After the King's Birthday interruptions, 'a large posse, quite a room full' came to shake hands with Barker and give him and each other their news on the latest incidents. Barker's hut represented a place to gather around and tell stories, where there was always a big pot of tea and biscuits to be had. On this afternoon Barker learnt that Wallangoli, the Wills man who was speared by Coolbun, had speared some King Ya-nup men before Taragon's death. Taragon's ghost was now reported to be stealing spears from the Wills people, an action he would not have been doing if Wallangoli had died from Coolbun's spear. However, Capacole, a 'very fine witch or wizzard', had recovered two of the stolen spears after mounting into the air one day at midday and returned with them in the afternoon.[54] These stories point to the belief by the King Ya-nup that sorcery was involved in Taragon's death and played a large role in their active social world.

Annoyed at the interruptions and frustrated at the myriad of 'stories' he was being told about the spearings, Barker wrote of what he thought was exaggerated gossip. 'The alarm of yesterday [the King's birthday]', he wrote, was 'something like the story of the three cows. Instead of three men there was only one, who proved to be Wannewar.' And a few weeks later the King Ya-nup were back to spearing fish on the beach with torches ablaze. It seemed that the fear of Wills people was ending.[55]

It is important to state that not all King Ya-nup participated in the spearings. Different individuals took part in different ways: for one particular spearing Talimamunde was known as *ator*, a peacemaker. He broke several spears of the stronger party to put a stop to a fight as he thought it was 'so unequal'.[56] And Numal, Wannewar's brother, was someone who never threw his spear. Mokaré told Barker that Numal 'talked a great deal to vent his anger, whenever it was excited, but speared nobody'.[57] He was considered a *moyen*, or 'one who kills nobody'. Not everyone was in agreement over the spearings, as Barker wrote about one incident in January 1831: 'Some objected, others agreed to it.'[58] Everybody, however, was involved in the circulation of stories about spearings, ensuring that the King Ya-nup community and Barker were kept informed.

Later in the year, in June, Waiter, another of Mokaré's brothers came to Barker's hut for tea and told him how two Wills men had just visited him at his camp. But this time they came in peace to invite people from 'King George', Mount Many Peaks, *Pepedyup* and *Kiangadarup* to a 'grand coroberi' and kangaroo feast at *Moorillup* Range in the season of *Minongal* (September – October). These were the same groups that had aligned to protect the King Ya-nup against the Wills people a few months earlier. Barker was pleased by this news, saying 'all spearing of King George's men by Wills people, it would seem, is now over and they are to shake hands.'[59]

Mokaré said that 'Black fellows now spear little, by and by *Minongal* … spear plenty,' and Barker wondered if 'a greater scarcity of food' put them 'in bad humour.'[60] This is an interesting connection. Mokaré announced the seasons to Barker in reference to animals or food rather than climate and this seasonal change most often coincided with stories of hostilities with the Wills people. But Mokaré suggested that it was not about food scarcity. In November 1830 he told Barker that the *Moorillup* men (in Wills country) to the north were 'very sulky' from eating too much and three brothers there were spearing each other. Mokaré contrasted the good humour of his men with the sulky *Moorillup* men.[61]

Mokaré talked to Barker about the seasonal aspect of these spearings. In April 1830 he told Barker that he had heard a story that a 'great number' of people from Wills country were soon to approach King George's Sound to look for King Ya-nup men to spear. All this spearing would be over by *Mondiaring*, around July. He said that by that time all of the Aborigines would say 'enough had suffered and it was time to give over and would all shake hands and be friends'.[62] In the meantime, Taragon's ghost was said to be stealing spears and the spearing of someone prevented his thefts, so Barker thought the spearings would continue until the evidence of his ghost had disappeared. This possibility about seasonal spearing is evidence again for the rules governing the times of violence.

Besides the occasional theft of spears by Taragon's ghost and a few mostly baseless stories of Wills men approaching, the excitement of spearings and hostile Wills people seemed to die down in the Aboriginal world, as far as Barker knew, until January 1831. The fears then rippled through the community once again. At this time the King Ya-nup had entered into a lucrative *towan* (parrot) trade with the soldiers and prisoners and any European visitors that stopped in at the garrison. They had also bartered their spears and *meara* with the crew of the *Sulphur* who had just visited; Mokaré getting a new shirt and trousers, and others getting ships' biscuits in exchange for spears and *towan*. Suddenly there was talk about the Wills people approaching and Barker looked out for their fires on the south side of the Porongurup Range. But the King Ya-nup had bartered all their spears to the *Sulphur*'s crew and had no weapons to meet the Wills people with. They started 'borrowing' back some spears that they had traded earlier to the soldiers and prisoners, offering them extra *towan*. But the soldiers and prisoners were angered by this and complained to Barker, who in turn, made the King Ya-nup give the spears back to their new owners. The King Ya-nup were left to quickly manufacture spears as best they could before the Wills people approached.[63] Even their trade with the British came second to the fear of Wills people. A similar incident had occurred in December 1830 when Barker discovered that Talimamunde and Maragnan were 'sulky with each other' over Maragnan's brother, Metyalpin having been speared. The soldiers locked up the spears that had been traded to them in the black hole – the solitary confinement used to punish wayward prisoners, as a measure against these men spearing each other.[64] Talimamunde borrowed spears from the newcomers on several occasions.[65] In November 1830 he had wanted to borrow Davis' glass-pointed spear, but had received two or three from the soldiers instead. This suggests that the glass-pointed spear was considered by some King Ya-nup as a technologically advanced spear.[66]

Stories about Wills people continued throughout February 1831. Barker was told they were 'sweeping King's River' on the way to King George's Sound. After Church one morning, Barker took Mokaré to the top of Mt Clarence to look out for them. Mokaré pointed out their fires (smoke) at *Oongarup* and *Copongerup*, on the south-eastern side of the Porongorup range. Barker wrote that Mokaré 'seemed to feel deeply the sight of an enemy bivouac in his country'.[67] Even though Barker's policy was to stay neutral in Aboriginal collective violence, he allowed himself at least emotionally, through the sympathy he felt for Mokaré, to be drawn into their regional politics. Mokaré mentioned to Barker that there were a few tribes or families of the Wills people who were still trying to preserve peace, 'chiefly those who lived nearest to the settlement'. The proximity of these families to the garrison may have been a reason why they wanted peace. A hand shake and biscuit from a powerful friend was one impetus to preserve peace. The 'great majority' of Wills people, however, had 'been stirred up to hostility by Wallangoli's family', Mokaré said. Wallangoli was the King's River man speared by Coolbun following Taragon's death. Tulicatwale had gone to *Cormo* country to persuade the Aborigines living there to support the King Ya-nup.[68] Since Wallangoli had recovered, he had been constantly going about exciting 'wrath and revenge' and had persuaded the young men of some tribes to come from a great distance. It was not just the King Ya-nup who saw the potential in forming alliances.[69]

Towards the end of February 1831, Barker was busy with the visit of Captain Thomas Bannister, who had finally arrived at King George's Sound after getting lost in his overland journey from Swan River. Barker detested Bannister whom he found arrogant and rude, and his attention was easily diverted to the business of the King Ya-nup. One morning as he was walking to the farm he saw an 'abundance of smoke' in the line of King's River and beyond. He was clearly anxious about seeing the smoke and asked Mokaré about it. Mokaré reassured him that none of it was Wills' smoke. They were still at a great distance. It is interesting that Barker was the one who was anxious about the smoke this time. When Barker and Mokaré returned from the farm two Wills men had just arrived in the settlement with, Barker wrote, 'tidings of a peaceable tendency'. The great assemblage of people was now retiring to their own country and would return at some time in the future, 'not in general hostility but to cause Tulicatwale and Coolbun to pass through the ordeal of the spear. After this Coolbun and Tulicatwale would give peace offerings of spears, skins etc' through the medium of a man at Mt Gardner and the 'two parties would then shake hands and be perfect friends'.[70] At least there was 'talk' of it.

◆

These stories appear quite tangled to outsiders, and undoubtedly Barker was confused too. What is most remarkable is the way in which the action was reported. Barker did not see anything of the violence: the battles, spearings or stealing of spears. He remained physically on the fringe. All the action happened away from the British stage, out of view of the garrison, revealing just how much the British were on the periphery of the Aboriginal world at this time. Barker discovered the violence through the compendium of stories he was told by these Aboriginal raconteurs. Mokaré was his main informant, and even he had often received the stories second or third hand. They were at times elaborate and unbelievable and always confusing for Barker.

What then can be gleaned from all these stories of heavy and perplexing action? The most striking revelation is that the King Ya-nup priorities and concerns in 1830 were not the newcomers. Their political issues remained with the feared Wills people, their long-time formidable neighbours. The newcomers were not the most important or worrying presence in the King Ya-nup world. At this time, they were not concerned with colonising or civilising the Aborigines or using much of their land. Their minds were still directed towards the sea. They were on the fringe of the Aboriginal world geographically and socially.

The newcomers still had an important and unexpected part to play in the Aboriginal world, albeit from the fringe. Throughout the violent activities that the King Ya-nup were involved in during 1830, they used Barker, the soldiers and the garrison as a safe haven for protection against their traditional enemies. When an attack from the Wills people was imminent, the King Ya-nup asked the soldiers to be on their guard. They also warned the soldiers not to interfere in any battle that might take place – perhaps they knew that the soldiers would not understand the very specific rules of play.

In 1832 Collie was put in a similar predicament when Waiter, who was living in Collie's hut, came racing into the settlement 'at full speed ... spreading evident dismay and exciting to battle or revenge' because of the presence of a hostile neighbouring group (probably the Wills). Collie wrote: 'Imagining a murderous strife was going forward, I caused a few of the military detachment to be sent to awe, if possible, the combatants to desist, without personally interfering.' The party of soldiers returned some time later, escorting the 'bulk, if not the whole of the party of old women and children.'[71]

Similar requests for protection were played out in other episodes. Barker was always informed of the King Ya-nup fears, mainly through Mokaré, and told when a spearing was due to take place. Barker was asked to 'protect' people who might be targeted. Mokaré even asked him to take Wannewar in the garrison's boat to Green Island in Oyster Harbour, possibly, because like the King Ya-nup, the Wills people did not swim and he thought he would be safe from their spears on the island. The soldiers' barrack seems to have had special importance as a safe place. There were always soldiers nearby who had access to loaded flintlocks. Mokaré saw an advantage in flintlocks over spears, he borrowed Barker's gun when he went hunting and Barker only made a few references to him carrying a spear, and that was only for fishing. The King Ya-nup were using the military garrison in the way it was designed to be used: as a military defence post against traditional enemies, but instead of the French being deterred it was to be the Wills people. The reported actions of the King Ya-nup suggest that they saw the military garrison, the soldiers and Barker as a force to protect them and aid them in their hostile dealings with the Wills people. Was the attraction their muskets, their uniforms or their added numbers?

A few years after Barker's departure from the garrison, Collie wrote about continuing King Ya-nup requests for protection and security from the newcomers. In 1832 he said: 'In our excursions in the bush, the [King Ya-nup] betrayed the greatest alarm of surprise, and often will not move from our sides.'[72] Collie also commented on the importance of guns, writing that the King Ya-nup would only travel in the bush with the newcomers if they were given a gun. 'This weapon,' he wrote, 'they hail as their sure protection – without its being prepared they will deem little security by the white's nocturnal fire.'[73]

◆

American historian Richard Metcalfe has written on historical approaches to American Indian cross-cultural history and points to useful ways of thinking about the fringe. His research focused on the internal political and strategic processes within American Indian community life in his analysis of Indian responses to white incursions on their land, permitting a 'simultaneous treatment of both the indigenous culture patterns and the white cultural inputs.'[74] Metcalfe powerfully argued that there had been an 'overestimation' of the role of white influences in 'creating Indian political behaviour' in American Indian contact histories. Most American-based studies of Indian politics up to the 1970s had focused on 'cleavages said to be directly due to white encroachment', Metcalfe wrote. Too much attention in indigenous politics, he argued, was given to white causality and white-related issues, making all Indian post-contact political activity, 'to have been directed at dealing with the white problem.'[75]

There has been a similar tendency in Australian Aboriginal historiography which has favoured the European presence at the centre of Aboriginal or cross-cultural narratives. While these histories focus on Aboriginal people's responses to the Europeans and analyse how they were treated or mistreated, they also ensure that Aboriginal action remains European focused with little consideration for ongoing regional politics and networks.[76]

Metcalfe was writing about a period of transition between first encounters with whites and 'total orientation' to 'white-provoked issues' in American history. During this transitional period, indigenous issues and problems continued to be the primary determinants of Indian political behaviour and, he argued, during this period the presence of Europeans was a 'minor issue'. The central concern of these Indians was not the white presence but the internal political context of their own communities. The Europeans, however, were not entirely disregarded: the indigenous people were exploiting them to promote personal and factional advantage within their regional communities.

Mokaré was the most eager of the King Ya-nup to be protected, either by a soldier, or by Barker, but this might not have been directly or solely about 'protection'. It could be read as an act of diplomacy. What sign would a military escort have given the Wills people? Being seen with a soldier was an image of a powerful friend, for other King Ya-nup and Aborigines around the whole region. This request for Barker to protect Mokaré reveals something more. Nind recorded a King Ya-nup custom in his report called *cotertie*: 'It is confined to boys,' he wrote, and he compared it to the western tradition of godfathers. 'It seems to be a promise of protection and assistance, and also adopting the boy as son-in-law.'[77] There are several instances when Mokaré sought protection from Barker. In January 1830 when Mokaré returned from the bush, 'alone and very tired', he said to Barker that he would 'not go again into the bush with blackfellows', he would only go with Barker.[78] This need for protection might also have had something to do with Mokaré's fear of being unable to dodge spears effectively. When admiring Chilloc's dexterous skill in spear dodging, Mokaré remarked to Barker that, 'formerly my sight was very fine in this way but I have lost it since living with the white fellows and should now be speared immediately'.[79] This small point about Mokaré's sight degrading since living in the settlement with the newcomers is a clear example of not only the effects of the fringe on the King Ya-nup – change was felt physically as well as cognitively – but also the pace in which some people felt those changes.

On a different scale and with differing levels of success, the King Ya-nup actions and requests anticipated those of indigenous New Caledonians. In New Caledonia, the Europeans were seen by Kanak as potential allies in redressing intertribal grievances. The King Ya-nup attempted to do just this with the British at King George's Sound.

While the intergroup spearings beyond the bounds of the settlement are seen as irrelevant to the British–Aboriginal relationship and are therefore absent from most histories, a closer reading of the action surrounding the spearings reveals an enormous amount about the developing relationships at King George's Sound in 1830 and shows that these activities were an integral element in the dynamics between the British and the King Ya-nup. The revelations from the action are surprising: we are not used to perceiving the British on the periphery of an Aboriginal world that they have encountered, and the hostile Indigenous group to the north at the centre of Aboriginal concerns. The King Ya-nup already had a strong trading alliance with the British but they also sought a political one, to strengthen their ability in regional warfare.

Reflection: Contexts of Violence

The spearing of Dennis Dineen by a group of eight King Ya-nup men in 1826 has been given at most a short paragraph by historians.[1] They perceived this incident as a story which Lockyer had already interpreted in his two journals. They disregarded it because it holds little relevance in the larger picture of Albany's progress. It certainly has not been given the iconic or mythic status that the spearing of Governor Arthur Phillip at Port Jackson received; it is seen rather, as an accidental, misdirected and irrelevant skirmish in an otherwise 'friendly frontier' by a historiography that glosses over the complexity of actions. The spearing of Dineen was not remembered by the community at King George's Sound for very long either. James Backhouse visited the settlement in 1837 and wrote in his narrative that 'no case is known of a white having been speared by them [Aborigines], nor by any other tribe within about seventy miles.'[2] Lockyer's Rough copy journal was not published and his Fair Copy was sent to the Colonial Secretary so it was probably not widely disseminated until much later.

Recent infatuation with colonial violence has distracted historians from the benefits of studying the fine-grained interaction that occurred in meetings such as this one between Lockyer's crew and the King Ya-nup. After interrogating Lockyer's texts, however, it is evident that this episode offers a unique and valuable clue to an important aspect of the Aboriginal social world at King George's Sound, hinting at how communication and negotiations were taking place in a volatile encounter. A critical ethnographic approach provides the ability to set actions in contexts for both cultures in search for meaning. Reflection on the different reactions to, and interpretations of, the violence by Lockyer in Chapter Four and Barker in Chapter Five, demands a more complex reading of the dynamics of power and control at King George's Sound at this time. The newcomers' reactions to the violence unearth some of their deeper thoughts and sensibilities as well as being reflections on colonial law more generally.

Lockyer's reaction to the spearing of Dineen is stated in his writing. He wrote down his response to it at the time and one month later that response was restated in the fair copy of his journal and in his official reports to the Colonial Secretary. He read the spearing in the following terms: the Aboriginal men who had been marooned on Michaelmas Island by white sealers sought revenge on whites, and when Lockyer's party arrived they took revenge in a random act of senseless violence. Lockyer wrote of the Aboriginal men's actions in primitivist terms. Their actions were 'not to be wondered at' because, 'as people in a state of nature, [they] seek revenge'.[3] Lockyer was explicitly eager to convey to the King Ya-nup that he disapproved of the way they were treated by the sealers, endeavouring to parade the majesty of British law, while being unaware that the very act of Dineen's spearing meant the fate of the marooned Aborigines and the death of one of their countrymen had been redressed by King Ya-nup law. Lockyer rendered the Aboriginal violence within his world and was unable to see that he, in turn, had entered an Aboriginal narrative.

Clendinnen shows how Governor Phillip, in a similar fashion, performed scenes of 'British justice' in front of an Aboriginal group at Port Jackson as a display of 'splendid impartiality' when a prisoner stole some fishing gear from an Aboriginal woman. Phillip flogged the prisoner in front of several Aboriginal people to make his law and order 'visible'. But as Clendinnen points out, the Aboriginal onlookers saw 'disgusting, wanton cruelty' in the flogging. One onlooker wept, while another, Barangaroo, 'leapt up, seized a stick, and made to wallop the flogger'.[4] Law and order in Lockyer's and Phillip's terms did not always transfer the same feelings to Aboriginal onlookers.

While the violence described in chapters Four and Five occurred under different circumstances, the British response to both incidents of violence is worth discussing together. Barker wholeheartedly disapproved of the spearings between the King Ya-nup and the Wills people, but he did not interpret the violence in primitivist terms, as criminal behaviour, or as simple acts of revenge. Unlike Lockyer, he did not explicitly express his interpretation of the spearings, but through his use of Napoleonic war language to describe the acts, it is evident he gave the violence a military, rather than criminal analysis. And this analysis had ramifications for the way he chose to respond

– he showed disapproval through his refusal to shake hands and stopped serving biscuits to the perpetrators, but he did not physically get involved in the intergroup grievances. If he had interpreted the acts as 'criminal', he might have intervened.

If Mokaré had been directly involved in the violence discussed in Chapter Five, if he had been speared, would Barker have kept refusing to shake hands with the perpetrators and barred them from tea, or would he have become physically involved himself, perhaps agreeing to join the King Ya-nup in settling their intergroup grievances and bringing the soldiers with their flintlocks as well?

After Dinneen's spearing, Lockyer did not allow any of his party to retaliate. However, it must be asked whether Lockyer's response would have been so lenient if it was an officer, such as Lt Festing, who had been speared. Lockyer's eagerness to have the sealers brought to justice under British criminal law for the murder of a man on Green Island and the atrocities against the four men and women was carried out with such determination possibly because it was his first week in a distant and foreign place and much rested on having amicable relations with the Aboriginal people.

Not all responses by newcomers to violence against them were as considered as Lockyer's response to Dineen's spearing. Lockyer's situation – newly arrived at an isolated place, without even a tent set up on shore – meant his reaction involved his concern and priority of establishing a friendship with the Aborigines; rough sealers he knew how to handle. However, Lockyer's successor, Wakefield, wrote with doubt about Lockyer's power in extending the arm of colonial law and punishment to the sealers in a place which did not have the rights or authority of British *possession*.

Anton Blok has observed that violence is not simple or universal, 'but it is contingent and context-dependent, shaped by social relations of power, force and dominance.'[5] Barker regarded the violence in 1830 between the King Ya-nup and the Wills people as 'senseless' and perhaps irrational. This reflects his understanding of the 'laws' of violence experienced in the Napoleonic wars where violence was performed in a different cultural context to spearings. British floggings of prisoners at Port Jackson were considered acts of violence by the Aboriginal outsiders; but for the British, the floggings were placed in the category of *punishments*, rather than violence. Such acts of violence, a flogging or a spearing, were actions that were rule-bound within their own context. Moreover, ritualised violence in both cultures took place in specific places and the presence or absence of particular people, sometimes in particular costumes, were vital. In the case of the British, floggings always took place in the Square; and in 1829 Lt Sleeman revealed how improper it was for the surgeon Nind to be absent for the flogging. Similarly, Mokaré notified Barker in advance the specific location for a spearing and the people, by name, who would be present and taking part.

Blok argues that violence in all its contexts should be viewed as 'a changing form of interaction and communication, as a historically developed and cultural form of meaningful action'. A Western bias of what constitutes violence indicates how violence gets divorced from its context, leading to rash misunderstandings. If we do not focus on what we don't understand about alien violent acts, we will, according to Blok, 'close off research precisely where it should start: with questions about form, meaning and context'.[6] This proposition is also helpful in reading the context in which Lockyer was forced to perform the flogging on prisoner Ryan in the Square at *Frederickstown*. His orders were disobeyed and nobody else believed it was their duty to act as *scourger*, knowing that it would not sit well in their social scene after the flogging was over.

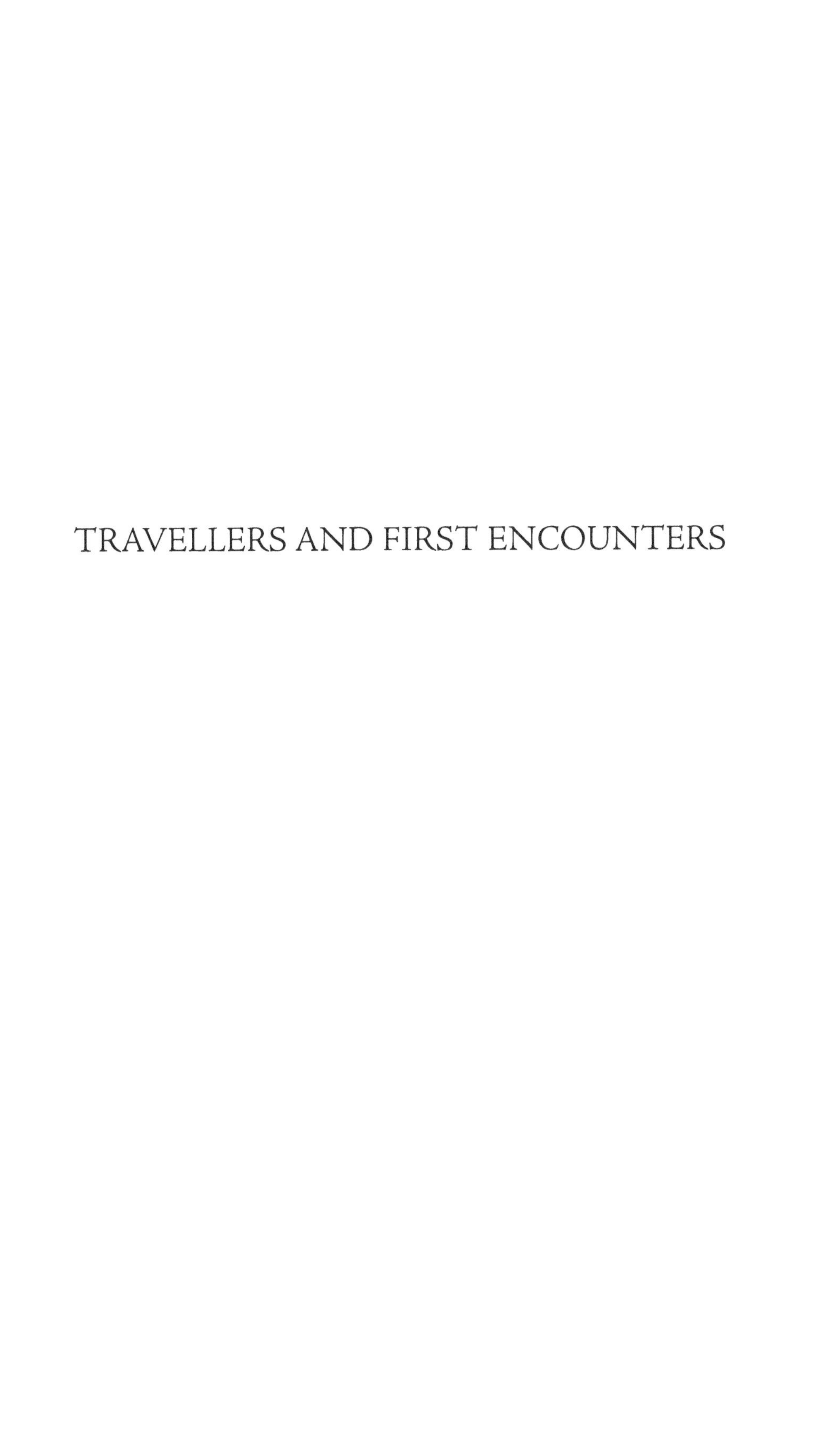

TRAVELLERS AND FIRST ENCOUNTERS

6

Caibre: The Ship as Symbol

I now return to the narrative with which I started: Phillip Parker King's visit to Oyster Harbour in 1821. Jack was taken on board the *Bathurst* on the second day where he stayed all afternoon, receiving food, clothes and other gifts from the crew. The Aboriginal group from the western shore, opposite to where Jack had boarded the boat, were in King's words, 'vociferous to visit' the *Bathurst*. They held long conversations with Jack, who replied to them in what King described as a 'song'. The group of men on shore sang a chorus back to Jack: *Cai, cai, cai, cai, caigh* with the final word, *caigh*, 'lengthened out with the breath'. This 'song', King wrote, 'was always repeated when anything was shewn that excited their surprise.'[1] In a vocabulary list which King collected during his visits to King George's Sound, *Cai, cai, cai, cai, caigh* was translated as 'surprise or admiration'.[2] This is King's translation and transcription of a foreign language, with meanings inferred through watching the actions of the Aborigines in their interactions with Jack and the visiting strangers.

King's manner of recording vocabularies makes me sceptical about their accuracy. At Exmouth Gulf in the north-west of Western Australia on an earlier expedition, King was supposed to collect a vocabulary list for the Colonial Office. He would do this, he said, by touching a part of an Aboriginal man's body and making an 'enquiring sound', then recording the phonetical reply. On one occasion, the Aboriginal man whom King was touching, turned the activity into a joke with 'hoots of laughter'.[3] When King touched the man's nose, he fingered King's nose back, smearing it with ochre.[4]

I am unconvinced about the meaning King gave to *cai cai cai cai caigh*. Could this phrase have been decoded by King as 'surprise or admiration' because it was sung rather than spoken? A song to King did not hold the same meanings as it did for Jack and his countrymen. Recitation was a form of conversing for the King Ya-nup. Perhaps King was reading Jack's and his respondents' song as a breathy tune of excitement and interest; what he missed was the meaning. These words were a sentence about a reality. Their meaning was embedded in the power play that these groups were engaged in over boarding the brig and the brig symbolised something significant too.

European vessels might also have had a deeper meaning for the Aboriginal people of the south-west coast. Marshall Sahlins and Greg Dening have both written on the importance and specifics that indigenous people in Hawaii placed on European visitors from the sea. Dening discussed the symbolic meanings that a ship conveyed to the local inhabitants and how the arrivals of European vessels shaped expectations of indigenous populations and directed their actions.[5] Although Pacific encounters often occurred between ship and canoe, interest in and knowledge of European vessels by indigenous peoples of the Pacific speaks to the context of Aboriginal expectations in the south-west, of strangers who came from the sea. George Fletcher Moore, a Commissioner of the Civil Court at Swan River, recorded what the Aborigines from the Swan River region thought when they saw the first European vessel: *Wundab-buri* was the name given to an English ship, 'from its shape like a shield'. The Aborigines of the Swan River 'describe with great vividness their impressions when they saw the first ship approach the land. They imagined it some huge winged monster of the deep, and there was a universal consternation.' One man, Moore wrote, 'fled inland for fourteen miles without stopping, and spread the terrifying news amongst his own friends.'[6] It is not known whether the King Ya-nup had the same initial response to these big vessels as the Swan River Aborigines. The King Ya-nup soon attributed a particular importance to these vessels and the visitors they housed – they brought different opportunities from visitors who travelled across country.

Conversations written down by Barker and the vocabulary list collected by Thomas Braidwood Wilson in 1829 suggest that a more specific conversation was occurring between Jack and the group of Aboriginal men on shore. Some of the King Ya-nup had become masters at reading a vessel from a distance by 1830. Wilson's vocabulary recorded that the King Ya-nup had different names for different-sized vessels – a boat was called a *potora*, and a man-of-war or a brig was called a *cay-bur-ugh*.[7] The King Ya-nup distinguished these vessels from afar by studying the number of masts, and the shape and size of the sails. They knew what sort of visitors to expect from the size of the vessel and the number of smaller boats that accompanied it. Wilson commented on the King Ya-nup knowledge of which visitors they might welcome and which they would not by reading a vessel. Sealers generally sailed up and down the coast in smaller open vessels. Wilson wrote: 'It is quite notorious on many parts of the coast, that if a small vessel makes her appearance, the natives get out of the way as fast as possible; while, if the ship be large, they come down to the beach, without mistrust or fear.'[8]

Barker participated in many conversations with groups of King Ya-nup men about boats and ships. Mokaré was curious about the nature of them: he enquired to Barker the age of ships and how long they would last before they broke up, or *died* as he called it. He wanted to know how the carpenters managed to build them on the water.[9] He and his countrymen had helped many visitors repair their vessels. Mokaré used the settlement's jolly boat on his own sometimes, although he was a repeated victim of seasickness. And Barker allowed some of the King Ya-nup to take the jolly boat if they wanted to cross Princess Royal Harbour or Oyster Harbour rather than walk around or wade across.[10] Boats were becoming a part of daily life, but ships still symbolised something more. Ships held significance for the prisoners too: they were a symbol of freedom to another world. Every time a vessel was visiting the Sound, the roll was called twice each day to ensure no prisoners had escaped.

In August 1830 Barker was in his hut talking to Marknaar, Warangoli and Nakinah, and this conversation suggests some possible interpretations of Jack's 'song'. The community – both British and King Ya-nup – had been expecting a vessel to arrive at the garrison for a week or so. The newcomers were keen for supplies, news and letters from home, and the King Ya-nup were eager about its arrival too, questioning Barker about when it might arrive. Barker wrote: 'Talking much about "Caibra", always an interesting subject to the [King Ya-nup]. Waran[goli] said he would go in a boat with me to it. Marknaar would be so glad to see a ship that he should not wait for a boat, but would wade to it.'[11] A week later they were still waiting for the ship and talking about when it might arrive. Barker wrote one word in his journal: *caibre*.[12] From Barker's conversations about *caibre/caibra* and Wilson's vocabulary list it can be deduced that Jack's lyrical: *cai cai cai cai caigh* was a song about a *caibre/cay-bur-ugh*, a large vessel. The words of the song, rather than being a breathy tune showing 'excitement and astonishment', were a conversation about Jack's being on the *Bathurst* and about the group on the western shore wanting to go on board also.

Why does this factual possibility from the archives matter? These vocabularies show the changing status and categorisation that such vessels were given by the King Ya-nup. Not only did the King Ya-nup have names for different-sized vessels, they categorised them according to their size and shape. A man-of-war created more excitement than a boat. King's encounter in 1821 and these vignettes that follow tell us why. *Caibra/cay-bur-ugh/cai cai cai cai caigh* symbolised trade.

The garrison created frequent and novel opportunities for the King Ya-nup to engage in trade with newcomers. The presence of the British meant that *caibre* visited the King Ya-nup shores more frequently, and *caibre* meant that intense periods of trade with strangers were possible as groups of King Ya-nup would go aboard, often spending the night. They knew the vessel *Governor Phillip* by sight, and as it was a common visitor, this vessel became a reference point for others, and each *caibre* was measured against it.

On 3 September 1830 the schooner HMS *Sulphur* arrived at King George's Sound, carrying Captain Irwin, Commander of the 63rd Regiment at Swan River, Captain Dance, the *Sulphur's* captain, and Governor Stirling and his wife. They came on shore and the King Ya-nup held a corroboree after dinner, which Barker thought, kept the visiting captains 'amused'.[13] Corroborees framed these large gatherings; they were performed to welcome the visitors. The following evening Barker dined on board the *Sulphur* with, he wrote, 'lots of blacks' some of whom had come from a distance. These Aborigines slept on board and were landed on shore early the next morning, 'very cold', Barker wrote, but 'pleased with their treatment'.[14] A merchant from Hobart, William Thomas Stocker, wrote about his exchanges with the King Ya-nup in 1832 while his vessel the *Mary Ann* was anchored in the harbour.[15] 'The natives [of King George's Sound] are very friendly. I was with them daily during my stay, and took one of them with me on board the cutter, they presented me with spears, waddies &c. in return for which I gave them biscuit …'[16] These visits and exchanges aboard occurred as often as a vessel arrived, and on shore the King Ya-nup always danced a corroboree for their visitors.

Not all visitors wanted to trade, however. In December 1830, the *Nimrod* was on its way from Launceston to Swan River carrying fresh provisions for the five hundred settlers who had recently arrived there. The following day a large number of King Ya-nup came into the settlement and Mokaré went aboard the *Nimrod* with the captain. A few other King Ya-nup went aboard also, but they did not receive any of the expected ships' biscuit. When they returned on shore they showed their disappointment with this *caibre*, saying that it was not like the *Governor Phillip* and other men-of-war ships that they knew. Most of the *Nimrod's* crew were Lascars, Indian seaman, and it seems that they were not interested in trading with the King Ya-nup. Barker wrote that the King Ya-nup who had not gone on board the *Nimrod* seemed to 'enjoy the joke' that their countrymen had not received any biscuit from the Lascars on board.[17]

Exchanges within the garrison were not often as intense as the ones that occurred on board the visiting *caibre*. The circumstances of trade slowly changed pace and shape within the garrison too. While there were times of daily bartering and manufacturing of items for trade, exchanges became manifested in the everyday activities of the garrison and the King Ya-nup world. They received fish from the prisoners when they hauled the seine. Barker was given King Ya-nup food as a gift and learnt only to accept it if he had something to give in return. The symbolism of the *caibre* was soon to be transformed, from opportunities for trade to a portal to another world.

7

Travelling Knowledge: 'Manyat's Sole Delight'

Fame [is] like a snowball increasing as it goes, among illiterate savages as well as among refined nations.[1]

Standing on the top of Mt Clarence, facing north, with one eye held closed, the other gazing steadily through the telescope, curious men could see two mountain ranges in the distance. One of the ranges, about 30 miles from the settlement, the King Ya-nup called *Porrengorup*; the other, a more distant and larger range, hovering in a lilac haze: *Koi-kyen-u-ruff*.[2]

During the early 1830s the seaward focus of the newcomers began slowly to shift from the fringe towards the interior. Several European visitors, based at King George's Sound or just passing through from Swan River or New South Wales, wanted to explore the inland. They held conversations (interrogations) with the King Ya-nup in which the beauties and riches of what the interior held were revealed to the colonists. Or at least, that is what they imagined: large freshwater lakes, rivers, cleared plains waiting for cattle, with a few 'well-wooded' forests.

There are often-told stories of colonial explorers, surveyors and botanists arriving in Australia eager to explore, map, name and take hold of the surrounding country. Once they had extracted samples for their botanical and geological collections and gained knowledge of the landscape, recording what it had to offer future emigrants, they passed this information back to Britain in official reports, letters and publications. Many of these explorers gained fame and prestigious connections for the natural knowledge they had collected and enjoyed a higher position in society as noble pioneers. At King George's Sound, visiting botanists were given a high status. They were esteemed as educated men engaged in an intellectual pursuit. Writing in March 1829, the commander Lt Sleeman wrote: 'In compliance with the instructions of His Excellency the Governor … I had the best vacant Hut on the settlement prepared for Mr Baxter (Botanist) when he landed; and, in order to contribute to his personal comfort, as well as to enable him to proceed with more expedition in collecting and preserving the most valuable Seeds and Plants in this neighbourhood, I gave him the exclusive Services of one of the most useful of the Crown Prisoners …'[3] Baxter sent 145 seed species back to Sydney in 1829, which he had collected during his stay at King George's Sound.[4] The King Ya-nup were around many people who had an interest in natural history collecting. Wakefield was a natural history collector too: he sent four boxes of soil to Sydney which he had collected on his travels around the region.[5]

Mary-Louise Pratt has described how, in late eighteenth-century Europe, natural history was viewed as a structure or system of knowledge, designed to classify all the plant species on the planet. This natural knowledge system created an impetus to travel towards the interior, as opposed to maritime exploration. Pratt calls this phase: 'planetary consciousness', which was marked 'by an orientation toward interior exploration and the construction of global-scale meaning through the descriptive apparatus of natural history'.[6] This 'planetary consciousness' created a new genre, while many travel writers, Pratt wrote, dissociated 'themselves from such traditions as survival literature, civic description, or navigational narrative, for they were to be engaged by the new knowledge-building project of natural history'.[7] The explorations by surveyors and botanists were acts of possession too, but conducted with a different mentality from the ritual that Lockyer performed in 1827. They were acts which David Malouf has called 'possession in the form of knowledge', by taking the country's 'spaces into our heads, and at last into our imagination and consciousness'.[8]

Many such expeditions into the interior in Australia included Aboriginal men, referred to as guides or cultural interpreters who showed the foreigners the way, found them water and food, and acted as intermediaries with other Aboriginal people. In some expeditions in the south-west, the benefits flowed both ways. Some of the Aboriginal travellers gained knowledge about new country, people and vegetation, and with that knowledge came a changed and elevated status, both from their kinsmen and women as they transferred knowledge back to their own communities, and in the minds of the colonials with whom they travelled.

This travelling knowledge gained high currency in the Aboriginal knowledge economy where information was a commodity, something to trade and get benefits from. A similar knowledge economy was important in both Aboriginal communities and among nineteenth-century naturalists and metropolitan savants who traded in natural history objects and anthropological information. Geographic knowledge and kin networks were extensive in Aboriginal cultures across Australia. One ritual that linked the King Ya-nup with their neighbours involved significant travel. As a part of their transition to adulthood, young men went to live with other Aboriginal groups, often in far distant places. Barker was informed about the different stages of male initiation by Mokaré, documenting some of the men who had travelled to King George's Sound for this ritual. Youths (*no beard*) would leave their family and travel to a far away group, sometimes living in this foreign country for up to a year. By the time they had completed this initiation into manhood they had built up a social network of friends and gained extensive geographic knowledge.[9] Neighbouring groups would travel in parties sometimes several hundred kilometres for exceptionally important ceremonies which King Ya-nup were a part of. Barker was told of one such meeting, held at the Porongurup Range in November 1830, where men had come from Wills country to the north and from far to the west for a male initiation ceremony.[10] Single men, in particular were said to 'wander a great deal'.[11] In January 1831, Talimamunde had 'lately been taking his travelling provisions' and travelling a lot, Barker wrote. This was because he 'had just fallen in love'.[12] Married men, Mokaré said, 'generally do not walk far, their wives persuading them to settle'.

Ceremonial requirements, initiation rites and having kin in far away country meant that the King Ya-nup travelled often and sometimes over vast distances. Travelling far was not desired by everyone, but there were a few, mostly elder men (*full beard*) who were revered as master travellers. Mokaré told Barker about Yetitole, who, in Barker's words, appeared 'to be a great traveller'. During one of his travels in the summer 'away from the sea', he went so long without drinking fresh water that he was 'obliged to drink his own blood', which he did by cutting his arms.[13] The newcomers revered these Aboriginal travellers too, extracting as much information as they could about the country.

Maragnan, was another well-travelled man. In June 1830, Barker was trying to gather information from the King Ya-nup as to the whereabouts of three escaped prisoners, who were believed to be heading towards Swan River.

Maragnan told Barker the places where he had seen traces of or heard about the escapees. These places were a series of campsites on a route from King George's Sound to the north of Augusta, a distance of over 300 kilometres. Maragnan described all the major harbours, lakes and river mouths that existed along the way. As well as giving Barker information about the escapees, Maragnan was also telling him about the land and waterways. 'Says Quarumbup is fit for ships ... very deep like [around] Green Island.'[14] Maragnan implied that he travelled along this long path often, mentioning several different journeys to Barker. He had a strong and extensive kin network that meant he could safely travel such a long distance, meeting with known groups along the way.[15] Mokaré told Barker that he did not speak the language at *Coconyup*, to the far west, but Maragnan knew the language well suggesting that Maragnan had travelled this distance often.[16]

In explaining the different harbours and landmarks along this path to Barker, Maragnan drew distances on the floor of Barker's hut. He described distances in reference to landmarks in King Ya-nup country: *Nornalup* is as far away from *Quaranup* as King George's Sound is from Green Island. Barker knew that he was talking about westward locations as Maragnan said that 'The sun in the summer sets in the sea, in the winter on the land, or part land and part water.'[17] Maragnan described the depth of each of the harbours and waterways on this route, mentioning which ones were large enough for ships and which ones would only fit boats. Barker interrogated Maragnan about the distances between harbours along the south west coast. Maragnan drew on the floor for clarity, but confused Barker even further. 'Nornalup about as far from Comandyup (Mount Hallowell) as this from [King George's Sound], but in shewing the distance on the floor he made it half as far again thus: N C KG'.[18] Whenever a great traveller was in the garrison, Barker pressed him for details about the coastline to the west. Metyalpin, Maragnan's brother was another traveller who was questioned about the knowledge that Maragnan had shared about Nornalup's harbour, and Barker was pleased that both accounts added up.[19]

King Ya-nup travel distance and travel time was measured differently from the way that the newcomers measured them. Mokaré expressed travel time to Barker in reference to the number of moons or sleeps.[20] Mt Many Peaks to the east, for example was two moons journey, whereas *Palerongup* was nine moons. These moons referred to how many sleeps it would take to arrive. Mokaré named stages, or camp sites along the way, with *Palerongup* being the final stage.[21] Distance was explained by relational land marks in King

Ya-nup country. Travelling would only be done across country boundaries at particular times of the year. It was a seasonal specific activity and the King Ya-nup would not act as guides during the hot summer months to particularly dry locations. In March 1830, Barker was trying to convince several of the King Ya-nup to travel north. He wrote of their reasons for declining: Wills country was 'Very hot, very hot, water bad'.[22]

From the ongoing conversations and constant questioning, the King Ya-nup learnt what it was the surveyors and explorers wanted to find in the interior: fertile land fit for agricultural production. In January 1832, Robert Dale, an ensign in the 63rd Regiment based at Swan River was visiting King George's Sound and went on an exploration of the *Koi-kyen-u-ruff* Ranges. Assistant surveyor at Swan River, Raphael Clint, joined him with three soldiers and 'chief' Nakinah who was to perform as 'native guide'. Governor Stirling had requested that Dale explore this mountain range in particular, to ascertain whether a story that the King Ya-nup had been telling the newcomers at King George's Sound was true. The story was this: *kiuk* and *quannet*, two types of grains, were said to be used by the Aborigines who lived near *Toodve-rup* in the vicinity of these ranges. Dale wrote, 'Several of the King George's Sound tribe describe these grains; the first or kiuk as growing to the North and Eastern foot Koikyeunruff, and the latter or Quannet to the N East of Koikyeunuruff and also on the northern base of Toodeverup.' The King Ya-nup described them:

> … the stalks on which they grow as being from Six to Eight feet high; the size of one's finger and protruding long ears which are pendant from a succession of joints, the Kiuk they say resembles our rice, and the Quannet grain is compared to a large pea for size.[23]

This story was not based on the King Ya-nup first hand account of the grains: they told the surveyors that none of them had ever laid eyes on them. But their information came from their interactions and exchanges with neighbours across country. They knew that the White Cockatoo people who lived in the district of *Toodverup*, ate the *kiuk* raw, but beat the *quannet*, tied it up in their skins and cooked it on hot ashes like a damper.[24] Nind was told a similar story about this mysterious grain: 'Rice,' he wrote, 'they call *kioc*, and say there is plenty, that it grows on a small shrub, and is of a reddish colour; that they shake it out into their cloak, and eat it uncooked.'[25] These native grains may have sounded promising to the British who were increasingly dependent for whatever food could be grown in the region.

The exploration party finally reached the vicinity of the mountain range. They killed a kangaroo and within an instant met a group of White Cockatoo and Wills people, Nakinah slipping easily into his job of 'interpreter'. The White Cockatoo group wanted to know where this party of strangers intended to go and after a discussion decided to accompany, or 'lead them'. On their return to the settlement six days later, Dale wrote,

> We were unsuccessful in our endeavours to find the Quannet and the Kiuk, the answers of the Natives from whom I had hoped to have gained some information, to our numerous interrogations on the subject were generally so very vague, that it was impossible to place any reliance upon them, but it does not appear they grow in the Neighbourhood of Toolbrunup.[26]

It seemed as though Dale and Governor Stirling were sold a good story. Perhaps Nakinah was keen to meet up with the White Cockatoo and Wills people in the presence of the newcomers; an alliance with the strangers had to be witnessed by groups who mattered. He had bribed Dale (and Stirling) with a tale about the grains, something he knew they would be persuaded by, and he travelled with them to meet with these neighbouring groups. Nakinah, perhaps more than any other King Ya-nup, was a good bargainer. He was in a strong position to bargain, considered by the newcomers as 'King of the tribe'. What is interesting in this little story about the (possibly fictional) grains is that the King Ya-nup had grasped what stories to tell the newcomers and were gaining from these travels in ways that the explorers were not aware of. There was, perhaps, not just an economy of knowledge, but also an economy of 'promises'.

A similar interrogation happened at Swan River in 1836–37. George Fletcher Moore, who was convinced that Australia had an inland sea attempted to retrieve information about such a sea from the Swan River groups. The Aborigines were happy to lead Moore on his futile search and he even published a book entitled *Evidences of an Inland Sea: Collected from the Natives of the Swan River settlement.*[27]

Nakinah's knowledge drew a high price. Just a month before his expedition with Dale, Nakinah embarked on an expedition to the north and west of King George's Sound with Surveyor General of Swan River, John Septimus Roe, and Governor Stirling. This description by Colonel Hanson of Nakinah's receipt in the exchange shows his bargaining powers:

> The Native Chief Nakainah, was dressed up in a most splendid uniform, to be given to him as a present, after he had accompanied the Governor into the interior, upon a journey he was then contemplating. It was a motley dress no doubt. Maude, the first Lieutenant of the *Sulphar*,[sic] furnished a Black Coat, I furnished a Red one, with which the black coat was trimmed – collar, cuffs, pockets &c.&c. The shoulders were then surmounted, by a pair of my largest embroidered Epaulettes, and every variety of Button was used that could be collected in the Ship – 'thereby (Maude said) *"to represent every department of state"*.' The man [Nakinah] was so delighted, when he found it was to be given to him on his return, that his gestures were quite ridiculous.[28] [see image 22]

Not all King Ya-nup were keen travellers. Some liked traversing long distances, whereas others, like Mokaré and Wannewar, seemingly did not. Wannewar was also to be a guide with Nakinah for Roe and Stirling in December 1831. However, whether he had cultural duties to attend to or whether he did not want to leave his country, we are told that he 'contrived to make himself scarce at the Settlement at the moment he should have accompanied Nakinna and the Soldiers …'[29] Despite travelling with the newcomers on several occasions, Mokaré felt uncomfortable when travelling, particularly when he was not on terrain that he knew well. In 1829 Thomas Braidwood Wilson, who had come to King George's Sound on his way to New South Wales after his ship had been wrecked near Raffles Bay, explored country to the west. He took Mokaré, intelligent and well versed in the habits of the newcomers by 1829, to guide him. Private Gough, who travelled with them, was heavily laden with rum, gin and brandy; Mokaré's only 'burden' was a fowling piece which, Wilson said, 'he would not go without; and, as he was a good shot', they thought he might be useful 'in procuring fresh provisions.'[30] They left the settlement via a 'native path', the usual exit from the settlement taken by these explorers, following the King Ya-nup' lead. Mokaré believed that the exploring party was heading towards the Porongurup range just as he had done with Wakefield the previous year. Wilson, however, intended on going 'a considerable distance' in the direction of Swan River (to the north-west of the settlement). He wrote, 'I had already to coax Mokaré, who, imagining we were going to Porrongorup … did not seem to relish taking any other direction.'[31]

A few days into the journey, while the party was camped near a stream, Mokaré seemed to be agitated. Wilson noted, 'whether it was that Mokaré had got into an enemy's country, we did not know, but he was particularly on the alert during the night. Some noise, not sufficient to arouse any other of the party, made him start up, seize his musket, and level it at something, which he afterwards said it was a *to-ort* (a dog)'.[32] Mokaré continued to feel uneasy over the following few days. While the party was having an after lunch sleep, 'Mokaré sprang on his legs, seized his musket, and ran forward', Wilson wrote, making what he described as 'a hideous noise'. They soon realised that Mokaré's noises were due to the approach of an Aboriginal man. Wilson ordered Mokaré not to fire his weapon at the stranger, but it was quickly revealed that Mokaré and this man knew each other. The man was on a kangaroo hunt, from Wills country and invited the whole party to join him, Wilson misunderstanding and writing that 'Will' would be glad to see them.[33] Mokaré was very keen to take up the invitation and visit these northern neighbours but Wilson declined, urging the party to press on in the other direction. Mokaré tried to persuade Wilson of the riches of the country to the north-east so that Wilson would agree to follow. Wilson wrote, 'From what I could learn, there is no doubt that a great extent of good land exists in that direction, to the northward of the Porrongorup and Moorillup Ranges. But as I had previously arranged, in my own mind, the plan of our journey, I did not wish to deviate from it.'[34] Wilson wrote that Mokaré was particularly 'chagrined' at the decline of the invitation from the Wills people and told the party that the land that they were headed in to the west was very barren, 'bad for travelling…and infested with snakes'.[35] Wilson misunderstood the importance of this invitation to Mokaré, sending instead his respects to Will 'and an invitation for him to visit King Ya-nup (the name the natives give the Sound), where he, and any of his tribe, would meet a friendly reception.'[36]

By 7 December, after they had been travelling for five days, Mokaré was beyond his known geographic range and reported to be feeling uneasy. Wilson wrote that Mokaré 'entered into a serious remonstrance' with him about travelling any further. The reasons that he gave Wilson were that they were a long way from home and did not have much food. He said 'the white fellows would cry', referring to Captain Barker and Lt Sleeman who were at the settlement negotiating the changeover of command. He also implied to Wilson that if he had known they were to travel this far before they left the settlement, he would have refused to be involved. 'He said, the expeditions of Captain Wakefield and the others had been *maatinip* [a short distance], while mine had been already *maatopen* [a long distance]'.[37] Trying to lift the spirits of the party (as Private Gough was also agitated by this stage), Wilson issued a 'double allowance of grog' and God save the King was sung with 'much vociferation, where it had never been chanted before'.[38] It was not until 11 December, when Mokaré was again on 'known ground', that he felt confident and began to lead the party through the bush towards the garrison.

Mokaré travelled with Barker over similar country and he later took another short expedition with Collie to the north of King George's Sound. It seemed as though Mokaré was happy to travel short distances with the explorers, but he was not keen on longer distance travel beyond his geographic knowledge. Interestingly, though, the idea of travel by sea was desirous to him in theory. There were several instances when opportunities arose for Mokaré to travel in a vessel to Sydney or Swan River in a *caibre*. But he never ended up leaving when the time came to depart.

When Lt Sleeman handed over control of the garrison to Captain Barker, Wilson wrote: Mokaré 'now wished to accompany him [Sleeman] to Sydney' aboard the man-of-war, and it was not until the very last minute before departure, that Mokaré said he would not go. According to Wilson, the reason given was that Mokaré would not have had 'an opportunity of getting back' to King George's Sound. And as he would be useful to Barker, Mokaré was 'willing to stay'.[39] And during HMS *Sulphur*'s visit in September 1830, Barker wrote in his journal that Mokaré was to travel to Swan River with Captain Irwin of the 63rd Regiment when the *Sulphur* departed.[40] He wrote, 'Blacks contented' with this proposal for Mokaré to travel, but 'Watyaquart said no.' When the *Sulphur* departed the following morning, Barker observed that Mokaré 'was well [contented]' when the vessel was off, adding that 'perhaps his heart failed him'.[41] The *Sulphur* visited again at Christmas that year, with the same visitors from Swan River. Between visits, Irwin had written a letter to Davis at the garrison, requesting Mokaré's 'leave' to visit Swan River. Davis, however, handled the situation badly, Barker thought, by abruptly announcing the matter to Governor Stirling over Christmas dinner, without his having any prior knowledge of the proposal. The Governor replied, 'Oh No!'[42]

Mokaré also requested to leave with Barker when he departed in March 1830, but remained on his country when Barker sailed. These requests to voyage are interesting. Why was Mokaré so eager to voyage, and yet he never actually departed? Were they false offers? Was he uneasy about the ocean? Or, were these requests a form of diplomacy, a show of alliance, or part of a ritual of initiation with a visiting group? King's Jack was also seemingly eager to depart with King's crew when the *Bathurst* was leaving in 1821. King thought it was seasickness that stopped him from voyaging, whereas Cunningham believed his decision went deeper, writing: 'The love of the place of our birth clings to us. He preferred his native arid shore…and a truly miserable comfortless existence, supported by a casual uncertain supply of food to an opportunity afforded him to better his condition by launching forth into an unbounded world of water.'[43] But perhaps the very suggestion of departing with them was as far as Jack's diplomacy went. Other King Ya-nup were eager voyagers and their embassies by sea will be discussed later.

◆

At the end of May 1832, the Resident Magistrate at King George's Sound, Dr Alexander Collie, asked Manyat, a King Ya-nup man, to be his guide on a journey that would take them more than 100 kilometres away from the settlement. John Henty, a new settler at King George's Sound, joined them with one servant and three soldiers, travelling to the north of the settlement over ten days. Collie reported that Manyat was given the job of 'fireman, not for extinguishing, but for lighting up and carrying a banksia cone.'[44] He was also to act as 'guide' to the explorers as they traversed the alien landscape and as 'interpreter' or 'intermediary' if and when they encountered Aborigines.[45] However, Collie was not aware initially that Manyat was travelling out of his known geographical range: it was foreign country for him as well as for Collie and he travelled far beyond his country's borders. As they did not meet one Aboriginal person on their journey, Manyat was not required to be an interpreter and put his efforts into other things, like the procuring of knowledge.

Explorers like Collie show how a landscape was filled differently by Aboriginal people and newcomers. Whereas Collie used previous explorers' maps and travel notes to guide him through the country, and helpful natives, Manyat's mind map was a collection of stories, of knowledge about the foreign country that he had been collecting all his life, that circulated within his kin groups and came from encounters with kinsmen from the west and strangers from the north. Collie's journals show him mapping out the land, his eyes searching for the important considerations – fertile land, cow pastures, hunting and grazing land – which he called the 'First Steps of Colonization.'[46] He was also, unwittingly, meticulously describing an already occupied land as he carefully copied down the native names for hills, swamps, valleys, vistas, trees and animals, changing the spellings of names as he got a better grasp of the pronunciations of the language (he thought). Throughout the journey, Manyat named places and plants. Collie reported that this naming came 'not from his actual knowledge but according to what he had heard from others never having been to this country before'. Manyat's itinerary, wrote Collie, was 'the recollection of accounts of others, which gave the names to most of the places and plants' that were encountered. He recognised a valley from his mind map and called it *Woorongurup*. Collie seemed amazed at this knowledge. A grassy bight was called by Manyat *Yambagallup*, wrote Collie, 'on the same hearsay evidence as before'.[47] Collie was creating material maps, for future explorers to rely on, scrutinise and alter; Manyat had a cartographic mind and his maps were retold and danced in story and ceremony.

It was an unfamiliar land for both Manyat and Collie, and Collie used the names that Manyat gave him throughout his diary, unless he had his own name or word to give it. He mentioned a large hill several times using Manyat's name for it, *Pwakkenbak*. By the end of his travel diary the name Mt Barker was written next to *Pwakkenbak* in brackets. Collie did not recognise the strange looking trees (Manyat recognised their descriptions) and so Collie adopted Manyat's naming of them: *wornt* and *moongirt* until he found something familiar, *she oak*, a reminder of the old world. Manyat did not just take knowledge with him from his community on his travels, but, importantly, he brought new knowledge home with him too. Collie recorded that Manyat,

> treasured up in his memory a detailed recollection of the various incidents and scenery [that he came across] arranged in the form of a Diary, where each day was designated by some leading distinctive mark, in place of numerals, as the killing of a kangaroo (1st day), cow meal; see a bullock (3rd day), and such like.[48]

Collie and Manyat both recorded this journey using their own culturally defined processes. They recorded the important parts of the journey: Collie writing down distances travelled, angles and vegetation; Manyat remembering the animals and new vegetation he saw and the food he ate. Laying eyes on a bullock, as Manyat did, would have produced much excitement: this was a new animal at King George's Sound, having wandered a long way south from

Swan River. They were forty-eight and a half miles from the settlement, near *Warre-up* when they saw this animal. Collie identified it as a 'Java bullock, in high condition', feeding on the banks of a stream.[49] Even the tracks of these animals were enough to create a series of rumours and much drama throughout the Aboriginal social world in the south-west during 1830. Collie used the sighting of this animal and a herd of fourteen cattle during another expedition, to promote the good country to Governor Stirling. The bullock was in 'high condition', and the herd of horned cattle were seen 'pasturing on the verdant slopes…Their high condition testified in favour of their feed'.[50]

It is important to note that Collie was the one who described Manyat's recollections as a diary. It was his interpretation of Manyat's remembering, but it may have meant something else to Manyat.

This knowledge and memory of the journey was not all stored in Manyat's mind. He was a collector of natural objects as well. A tree that the travellers came across was one such thing that captured Manyat's interest and Collie recorded: 'Its native name is Wang, and such importance did Manyat attach to it that he took a specimen as well as myself.'[51] In his work on flora of the south-west, botanist Stephen Hopper gave important detail about this tree. It was a peach *Santalum acuminatum* or quondong. 'Noongars knew this plant as wolgol, and its richly-coloured fruits with single pitted seed is gunnar.'[52] Perhaps Manyat had watched the many naturalists and botanists collecting specimens during their visits to King George's Sound. Barker was a preserver of different types of moss and Mokaré helped him to stick his moss specimens down on paper or between pieces of glass, even though Barker said that he could not understand why Barker wanted to collect it and laughed at the idea 'of preserving such things.'[53] Jack had also assisted Cunningham collect his natural specimens in 1821. Collie believed that this collecting of plants and specimens by Manyat was to 'show his comparatively untravelled friends at King George's Sound his far travelling or Some other advantage in which he prided himself over them.'[54]

Collie certainly saw the value and esteem in this natural knowledge collecting. He was, after all, a botanist himself; as a medical student of the Scottish Enlightenment it was common for surgeons to be educated in natural history as part of their training. In 1825 Collie joined Captain Beechey's voyage of discovery to the Arctic as Surgeon/Naturalist. This combined position was frequent in such expeditions in the late eighteenth and early nineteenth centuries. Prior to Collie's departure with Beechey he became a fellow of the

Linnean Society in London, which houses one of his natural history reports from that voyage.[55] Famed naturalist Charles Darwin wrote about Collie's fossil collections from the Beechey voyage in 1844.

In 1830 Collie wrote a letter about the 'mode of generation in the kangaroo' to the Zoological Society of London. This letter is now considered to be the first European recorded observation of the transference of a kangaroo embryo to its mother's pouch, rather than from its mother's nipples.[56] In one of his letters to his brother George, Collie wrote modestly about his hobby:

> As usual I wander a little bit into the woods and gather a few bits o' floors to make me think myself a Botanist, a great naturalist, whereas others most likely set me down as a great natural…Sometimes I get hold of a rotten stone, a kangaroo's toe and ruminate a propos.[57]

Collie's prediction of Manyat's reasons for collecting the specimen of the tree *Wang*, proved to be correct. Collie recorded a dramatic image of Manyat being celebrated by his friends. On his return home after ten days journeying, Manyat rehearsed his diary to a crowd of 'curious and eager countrymen'. This, Collie wrote, crowned Manyat's joy 'and afforded no little amusement to the dingy groups which assembled round him'.[58] We can only imagine what he reported back to them: obviously the landmarks and animals he saw, the bullock would have been of particular interest, but also the plant species of which he brought home samples and the new terrain he had 'discovered'. This image of curious Aborigines gathered around the returned traveller was also conjured up by Wilson of Mokaré. On his return in 1829 he wrote: 'The natives crowded around Mokaré, eager to hear the news from a far country'. This was not just a native novelty as the soldiers also besieged Private Gough for the same purpose. He did not report on anything, however, until they brought him some food.[59]

It is impossible to know what Manyat's plant sample symbolised for him – Collie wrote down what he thought it meant. Was it exciting to Manyat because he had never seen this plant before or was it a marker of distance, showing his friends how far he had travelled, perhaps in hostile territory? Manyat's 'vanity', Collie wrote, 'revelled in the idea, that he had penetrated farther from King George's Sound than Nakina [King of his tribe] or any other acquaintance'. It is difficult to ascertain whether this is Collie's assumption of

Manyat's experience, or if Manyat actually felt proud and dignified from his travel. Collie wrote that the 'excursion seemed to afford Manyat considerable pleasure'. He was treated to ample rations as well as procuring as much food as he could for himself along the way.[60] But, Collie warned, his 'sole delight must not be supposed to have consisted after all, in animal gratification'. Rather, Collie believed, it was the 'mental treat of travelling over unknown and far distant ground, seeing, touching, and even collecting and preserving portions of trees which he had hitherto only known to exist in name'.[61] It might have been as exciting to travel over well-known but dangerous ground, especially in the presence (protection) of a powerful foreigner.

Paul Turnbull has written about the necessity for colonial naturalists to draw heavily on Indigenous knowledge in the nineteenth century. In their travels naturalists 'invariably relied on Indigenous people to locate specimens of flora and fauna', he wrote.[62] Turnbull described a cross-cultural relationship similar to that between Collie and Manyat in a narrative about the botanist George Caley and his friendship with a *Eora* man named Moowat'tin. Caley relied on his friend to help him collect natural specimens in the bush. Of their expeditions to Norfolk Island and Tasmania together in 1805, Turnbull wrote: 'it would seem that this expedition proved a fascinating cross-cultural engagement in which two individuals schooled in radically different knowledge traditions worked closely together to make sense of the ecology of places to which both were equally strangers'.[63]

Aboriginal travellers like Manyat, who returned home with valuable knowledge of far away country, gained a higher status within their community. Manyat was offered a wife soon after he returned home. He also gained credit in the imagination of Collie who wrote with remarkable admiration of his new 'knowledgeable' friend. Months after their journey, Collie wrote of Manyat: 'His name will be handed down as another Bruce to the rising generation,' likening him to James Bruce the famed traveller of Africa.[64]

Collie's travel writing invokes not only Manyat's increasing mobility, but also the changes in status he experienced as a result of the new knowledge that he brought home to his community and the elevation of the calibre of his character in the minds of the colonists. In a report in 1832 to Governor Stirling, Collie wrote of the effect of travel on the Aboriginal 'knowledge economy' at King George's Sound in the following terms:

Their vanity is perhaps a beneficial quality, even in their intercourse with each other, and certainly so, to a considerable degree with us. They make a boast of the learning obtained from the white people among the more distant tribes; and if I have deduced a correct inference from the details which some of them ...have given me, this ostentation not only affords them delight at the time, but the bare recollection of the astonishment, wonder and envy it excited, gives them an ecstasy of pleasure. Their vanity, too, prompts them to procure those things which distinguish the learned, admired and envied foreigner from the ignorant and despised savage; and this may be advantageously cultivated until the capricious hunter grows into the steady labourer.[65]

This romantic vision of Collie's explained the importance and vitality of Aboriginal gossip and knowledge networks in the south-west. He saw the value and advantage of these journeys for the King Ya-nup who were not passive guides to European adventurers. We cannot know to what extent Collie's interpretation was also the King Ya-nup. Collie saw travelling as a civilising ritual, an educational process. In Britain in the early nineteenth century, the notion of the 'Grand Tour' was, according to James Buzard, an exercise to 'round out the education of young men of the ruling classes by exposing them to the treasured artefacts and enobling society of the Continent.'[66] Travel was seen as a social ritual and was intended to prepare young men to 'assume leadership positions preordained for them at home'. It was intended as an educative and preparatory initiation.[67] But did the King Ya-nup view it this way? The reception of Manyat's return home suggests that they did.

Historical anthropologist Anne Salmond has written persuasively about Tahitian voyagers and navigators of the South Seas who acted strategically in their positions as 'navigators' or 'guides'. She described culturally defined 'way-finding' devices; Europeans and Tahitians combining their very different knowledge and navigational systems to traverse the South Seas.[68] Such shared voyages in the Pacific and in the south-west of Australia allow us to see the mutual impacts that the indigenous people and newcomers had on each other. Some of the histories that utilise these travel narratives render the Aboriginal 'guides' as passive troupers, side players in European heroic efforts at discovery of 'new' land. Aboriginal accounts are trivialised or ignored and their intentions and purposes for travel are obscured under the topics of 'guides', 'interpreters' or other aids to the Europeans.

Explorers generally appreciated their guides and were aware of their own reliance on them, but earlier historiographies are to blame for the negative image of passive Aborigines. Henry Reynolds helped to redress the negative passive image of Aborigines in European expeditions in *With the White People*, showing how explorers could not have 'discovered' the inland of Australia without the expert guidance and knowledge of Aboriginal people, whom Reynolds referred to as 'black pioneers'.[69] Some Aboriginal guides have recently gained recognition for their participation in exploring the inland of Western Australia. In 1977 the ranger of the Porongurup National Park changed the name of a mountain peak in the range from 'Daisy Summit' (after anthropologist Daisy Bates) to 'Manyat Peak'. His nomenclature decision came after reading Collie's journal which described his journey with Manyat to this area.[70]

A closer look at these stories of south-west expeditions, with Aboriginal characters who are becoming familiar, shows that some of these expeditions were collaborative accomplishments to which the King Ya-nup and their knowledge systems made significant contributions. When scrutinised, the Europeans' travel writing reveals the complex, multi-layered dynamics of cross-cultural engagements around the south-west and shows the specifics of an Aboriginal cartography.

8

Aboriginal Voyagers

In the year 1833 a series of unprecedented diplomatic meetings took place. Manyat, a master traveller by this stage, embarked on what was to be an epic voyage with Gyallipert, hundreds of kilometres along the rough and rugged coastline to the Swan River with the purpose, according to the colonists, of holding 'an interview' with the Aboriginal men there. Donald McLeod, who had taken over from Alexander Collie as the Government Resident at King George's Sound in November 1832, wrote that he 'acceded to an urgent request' from Manyat and Gyallipert to visit Swan River in the schooner *Thistle* 'and to return back by the next [opportunity] that [was] offered'.[1] But before the narrative of that voyage can begin, some background about the Swan River world is needed.

The reasons for the establishment of a British settlement at Swan River were very different from those for the military outpost at King George's Sound. The colony was set up as a free settlement, clean of crown prisoners, and it was established on the basis of land grants to settlers. There was a strong enticement for emigrants who were granted land in proportion to the value of assets and labour that they brought to the colony. Compared to the fairly small and fixed number of people at King George's Sound, floods of newcomers migrated to Swan River. In the first six months 625 people arrived, including a detachment of the 63rd Regiment under the command of Captain Frederick Chidley Irwin. In 1830 there were 1125 more. In the years after that, however, the floods petered out to just a trickle, with some of the arrivals leaving for home after a bitter taste of an isolated colony.

King George's Sound was a limpet-like garrison, sitting on the fringe of the Aboriginal world, looking out to sea for the French. But Swan River townships, which were hastily set up at Perth and Guildford in the north and east, looked inwards towards the rivers and the country with Fremantle as the settlement's port town. By January 1830 the town plans for Fremantle and Perth had been laid out and soon after that all habitable land around the Swan and Canning rivers had been allocated to migrants.[2] The different focus of King George's Sound and Swan River helped to shape the relationships with the Aboriginal groups at each settlement. The motivation of the Swan River settlement was colonisation of the landscape and the people, ensuring that the spaces were occupied with a superior confidence of ownership. Stirling's instructions from the colonial authorities required him to do his utmost to promote religion and civilisation to the Aboriginal inhabitants. Lockyer was told to conciliate them with 'Tomahawks and Blankets'.

In 1833, the year that Manyat and Gyallipert's epic voyage took place, little cottages had been built in Fremantle. The cottages were mostly white, matching the colour of the sand that was said to blow about 'incessantly', forming hillocks in the streets.[3] Families were growing gardens and establishing their livestock; branding their mark in ways they knew how on what was to many of them an alien, untouched new world. Perth and Guildford in the north did not have as many buildings as Fremantle in 1833. Perth was establishing its government buildings, but at this stage most business was conducted in wattle and daub tent-like structures, made from the thick clay that was stacked up along the Swan River foreshore.[4]

The migrants and colonists who were creating the Swan River colony had built themselves onto and laid their structures over three different Aboriginal 'territories'.[5] The people of these territories were described and somewhat loosely defined by Francis Armstrong in 1836, who had the job of 'Native Interpreter', and Robert Menli Lyon in 1833, a man who expressed much interest in and concern over the Aborigines. To the south was a group called *Beeliar*, whose country was bounded by Melville Water and the Canning River on the north, by the Darling mountain range on the east, by the Indian Ocean to the west and by a line drawn east from Mangles Bay in the south.[6] The men given the most prominence by the newcomers in this country were Midgegooroo and his son Yagan. Next to *Beeliar* was *Beeloo* country, the custodian being a man named Munday. The *Beeloo* estate was bounded on the south by the other side of Canning River, on the west by Melville Water, on the north by the Swan River and Ellen's Brook, and by the mountains on the east. The country to the north of the Swan River was *Mooro* country and the prominent figure from this country was Yellagonga.[7] (see map, image 5) The *Beeliar, Beeloo* and *Mooro* shared a complex and vital kin network, with family connections and individual tracts of land custodianship extending across them: all of which were affected by the rapidly expanding colony. Unlike King George's Sound, migrants and colonists at Swan River were attracted to the same landscapes as the Aborigines, settling inland along the rivers and coastal plain.

As discussed earlier, the King Ya-nup were constantly characterised by their 'friendly' behaviour towards the newcomers. At Swan River, the Aborigines were given the polar opposite of that categorisation: they were the foes. The relationships between these Aborigines and the migrants were not as idyllic as those at King George's Sound: when the settlements at Perth, Guildford and Fremantle began, spearings and shootings quickly followed. The migrants defined the conflicts as land-and-food related (the Aborigines were spearing their livestock and 'plundering' their houses). Unlike King George's Sound where the newcomers and King Ya-nup were not threatening each other's food resources, for the Aborigines at Swan River dramatic lifestyle changes were brought about at a quicker pace as some groups were quickly moved off their hunting grounds. There were, perhaps, fewer opportunities for patient and considered negotiations of the increasingly 'shared' space.

The most notorious of the Aboriginal 'foes' was a man from *Beeliar* country called Yagan. His story, a well-known Western Australian narrative now, overlaps this one and so he deserves a larger introduction. Yagan was the son of Midgegoroo, 'chief' of *Beeliar*.[8] He was first mentioned in 1832 when the Swan River migrants became aware of a particular Aboriginal man 'with striking appearance' who was apparently leading 'attacks' on their properties and on people along the Canning and Swan rivers. In May that year, a labourer called William Gaze was speared and died, and Yagan was identified as the perpetrator. A reward of £20 was set on the young man's head, but he eluded capture for four months, until September when he and two other Aboriginal men Donmera and Ningina, who were fishing, were enticed into a boat with bread by three colonists. They were bound up together and taken to Fremantle gaol, a whitewashed roundhouse which dominated the port township.[9] The Executive Council of Western Australia decided that Yagan and his fellow prisoners be sent to Carnac Island, off the coast south of Fremantle, to be overseen by two soldiers. Like Lockyer, the Western Australian authorities saw the advantage in offshore penitentiaries.

Robert Menli Lyon, who was fascinated by the ways and life of the Aborigines and concerned for their welfare, requested to be exiled with them on Carnac Island in order to study the ways and speech of the Aboriginal prisoners. Lyon's self-exile was motivated by a desire that his knowledge of the Aboriginal languages of the Swan and Canning rivers would improve relationships between Aborigines and migrants. The key for peace was often thought to be made through language or effective communication with the thought that if the Aborigines understood the intentions of the migrants all would be well. Being a religious man (he later became a minister) Lyon also had a Christianising motive. He wrote passionately about the devastation which he saw, caused by the presence of the migrants on the Aboriginal populations and the disruption of their intricate social world. He wrote with strong emotion to the *Perth Gazette*, the Executive Council and to Colonial Secretary, Hay. Lyon's writing gives glimpses of Yagan and of the tragic and different cross-cultural engagements at Swan River. Lyon's exile was not going to be an easy task. As he did not speak Yagan's language, he thought it would be necessary to solicit some help from the friendly, peaceful, pidgin English-speaking King George's Sound Aborigines. Lyon sailed to the Sound to meet and discuss his plans with the newcomers (and possibly the King Ya-nup) in the hope that some of the King Ya-nup might join him. However, Lyon's proposition was not approved by the Colonial Secretary or the Executive Council and he went to Carnac Island alone.[10]

Two soldiers rowed the three Aboriginal prisoners and Lyon out to Carnac Island in late 1832. Unfortunately for Lyon, his education in Aboriginal language and life was halted early. Yagan and his comrades escaped. After one month of living on Carnac, in the dead of night, Yagan, Donmera and Ningina took the island's only boat and rowed back to the mainland. The boat was later found, with one oar, on the shores of the Swan near Point Walter.

◆

Enter Manyat and Gyallipert. Although the King Ya-nup were initially asked by Lyon to help him on Carnac Island in his humanitarian pilgrimage, Gyallipert and Manyat's voyage was not a government-sponsored mission. These two men (who must have heard about the difficulties at Swan River) not only volunteered, but, it was said, urgently 'requested' to take the voyage to Swan River and to meet with the Aborigines living there.

So far as is known, the King Ya-nup had never met any Swan River Aborigines before. They had travelled extensively by land and had kin in far away places. As part of their transition to adulthood, young men went to live with other Aboriginal groups, sometimes quite far away, to gain valuable education, to extend their kin networks and to develop 'extensive geographic knowledge'.[11] But it is very unlikely that any King Ya-nup had ventured to the Swan River before – a distance of several hundred kilometres along the coast – and what made Gyallipert and Manyat's voyage so innovative is that these two men travelled there in a *caibre*.

The textual traces left behind by these two King Ya-nup are scant in comparison to those of Mokaré's daily activities, but what is recorded is remarkable, revealing enigmatic Aboriginal behaviour. Manyat previously featured in this story through Alexander Collie's admiration. He had behind him the experience of travel beyond his country and was possibly keen to travel further than before. Gyallipert, however, was written about only briefly before this epic voyage. He is less identifiable in the archives, probably because his name was a complicated one for a non-Aboriginal ear and thus it was spelt differently by every recorder (including several different spellings by Barker). It is most likely that he and his family had strong connections with groups towards the west of King George's Sound, in *Murrum* country or were *Murrum* people who travelled frequently to King George's Sound. Barker wrote about him under three names: Tetialtipert/Tichtipert/ Chaltipert. According to Barker, he was 'the troublesome boy that used to be constantly at [Private] Langton's'.[12] These three different names probably all refer to the same person who was later recorded as Gyallipert (but never by Barker). Given nineteenth-century spelling and phonemics, it is most likely that he was the Gyallipert of this narrative. It was common for Barker frequently to change the spelling of Aboriginal names, presumably becoming more accurate in the pronunciation the more he heard them.

Government Resident Donald McLeod wrote that Gyallipert and Manyat were not allowed to embark on the epic voyage until they had received 'full consent from their tribe'.[13] They expressed to McLeod a wish that their friends might also be permitted to go to Swan River on a subsequent voyage, but only on the condition of their own safe return to King George's Sound.[14] Negotiations, bribery, exchange: the King Ya-nup were masters at this. They knew how to strike a good deal and gain well from such transactions. They farewelled their countrymen at the settlement and boarded the schooner *Thistle* (a ship owned by James Henty from Portland) to begin the rough ten-day journey to Swan River.

These men were not traditionally seafarers, although many of the King Ya-nup had boarded and travelled in small boats before. This experience was limited to the harbours around the settlement and to King and French's River where they utilised the opportunity of being ferried around rather than walking. Almost as soon as Europeans arrived on their shores, the King Ya-nup were keen to negotiate the use of the newcomers' boats, seemingly to their own advantage, although with disastrous outcomes with respect to the sealers in 1826. Ships, however, were still novel in 1833.

The historical record does not reveal whether this was Manyat and Gyallipert's first time on board a ship. It was certainly the first time they had sailed out of the protective haven of Princess Royal Harbour and headed into the unknown of the Southern Ocean. This was an epic voyage. They would have seen their country with new eyes, from a new perspective. The scale of the country changed as did the well-known shapes and contours. They would examine the windings of the coast for the first time.

By Thursday morning, 18 January 1833, the voyagers had arrived at the port town of Fremantle. They were met by Richard McBryde Brown, the Government Registrar and Collector of Revenue, and Alexander Collie, whom they knew from King George's Sound. It is impossible to know what Gyallipert and Manyat were expecting when they stepped off the *caibre* at Fremantle. The Swan River settlement was very different from King George's Sound, not only in layout and landscape, but also in population and character.

The *Perth Gazette* reported on Gyallipert and Manyat's travels and meetings while in town. Their presence was very much of interest to the newcomers; they featured in every edition of the paper during their stay. The Swan River colonists had sanguine expectations about the visit from these friendly King Ya-nup. They needed a happy and hasty resolution to their Aboriginal 'problem'. Gyallipert and Manyat, who insisted on their embassy, were warmly welcomed by the desperate colonials. Great things were expected.

Collie and Brown, who met them at the port, were to take them to Monger's Lake, north of the Swan River, to meet Yellagonga of the *Mooro* group who was thought to be camped there with 'considerable numbers' of Aborigines.[15] This was to be a different meeting to witness, in which expectations of what constituted 'outsiders' was reversed. This time it was Collie's turn to act as 'guide' and 'cultural mediator' as he showed these foreigners the way to the lake and helped negotiate the terms of this meeting between strangers. From the newspaper report it seemed that Yellagonga was not expecting Gyallipert and Manyat.

John Henry Monger who owned a house on the lake (his name was given to it) joined the party. Monger was the first migrant to be granted land at the lake in appreciation of a sawpit business he established in the colony.[16] His presence at this meeting, according to the *Perth Gazette*, was much needed to ensure cooperation from Yellagonga's group. Monger conversed with some of the *Mooro* who were often on his property and he understood a few of their words but it was reported in the paper that he mostly communicated with them through 'gestures'.[17] Monger was to be the mediator for the local group whereas Collie would mediate the foreigners from King George's Sound. Some of the Aborigines at Swan River communicated with the migrants in an undeveloped pidgin-like language, but this language was still in the early stages of its creation, compared to the fairly developed King George's Sound pidgin, and not as widely spoken by Aborigines or migrants alike. Conversations still relied on the language of the body as much as the voice at Swan River in early 1833. Migrants were looking for the security of language to measure success and understanding in communication with the Aborigines, but the body 'spoke' as well. As Mary Douglas has written, 'the body comes into play to support the meanings of a spoken communication. Posture, voice, speed, articulation, tonality all contribute to the meaning. The words alone mean very little'.[18] Historians unduly privilege language over bodily actions in search for past meaning. John Henry Monger was aware how much he relied on his body and his reading of Aboriginal bodies in his meetings at Monger's Lake.

Yellagonga's camp site had only recently moved to the lake from the banks of the Swan River.[19] A favourite camping site for him and his family was previously on the slopes of the hill *Byerbup* on the northern banks. Before the arrival of newcomers in *Mooro* country, the camping spot offered a superior view of *Matta Gerup*, or 'knee-deep' crossing where visiting groups would cross the river, taking advantage of the sand flats. In 1833, Robert Menli Lyon described Yellagonga's campsite which had become a government food depot in late 1832:

> The camp of Yellagonga, bearing this name (Byerbup) stood beside the Springs at the west end of town, as you descend from Mt Eliza; and on this very spot did the 63rd pitch their tents, when they came to take possession. So that the headquarters of the King of Mooro are now become the head-quarters of the territories of the British King in Western Australia. On

this spot too the King of Mooro, now holds out his hand to beg a crust of bread.[20]

It is telling that the meeting was held at Monger's Lake, or *Kalup* as the *Mooro* called it. Even though it was not where Yellagonga had previously camped, the *Mooro* had an ancient camping ground on the west and south side of the lake and it held spiritual importance too. The ancestral serpent the *waugal*, in his journey towards the sea, deviated from his route and emerged from the ground, creating *Kalup*. The lake played a significant part in the spiritual beliefs associated with the cycle of births and deaths of the *Mooro* and large and important ceremonies were conducted on the lake's southern shore. The *Mooro* also buried their dead there. It would soon gain a new significance. In 1832 and 1833, government food depots were set up on the outskirts of the settlements to reduce the flow of Aboriginal traffic into the settled districts to stop the Aboriginal 'raids' on migrants' stock and food. One of these depots was set up at Monger's Lake in March 1833.[21]

Yellagonga and the other *Mooro* were hosting this meeting on their country and at a significant site. Gyallipert and Manyat might have recognised the markers of this sacred place: did they see graves at the burial ground or broken spears strewn on the ground from battles or remnants of paint or clay after a ceremony? The visitors were acting in terms of the knowledge and conventions of their social system and approached this meeting with their own (and probably very different) expectations. They arrived wearing their skin cloaks. The hosts wore them too.

The editor of the *Perth Gazette* recorded the meeting: Yellagonga's tribe received the King Ya-nup with 'considerable diffidence'; their languages were so dissimilar, the paper reported, that they could only 'interchange of the names of their respective districts, and those of some of the adjoining tribes.' Yellagonga's group, however, eagerly entered into conversation with Manyat and Gyallipert.'[22] Then, Gyallipert and a man named Mundee (Munday) exchanged skin cloaks and just before the meeting ended, the paper recorded, Gyallipert received 'a most hearty salutation on both sides of the face from an aged lady as a seal of this testimony of friendship.'[23] In a letter to Lord Goderich, Francis Chidley Irwin, who was Acting Governor during Governor Stirling's visit to England, wrote, 'The Tribe in this neighbourhood [Swan River] ... gave them a cordial reception tho from the dissimilarity of their dialects they appear to have imperfectly understood each other.'[24] Some of the specifics of this meeting – observed and described through heavy cultural smog – need to be clarified.

Yellagonga received the visitors with 'considerable diffidence'. Without any prior notification about these strangers' arrival on his country, it was appropriate for the host of such a meeting to be indifferent to foreign visitors until they knew how to categorise and place them, particularly visitors who came from the sea. After the initial allusiveness they started talking. They spoke different languages, so the words they exchanged were the necessary ones: names of their country and the country that neighboured theirs. They might both have heard of the intermediate neighbouring groups, but it seems that they did not know the specifics of each other's region. Lyon included in his vocabulary (written two months after Gyallipert and Manyat's visit) the Swan River Aboriginal name for King George's Sound: *Monkbeelven*, suggesting they had heard of groups from the south.[25] The Swan River Aborigines were not described as great travellers by the colonials. Francis Armstrong wrote in 1836, 'There is good reason to believe that few, if any, of the Swan men have been further from the Swan than 80 to 90 miles, unless with settlers.'[26] Yellagonga would have possibly heard of King George's Sound, but had not travelled that far. How would these far from home voyagers been perceived by the comparatively less-travelled Swan River groups?

Back to the meeting: importantly, an exchange of skin cloaks took place. The cloak exchange was symbolic, heralding that the meeting would be a friendly one and these exchanged cloaks would be proof back home of the distance they had travelled and the type of transactions they engaged in. Exchanges could only take place once the status of the visitor was secured.[27] The meeting ended with Gyallipert receiving a 'hearty salutation' – a kiss – on both his cheeks from an old woman. This kiss is an interesting Aboriginal action. There are glimpses of similar actions in texts elsewhere in the south-west. The migrants read the salutation as intimate, a 'testimony of friendship', but it must be questioned whether it held the same gendered intimacy to these Aboriginal people as it did for the newcomers. Without being able to conclude what the kiss might have symbolised, it is worth deliberating about the significance of an old lady's presence at Yellagonga's meeting, and it was her drama, her kiss, which called an end to the meeting.

The colonists at Swan River held high hopes for the meeting. The success of the colony in many ways depended on their having an ongoing amicable relationship with the Aborigines, and if the King Ya-nup could convince

Yellagonga and his countrymen to stop spearing their stock and stealing their provisions, life in this new world would be easier. The editor of *Perth Gazette* wrote: 'The arrival of these natives will lead in every probability to the ultimate establishment of an amicable intercourse with the original possessors of the country, throughout the Colony, a result most sincerely desired.'[28] Irwin believed that the friendly disposition of Gyallipert and Manyat was a 'good reason to expect that [they] may render [an] essential service towards forwarding the object the local Government hopes to effect namely the placing on a permanent basis the good understanding now maintained with the tribes in these districts.'[29]

It is unlikely that the different Aboriginal protagonists saw their meetings and the epic voyage from King George's Sound in the same light as the colonists. Aboriginal motivations were always much more complicated and consciously directed than at first glance. Rather than Manyat and Gyallipert voyaging so far from their country to help the Swan River authorities, it is more probable that their request to travel to meet these strangers held strategic and diplomatic advantages for themselves.

◆

News travels fast in a small community. It was not long before the news about the two outsiders from a foreign place had whispered its way through the Swan River gossip networks, white and black. Yagan, an outlaw in the eyes of the colonials, but allowed to roam free since his escape, had got word that Manyat and Gyallipert were visiting the Swan River and had already met with Yellagonga. He expressed his wishes to the colonials to meet with them.[30] Accordingly, one week after Manyat and Gyallipert's first encounter with Yellagonga and the *Mooro*, Robert Dale, who visited King George's Sound in 1832 and travelled with Nakinah, and George Smythe of the Surveyor General's Department, guided the King Ya-nup men to Monger's Lake again, this time to meet with the infamous Yagan.

It is puzzling that this meeting with Yagan took place at the lake as it was not Yagan's country. Even more curious, although Yagan was 'outlawed' by the colonists (despite several months in 1833 where there was no attempt to capture him), he was about to be put in charge of the bread distribution at the food depot at Monger's Lake. Lyon wrote a letter to the *Perth Gazette* complaining that Yagan's role was very inappropriate. He wrote: 'The propriety of allowing any of the natives to do this at present, is, perhaps questionable. But the conferring this honor upon Yagan is a gross insult to Yellowgonga, who is the leading Chief on this side of the water.'[31] If Lyon realised this was a strange place for Yagan to be given authority, it is even more curious that he was hosting a meeting with these strangers from King George's Sound on Yellagonga's country.

This meeting was markedly different from Gyallipert and Manyat's meeting with Yellagonga and the *Mooro*. It was a planned, premeditated meeting, which meant that Yagan was acting as a host and was prepared for the arrival of the strangers. Shortly after Gyallipert and Manyat arrived at Monger's Lake, Yagan and about ten Aboriginal men 'made their appearance well armed' the *Perth Gazette* recorded. So the hosts arrived after their visitors. Yagan welcomed Gyallipert and Manyat in what was described as a 'cordial manner'. First, a corroboree was danced before an exchange of names and spears took place. The *Perth Gazette* reported that the 'Dialects of either party was perfectly unintelligible to the others' and they seemed to apprehend each other's meaning in 'some few instances rather from gestures than language...'[32] This bodily communication was vital in Aboriginal cross-cultural meetings as well as with Europeans.

Despite their lack of understanding through language, the King Ya-nup men and Yagan's group persisted in searching for a common understanding throughout the meeting. The *Perth Gazette* described a spear throwing trial which took place between Yagan and Gyallipert; Yagan 'struck down a walking stick' which was placed in a vertical position, at a distance of 30 metres. The *Perth Gazette* suggests that he won this trial of skill, but it needs to be questioned if it was such a 'trial' in the British sense of competition. The meeting lasted for about four hours. As the King Ya-nup were leaving, Yagan invited them to meet him again the following morning at the same place. However, according to the *Perth Gazette*, 'circumstances prevented' the second meeting.

The newcomers who were present at the meeting, although not involved in it, thought that the 'interview' included the following: for Gyallipert and Manyat, a:

> description of their native District, detail of the kind treatment and benefit they had received from the 'white people' and an exhortation to Yagan and his followers to conduct themselves in a peaceable and friendly manner towards their white neighbours.[33]

This is an outsider's perception of how the conversation went. Gyallipert also relayed this meeting to George Fletcher Moore later on, who recorded in his diary what Gyallipert said to Yagan. Gyallipert conversed with Moore in King Ya-nup 'pidgin-English':

> me wonka (tell) black man pear white man cow, white man yeep (sheep), white man kill black man: black man no pear (spear) cow, no pear yeep, white man give black man jacket, towlyer, yerk (shirt) and bikket (biscuit) plenty; black man wonka (say) no pear no more.[34]

According to the *Perth Gazette*, Yagan's 'conversation' with the King Ya-nup included 'a seeming adoption of his visitors into his own tribe by exchange of names, a description of his late imprisonment and escape [from Carnac Island], and the nature of their connection with their white associates'.[35] This last point: 'the nature of their connection', is worth further thought. The King Ya-nup connection with the newcomers was seen as an important alliance for Gyallipert and Manyat, who had come on a very public embassy under the auspices of helping their 'white associates'.

The newspaper's analysis of the meeting was filled with presumptions about native behaviour: a simple exchange of names would not have translated as a welcome into the 'tribe'. The paper reported a successful interaction with a positive outcome for the colonists – the King Ya-nup men had told Yagan how to behave and it is likely that Yagan's conversation was 'guessed' by the newcomers who were present. But for Yagan and his group and for Gyallipert and Manyat the expectations of this meeting might have been quite different from what the colonists had in mind.

Although this encounter with Yagan was held in similar circumstances to the meeting with Yellagonga, it had important differences. First, there were no women present. Yagan and his group made their appearance 'well armed' and this might have established the protocols for the meeting. As was apparent in Lockyer's first meeting with the King Ya-nup when Dineen was speared, the presence or absence of spears in a meeting with foreigners was a deliberate and overt action. It sent a signal to the outsiders. Unlike the meeting with Yellagonga, a corroboree was danced. This performance was often enacted as a formal protocol before the 'business' of a meeting was conducted.[36] And then an exchange of 'names and spears', demonstrating that Gyallipert and Manyat also had spears at this meeting (and I wonder if they brought them with them from King George's Sound, or exchanged parts of their English dress or rations for them in the town). Once the status and kin groups had been established, the exchange of spears took place; a sign heralding that this meeting was to be a friendly one. After heavily gestured 'conversations', in which they attempted to swap stories about their treatment by, and relationships with, the newcomers, they finally spoke a language that was mutually understood: in the form of a spear throwing competition. Perhaps a trial of skill, or was it more symbolic than a competition? Interestingly, Gyallipert played an important part in both meetings. With Yellagonga he received a kiss from an old woman and with Yagan, it was he rather than Manyat, who took part in throwing his spear.

While the colonists deemed these interviews a success because they had brought together two foreign groups of people to better their own situation, the Aboriginal groups had different experiences in these encounters: they were not passive pawns in the colonists' strategies but had their own agendas. They talked about the colonists – Gyallipert allegedly told Yagan how to 'behave' and Yagan talked about his imprisonment and radical escape – but there is no evidence to suggest that this meeting made the cross-cultural dynamics at Swan River any better. On the contrary, they got worse.

During Gyallipert and Manyat's stay at Swan River, John Henry Monger, who had been a mediator in the first meeting at the lake, reported that the Aborigines who were camped near his property had become so troublesome that he had applied for a military force to 'repel them'.[37] The number of Aborigines at the lake had 'greatly increased by', he thought, 'accessions from other tribes' and they were 'all larger and more powerful men than those we are accustomed to see', he informed the *Perth Gazette*. These increasingly large gatherings of Aboriginal men, during the time of Gyallipert and Manyat's embassy, and on the very spot where the strangers met, may have been a connected circumstance. The two different meetings – one with Yellagonga, the other with Yagan, both very different and both conducted on Yellagonga's country – and the swelling numbers of Aboriginal men at Monger's Lake convey something of the dynamics of the Aboriginal social world at Swan River at this time. These groups, whose words were rapidly changing, were probably in a power struggle and trying to gain politically in these meetings with strangers from the south (and the sea).

◆

A week after Gyallipert and Manyat met with Yagan, on Thursday 7 February, they were guided to the Bush Inn by the Sergeant Major. The Bush Inn was the first licensed public house in the colony of Western Australia, also known as the 'Half-way house' as it sat on the Perth to Fremantle road, conveniently halfway between the two townships. And it was here that they were to have a second meeting with, as the *Perth Gazette* put it, 'the tribes of this place', probably Yellagonga as it was *Mooro* country. The Inn was owned by John Butler who lived with his wife and three children on lot 86, a property which stretched from Butler's Hump at Freshwater Bay on Swan River to the coast. Butler's Bush Inn was a stone building, some reports say of two storeys, 'rigged out with native mahogony'.[38] It was a busy public house, as they could be in isolated settlements, and Butler must have been considered by the colonial authorities to be providing a good service for the community as he was exempted from paying his license duty on two occasions.[39] The Inn was in an ideal location for the thirsty pilgrims travelling between Perth and Fremantle, and as it was near the river it was also a popular spot for passing bargies.[40]

Despite the loyalty from travellers with a strong taste for grog, the Bush Inn was an isolated place in 1833. It was also a site heavy with significance for the Aborigines who knew the area around the Inn as *Beegeerup*.[41] In 1697, it was recorded as being an area in which the Aborigines had a camp. The Dutch explorer Willem de Vlamingh came across one of these campsites near Freshwater Bay which he compared to the 'Hottentots at the Cape of Good Hope'.[42] There was a fresh stream of water which trickled from the high ridges down into the bay and there were wide sand flats across the river near this point. It was the place where the Aborigines crossed the river from north to south, similar to the 'knee-deep' crossing near Yellagonga's old camp site in Perth. This place, where the rough rocks jutted and hung high over the river, was also a lookout point where one could watch, with a commanding eye, the approach of a visitor. It was here that de Vlamingh also spotted a tree with notches cut into its trunk, for those who wanted a superior view.[43] The Aborigines danced their corroborees there; it was a place where meetings were held and large groups gathered together. It became a place where meetings between the migrants and Aborigines took place in the first few years of the Swan River settlement. And it was the setting for the meeting of Gyallipert and Manyat with the *Mooro*, another cross-cultural encounter.

The *Mooro* had a good relationship with John Butler: they had even helped him build the Bush Inn. As Lyon wrote in a letter to the *Perth Gazette*, 'The whole of the timber, if I am correctly informed, for the Bush Inn, was carried to the site by them [Aborigines]. They carried in one day 8000 feet [of timber].'[44] Large numbers of the *Mooro* were often seen in and around the Bush Inn, and Butler has been described as a migrant who showed conciliation and moderation with the Aborigines that he came to know. He often requested (and was often refused) rations from the colonial authorities to offer the Aborigines when his personal stores were low.[45]

Unfortunately, no details exist of the actual meeting held at the Bush Inn between Yellagonga and the King Ya-nup. The *Perth Gazette* did report that the two groups promised to meet again the following morning, but they 'did not appear'. Despite the lack of records of the meeting, a lot of information about the transforming Swan River Aboriginal social world is suggested by the fact of its having occurred and the place where they met. The Swan River Aboriginal groups were organising diplomatic meetings on their own terms, using the colonists as negotiators, or intermediaries – the King Ya-nup were using them as guides too – and they were holding these meetings in specific places which held ongoing significance to them. The Bush Inn was one such site for the *Mooro*, a place where they were meeting quite regularly with Butler and his thirsty travellers. It is a place where first contacts occurred between white and black, and now a similar encounter was taking place, but this time between two foreign Aboriginal groups. Yellagonga's first encounter with Gyallipert and Manyat was at Monger's Lake, a site of high importance. Now that he knew them better and knew their intentions, perhaps, it was safe and diplomatic to meet them again, this time at the Bush Inn, showing that they too aligned with powerful white friends.

Another important issue here worthy of consideration is why, at two of these meetings, a promise was made by the hosts to meet with the visitors again the next day, and each time the promise was unfulfilled. How would Yagan and Yellagonga have viewed Gyallipert and Manyat? Two strangers who arrived at Swan River in a colonists' vessel? Ships were significant to the Swan River Aborigines too. In 1837 James Backhouse noted that Aboriginal groups gathered about Fremantle and Perth particularly when ships were in port because the town was bustling with what the Aborigines called *kibra men*, which Backhouse translated as: 'the people coming and going in ships.'[46] They would later express a desire to travel with the colonists in their vessels when the *kibra walks*, or the ship sails.[47]

◆

Gyallipert and Manyat stayed at the Swan River for a month. They were somewhat celebrated during their visit, impressing the colonists and curious migrants with their so-called 'civilised', yet 'native' ways. Irwin, who admired the character of these men, authorised Collie to give them each a blanket, trousers, shirt and jacket from the stores of the colonial hospital. The storekeeper also issued them flour, salt meat, tea and sugar.[48] It appeared they enjoyed this newly found fame from both Swan River Aborigines and colonists. Irwin wrote that these two King Ya-nup men had 'some knowledge of our language and manners and … exhibited a docile and very friendly disposition.'[49] They met many of the migrants at Swan River, staying with different people as house guests and 'prancing' along the town streets, putting on spectacular performances. They made a great impression on the migrants and colonists who categorised them differently to the Swan River 'natives.' The *Perth Gazette* wrote: 'The attention which is shown them, and the general interest they excite from their good behaviour, has instilled into them a degree of pride, which is frequently most ludicrously displayed.'[50] A lovely image of Manyat unblushingly flaunting himself for the onlookers is conveyed in the *Perth Gazette*: 'The stately air of Manyat, as he parades the streets with his feather-tufted stick, and feathered cap, approaching closely to some of our most dignified and polished actions, acquired by art, has led us to reflect how unjustly we estimate the savage, by our own acquirements.'[51] Manyat must have engaged in some serious bartering to acquire the feathered cap and stick. Ornaments like feathers were worn proudly by men of high degree at King George's Sound. Perhaps Manyat thought he was now worthy. The presence and performances of these men changed the opinion of 'natives' more generally at Swan River.

During part of their stay, Gyallipert and Manyat stayed with John Morgan. Morgan was a controversial character in the colony. He arrived with the first migrants on the *Parmelia* in 1829 with his family to take up the position as Colonial Storekeeper, first on Garden Island and then on the mainland. He was then made Justice of the Peace and Government Resident of Perth. In 1834 he left the Swan River to go to Van Diemen's Land. There, he interviewed William Buckley the escaped crown prisoner who spent thirty-two years living 'wild' with the Aborigines of Port Phillip. Morgan transcribed and significantly edited Buckley's story which was published in 1852 as *The Life and Adventures of William Buckley*. Morgan clearly had an interest in things 'native' as he also provided another valuable record.

At the Swan River on 28 January, Gyallipert was spending time with Morgan at his house. Morgan was busy writing a letter to Colonial Secretary

Hay in London, and Gyallipert was given paper and Morgan's quill and ink to keep himself busy. In his letter to Hay, Morgan described daily life in the colony, the recent exploration he had been involved in and the dismal situation between Aborigines and migrants at Swan River. He also mentioned that Gyallipert was with him at the table. Gyallipert 'has been with me the greater part of the time I have been writing this Letter', he wrote, 'and after amusing himself with a pen, at my table, which he now holds tolerably well, – he has just now drawn for me, a sketch of a Native encampment'. Luckily Morgan saw the value in this remarkable sketch. He wrote that it was 'the first sketch certainly drawn by any Aborigine of this Country'.[52] Morgan slipped it into the back of the letter he was writing to the Colonial Secretary and it is now deposited, in a fragile state, in the Public Records Office in Kew, London. It has been little used as a historical source, perhaps due to its distant location. It is the oldest surviving Aboriginal plan or 'mud map' drawn on paper.[53] (see image 16)

Morgan was clearly impressed with Gyallipert's learning to draw, although he had most probably been inscribing pictures, stories and maps in the sand with a stick for many years. It was the first time he had picked up a quill and dipped the nib in a pot of ink; this is evident by his scratchy first-timer sketch. The newcomers often commented that the Aborigines of this area had no art. Perhaps they did but it was not preserved and displayed in a fashion that the newcomers recognised as art. Morgan was also impressed with Gyallipert and Manyat's 'behaviour' in general: 'I am certain,' he wrote, 'that both Manyat and Galyput, would very soon learn to write our language, and to understand it sufficiently for promoting a friendly intercourse with the tribes in this neighbourhood.' Their civilised ways had a purpose for the colonials.

Gyallipert and Manyat were not just visiting the Swan River to meet with the Aborigines. They were moving cross-culturally in other ways too: ways that were becoming less cross-cultural and more conventional. Morgan explained:

> They have both been, to divine Service, this being Sunday, and behaved far better than several of the 'Civilized' part of the Congregation. They have dined and breakfasted at my table twice, are decently cloth'd, and are exceedingly well behaved Men'. Morgan was hopeful that they would be impressed by the colonists too. He wrote: 'I <u>hope</u> from <u>all</u> that has pass'd, that this impression will be mutual, – but from the drinking habits of the lower class of the people here, I fear this can hardly be expected.[54]

George Fletcher Moore, Justice of the Peace and later Advocate General of Swan River, was also impressed by the King Ya-nup men. He was introduced to them by Irwin: 'They were both dressed in shirt, trowsers and cap, good humoured, quiet fellows. They intimated that they were coming to pay white men at "Wan River" a visit.'[55] On 10 February it was Moore's turn as *guide*. He took Gyallipert and Manyat to visit the house of the Civil Commissioner George Leake for tea. Leake's wife, who had just arrived in the colony, played the piano for them. Moore painted the scene in his Diary:

> The two natives of King George's Sound...were greatly delighted with the music; they danced the kangaroo dance, and did everything in their power to show that they were pleased and grateful – 'tank you mem, very pretty'. Their dance appeared to be in imitation of the chase of the kangaroo, the motions of the animal, and the panting and gestures of the person in chase. This dance was divided into different scenes or parts... Afterwards they seated themselves in arm-chairs, with the greatest self-complacency, and drank tea.[56]

Dancing on country with Aboriginal groups and colonists made this diplomatic mission a significant one for the King Ya-nup. Moore's account suggests that Manyat and Gyallipert probably felt confident in these surrounds. They often sat in the British huts in the settlement at King George's Sound and were served tea and biscuit by the commandant. It was a ritual that they knew, understood and enjoyed.

Moore also described Gyallipert and Manyat's visit to Swan River as of 'great service'. Many Aborigines subsequently came into Perth and Fremantle and 'intimated their desire to live on friendly terms' with the migrants and to refrain from spearing them or their cattle.[57] But if such a restraint was in any way intentional or a consequence of the visit, it was also brief. Between April and July 1833 conflict between the *Beeloo* and *Mooro* and the migrants increased. Midgegooroo was executed by a firing squad for his group's involvement in the death of two migrants in April 1833 and Yagan's status as outlaw was re-instated following the retribution caused by his father's death. He was shot by two young boys who claimed the £30 bounty for his head.[58]

◆

On 15 February Gyallipert and Manyat boarded the schooner *Ellen* bound for home after a busy month of journeying. Around ninety Aboriginal people from around the region came and camped for two days before Gyallipert and Manyat left under the pretences, according to the *Perth Gazette*, of bidding them farewell, but they were also there to receive bread.[59] On board the *Ellen*, the King Ya-nup were accompanied by Moore, Irwin and Dale, all keen to investigate the progress of the settlements at Augusta and King George's Sound. Due to a strong head wind they had to camp one night at Garden Island and another night at Carnac Island, where Gyallipert and Manyat caught a fish dinner for all the passengers with the spears they had exchanged during their meeting with Yagan.[60] One wonders how they felt about visiting Carnac Island, soon after hearing Yagan's story of his recent imprisonment there.

On the morning of 21 February, they disembarked at the settlement on the shore of Princess Royal Harbour. Moore explained that the travellers were welcomed by the 'clamouring "allalo" (how d'ye do) of a dozen natives, who expressed the greatest joy at seeing their friends Manyat and Gyallipert again'.[61] An anonymous source (probably Dale) who published his account of the excursion in the *Perth Gazette*, wrote that the return of Manyat and Gyallipert 'was very seasonable as the tribe began to shew symptoms of uneasiness at their protracted stay, and inclined to impute a want of faith to the white people on that account'.[62] They had made a deal and the newcomers had to stick to their side of the bargain. Irwin wrote that their return home was 'hailed by their Tribe with great satisfaction, and increased confidence in our good faith and friendship'.[63] They were 'received with every sign of attachment, and several of the neighbouring tribes came in to welcome them; and held their corrobaries every night, in honor of the presence of the Governor, before whom they seemed proud to display every variety of their singular mode of dancing'.[64] This was an epic journey and they were welcomed back accordingly.

Filled with the excitement, knowledge and newly found status from their journey to the strange new world of Swan River, Gyallipert and Manyat informed the other King Ya-nup about their voyage. They had tradeable knowledge of distant country and had met and exchanged with several foreign groups, black and white. They had also gained respect and praise from the colonists and migrants, something that was evidently highly regarded.

Moore, Dale and Irwin explored Oyster Harbour, King and French's rivers while at the Sound, guided by Eye-nan, a King Ya-nup man.[65] After two weeks of exploration, preparations were underway for the *Ellen's* voyage back to Swan River. Moore wrote that a large group of King Ya-nup were 'drawn up in line' in the settlement to be chosen to visit the Swan River. Morley, the storekeeper, addressed the congregation in King Ya-nup pidgin, a language he had learnt quickly, which may have sounded humorous to Moore and Dale who were trying their hardest to look 'most ludicrously grave'.[66] Morley:

> Now now twonk, Gubbernor wonka me wonka black fellow, black fellow pear white man white man poot. Black fellow queeple no good. Black fellow pear black fellow no good. Black fellow plenty shake hand black fellow, no black fellow no queeple, black fellow give him white man wallabies, wood come here, water come here, white man plenty shake hand black man, plenty give it him bikket, plenty ehtah, plenty blanket, arrack, tomahawk. Now now Gubbernor wonka me give it him one guy black fellow one guy knaif.

This translated to:

> Now attend, the Governor desires me to tell the black man if the black man spear the white man the white men will shoot them. If a black man steal it is not good. If the black man be friendly with the black man, if the black man do not steal, if the black man give the white man wallabies, bring wood, and bring water, white man will befriend the black man, and give him plenty of biscuits, plenty to eat, and give him blankets, rice, tomahawk. Now the Governor desires me to give each black man one knife.[67]

While the pidgin language was useful, Moore found it humorous, writing: 'There's a speech. Ha. Ha. Ha. Help me to laugh.'[68] Morley's verbal statement resembles Governor Arthur's proclamation in pictures that was hung on trees around Van Diemen's Land in the 1830s. And it sounds very similar to the sentence that Gyallipert relayed to Moore regarding his exchange with Yagan. Each Aboriginal man present was given a knife, suspended by a 'riband around his neck'. And presents of tomahawks and blankets were given to the most 'deserving' Aborigines.[69] The inclusion of one of the above requests is telling: *if the black man be friendly with the black man*: a warning to stop the violence between themselves too.

According to the anonymous source, every unmarried Aboriginal man volunteered 'without exception' to travel to Swan River, and the six most 'intelligent and docile' were selected.[70] It is a telling sign that the single men were the ones keen for the adventure to Swan River. They were at a stage in their lives when they were not burdened with heavy family obligations and could afford the time to travel, but also, importantly, adding a voyage to Swan River to their repertoire with the geographic knowledge it offered, must have been a desirous attribute, helpful when trying to find a wife. There was some sort of competition between the King Ya-nup men to see who would be allowed to travel and Moore explained that 'we brought six natives, at their urgent request …' showing that the King Ya-nup were active in their choices to travel.[71] As they departed for Swan River, the relatives of the six chosen men bid them farewell, and were yet again anxious about their safety.[72]

Gyallipert and Manyat, obvious favourites already with Moore and the Governor, were chosen to travel again. They were joined by four others, Tatan – Dr Uredale's son and nephew of Coolbun; Moopey/Mopey; Wayton Walter who took over Nakinah's title of 'King' of the King George tribe following Nakinah's death so most likely Waiter, Mokaré and Nakinah's other brother; and Ionen/Eye-nan/Ayennan who had been the guide for the Governor and his entourage a few days earlier.[73] These six Aboriginal men were on 'a clear understanding', Irwin wrote, that they would not return to King George's Sound 'before a lapse of twelve months'.[74]

One year might seem a long time away from country and family for these young, single men. However, Barker recorded in his diary that youths (*no beard*) would leave their family and travel to a far away group, sometimes living in this foreign country for up to a year. By the time they had completed this initiation into manhood they had built up a social network of friends and gained extensive geographic knowledge.[75] So this long absence was part of a traditional initiation which youths in this region were expected to undertake.

The return voyage got underway with the new eager travellers on board. On the way to Swan River, the schooner *Ellen* stopped at the Vasse near the small settlement of Augusta, and Moore, Dale and Stirling superficially explored the country. The following morning the party was preparing to leave Augusta, when Moore realised that Gyallipert was missing. 'On searching for him I suddenly found myself among a large body of natives on the beach. Seeing me hesitate they called out "abba" (their friendly salutation). I immediately joined them and found our runaway among them.' Gyallipert had spent the night with this group of Augusta Aborigines and 'declared his intention of remaining some time to visit them, and then walking by land to K.G.S.'[76] Moore accepted Gyallipert's abandonment of the Swan River voyagers and felt that he would be safe on his return to King George's Sound as the group of Aborigines that he had met were 'numerous, well armed and able, though good looking-men'. Perhaps their strength and numbers convinced Moore not to argue with Gyallipert. He reflected that if Gyallipert was to reach King George's Sound in safety, it would benefit the colony as Gyallipert might open a 'friendly intercourse' between the colonists and the 'natives of this district'.[77] Luckily, Mopey had accompanied Moore in his search for Gyallipret and he was able to inform the remaining travellers Gyallipert's intentions. Dale also thought that Gyallipret's travel on foot would be advantageous to the colonists, if he reached King George's Sound safely: 'it may serve to spread more effectually among them, the knowledge both of our power and good will towards them'.[78] Thinking all the time about how such cross-cultural meetings could benefit them, the colonists did not pause to consider this voyage from Gyallipert's perspective and what he might have gained from it.

Gyallipert's father was Maragnan who was mentioned in the previous episode as Barker's informant about the escaped crown prisoners. Essentially, he listed to Barker a series of camp sites close to the coast between Albany and Augusta (and possibly further north). Barker called these places – near rivers, harbours and inlets – 'sleeping sites'. Maragnan had travelled to Augusta previously, perhaps many times and as Maragnan's son making the same journey, Gyallipert was possibly extending his kin networks, geographic knowledge or meeting up with relatives. One wonders how the Vasse region people would have received Gyallipert and how his status would have altered arriving in their country from the sea and in the company of powerful white strangers. While constantly pushing the powerful newcomers to the margins of their world, King Ya-nup like Gyallipert were using their presence to create a 'friendly' alliance and exploit it in ways that would advantage them; he was gaining prestige and power which seemingly enabled him to step easily into both worlds.

Gyallipert's independent decision to stay with the Aboriginal people at Augusta shows that for some King Ya-nup the newcomers remained on the fringes of their world for a long time. With Gyallipert left at Augusta to walk home, the other six King Ya-nup went on to Swan River where they were greeted warmly by the colonists. Irwin had this to say about their visit:

> … one of the [King George's sound men] chose to remain with the tribe there, the remainder since their arrival, have been stationed at Perth, where they have had almost daily intercourse with the Swan and Canning River Tribes, with

the most perceptibly beneficial results; so much so, that I have directed three of them to be clothed and rationed at the public expense, and attached them to the Superintendent of Native Tribes; and I attribute their intervention no inconsiderable share in the success which I am happy to say, has attended his daily intercourse with the Tribes of these districts … The conduct of all of them has been highly satisfactory, and encouraging, tho they had a difficulty in conveying their meaning to the tribe here, the dialect differing considerably, yet both parties are becoming more and more intelligible to each other by repeated intercourse, and I feel warranted in saying, that we can obtain, by means of the King George's Sound Natives, earlier and clearer information of the existing feelings and intended movements of the local tribes, than from the most friendly and familiar of the latter.[79]

♦

These meetings invert the typical 'colonial encounter' as the Aborigines can be seen to have used the newcomers as 'guides' on journeys to a place they had never visited previously. Alexander Collie and other colonials were acting as cultural intermediaries as they accompanied Gyallipert and Manyat to Monger's Lake and the Bush Inn. But they stood detached from the meetings; this was a position usually occupied by Aborigines in colonial encounters between whites and blacks, when language and cultural systems were barriers to communication.

Manyat and Gyallipert's movement and procurement of knowledge suggest an Indigenous use of colonial resources to improve their wealth in a knowledge economy. Whether the embassy of these two men to *Beeliar* country was to help the colonists in their race relations, or not, from these remarkable journeys across land, sea and culture, and from the details and descriptions of the cross-cultural meetings, there is evidence that the King Ya-nup men were gaining too. Rather than being the focus or purpose of the Aboriginal journeys, the colonists were being used strategically by these men. A colonial vessel took the Aboriginal men to a distant place, the newcomers were used as 'guides' and 'mediators' for the Aboriginal interactions, and they acted as hosts to Manyat and Gyallipert, the celebrated visitors. But the newcomers remained on the edges of the Aboriginal world as the meetings with Swan River groups and the advantages to be gained from such exchanges were evidently of the highest importance to the King Ya-nup.

Reflection: Amphibians: Voyaging Across the Fringe

In 1856 James Browne, who spent his boyhood among the Aborigines at Albany, reflected on his first sighting of a man of the group he called 'Kincinnup' as he sailed into Princess Royal Harbour:

> ...on a bright morning in the month of May...I obtained my first sight of the aborigines of the southern continent. The first impression produced by a sight of the grinning native in the bow of the harbour master's boat – black as coal, but with a pair of keen sparkling eyes...Such was Wan-e-war, the first of the aborigines of Australia it was my fortune to see...[1]

Manyat and Gyallipert's voyage was the start of several seafaring journeys that particular King Ya-nup engaged in. They travelled beyond the fringe of their world and became outsiders as they engaged cross-culturally at Swan River. This voyage signalled a shift in the symbolism of the *caibre*. Once a signifier of intense trading opportunities, the *caibre* began to represent experiences for those who wanted to voyage; it symbolised a transforming diplomatic mission and for others like Wannewar in Browne's story, a boat was also seen as a utility. These new opportunities included trade, not on board but onshore in the distant new world of Swan River. *Caibre* were used as vehicles for significantly extending kin networks and enhancing geographic knowledge and perspectives of country. Once these networks were established at Swan River, the voyaging continued and was extended.

These voyages and meetings at Swan River would not have occurred without the aid of the newcomers. They provided the means and impetus to travel such distances. And the reasons for voyaging were unexpected. Aboriginal desires to travel and the significance of it were constantly misunderstood by the colonists at Swan River and the garrison at King George's Sound. Aboriginal voyagers were represented only in terms of the British world, and the British could not see that there was an Aboriginal world, or with Gyallipert and Manyat's voyages, several Aboriginal worlds alongside the colonial one.

In May 1838, twelve King George's Sound men arrived at Swan River. They had travelled overland for more than 280 miles, walking for fourteen days. The *Perth Gazette* reported that it was the first visit that the colonists were aware of in which the Aborigines had travelled in such a large number beyond the borders of their country, unaccompanied by any newcomers.[2] The object of their epic journey, according to the colonists, was to pay their respects to Governor Stirling and the Swan River community and deliver letters from the newcomers at King George's Sound. However, their real desires for travelling soon became apparent: they had come to spear some of the Murray River Aborigines who had been involved in the 'disappearance' of one of their countrymen a year earlier.[3] Their countryman, recorded as William Knott, was employed as a servant of Patrick Taylor at King George's Sound. Knott accompanied Taylor on a voyage to Swan River in 1837. On the return voyage he was joined by two Murray River Aboriginal men. The weather forced the vessel to stop at Garden Island and the three Aboriginal men, who were all seasick, slept on shore for the night. In the morning, William Knott had 'disappeared' and it was suspected that he had been killed by the two other Murray River men. It was alleged that Knott was killed because he had travelled 'too far from his homeland'.[4] And so the twelve men from King George's Sound – a large number to carry a few messages – who arrived at Swan River in May 1838 had used the guise of carrying the colonists' letters to travel strategically to Swan River to enact a spearing against the Murray River group.

The arrival of these men at the Swan put the colonials in a moral dilemma – should they protect the Murray River men who were to be speared or the King George's Sound visitors whom they were hosting in the town? The presence of these visitors again added to the power plays within the Aboriginal social world at Swan River. The *Perth Gazette* reported that the Swan River groups were constantly inquiring: 'What for Governor give it em black fellow, King George's Sound man, flour; give it em Perth black fellow no?'[5] The *Perth Gazette* explained that the Swan River men receive ample rations for their labour within the colony and that they did not require the 'same attention which it is prudent to show to the strangers' from King George's Sound.[6] The death of Knott and the visit of revenging King Ya-nup caused the *Perth Gazette* to query about Aboriginal travel: 'These accidents may lead us to question the policy of removing the natives from their own districts, or of encouraging a communication between different tribes. It may be attended with present advantage but it appears liable to produce a prospective evil.'[7]

The voyaging of Gyallipert and Manyat joins other narratives of indigenous voyagers across Oceania, such as Tupaia and Omai/Mai who travelled or navigated with Captain James Cook. Tupaia, who helped Cook and his crew navigate through the South Seas, learned from the botanist Joseph Banks to paint with watercolours and he painted several ethnographic pictures during the voyage.[8] Manyat assisted Collie to navigate his way through country to the north of King George's Sound and Gyallipert picked up a new artistic skill during his voyage also, sketching for the first time with Morgan's quill and ink. Bong-ree/Bungaree and Bundell were two Aboriginal men from Port Jackson who travelled with Matthew Flinders and Phillip Parker King to help these explorers with their cross-cultural encounters on shore. However, as Bronwen Douglas has written, when Bong-ree travelled with Flinders to Moreton Bay during his circumnavigation of Australia, Bong-ree was the only crew member who participated in a cross-cultural, reciprocal encounter with the Moreton Bay Aboriginal people. This meeting in which Bong-ree was the main protagonist was, Douglas argues, a 'genuinely cross-cultural act which symbolised a reciprocal rather than a hierarchical relationship and belies the reified idea of the cross-cultural as a binary divide between opposed, homogenised cultures.'[9] In meetings such as these, indigenous voyagers were engaging with foreigners who spoke a different language and had a different repertoire from their own.

The newcomers brought with them a foreign material culture and an alien way of life which stimulated changes in the lifestyle of many of the King Ya-nup. Some of the changes were subtle and some King Ya-nup, like Mokaré, Manyat and Gyallipert, adapted these new materials and ways into their world with ease and advantage. What the newcomers and their material culture offered were new situations and opportunities. They did not stop the Aborigines from travelling across country for diplomatic meetings and visiting kin. In some instances the newcomers helped (unknowingly) to extend such visiting, increasing the mobility of some King Ya-nup not only in the method of travel – from foot to boat – but geographically and culturally too. 'Traditional' activities continued, but in new ways, with new people and new intentions. This amphibious transformation allowed particular King Ya-nup to voyage across the fringe: to travel beyond it literally and step outside it metaphorically, adapting some British rituals into their own daily life, and extending their networks and knowledge.

CULTURAL VOYAGES

9

Peter Pindar's Razors

When Phillip Parker King left King George's Sound after more than two weeks of lucrative exchanges for both his crew and the Aboriginal people in Oyster Harbour, he had collected 'one hundred spears, thirty throwing-sticks, forty hammers, one hundred and fifty knives and a few hand-clubs', costing his party one eighth of a biscuit for each piece.[1] As a collector, King's instinct was to describe, categorise and judge these items against others he had seen or collected from previous encounters. King noted that the throwing sticks he collected from Oyster Harbour 'were much more ingeniously formed than others' he had seen elsewhere, thereby adding them into his taxonomy of Aboriginal material culture. He spent several pages in his narrative detailing and sketching these Aboriginal tools. He was impressed with the portability of them, including a spear sharpener which was fixed in a knob at the handle and made out of *Xanthorrhoea* gum. It was a 'small sharp-edged shell, or piece of quartz' and was used to scrape the points of the spears while hunting on the move.[2] The spears were very slender, he thought. They varied in length from nine to ten feet long, and all of them were barbed 'with a piece of hard wood, fastened on by a ligature of bark gummed over'. The spears had a hole at one end so that they could be attached to the hooked point of the *meara*. The slender spears were cradled in the spear thrower and launched with remarkable speed and accuracy.[3] King witnessed the skill with which these spears were handled when a seal that had beached itself in the shallows of Oyster Harbour was struck with one in the neck.

King knew that the spears, hammers and throwing sticks that he received from the Aborigines at Oyster Harbour were not perfect artefacts. They were, he thought, 'like Peter Pindar's razors' and only made for sale. Peter Pindar was an eighteenth-century English satirist who wrote allegorical poetry. King was referring to the famous Pindar poem about a man named Hodge who was sold a pack of razors very cheaply, thinking that he had bought them for a bargain price. However, these razors did not cut his beard and when he tried to return them to the vendor, so the poem goes: with a 'voice not much unlike an Indian yell; 'What were they made for then, you dog?' he cries – 'Made!' quoth the Fellow with a smile, – 'to sell.'[4] Pindar's poem was a comment on the temperament of commercialism and bargain hunters in early nineteenth-century England.

Allan Cunningham, King's botanist on the 1821 voyage, also saw the artefacts as more of an Aboriginal tourist trade than a fair exchange. In the first few days of their encounter with King's crew the Aborigines had sold their 'entire stock of [ready] weapons' and had to manufacture more to 'secure themselves of continued meals of bread', Cunningham wrote. Rather than Pindar's razors, Cunningham called up his anti-semitic sentiments as he likened these imperfect weapons to 'Jew's Hatchets'. Some of the weapons were so 'hastily finish'd off and so badly were the handles cemented with Gum [of the] Xanthorrhoea' that they were made 'simply for sale', he thought.[5] King seemed to enjoy the joke of this tourist trade, laughing with Jack about his crew getting the bad end of the deal. King was not aware of the second joke, however, that the King Ya-nup were manufacturing their hunting and fishing style of spear to trade with him and not the highly valuable spears which they used in warfare. King did not realise that these Aborigines had more than one spear and King only understood one metaphor for Aboriginal spears; the King Ya-nup had several. The hunting and fishing spears held less value for the King Ya-nup because they were an easier and quicker tool to construct and suitable for quick trade, when opportunities arose. These spears – hunting, fishing and trading spears – were called *maungull*.[6] The war spears, or *keit*, demanded longer labour and were a highly valuable weapon to the King Ya-nup – not something to be traded. *Keit* were significantly longer and heavier and were rotated over the fire until they were hard and straight. At the weapon's point the King Ya-nup stuck pieces of sharp stones into the warm and sticky *Xanthorrhoea* gum, fixing them in place. These stones formed a six inch line up the shaft from the point. Nind thought they resembled 'the teeth of a saw'.[7] *Keit* were designed to inflict damage; the sharp stones splintering and shattering inside the body on impact. These spears took three or four days to make and Barker recorded that the King Ya-nup had different names for 'each particular part of the operation.'[8] *Keit* were not traded with King. Their trading spears were indeed like Peter Pindar's razors; they were manufactured to sell. The Aborigines enjoyed the joke as well.

In early October 1830, a large group of King Ya-nup were visiting the settlement. They spent all day manufacturing *meara* and knives for Dr Davis in exchange for biscuit. These trading goods had gone up in value since King's visit in 1821; King had only given the Aborigines one-eighth of a biscuit for each piece. Davis offered 2lb of biscuit for each *meara*: a decent amount considering the prisoners received 7lb of biscuit in their weekly ration, and these Aborigines were trading *meara* and knives all day long. It was not just the value which had changed in these exchanges, but also the construction. Barker noticed the subtle changes in the way these articles were manufactured. He wrote that 'Their knives [were] formerly made by fixing with the grass tree resin, sharp pieces of quartz on a piece of stick about a foot long. They now substitute for the quartz pieces of broken glass bottles, broken or sharpened so ingeniously that they can shave themselves with them.'[9] Glass spearheads were a common technological change in Aboriginal communities across the country where intercultural contact occurred. This small change in the way the King Ya-nup manufactured their knives is revealing of the subtle form in which their world was transforming. And with an increase in the value of their knives and *meara*, these changes were most likely to have been viewed positively within the community.

In the first few months of the settlement party's arrival in 1826, the King Ya-nup sought out encounters with the newcomers, particularly when they wanted to barter. They knew from previous meetings which items these people gave status to. They knew the value of their hunting and fishing spears to the foreigners. On 17 March 1827, along the beach to the west, fifty or sixty Aborigines were seen by Lockyer spearing fish; the group included women and children. The prisoners were in the adjacent woods cutting down trees and the Aborigines went into the woods to approach some of the prisoners whom they 'offered' their spears to.[10] Lockyer tried to clarify in his journal that this present of spears was in 'token that they were only fishing and did not intend to molest any person', reading it as an Aboriginal act of reassurance. But a similar encounter a few days earlier points to what was going on. Several of the King Ya-nup had come into the camp bringing, Lockyer wrote, 'spears as presents to different individuals'.[11] They spent time, he thought, looking about for the person for whom they were intended.[12] Rather than an act of reassurance or a friendly gift, images of King's daily barter in 1821 come to mind. Gifts were rarely given without an expectation of reciprocation. Lockyer misread this Aboriginal initiative and no consistent program of material exchange was recorded under his command.

In December 1830 Barker documented another subtle transformation within the King Ya-nup world: a change in King Ya-nup knowledge of what items could be traded with the newcomers. During Nind's time at the settlement (between December 1826 and early 1829), Nind had told Mokaré that he was interested in the beautiful parrots he had seen around the garrison. They were a rare species he thought, different from the ones he had seen at Port Jackson.[13] Mokaré brought one to him, which he kept in his hut. By December 1830 a seasonal trade had been established every *Mandianary* (November–December), when the *towan*, or parrots, were nesting near the settlement at *Woollyongup*. It seems that the idea to trade these birds started slowly. Barker was teaching Mokaré to skin some birds that Barker had collected for whom he called 'the Colonel' in Sydney.[14] Commissariat officer John Kent gave Mokaré a lesson in skinning birds, but Mokaré had a short attention span for this activity.[15] Then, in late November, Mokaré asked Barker for 'permission' to bring him two *towan*, saying jokingly that Barker was to give them to the Governor when he went to Sydney.[16] A few days later Mokaré went with Talwyn and Davis to search for *towan*. They went west beyond the lagoon at *Kiangadarup* where Mokaré climbed trees with the help of his tomahawk; he cut foot holes in the trunk as he ascended. They returned tired and empty handèd, having found no birds that had hatched. He knew there would be plenty of birds at King's River and some to the west in about a month.[17] And by early December Tringoli, Talwyn and Wannewar were all aware of the new currency. Soldiers and prisoners had seen these brightly coloured birds brought in by Mokaré and given him requests for them. With Mokaré, Talwyn, Wannewar and Tringole went as far as Mt Many Peaks to collect *towan* for trade in the settlement.[18]

This new item of trade created some issues within the King Ya-nup world which show how trade with the newcomers had become one of the most important engagements for some individuals. On 6 December 1830, Dr Uredale, the highly esteemed *mulgarradock* died and was buried at Duck Pond Hill, near *Tondirrup* to the west across the harbour. He had been ill for a long time with influenza. His brother Coolbun and many others had to leave

King George's Sound for a month or two to 'go bush' as part of their grievance rituals. But Dr Uredale's death coincided with the *towan* season. Several of the soldiers and prisoners had already put their orders in for *towan* and the King Ya-nup did not want to miss a trading opportunity so they deferred going bush to grieve for Dr Uredale until they had traded a sufficient number of *towan*. Mokaré went to *Woollyongup* the next day where there were known to be *towan* nests, but returned very angry because the young birds had already been eaten by Tipatroit's party, he thought. Barker wrote that the young birds were previously always eaten by the King Ya-nup, 'formerly being considered a great delicacy, till the white people came and set such a value on them, for keeping.'[19] A few days later this anger over the *towan* being eaten had turned into a conflict and a spearing occurred as a result on 12 December.[20]

In April 1832, Gyallipert was 'punished' by Alexander Collie who confiscated his kangaroo skin cloak for 'having wantonly killed two private parakeets.' Gyallipert 'strenuously denied' this act until Collie confronted him with the 'wing of one of them.'[21] The *towan* were brought in alive for the newcomers to keep as pets, but some King Ya-nup, like Gyallipert, continued to regard them as good for eating. The creation of the *towan* trade is revealing of how the Aborigines' daily narrative was both transforming and resisting. The King Ya-nup deferred the grieving process of their esteemed *mulgarradock* and it caused a conflict between those who wanted to trade the birds and those who continued to eat them.

◆

In 1832, James Purkis, Postmaster General at Swan River, wrote that Nakinah 'the chief' at King George's Sound 'wears an old naval uniform of the rank of Captain, with a cocked hat and gold epaulettes.' He was, Purkis thought, 'a very intelligent fellow, and well disposed towards the settlers; he dines mostly with the Officer in command, eats with a knife and fork and drinks "king of Ingle and much life" as his standing toast.'[22] The King Ya-nup use of British material culture was often misunderstood by the newcomers who did not see the Aboriginal motivations for some of its utility. Purkis perceived Nakinah as a successfully civilised Aboriginal man, who had taken up British cultural items and rituals, thereby largely divorcing himself from his own cultural language. However, Purkis and other newcomers did not necessarily understand that the adoption of British cultural items, such as clothes and blankets, did not mean the adoption of the cultural metaphors that went together with those items. Similarly, historian Ferguson collapsed the depth of the King Ya-nup culture when he wrote of Mokaré in the following terms: 'He eventually discarded his kangaroo skins for European clothes and became an excellent shot with a rifle.'[23]

It was not just Aboriginal material culture that was hastily manufactured for trade. In encounters with Aborigines, Europeans became expert improvisers, redefining their cultural items as 'native gifts'. Discarded buttons, ball bearings, mirrors, handkerchiefs and beads were transformed into what the Europeans thought the Aboriginal receivers considered 'objects of desire'. The Aborigines at King George's Sound received many gifts from European visitors from the end of the eighteenth century. Jack was clothed by King and christened by the crew in an attempt to mask his 'native' identity. Many discarded European items which were given as gifts, were in turn discarded by the Aborigines who received them. Baudin's midshipman, Ransonnet, who visited in 1803, was surprised that his gifts to the Aborigines near Mt Gardner were returned to him and other crew members and, when the gifts were given to the Aborigines again, Ransonnet later found them rejected and left on the rocks.[24] The French artist travelling with d'Urville, de Sainson, sketched a picture of a group of Aboriginal men in high glee as they received gifts from d'Urville's crew in October 1826. The sealers whom Lockyer met had visited King George's Sound at the same time as d'Urville and recounted to Lockyer their discovery of a 'Pocket Compass and a knife' that had been given to the Aborigines by d'Urville. These items were seen hanging from the trees near the sealers' camps.[25] Gifts were transported across cultures but their utility often transformed in the process.

Some King Ya-nup exchanged spears, *meara* and *towan* for British clothing, either in the settlement or when *caibre* were visiting. Mokaré wore a shirt and trousers. He was also given a seal pup skin jacket and cap that Sleeman had the prisoners make for him in 1829.[26] In his 1834 report Collie reflected that Mokaré always wore a kangaroo skin cap.[27] And Barker described how Mokaré laughed at the thought that his worn out trousers would make good paper.[28] Other King Ya-nup were also clothed in English dress: recall Nakinah's bargaining powers and his receipt of the naval jacket for his help in guiding the Governor on an expedition in 1832. These English materials did not simply replace the Aboriginal ones but were used in a particular and revealing way. Several newcomers commented on the temporary use of the English dress by the King Ya-nup and the alternative ways in which some items were refashioned. Just as painting their bodies was done for particular ceremonial reasons, the King Ya-nup English dress was only donned at particular times.

When the King Ya-nup went bush they left their new clothes with the newcomers in the settlement, or gave them to a King Ya-nup who was to remain in the settlement. When one of Nakinah's brothers died in 1831, Nakinah went bush for about a month. Dr Uredale's son, Talwyn, returned to the settlement before Nakinah, bringing with him Nakinah's English dress to give to Collie for safekeeping. Nakinah had appropriated 'half a blanket' which Collie had given to Talwyn before he went bush. When he returned to the settlement a few weeks later he was still wearing the half-blanket. He examined the English clothes which he had left at the settlement, but, Collie wrote, 'they had been little cared for and sent up an agreeable effluvia to his nostrils…'[29] Collie ordered them to be washed while Nakinah 'retired to his native quarters close to the Settlement, saying that he would get washed and shaved before he changed his dresses.'[30] This vignette shows that Nakinah only wore his English dress in the company of the English; when he went bush, his dress stayed behind, while he wore a blanket in the way he would have worn his kangaroo skin cloak. When he returned and slipped once again into his English dress, it was done with formalities. He wanted to wash and shave first, just as the newcomers did.

The ways in which certain individuals used and rejected the new articles of clothing and items of trade reveals that the Aboriginal metaphors continued to hold sway on the fringe. When Manyat and Gyallipert travelled to Swan River they paraded through the streets of the townships dressed in formal English clothes, Manyat with a feather tufted stick and cap. But when they met Yagan and Yellagonga they donned their kangaroo skin cloaks; Yagan and Yellagonga wore them too. These English clothes did not take over but were used in a ceremonial manner: worn only in the presence of their powerful new acquaintances.

Some individuals wore a shirt and trousers more often than others because they spent more time in the settlement or were often in the presence of the newcomers. But when these clothes inhibited them, they were quickly shed. Wilson and Collie both wrote about King Ya-nup stripping off their cloaks or clothes when hunting so that they would not be inhibited by them. Mokaré, 'irritated by repeated disappointments' when hunting with Wilson, 'stripped himself naked' to make himself more steady in the chase of the kangaroo.[31] Recall the story that Barker recorded of Little Wapere being in fear of the approach of Wills people in 1830. He thought he saw some Wills men near the sawyers' place over the harbour and was terrified; he pulled his trousers off so that he could run faster back to the settlement. In the transfer from British hand to Aboriginal, the English metaphor and social behaviour that those trousers represented were lost. Materials were quickly taken up, cultural contexts were not.

Most of the materials that the King Ya-nup were given by the English were used in a different way from that intended. Blankets were worn fastened at the shoulder in the same manner in which the King Ya-nup kangaroo skin cloaks were.[32] (See image 24) Other clothing included King Ya-nup materials but the construction and designs were English. Mokaré's kangaroo skin cap is one example of this. A cap was not a traditional Aboriginal item, but the kangaroo skin was. There was improvisation by both the Aborigines and the newcomers.

With the *towan* trade the newcomers were including an aspect of the King Ya-nup culture into theirs, but rather than eating the birds they kept them as pets. The use of English clothing and other materials by the King Ya-nup shows how some individuals were appropriating aspects of the British world into their own. The intended meanings that these new items held were transformed in the exchange and a new cultural context was created for them. These incidents might not seem remarkable. But it is the purpose of this history to discover both the resilience and creativity of cultures in contact. Microhistories such as these give an accurate idea to the pace of the changes and of the individuals resisting the changes occurring in the Aboriginal world at this time.

10

A Delicate Friendship

It was a cold August day in 1831 when Mokaré died. He had left the settlement a month before and 'gone bush' without the permission of Alexander Collie and against Collie's strict 'injunctions' not to 'expose himself' too much to the natural elements; but he left the settlement anyway. Collie thought that it was unusual and out of character for Mokaré to just leave. He quickly excused his friend's absence, however, as his 'predilection of the savage life'.[1] Mokaré returned to King George's Sound at the end of July a physically different man to when he left. Collie described him as 'much reduced in flesh and strength' and believed that he was 'labouring under…organic disease'.[2] In a letter to his brother George in early August, Collie wrote that 'a great many' King Ya-nup were very sick and some had come into the settlement 'in consequence'. He added that Mokaré 'had just returned from the bush…so ill that I doubt whether he will recover'.[3]

When Mokaré returned he went straight back to Collie's hut. It was, by 1831, Mokaré's hut too; it was where he had slept most often for several years. His house companions had changed – from Lt Sleeman, to Captain Barker and now Collie – but it was always the same hut. He curved his lean body around the shape of the fire in the living room and Collie kept a close watch on him. Nakinah came in to see his brother too and Collie gave them space to spend time together; he listened to their conversations from his bedroom.

On the morning of the 9 August, Collie heard Nakinah calling out his brother's name earnestly: 'Mokaré, Mokaré'. Mokaré was sitting with his back against the wall near the fire and Nakinah was leaning down, looking into his face. Collie interrupted their intimate moment as he feared that Mokaré was about to die. He watched Mokaré's eyes in what he described as a 'vacant roll of delirium'. In case Nakinah had not already realised it, Collie now warned him that Mokaré was dying; he told him to collect the other King Ya-nup to come and farewell their friend. The elder King Ya-nup men came and visited Mokaré, holding a sort of vigil all day inside the hut. They spoke to him 'affectionately', Collie thought.[4] Perhaps some of the newcomers also attended the vigil. Did they come to pay their respects to this well-known and much liked Aboriginal man? Collie did not say.

At about two o'clock in the afternoon, Mokaré turned his head slightly as if to acknowledge his gathered countrymen. His eyes then rolled back and his lids closed, 'to be forever veiled in darkness', Collie wrote dramatically. Nakinah, who had stayed by Mokaré's side all day, immediately started preparing his brother's body for burial: the face was touched gently and the head brought forward; the arms were bent downwards and the hands crossed and placed near the neck; the knees were bent and brought forward towards the chest and a blanket was tucked underneath the tightly cuddled body. As soon as these important procedures had taken place, Nakinah moved onto the next part of the process. He stood up and asked Collie for 'pear, pear (give me spears)' which the King Ya-nup were forbidden to bring into the settlement. There had been a ban on spears within the bounds of the settlement since Collie's arrival as Resident Magistrate in April 1831. There were still spears in the newcomers' huts that they had received when trading with the King Ya-nup, but these were deemed *collected artefacts* by their new owners, not weapons. They were, however, traded to and fro between the King Ya-nup and the newcomers, if the King Ya-nup were in times of need. Mokaré's death needed to be put to rights with a retaliatory spearing and when Collie said no to spears, Nakinah was able to get a spear easily from one of the other huts in the settlement. It was retrieved however, when the purpose for borrowing the spear had been whispered from hut to hut.

Collie asked Nakinah if he would prefer Mokaré's body to be laid out straight like the corpse of a newcomer, or would he prefer it to be prepared in the King Ya-nup custom? But all that Collie understood from Nakinah was that Mokaré would be buried the following day, and Nakinah left the settlement leaving his brother's body in Collie's care.

Collie knew that Mokaré's death was going to be an important moment at King George's Sound, within the settlement and in the Aboriginal world which surrounded it. Mokaré was thought of as an essential intermediary by the newcomers, an interlocutor or half-way man who managed to bridge some parts of the gap for the newcomers and the King Ya-nup in their negotiations with each other. Would he be easily replaced by another 'friendly' native?

While Collie was absent from the hut, something happened to Mokaré's body which could have put the relationship between the King Ya-nup and the newcomers in danger, or so Collie thought. Collie's house-help went into the living room and stretched Mokaré's body out into the 'full length in proper English position'.[5] The rigidity of the joints was destroyed in this act. When Collie returned and found the corpse stretched out with joints loose and mobile, he was shocked and worried that he might be 'seriously embroiled' with Nakinah and his countrymen when they found out. He quickly tried to reposition the body to its prior, seated position, meticulously going over Nakinah's preparations from the previous day. Collie feared also, that Nakinah might suspect Collie to have poisoned Mokaré, which was one cause for a corpse's joints and limbs to loosen thereby changing Nakinah's intention from spearing 'black fellow' to spearing 'white fellow'.[6] There were many delicate situations in the ongoing negotiations of living on the fringe but, for Collie, this was the most pressing danger yet. He managed, however, to avert any issues with Nakinah who did not notice, or did not show that he noticed the manhandling of Mokaré's body.

The burial took place the following morning, as Nakinah had wanted. All Aborigines from the 'neighbourhood', Collie wrote, 'men, women and children', assembled in the settlement.[7] Collie thought they had come for the burial ritual; they seemed, however, to have come for biscuit, which they all received, and only the men participated in the burial. The motivations for Aboriginal presence and participation were rarely clear to the newcomers. Nakinah brought with him a spear and *meara* which had belonged to Mokaré, along with the kangaroo skin cap that he wore. Several newcomers were there too and they carried Mokaré's body up the hill – a duty which the King Ya-nup would usually have performed themselves. This was the first Aboriginal burial at which the newcomers were allowed to be present.[8] They were not only witnesses to the event, they participated too. The oval shaped grave – four by three by nine feet – was traced out by Nakinah, but the digging of the grave, which again was usually carried out by the King Ya-nup men, was laboured over by several newcomers who had brought their tools for the purpose. Nakinah stood by and dictated the exact procedures to them. The grave was to be dug east-west in length, inclining a little to the south-east and north-west. The soil was to be dug up and placed on the south side of the grave for Nakinah to break up the chunks of soil with his hands, forming it into a crescent shaped mound. When the newcomers reached water at three and a half feet, Nakinah called to them to stop digging while the King Ya-nup men who were standing around watching, grounded the grave with branches of trees and leaves. Mokaré's body was rolled onto the right side and placed on top of the branches with his head facing east. Collie was surprised to witness that Mokaré's body was covered with soil taken from the north of the grave, not with the soil that Nakinah had broken up. He had not witnessed an Aboriginal burial so closely before. The grave was covered completely and Nakinah finished the job by sweeping the surface smooth; the broom made of branches was then thrown on top of the grave. A fire was made to the north of the grave near the head of the corpse. Nakinah broke Mokaré's spear so that it was bent but still in one piece and laid it on the edge of the grave and the *meara* was stuck into the ground with the kangaroo skin cap placed near the head. He was buried with all his possessions. Barker noted that when a King Ya-nup died it was considered 'dishonourable for another to possess any of his property. It is all buried, or left at his grave or destroyed'.[9] The King Ya-nup men who were gathered around, cried in loud sobs for a few moments at a time. Nakinah, however, did not express grief. Close relatives of the deceased in King Ya-nup culture did not show their grief in ways that the newcomers could recognise and a few British observers commented on the 'unfeeling' they showed towards their dead.

After the funeral Collie treated every Aboriginal in the settlement to as much tea and biscuit as they wanted, before the whole assembly departed with some King Ya-nup, including Nakinah, 'going bush' for a period of time as part of their grievance rituals.

◆

Mokaré died from what Collie described as an 'organic disease', probably some kind of influenza or tuberculosis. He had been sick with the same flu-like symptoms for much of 1830. While almost all Commanders commented on Aboriginal ill health, Barker was the only newcomer in this period to connect it with the volatile friendship between the King Ya-nup and the newcomers, writing in his journal that the acquaintance made some of the King Ya-nup 'delicate'.[10] The delicate nature of the friendship resulted from what modern medical science knows as the exchange of organisms such as viruses and bacteria. The very constitution of their friendship, which was tirelessly worked at by both the newcomers and the King Ya-nup – the close living, the sharing of space, food and, with increasing importance, clothes – would also have been a major factor in the devastation of the King Ya-nup community. This close sharing had a profound effect on the naive immune system of the King Ya-nup. The powerful handshaking ritual which was a useful and significant symbol was also a dangerous one as bacteria in the droplets from coughing and sneezing passed from one hand to the other. Many King Ya-nup slept the night on board visiting vessels in order to take advantage of trading possibilities with the crew, but while on board they unwittingly traded in diseases too. The intimacy which their friendship created would also lead to devastation.

Barry Smith has written that disease introduced by Europeans on the east coast of Australia had a more devastating effect on Aboriginal populations than any other factor from contact situations.[11] Tuberculosis and influenza were new diseases for the King Ya-nup and Mokaré was not the first to die from them. Many King Ya-nup deaths were recorded by the newcomers from 1826 to the early 1830s, and while it is hard to tell what exactly caused some of the deaths, it is most likely that many of them were caused by introduced diseases or ill health due to changes in diet and in the way that the King Ya-nup dressed.

Francis Armstrong, Native Interpreter at Swan River, noted that the Aborigines at the Swan had 'no recollection or record of any disease of an epidemic, or contagious or infectious kind having occurred among them; at least before the arrival of the Colonists'.[12] At King George's Sound, Lockyer described the Aborigines that he saw around the settlement in early 1827 as healthy, writing that they 'appear quite free from any sort of disease and their skins are perfectly clean without any irruption or blemish'.[13] He might have been surprised that they had no illnesses. He would have known about the smallpox epidemic at Port Jackson in 1789 and perhaps witnessed pockmarked survivors. Lockyer might have also suspected that the Aboriginal women who had been abducted by the sealers in 1826 had contracted venereal disease: sealing and whaling communities were rife with them.

Isaac Scott Nind who left the settlement in mid-1829 thought that in general the King Ya-nup had 'few ailments'. But he added in his report that 'the complaints to which they are most subject are those arising from cold, sore throat, and bowel complaints, which are frequently terminated by death, particularly with children.'[14]

Aboriginal immune systems had certainly been challenged by infections before European contacts occurred. As Smith has documented, archaeologists discovered evidence that suggests that Aboriginal people three to four thousand years ago might have carried parasites and contracted bacterial and viral ailments by living with dingoes and other native dogs and ingesting semi-cooked meats.[15] Judy Campbell added to this that 'the relatively few important and widespread infectious diseases that occurred in pre-contact Australia were caused by bacteria, protozoa and viruses that were established in the region, and Aboriginal people lived with them for thousands of years.[16] The impacts of introduced disease on the south-west Aboriginal population would get much worse in the 1840s as settlement to the area increased. The settlers would then point the blame towards the 'refuse of [the] whaling crews.'[17] In the late eighteenth and early nineteenth centuries, many migrants travelling from England for North America and Australia were infected with tuberculosis as England was experiencing an epidemic of that disease.[18] Tuberculosis was also one of the most widespread and damaging diseases introduced to North America by the British. Campbell has recorded anecdotal evidence from English migrants in Australia which indicates that 'first introductions of tuberculosis,' otherwise known as the 'white plague,' 'had unusually severe effects on Indigenous Australians, as they did on North Americans.'[19] But death from disease was never as prominent in the south-west as the epidemics of smallpox experienced by the Aborigines on the east coast of Australia around Port Jackson, Botany Bay, the Hawkesbury River and in South Australia.

The winter of 1831 was particularly bad for illness and death in the King Ya-nup world. Collie, who had an interest in Aboriginal health, wrote a letter to his brother George, describing the effects of what he called the 'open winter' of 1831.[20] 'So far as the poor natives have been concerned,' he wrote, 'it has had the usual effect of open winters in your part of the world [Scotland] that of being very unhealthy. Many of the [King Ya-nup] have died, generally of pulmonary disease, and a few of liver.'[21] Collie believed that the cold and wet weather was felt 'strongly' by the King Ya-nup because of their 'slender and unprotected bodies.'[22] The 'open winter' affected the newcomers too – as infections spread from hut to barrack.

Collie made a connection between European clothes and Aboriginal ill health at King George's Sound. In a letter to Governor Stirling in January 1832 he wrote about the 'baneful influence' of European clothing on the 'wandering native', as he believed it laid the 'foundation of organic disease that has often had a fatal termination.' When the Aborigines exchanged their kangaroo skin cloaks for a 'dress of cotton or worsted', the newcomer, Collie thought, 'should either keep the native dress that he thus supersedes till his fickle servant may want it again for the bush, or provide him with such substantial covering as shall be adequate protection when exposed anew to the inclemency's [sic] of the weather'.[23] However, neither Collie nor the King Ya-nup knew the other 'baneful influence' of sharing cloth: bacteria were transmitted through clothes, sheets and blankets.

Collie's expression of concern about Aboriginal health and clothing reveals something more of the way in which some of the King Ya-nup were utilising the British presence. They came and went from the houses in the settlement as they pleased, working when they wanted to and using the European frock and trousers only when they were on the fringe, reverting back to their kangaroo skin cloaks when they went bush. Barker also connected a lack of protection from the elements with illnesses. When Mokaré returned from the lagoon at *Kiangadarup* in April 1830, he went to bed with a headache, a hoarse voice and a hot, dry skin. Barker wrote, 'he had in fact a severe cold, most likely from sleeping in the bush without his blanket.'[24]

Barker and Mokaré often talked of sickness and death. Barker was interested in Aboriginal burial customs and their long grieving process in which they went bush for several months, while Mokaré asked Barker questions in return, such as: did 'white people [die] in England?', telling Barker that 'Black fellow die plenty' at King George.[25] They talked about the causes of particular illnesses. Mokaré explained to Barker that if a King Ya-nup stole (*quipple*), then they would get sick as a result of their action. He asked Barker what made white people sick, but Barker wrote: 'Not being able with our paucity of each other's language to explain the immediate causes', he simplified his answer and told him that it was the will of 'God' who made the newcomers sick and that all men are, 'subject to sickness', adding that they will 'all die sooner or later'.[26] This conversation reveals that both the newcomers and the King Ya-nup had a belief that the extra-human forces were associated with ill-health and death.

Mokaré's experience of the newcomers was manifest in many different ways. He noticed subtle physical changes which he told Barker about: his eyesight was not as sharp as it was and his hearing not as astute. When admiring Chilloc's dexterous skill in spear dodging in July 1830, Mokaré remarked to Barker that, 'formerly my sight was very fine in this way but I have lost it since living with the white fellows and should now be speared immediately.'[27] Interestingly, it seems Mokaré had foresight that these physical changes would happen. In September 1830, Mokaré told Barker that he was getting very forgetful, which, Barker wrote, 'he told me he had warned me about. He had spoken some time since of his sickness [eating] him'. Barker thought that he was probably talking about his deafness.[28]

When Mokaré was unwell, Barker was very protective of him. He put off his expedition to the west of the settlement when Mokaré was sick in February 1830, insisting that he could not go without Mokaré after 'promising' he could accompany them.[29] Barker did believe, however, that Mokaré and some of his countrymen complained too much and did not suffer their sickness well. In August 1830 he wrote, 'Mokaré moaning dismally … they seem to have a set form of complaining when sick.' All King Ya-nup, Barker thought, moaned with the same 'sound and measure' no matter what their ailment and Mokaré made a 'great deal of anything [illness] new to him'. [30] In October Mokaré's moaning and complaining was getting on Barker's nerves. 'I wish he could bear it better', he wrote, 'for he destroys one's compassion for him by sometimes making such a rot about a finger ache.'[31] The King Ya-nup were not attuned to the newcomer's expectation of suffering an illness. And Barker was not aware that it went deeper than a frustrating 'complaint'. Mokaré's overt expression of his illnesses was one of the ways he dealt with feeling unwell. Barker described him breaking into a 'kind of abuse' of it. 'At this moment,' Barker wrote in October, 'he is giving vent to what I imagine are some imprecations of against [his illness] in which the words 'câro' or 'cairo' repeated three times energetically are conspicuous.'[32] This moaning and chanting was part of Mokaré's treatment.

Mokaré was not the only King Ya-nup who was often unwell. Barker recorded his symptoms most often because of their close relationship. Many other King Ya-nup experienced sickness such as catarrh, colds, stomach aches, headaches, liver problems and sore teeth. It is possible that this last complaint was caused by an increasing desire of the King Ya-nup for the newcomer's diet. Aborigines in the settlement received biscuit, tea, plums, raisins and damper. Gorging on this food – as was their manner of eating – created indigestion, bowel problems and toothaches. Traditional food was not replaced with these new items, but added to. Collie commented on the changing nature of the

King Ya-nup diet in 1832. The King Ya-nup did not give up their favourite food of kangaroo, 'although the stated meals of biscuit, beef (salt), cabbage and rice with tea may be very acceptable to the uncultivated palates of the savage, still there can be no marvel excited by the wish to gratify their old habits by gorging on fresh kangaroo.'[33]

When Nakinah returned to the settlement after one month in the bush following Mokaré's death, Collie noticed that he had gone from hut to hut to receive large meals three times a day. As Collie predicted, this overeating brought on a severe indigestion and rheumatism and Nakinah demanded 'physic' from Collie. He was given purgative treatments to soothe his bloat.[34]

◆

Mokaré had gone into the bush for a month before he returned and died in Collie's hut. Collie believed it was his 'natural predilection' for savage life that drew him back to the bush. This 'savage life' however, included an Aboriginal medical system, established with methods of prevention, cures and pharmacopeia. It is probable that Mokaré went 'bush' for a month to meet with a *mulgarradock*, or medicine man, to help him cure his illness – King Ya-nup style. He did not ask for Collie's permission to go bush to see a *mulgarradock*, because he knew Collie would disapprove. And when after a month of being treated by a *mulgarradock* he was still unwell, he returned to the settlement to receive Collie's medical assistance and nurturing.

Both the newcomers' and the King Ya-nup medical systems were a combination of empirical scientific observations and spiritual beliefs. As Pat Jalland has written, it was not until later in the nineteenth century that death was thought to be caused solely by particular illnesses, rather than the will of God.[35] Just as the newcomers had their spiritual beliefs in illness and death, so too did the King Ya-nup: they were spiritual and believed that all sickness was caused by acts associated with sorcery. Their *mulgarradock* had supernatural powers and were always called on if the King Ya-nup were unwell, to heal their spear wounds, to transfer their sickness or 'blow it away' from their bodies. The female equivalent of a *mulgarradock* was a witch or *wirago* and these spiritual women also held enormous power. Their activities were not revealed to many of the newcomers, possibly because they had sacred gendered roles which the single men were not allowed to know about; Barker, however, knew of their existence. Dr Uredale was a King Ya-nup *mulgarradock* and he was known to have strength and a highly esteemed status within the community. Dr Uredale also had respect on the fringe where several white medical men spent time with the King Ya-nup, and had a varying interest in Aboriginal health, medicine and death. Nind, Wilson and Collie seemed to have an interest in the *mulgarradock* and Aboriginal wellbeing in general. Dr Davis, Collie and Wilson, however, remained sceptical of Aboriginal medical treatments. Although not a medical man, Barker had a deep respect for the Aboriginal *mulgarradock* and always accorded Uredale the title of Dr when writing about him in his journal, often just writing 'Dr. U'. He was also interested in how Dr Uredale had become a *mulgarradock*. Mokaré told him: 'Before they become Dr.'s or wirago's [sic] they feel unwell, then they fly into the air, come back on thunder and are dubbed Dr.'[36] Likewise, Mokaré was keen to know how Dr Davis became a doctor – was he sick first? Mokaré told Barker that there was a lake of 'fine water' in the air out of which the *wirago* drinks and Dr Uredale had given Mokaré accounts of his 'aerial excursions.'[37] Barker understood the spiritual nature of the King Ya-nup medical system, writing that the Aboriginal doctors and 'wizards' have a joint profession because 'their doctors [use] a few remedies besides charms.'[38]

On the fringe, the complicated and at times tense relationship between these two different medical systems reveals ongoing negotiations between some of the King Ya-nup and the newcomers in charge of the garrison. The King Ya-nup held a mixture of respect and suspicion for the white doctors and their treatments; they sometimes trusted them and used them and at other times they were doubtful of the tenets of the treatments and avoided them. There was a similar level of interest in and arrogance over the *mulgarradock* by some of the white medical associates.

Wilson submitted himself to an Aboriginal medical treatment on Mokaré's insistence in 1829. When Wilson and Mokaré returned to the settlement after their journey to the west of King George's Sound, Mokaré took Wilson to visit Dr Uredale, who said he was a 'relation', to cure Wilson's sore ankle which he sprained during his climb up Mt Lindesay. Wilson described Dr Uredale as 'a man of mild and grave aspect' who was 'evidently highly esteemed by and possessed much authority over, the other natives.'[39] Of his treatment by Dr Uredale, Wilson wrote:

> I thanked Eural for his kindness, and submitted my ankle, now much swelled and exceedingly painful, to his examination. He immediately began to press it with his fingers, blowing on it at the same time; I bore this painful operation as long as I could, and then told Dr Eural (so he was called), that I thought he had

done me much benefit, and that there was no occasion for his giving himself any
further trouble; but he gave it another squeeze or two, and then went to the door,
and blew over his fingers, and also over his kangaroo skin, thus, as I was told, first
taking the disease from me to himself, and then blowing it away; he was pleased
that he had been of service to me, and seemed to understand medical etiquette
too well, to receive any remuneration from a number of the profession.[40]

Although Wilson surrendered his ankle to Dr Uredale, he did it to appease
Mokaré and out of curiosity for the Aboriginal medical art form. He was a
sceptic of the *mulgarradock* complaining that Dr Uredale had aggravated his
sprain. After bearing the treatment, he went straight to Davis from whose
assistance, Wilson wrote, 'I derived more benefit…than I was likely to do,
from the Aboriginal Æsculapius.'[41] Dr Uredale also sought treatment from
the white doctors in the settlement. Davis treated his sore foot in February
1830 and Barker was impressed when he observed that Dr Uredale 'seemed
aware of the use of cleanliness for the wound.'[42]

As they spent more time on the fringe, the King Ya-nup began calling
on the settlement's doctors and commanders for assistance, but they never
completely gave up the belief in and treatment by their *mulgarradock*. They
used both systems, consulting the experts from both worlds.

The King Ya-nup and the newcomers studied each other's medical
techniques and treatments and Wilson and Collie both noted the similarities
of some of them. Collie administered several King Ya-nup with various
treatments during 1831–32. Interestingly, the two procedures that the King Ya-
nup 'readily submitted to' more than any others were scarification and cupping.
Collie recognised that this was probably because these two procedures were
similar to the ones which some of the King Ya-nup men performed traditionally.
Collie maintained that his procedure of scarification was far superior to the
'native substitute' called *umbin* which was conducted with a burning piece
of wood or a sharpened kangaroo claw. Many of the King Ya-nup men had
umbin on their upper chests marking a significant initiation process which
symbolised a man's age and status. Collie wrote that the newcomers and the
King Ya-nup had this scarification process as one 'common custom' between
them.[43] This procedure was probably 'submitted to' because the King Ya-nup
men could relate to it, seeing it perhaps as less of a treatment and more of
an initiation process by the newcomers; a procedure as part of a developing
relationship.

Wilson observed another medical technique which he initially assumed was a common custom of the King Ya-nup and newcomers. When Wilson sprained his ankle while exploring with Mokaré, Wilson immediately placed it in a stream to cool it down and prevent any swelling. He noticed that several leeches had attached themselves to his ankle, which he thought was an 'excellent, though unexpected remedy'.[44] Mokaré, who saw the leeches, told Wilson that the King Ya-nup also applied them to their bodies in 'certain cases'. But after Wilson quizzed him further, it seemed as though Mokaré had picked up his knowledge of the leeches' utility from seeing their application by the doctor at the settlement. Mokaré said the leeches were 'very good for white fellow, but very bad for the blacks', who drank from streams with caution in case the leeches entered their mouths, which had in some instances led to death.[45]

Not surprisingly, the newcomers were often sick at the same time as the King Ya-nup, all suffering from the same infectious disease. In October 1830 Barker wrote that there was a 'kind of influenza' going around, which most of the King Ya-nup had been suffering from.[46] The King Ya-nup realised the infection was contagious and Mokaré thought he caught it during his visit to Dr Uredale a few days earlier, whom he had gone to 'condole'. The newcomers were sick with it too. Barker had been confined to his bed with fever and constant vomiting and Dr Davis came and rubbed his temples with acetic acid, ordering him to lie down in the sun.[47] Davis became contaminated as well as Officer Kent and three of the prisoners. The King Ya-nup who contracted the influenza sought help from their *mulgarradock*. But Dr Uredale was sick too and could not cure anyone, so several King Ya-nup travelled far to the north to *Cojinerup* (Barker's term for The Stirling Range) where other *mulgarradock* were living. Some of the Aborigines blamed their sickness on the heavy thunder and lightning that was prevalent. Mokaré said that the people living at *Cojinerup* to the north (the Wills people) would be 'sulky' at the King Ya-nup for visiting them as they would expect to catch the sickness from them. Capacole who lived there was the most famous doctor in the whole region. He was married to a 'doctress' as Barker called her, and they were both better doctors than Dr Uredale who was considered only a 'middling one' by Mokaré.[48] This comment that Dr Uredale was considered a 'middling' doctor could be interpreted that his status in the Aboriginal world was connected to the amount of illness within his community or his ability to effectively treat people. Or was Capacole, the famous doctor from *Cojinerup*, considered superior because he was a Wills man? The Wills people were considered by the King Ya-nup as a formidable and all-important group. Perhaps Dr Uredale's reputation dwindled as the impact of new diseases were taking their effect on the community.

Most of the King Ya-nup travelled to *Cojinerup* and Mokaré went to Mt Melville to see the ailing Dr Uredale and his sister Mullet, who was also sick. He was gone for several days, which made Barker upset, for not telling him in the first place of his intention to leave the settlement. When he returned Barker told him off, but Mokaré's excuse was that he 'felt ill always at King George'.[49]

During 1830 Barker recorded often that the King Ya-nup and their neighbours were very sick and there was a high rate of deaths due to disease, most probably introduced by the newcomers living in or visiting the settlement. At the same time that the King Ya-nup had gone to *Cojinerup*, Waiter told Barker that the government farm was 'plenty sick' and that he would sleep at the settlement as a consequence.[50] And again in December Mokaré came to the settlement with a group of Aborigines including Maragnan who was 'very sick'. Barker wrote that '8 or 9 women had died and 1 man – all apparently from severe colds or catarrh'.[51]

Throughout this time of illness and death in the Aboriginal world, some of the tensions in the King Ya-nup relationship with the newcomers is evident. Some King Ya-nup were torn between the respect for and belief in their *mulgarradock* and the convenience and comfort of the settlement doctors. They wavered between these two systems, tugged to and fro by custom and their loyalty to their medicine men, but were also drawn to the utility of the fringe. As in all issues that developed on the fringe, this tension was greater for some than others.

Dr Davis was represented in Barker's journal on several occasions as being tactless when it came to dealing with the King Ya-nup. Nakinah partly blamed Davis for the death of his brother, Taragon, as Davis had treated Taragon for a snakebite with purgatives and rubbed the wound vigorously, thereby spreading the venom; Davis told Nakinah off for not following his medical instructions. Taragon's death brought Davis' medical treatments into question for several of the King Ya-nup in a very public manner. Barker and Mokaré negotiated through this situation, which was fraught with danger from misunderstood intentions. Barker, however, had also been anxious about caring for Taragon and tried to persuade Mokaré into allowing Taragon to come into the settlement. But when the King Ya-nup refused to bring him in, Barker wrote with frustration: 'They seem anxious enough about him at the moment of apprehending danger, but greatly apathetic as to using any active remedies.'[52] And when Mokaré asked Barker his opinion of Taragon's mortality, Barker told him that he would not be in danger if Taragon was brought back into the settlement 'for us to look after him', but it was impossible for Davis to be with him in the bush and especially dangerous if the King Ya-nup did not administer Davis's medicine to him. Mokaré acknowledged Barker's concern, but insisted that: 'Physic very good white fellow, no good black fellow.'[53] After the public failure of Davis's medical procedure on Taragon, the King Ya-nup did not take any more of the newcomers' advice for Taragon's health. Dr Uredale treated Taragon in the bush and was an important presence on his deathbed, at his funeral and in the retributive activities that followed.[54]

The *mulgarradock* treatments were rarely witnessed by the newcomers. And any information again comes from Mokaré's stories. It is clear that the treatments were both scientific and spiritual. Nind was told of some of their powers by Mokaré: 'the hand of the Mulgarradock is … supposed to confer strength or dexterity, and the natives frequently apply to them for that purpose'. Nind continued: 'The operation consists in simply drawing his hand repeatedly, with a firm pressure, from the shoulder downwards to the fingers, which he afterwards extends until the joints crack.' *Mulgarradock* also gave doses of what Nind recognised as medicine to their ailing countrymen: 'in cases of dysentery, for example, to which the [King Ya-nup] are very subject, they administer to the patient the gum of the grass tree, and sometimes the green stems of the meernes [red root]'.[55] Barker also noted the grass tree gum was eaten when King Ya-nup were sick.[56] Other cures of sickness included talking to ghosts about the symptoms of the disease, as Barker witnessed with Mokaré's chanting and moaning.[57] George Fletcher Moore described a species 'of shrub' called *kurren*, which he believed the King Ya-nup attributed medical properties to: 'It is a sensitive plant … and emits a smell like most powerful garlic; in this state the natives use it in cases of headache, waving it under the nose of the patient.'[58] Nind believed that the King Ya-nup probably had 'many other remedies' besides the gum and meern, as they were 'partial to medicines' and would swallow the most 'nauseous dose to the dregs'.[59]

Even though the newcomers generally respected the King Ya-nup medical beliefs, they did not believe in them themselves, trying to persuade the King Ya-nup to seek assistance from the settlement's doctors. The King Ya-nup increasingly came into the settlement when people were sick, sometimes getting medical advice or medicine from Davis. In July 1830, Coolbun brought his wife Neerwenga and their two-month-old baby girl into the settlement. Neerwenga and her baby were unwell, and they asked for some 'physic' for the child 'for whose sake they appeared to have come', Barker wrote. They were pleased to find out from Davis that the ailment was not serious, but one which 'children at the breast were subject to'.[60]

Other King Ya-nup came into the settlement only to receive the much sought-after 'gruel' from Davis. Gruel was a soupy porridge of boiled barley or oats and water which was administered to the sick as it was easy to digest. In July, Nakinah visited Davis' hut, with, Barker wrote, a 'doleful face' and complaining of being unwell. Davis examined him but could not find anything wrong with him, except a moderately sore finger. Barker wrote that this was not the treatment that Nakinah had come for and 'keeping up the complaining tone he at last hinted' to Davis 'that a little gruel would be very good'. Nakinah had noticed that the King Ya-nup who had been sick at the time were all receiving gruel and, Barker wrote, he 'thought it no bad thing to be on the Dr's list for such an agreeable medicine'.[61] While Nakinah and others saw the benefits in the service of the settlement's doctors, not all the King Ya-nup were interested in or dependent upon the settlement for food or treatments such as gruel.

Throughout this period, the tensions between the King Ya-nup and the newcomers were at their strongest in times of illness and death. Mokaré was often caught between the fringe and the Aboriginal world, but his loyalty clearly remained to his Aboriginal traditions.

In August 1830 Mokaré was unwell again. He had been to see Dr Davis who 'blooded' him. Barker was trying to keep Mokaré in his hut and prevent him from 'going bush' to seek Dr Uredale's help. However, several King Ya-nup came in to the hut to see Mokaré and were 'very urgent with him … to go into the bush, and so worked on him', Barker wrote, 'that he actually left us to do so'. Barker told him plainly 'that it would kill him' to go bush now and said all he could to 'no purpose'. Barker sent for Davis who reiterated Barker's warning. But Mokaré felt strongly about going to see Dr Uredale in the hope that he might cure what Mokaré referred to as his 'yony yony'.[62] Barker allowed him to take leave to the bush. Davis, however, thought he should have been forced to remain in the settlement but Barker finally decided that it would do him good to go.[63]

Collie also urged Mokaré to stay in the settlement when he was unwell, however, he left to go and see Coolbun, who had inherited his brother Dr Uredale's status of *mulgarradock* when Uredale died in December 1830. Coolbun was eager to keep the esteem associated with his new status by persuading the King Ya-nup to seek his assistance when they were unwell, rather than allowing the newcomers to hold the power in looking after them. Not long after Mokaré died, Talwyn (Coolbun's nephew) had signs of deteriorating health; he was suffering with the same flu-like symptoms that Mokaré had been. Collie was eager for him to stay within the settlement until he had completely recovered. Collie wrote:

> and had I once seen that he was inclined to abide by this rule, I would have assisted him still further with medicine; but, as Mokaré had evaded my good intentions, and by his conduct tended to throw great discredit on the whites, I determined to administer no more medicine to my black patients until I thought I might trust to their observance of the requisite injunctions to keep within doors.[64]

Did Mokaré's actions hold sway within the Aboriginal world, or did Collie assume that his actions had a strong effect on his countrymen? It is difficult to know. Talwyn disobeyed Collie and went bush to the 'bivouac of his native advisers', to Collie's disapproval. Talwyn told Collie that he was under the orders of Coolbun, who continued to hold power and influence within the group. However, after staying in the bush not far from the settlement, Talwyn 'took his chance' among the newcomers, abandoning Coolbun and returning to the settlement to be looked after by the Commander and his wife. Talwyn died in the settlement and was buried next to Mokaré on 24 August 1831. Collie wrote of his anger at Coolbun for having persuaded Talwyn to leave the settlement, taking him to the 'cold native bivouacs' which caused Talwyn's 'premature decease'.[65]

Collie disliked the King Ya-nup 'going bush'. In his letter to Governor Stirling describing the characteristics of the Aborigines of King George's Sound, he wrote of their 'love of ease' which stopped them from attaching themselves to civilised society:

> At any moment they can obtain the Necessaries of life in the wilds of their own Country, with less trouble than at the house of the Settler; at that moment they

will be ready to desert those who may have been considering themselves as their protectors and benefactors, without Ceremony of applying for permission to depart.[66]

Coolbun also tried to retain his power when another young boy, Charlie Brown, was unwell. Coolbun came into the settlement, guiding Charlie Brown out and towards his camp where he treated him. When in the settlement, Charlie Brown refused all Collie's medical suggestions, perhaps following Coolbun's wishes. Collie wrote that no amount of persuasion could overcome his 'inclination for the bush'. Collie was under the belief that two King Ya-nup – Gyallipert and Tatan – were helping Coolbun persuade Charlie Brown to stay in the settlement. Gyallipert and Tatan succeeded in getting Charlie Brown to stay for one night, telling Collie that they would make sure he kept within the settlement bounds. However, as Collie wrote, 'the dark motives of my swarthy friends were unblushingly exposed' when it was realised that these men were actually trying to receive some extra supplies of biscuit, which they did; Gyallipert laughing heartily at his cunning success. Charlie Brown had himself been a part of the trick, getting biscuit from his two friends for staying in the settlement.[67]

It seems that some of the newcomers blamed the Aboriginal deaths on the King Ya-nup 'wandering propensity' and strongly believed in the safety and health of the settlement. Explorer Robert Dale wrote in 1834 that Nakinah's way of life had changed so remarkably due to the arrival of the newcomers that he lived 'almost entirely in the settlement'. But, Nakinah's 'wandering propensities at last prevailed', Dale wrote, and he 'rejoined his companions in the woods, where he shortly afterwards died'.[68] Nakinah also returned to the bush, probably to receive treatment from Coolbun, before he died.

With the deaths of Mokaré, Talwyn and Charlie Brown all occurring in Collie's hut, Collie became concerned that Nakinah and other senior King Ya-nup men would be superstitious about so many King Ya-nup deaths in the presence of the newcomers. But Collie's fears were allayed by Nakinah and his brother Waiter's constant requests for 'physic' and other medical treatments from Collie and the suspicion of the newcomers was never confirmed overtly by the King Ya-nup.

Disease and death had a significant effect on the King Ya-nup world. New diseases such as influenza and tuberculosis were part of the devastation amid which the King Ya-nup experienced the fringe. The very nature of their close relationship with the newcomers meant that the delicate immune systems of the King Ya-nup suffered, and with the push-and-pull tension between their traditional medicine and the settlement's doctors, their friendship was, at times, at risk of being damaged also. The King Ya-nup never lost faith in their *mulgarradock*. As they continued to push the newcomers to the fringes of their world, they utilised both the settlement doctors and their own medicine men.

Epilogue

'Nothing in Collet Barker's courageous life approached the tragic irony of his violent death on 30 April 1831,' wrote John Mulvaney and Neville Green in their introduction to Barker's journals.[1] It is true that the part of Barker's life that is most well known is his death. However, after living intimately with his journals for more than four years I felt that I could not kill him off so readily.

His life and experiences were so remarkable that they should not be written away as a prelude to his death. His journals would most likely have been published and his stories – and those he recorded – would have been well known if he had not died before his next posting. He was to be given the job of a Government Resident in New Zealand.[2] The tragic irony that Mulvaney and Green mentioned refers to Barker's patient interest in and acceptance of the Aborigines with whom he met and lived, only to be fatally speared by a group of Aborigines from southern South Australia. It has been assumed by Barker's contemparies and later historians that these Aborigines mistook Barker for a rapacious sealer who had been carrying off women from that coastline and living with them on Kangaroo Island, near the mainland. Mulvaney and Green lamented that the Aborigines who killed Barker 'got it terribly wrong', choosing as their 'payback victim one of the most humane friends that Aboriginal people had encountered in a responsible post since 1788'.[3] While Barker's death was tragic and could be seen as ironic, I feel that we can draw more from Barker's death than a sad reflection on the tragedy and irony of it.

Barker left King George's Sound in March 1831 and was instructed to proceed – with Captain Charles Sturt en route to Port Jackson – to the eastern shore of St Vincent's Gulf in what is now South Australia. He was to explore the coastline to the east of Cape Jervis and carry out a survey of the Murray River to ascertain whether it had any communication with the sea. Barker, accompanied by a small exploring party, including his servant James Mills, Officer John Kent from the commissariat and Dr Davis, set out to determine the river's outlet. They saw that the shore of the gulf lay to the north north-west of where the boat had landed them and so they started out in that direction. After a few days of travelling through the country close to the coast, Barker obtained a view of the Murray River and its mouth to the north-east. He had to cross a channel which was judged to be a quarter of a mile in width and Barker decided to swim across it to the sand hill on the other side to take some bearings. Being the only member of the party who could swim, he stripped to his skin and attached a compass to his head, swimming across to the opposite bank. The rest of the party saw him climb the sand hill and disappear over the other side. They waited for him for several hours and started to prepare some food when they heard a 'distant shout or cry' which, Kent thought, 'resembled the call of the natives'. The soldiers, however, 'positively declared [it] to be the voice of a white man'.[4] Was that call that they heard similar to the King Ya-nup *coo-wee*? This *coo-wee* was a call that was used in the bush and had slightly different meanings in different situations: it warned strangers that you were approaching, it meant that you came in peace and it also meant 'come here' and 'come back'.[5] It is possible that Barker, seeing Aborigines approach him with their spears, called up his knowledge of Aboriginal communication in a desperate attempt to pacify this foreign group.

That night as the rest of the party waited anxiously they noticed smoke from a line of small camp fires around where Barker had ascended the sand dunes and some Aboriginal women were heard chanting a 'melancholy dirge'.[6] Fearing the worst, the party started to head back to the *Isabella* to inform the remaining expedition members the likelihood of Barker's fate. The expedition party wanted to know if he had been speared by Aborigines or if he was being kept hostage. Sturt had encountered a group of hostile local people on an earlier expedition and he suspected Barker had been attacked by the same group. Davis went in a boat to Encounter Bay on the mainland to try to meet some of the local Aborigines to ascertain information about Barker. On the mainland Davis met Sally, an Aboriginal woman who spoke English 'tolerably well'. Remarkably, she was recognised by others aboard the schooner *Isabella* from her visit and stay at King George's Sound in early 1827. She had been brought there by John Randall's sealing gang, who abducted the women from King George's Sound and murdered the man on Green Island before marooning the four Aboriginal men on Michaelmas Island. It is unclear whether she too had been abducted: it is likely she learnt her English from the sealers.

Sally was persuaded to help Davis find out what had happened to Barker. She led Davis to a party of sealers living on Kangaroo Island just opposite the mainland. Davis knew about these rough sealers and their 'bad acts'. They had been living on the islands around the coast for some time and regularly visiting the mainland where they carried off women and killed the men if they had to. Two sealers living there were bribed with money by Davis to take him and Sally to mediate between them and the local inhabitants on the mainland. They were accompanied by Sally's father, Condoy, and her uncle. The group landed at Cape Jervis and crossed the Murray River on a traditional reed raft – a local device that the sealers had adopted – and met with the local Aboriginal group near to where Barker's last call was heard. Sally talked to them and recounted to Davis the sad news. Cummarringgeree, Pennegoora and Wannangetta had thrown one spear each. Barker had run into the surf and made signs with his hands, calling them to stop. Their spears killed Barker, and his body was thrown into the sea.[7] These three men told Sally that they came across Barker's footprints in the sand. They followed them until they saw him, but were hesitant to approach because of the strange looking instrument which he had attached to his head. They approached him slowly and Barker tried to soothe them (perhaps with the familiar King Ya-nup *coo-ee* that Kent recognised), but they were determined to attack him. He ran for the ocean, perhaps thinking he was safe there from his knowledge of King Ya-nup fear of deep water. But a spear struck him in the hip, then another in the shoulder. He turned around to face the Aboriginal attackers and received a third one in his breast. On recounting the events to Kent, Sally reported that the perpetrators were 'influenced by no other motive than curiosity to ascertain if they had power to kill a white man'. Sturt and the other members of the expedition, however, thought that the Aboriginal motivations were more likely in response to the 'cruelties exercised by the sealers towards the blacks along the south coast', encouraging these three men to 'take vengeance' on the 'innocent as well as the guilty'.[8]

Barker was killed by three Lake Alexandrina men. It is possible that they might have thought he was part of a sealing group, representing one of their 'tribe', but that is not certain. His death could have been, as Sturt suggested, part of a retribution for the mayhem inflicted on the Aboriginal people by the sealers who worked and lived on the islands and coastline of the south. Or perhaps Barker was attacked because of the alien-looking compass on his head – the only item he was wearing. Perhaps he was more vulnerable wearing just his skin; stripped of his authority. Perhaps his nudity related to the Aborigines' curiosity of whether they could exert power over this strange, naked visitor.

The spearing had differences from and similarities to Dineen's spearing in 1826 – the King Ya-nup did not want to kill Dineen – but for the British these spearings occurred under the same circumstances. Because Barker's attack was fatal, the Lake Alexandrina people have been blamed by contemparies and historians. If the atrocities of sealers were responsible for both spearings, as the British recorders suggest, why were the King Ya-nup who speared Dineen viewed as victims, and the Lake Alexandrina people deemed murderers? Barker's death in this history becomes especially ironic when told next to the story of Lockyer's settlement party arrival and the spearing of Dineen. One paragraph is devoted to Dineen and that unfortunate 'skirmish' in history books of Albany, while Barker's death has more pages written about it than his remarkable life.

◆

Barker's treatment of and respect for the King Ya-nup were remembered by a later migrant to Albany, James Browne, who wrote that Barker 'took great interest in the natives' and it was because of his 'acts of kindness and justice, and by protecting them from insult and injury in fact doing everything in his power to conciliate them, [that] laid the foundation of the present amicable understanding between the settlers and natives of King George's Sound'.[9] Collie also wrote with admiration of Barker and his Aboriginal 'policy'. He urged Governor Stirling to encourage each successive Resident at Albany to uphold Barker's principles of kindness and respect towards the Aborigines.[10] Browne's statement also included a comment on the King Ya-nup knowledge of, and response to, Barker's death. He wrote: 'The natives to this day lament the loss of Captain Barker, and when they heard that he had been killed on the coast, on his way to Sydney, wished to be taken down to the place that they might revenge his death.'[11] The King Ya-nup desire to revenge Barker's death – to be taken as a group in a *caibre* to the mouth of Lake Alexandrina to spear some Aboriginal strangers – is a profound statement. It reveals that the

King Ya-nup were protective of Barker, just as he had been protective of them against their own traditional enemies. It perhaps also shows that Barker was adopted and accepted by them, as one of them. To some King Ya-nup, Barker represented a *cotertie*, a protective guardian or 'godfather' and his death needed to be avenged. Barker was one newcomer who stepped metaphorically beyond the fringe and engaged with the King Ya-nup in their world and largely on their terms.

Mokaré's death was strongly felt by the newcomers too. Collie's unusual dying wish reveals his respect and admiration for Mokaré in a similar way to the King Ya-nup response to the news of Barker's fatal spearing. Collie died in Albany in October 1835 in the house of his friend and fellow Scot, George Cheyne. He had been suffering with what he called his 'asthma' for a long time, but it was most likely tuberculosis that killed him. He had been living at Swan River from November 1832 onwards and left in 1835 with the hope of returning to Scotland to die near his family: but he had made the decision to leave too late. His legs had already begun to swell.[12] His condition deteriorated on board and when the vessel made a stopover in Albany, Collie was carried on shore and died there on 8 November. Collie's friend Richard Scholl wrote to Collie's brother George, explaining that Collie's dying request was to be 'laid beside the Native Chief Morkew [Mokaré], who he himself buried, when Resident of that part of the colony.'[13] His request was respected and he was interred beside Mokaré's grave. The details of his burial and funeral were not recorded and so it is not clear whether Collie was buried in a coffin or an Aboriginal grave. I know of no other burials recorded in Australia in the nineteenth century in which a newcomer requested to be interred with an Aboriginal person.[14] This unusual burial represents Collie's deep respect for Mokaré. They had spent a lot of time together, lived in the same hut for several months in 1831 and Collie considered him *one of us*. These deaths and the responses to them are telling of what the fringe had forged. The close, yet complicated relationships that developed between particular individuals like Collie and Mokaré meant that there was a cultural sharing in life and in death. Barker died a traditionally Aboriginal way and, just as tragically, Collie and Mokaré died of the same European disease. Gwen Chessel has noted that Mokaré is also remembered obscurely in Aberdeen, Scotland. After Alexander's death George Collie acquired a piece of land in Aberdeen and named his house 'Morkeu', after his brother's companion. The name remains intact.[15]

In October 1840, five years after Collie's death, the colony's surveyor, John Septimus Roe travelled to Albany at the request of Governor Hutt to have the body of his late friend removed from the side of Mokaré and re-interred in the new Albany cemetery situated on the farm road. Roe mentioned that 'The Governor and every respectable inhabitant of the Town and neighbourhood as well as several of the humble class and 7 or 8 of the natives who had known him in life, attended the removal...'[16] Nothing was mentioned however, of Mokaré's grave or the reneging of Collie's dying wish to be buried next to his friend.

In 1888 a grand town hall was erected on the site near to Mokaré's grave in what is now the main street of Albany. In 1963 during an excavation behind the Town Hall, two bodies were discovered, wrapped in blankets. Local radio reporter Les Johnson speculated that these two bodies were probably Mokaré and Talwyn, who died a month after Mokaré, but the local community believed them to be sailors who died during the garrison period. In the 1970s a car park was established on top of the graves, deeply burying them with infill spoil which was used to create the car park.

In 1995 local historian Bob Howard wrote an article in the *Albany Advertiser* criticising the council for not acknowledging Mokaré's role in the town's history or locating and marking his grave in the town today.[17] Mokaré's memorial, *Man of Peace*, was erected two years after Howard's article, possibly as a compensation for the loss of Mokaré's grave under the town hall car park. Public histories often say more about contemporary sensibilities than past happenings. Two months after the memorial was erected it was vandalised. Swastikas and the letters 'KKK' were drawn all over the figure, battery acid was poured onto it and the spear had been snapped from Mokaré's hand.[18] The local papers reported the vandalism, blaming racist youths for the outrage.[19] However, the irony of the violent performance against the *man of peace* was not publicly stated. Symbols of reconciliation – such as this memorial – and acts of violence seem to go hand in hand. Perhaps Western Australians were becoming used to seeing Aboriginal memorials defaced: another statue of a Western Australian Aboriginal figure, Yagan, was decapitated several times in the same year as Mokaré's memorial was vandalised; an act which mirrored what had happened to Yagan's actual head in the name of science in 1834.[20] These public memorials translate these Aboriginal men into the British narrative; and the violent acts clearly show that their inclusion is a contested one. The micro-narratives in my history have aimed to go beyond these

Reconciliation statues and unearth something of the ways in which particular Aboriginal people experienced the presence of the British on their country and in what ways they conceived them in their world.

◆

The newcomers to King George's Sound brought an unintentional balance of promise and menace for the King Ya-nup during the period of this history. The permanency of the British presence on the edges of King Ya-nup country was not a destructive force initially, but a subtly transforming one with advantages in exchange and political gain for the King Ya-nup within their region and beyond. By the time Barker arrived in November 1829, three years after the garrison's beginnings, the boundaries of the British world at King George's Sound were seemingly porous for the King Ya-nup who came and went as they pleased, utilising the best of both worlds and improvising with new materials.

Mokaré's use of the fringe was partly a diplomatic one but also included individual gain. His ongoing illness and death show that he never gave up the King Ya-nup world completely, but was drawn backwards and forwards between the two worlds to suit his desires and ongoing beliefs. The coming and going of the King Ya-nup between the Aboriginal world and the fringe were not without their complications. As mentioned previously, Mokaré noticed physical changes and he often feared being speared in the bush after a prolonged time in the settlement. Mokaré sometimes acted as a gatekeeper of the fringe too: he sent King Ya-nup back to the bush if they were becoming too 'saucy': little Wapere was sent back on a number of occasions, probably for being blasé about his cultural obligations, or outstaying the settlement's welcome.[21]

These episodes also show the slow transformation of an Aboriginal landscape. For the King Ya-nup, their spaces and culture changed at a pace and in ways that they could partly control. With *caibre* their geographical knowledge was opened up and their world expanded. The slow pace of change meant they could largely control the ways in which they utilised the British presence. Protection from the Wills people, clothing and knowledge collection are good examples of their unrelenting control on the fringe and their gains in strength in the region generally. The episodes of travel, knowledge collection – geographical and natural – and trade also reveal how the newcomers were incorporated into a transforming Aboriginal narrative through the strategic use of the fringe by the King Ya-nup and all the new and continuing possibilities it held.

With disease and death increasing and large groups of migrants arriving to take up Aboriginal land, the Aboriginal worlds of the region would soon change at a quicker pace. The fringe would eventually become inverted as Aboriginal families migrated from around the region, becoming 'fringe dwellers' themselves – morally and physically – on the edges of a rapidly changing colonial world. Micro-social histories, such as this one, slow down the pace of studies of past people and events to display something of the culture of a British garrison. In this period there was room, and need, for the development of new cultural vocabularies. Fine-grained episodes enable revelations of remarkable characters, such as Barker, Collie and Nind, as they struggled with issues such as 'law and order' and 'peace' in the volatile and slippery cultural space of the fringe.

Research and writing this history has deepened my attachment to this place. Visiting the region now, I witness a landscape which is littered with hints from these long-ago people and echoes of their stories, and I am constantly aware of the past moments of shared laughter, misunderstandings, violence and handshakes that took place on the fringe and beyond it. I believe there is an ethical importance in celebrating moments of friendship, reciprocity and respectful interaction in Aboriginal relations with non-indigenous people, given the generally parlous, ongoing colonial history of Australia. Such moments may be read as precedents for genuine reconciliation, as alternative paths which might have been taken and perhaps still can be.

Main Characters

Characters are listed in chronological order within their groupings.

Explorers

Nuyts, Peter: Dutch explorer aboard the ship *Gulden Zeepardt*, sailed past what would later be King George's Sound in 1627.

Vancouver, Captain George: English explorer, visited and named King George the Third's Sound in HMS Sloop *Discovery* and HMS *Chatham* from 30 September to 12 October 1791, and took possession of the entire southern coast for Britain.

Flinders, Captain Matthew: The first British naval officer to circumnavigate Australia. He visited King George's Sound for three and a half weeks from 9 December 1801 to 5 January 1802. He was the first European visitor to record encounters with the Indigenous people of the area.

Baudin, Post Captain Nicolas: French navigata. His expedition visited King George's Sound in 1803.

King, Phillip Parker: British maritime surveyor, visited King George's Sound in 1818, 1821 and 1822.

d'Urville, Jules Sebastien Cesar Dumont: Navigata-naturalist, visited the region in October 1826. His crew spent a night on shore with Mokaré and his family. They also encountered two sealing crews while visiting the area.

The Garrison

Lockyer, Major Edmund: Founding commander at King George's Sound. His settlement party arrived to set up the garrison in December 1826 to deter the French from settling.

Wakefield, Captain Joseph: Took over from Lockyer as commander of the garrison in April 1827 until September 1828.

Nind, Isaac Scott: First doctor at garrison.

Sleeman, Lieutenant: Commander at the garrison from September 1828 to December 1829.

Barker, Captain Collet: Fourth commander of the garrison at King George's Sound. He arrived at King George's Sound from Raffles Bay on 29 November 1829 and took up his post in early December. His journal records the period from 18 January 1830 to 26 March 1831.

Wilson, Thomas Braidwood: Explorer and Scottish surgeon, visited King George's Sound in November 1829.

Collie, Dr Alexander: Scottish surgeon of the Royal Navy, Collie was appointed first Government Resident of Albany when the garrison became a free settlement under control of Swan River and Western Australia in April 1831.

Davis, Dr. R. M: Second doctor at the garrison, left with Barker in March 1831.

Major Aboriginal Characters

Jack 1: A King George's Sound man named 'Jack' by King's crew in 1821.

Jack 2: Lockyer named this Aboriginal man 'Jack' in 1826, 'on the supposition that he was the Jack of Cptn. King.'

Mokaré: 1800–August 1831. A King Ya-nup man who lived in the settlement with several commanders.

Dr Uredale: A senior *mulgarradock* in the King Ya-nup community and relative of Mokaré.

Nakinah: Mokaré's eldest brother. Considered 'King' of his 'tribe' by many of the newcomers.

Coolbun: Dr Uredale's brother.

Gyallipert: Maragnan's son. Travelled with Manyat to Swan River in 1833.

Maragnan: From the west, possibly a *Murrum* man. Revered traveller, father of Gyallipert.

Manyat: King Ya-nup voyager and traveller who visited Swan River in 1833 and guided Collie in 1831 and 1832.

Wannewar, Patyet and Numal: Brothers involved in the 1830 spearings, Chapter Five.

Glossary of Aboriginal Terms

All words are King Ya-nup unless stated otherwise.

Ba-doo – Port Jackson word for water
Bo-ken-yen-na – Shall I go on board?
Caibre/Cay-bur-ugh/ Cai cai cai cai caigh – European ship
Canpie – the Coconyup word for water
Carl – fire
Cau-wha – Come here
Cyrye – frogs
Djanga – Swan River word for ghosts of the dead/returned ancestors
Keit – war spears
Kibra – European Ship (Swan river word)
Maatinip – a short distance
Maatopen – a long distance
Man-jah-lies – unmarried man
Maungull – hunting, fishing and trading spears
Meara – spear thrower/throwing stick
Mialopen – someone who watches
Moolyert – song cycle
Moyen – one who 'kills nobody'
Mulgarradock – medicine man/sorcerer, who holds power in the community
Murtagh – very deep water
Noodle-bul – waistband made with possum fur
Paloil – ochre used in ceremony and worn in formal meetings with visitors
Peep-anger – an infant

Polgen – song cycle

Potora – English boat

Quipple – to steal

Toortungurr – ceremonial dance, known elsewhere as 'corroboree'

Towan – parrot

Turloit – a hut

Urelap – hungry and thirsty

Umbin – ceremonial scars, made with a burning stick or kangaroo claw

Wirago – spiritual and powerful woman

Woortil – neck band made with possum fur, worn by young girls

Wundab-buri – English boat at Swan River

Yockadock/Parn Yocker – married man

Yuredanger – somebody who marries outside their 'tribal' division

Notes

Prologue

1   E.P. Thompson, 'The Moral Economy of the English Working Class', in *Past and Present*, no. 50, February 1971, p. 78.

2   D. Watson, *Caledonia Australis: Scottish Highlanders on the Frontier of Australia*, Collins, Sydney, 1984, p. x.

3   Only the large outer harbour is known today as King George Sound. However, during the period of this history, the whole region, including the settlement and the harbour was referred to as 'King George's Sound'. I also refer to the whole region as well as the settlement as King George's Sound.

1 Stepping Ashore, Stepping Aboard

1   P. P. King, *Narrative of a Survey of the Intertropical and Western Coasts of Australia. Performed between the Years 1818 and 1822 by Captain Phillip Parker King, RN*, vol. II, John Murray, London, 1827, facsimile edition, Libraries Board of South Australia, Adelaide, 1969, p. 144.

2   I am using King's published account of his expedition. His original log books of the voyage, which offer a briefer and more immediate experience, are held in the National Archives, Kew, UK.

3   King, *Narrative*, vol. II, 24 December 1821, pp. 120–1.

4   ibid., p. 119.

5   A. Cunningham, *Journal of the brig Bathurst 1821–1822*, CSO papers 1788–1825, NLA, AO Reel no. 6034, SZ8, 24 December 1821.

6   ibid.

7   King, *Narrative*, vol. II, 24 December 1821, p. 121.

8   ibid., p. 122.

9   ibid., p. 125.

10   ibid., 25 December 1821, p. 130.

11   ibid., 26 December 1821, pp. 130–1.

12   Cunningham does not refer to Jack as a 'hostage' anywhere in his log, but writes about Jack's 'eagerness to help him collect plants and arrange the specimens on paper'. Cunningham, *Journal*, 28 December 1821.

13   Cunningham makes reference to Brown's work several times in King's *Narrative*. The species he referred to was *Kingia Australis*, named by Robert Brown, in honour of Captain Phillip

Parker King and in memory of King's father, Phillip Gidley King. This was written about by Brown and Cunningham in 'Appendix to the Account of the Voyages of Captain King', in King, *Narrative*, vol. II, pp. 534–8.

14   M. Hordern, *King of the Australian Coast: The Voyages of Phillip Parker King in the Mermaid and Bathurst*, Melbourne University Press, Carlton, Vic, 1997, p. 275.

15   King, *Narrative*, vol. II, 27–28 December 1821, p. 132.

16   ibid., 31 December, 1821, pp. 137–8.

17   ibid., 29 December 1821, p. 133.

18   ibid., p. 134.

19   ibid., 30 December 1821, p. 135.

20   ibid., p. 136.

21   ibid.

22   G. Beer, 'Travelling the Other Way', N. Jardine, J.A. Secord and E.C. Spary (eds), *Cultures of Natural History*, Cambridge University Press, London, New York, 1996, p. 329.

23   King, *Narrative*, vol. II, 27–28 December 1821, p. 132.

24   R. Appleyard, and T. Manford (eds), *The Beginning: European Discovery and Early Settlement of Swan River Western Australia*, University of Western Australia Press, Nedlands, WA, 1979, pp. 14–18.

25   R. Dickson, *To King George the Third Sound for Whales: A Voyage Aboard the British Whaling Vessel Kingston of London, Captain Thomas Dennis, 1800–1802*, transcribed from the original ship's log by Rod Dickson, Hesperian Press, Carlisle, WA, 2006, p. viii.

26   G. Vancouver, *A Voyage of Discovery to the North Pacific Ocean and Round the World 1791–1795*, vol. I, first published in 1798, Lamb, W. Kaye (ed.), The Hakluyt Society, London, 1984, p. 336.

27   ibid., p. 337.

28   ibid., p. 338.

29   ibid., pp. 340–1.

30   D. S. Garden, *Albany: A Panorama of the Sound from 1827*, Thomas Nelson, West Melbourne, Vic., 1977, p. 9.

31   Dickson, *To King George the Third Sound for Whales*, p. x.

32   ibid., p. viii.

33   M. Flinders, *Voyage to Terra Australis: Undertaken for the purpose of completing the discovery of that vast country and prosecuted in the years 1801, 1802 and 1803, in His Majesty's ship Investigator and subsequently in the armed vessel Porpoise and Cumberland schooner: with an account of the shipwreck of the Porpoise, arrival of the Cumberland at Mauritius, and imprisonment of the Commander during six years and a half in that island*, 9 December 1801, Facsimile edition, Libraries Board of South Australia, Adelaide, 1966 (1814), p. 53.

34   ibid., 14 December 1801, p. 57.

35   ibid., 15 December 1801, p. 58.

36   ibid., 30 December 1801, p. 60.

37   ibid., p. 61.

38   I. White, 'The Birth and Death of a Ceremony', *Aboriginal History*, vol. 4, 1980.

39   'Anatomical measurements by Hugh Bell', in Flinders, *Voyage to Terra Australis*, January 1802, p. 67. This vocabulary is listed and compared to an Aboriginal language at Port Jackson collected by David Collins and D'Entrecasteaux's Van Diemen's Land vocabulary lists.

40   F. Péron, *Voyage of Discovery to the Southern Lands*, 2nd ed., 1824, Book I to III, comprising chapters I to XXI, by François Péron, continued by Louis de Freycinet, Christine Cornell (tr. and ed.), Friends of the State Library of South Australia, Adelaide, 2006, p. 122.

41   J. Ransonnet, 'Report written on board the *Geographe* in 1803 to Captain Baudin from

midshipman Ransonnet about Ransonnet's exploration of the King George Sound area, Mt Gardner and Bald Island and his meeting with Aborigines', typescript of translation by P. Bevan, 1975, BL, PR10532.

42   Péron, *Voyage of Discovery*, pp. 120–1.

43   For a chronology of characters see Main Characters p. 217.

Reflection: Finding My Own Vocabulary for Encounters

1   For a remarkable recent indigenous history of this region see K. Scott and H. Brown, *Kayang and Me*, Fremantle Arts Centre Press, Fremantle, 2005.

2   B. Douglas, 'Encountering Agency: Islanders, European Voyagers, and the Production of Race in Oceania', in Elfriede Hermann (ed.), 'Changing Contexts – Shifting Meanings: Transformations of Cultural Traditions in Oceania', forthcoming, footnote 1.

3   J. Bruner, *Acts of Meaning: Four Lectures on Mind and Culture*, Jerusalem–Harvard Lectures, Harvard University Press, Cambridge, MA, 1990, p. 9.

4   E. Lockyer, 'Journal at King George's Sound', [Fair Copy] in *HRA*, series III, vol. VI, pp. 453–548, original held at AO NSW (CSO relating to King George's Sound 4/2092); E. Lockyer, 'Journal of Major Lockyer: Commandant of the Expedition sent from Sydney in 1826 to found a settlement at King George's Sound, Western Australia, [Rough Copy], in BL (919.412/ALB); I. S. Nind, 'Description of the natives of King George's Sound (Swan River Colony) and adjoining country', written by Isaac Scott Nind and communicated by Robert Brown, *Royal Geographical Society*, vol. I, 1831, London, 1832, pp. 21–51; C. Barker, 'Journal at King George's Sound January 1830–March 1831', BL microfilm (ACC 2545A); A. Collie, 'Anecdotes and Remarks relative to the Aborigines at King George's Sound' in *Perth Gazette and Western Australian Journal*, 5, 12, 26 July and 2, 9, 16 August 1834, pp. 315–40; A. Collie, *Letters with Respect to the Early History of the Swan River Settlement 1828–1835, written by Dr Alexander Collie to his brother George*, BL microfilm (ACC 332A.).

5   R. Isaac, *The Transformation of Virginia, 1740–1790*, Chapel Hill, University of North Carolina Press, Chapel Hill, Williamsburg, 1982, p. 324.

6   I. Clendinnen, 'Spearing the Governor', K. Darian-Smith (ed.), *Challenging Histories: Reflections on Australian History, Special Issue of Australian Historical Studies*, 2002, p. 163.

7   The French *Annales* school first wrote about the history of mentalities. See P. Ricoeur, *Memory, History, Forgetting*, University of Chicago Press, Chicago, London, 2004, pp. 188–200.

8   C. Geertz, 'On the Nature of Anthropological Understanding', *American Scientist*, vol. 63, no. 1, January–February 1975, p. 53.

9   G. Dening, *Readings/Writings*, Melbourne University Press, Carlton, Vic, 1998, p. 78.

10   V. Turner, 'Social Dramas and Stories about them', in W. J. T. Mitchell (ed.), *On Narrative*, University of Chicago Press, Chicago and London, 1980, pp. 137–64; C. Geertz, *The Interpretation of Cultures: A Selection of Essays*, Basic Books, New York, 1973.

11   Dening, *Readings/Writings*, p. 48.

12   The books I have found most helpful are D. Merwick, *Death of a Notary: Conquest and Change in Colonial New York*, Ithaca, Cornell University Press, New York, 1999, and D. Merwick, *The Shame and the Sorrow: Dutch-Amerindian Encounters in New Netherland*, University of Pennsylvania Press, Philadelphia, 2006.

13   I. Clendinnen, 'Response to Correspondence' in R. Davidson, 'No Fixed Address: Nomads and the Fate of the Planet', *Quarterly Essay*, issue 24, 2006, p. 84.

14   H. White, 'The Value of Narrativity in the Representation of Reality', in Mitchell, *On Narrative*, p. 4.

2 Beyond the Littoral: Reading the King Ya-nup World

1. J. B. Jackson, cited in L. R. Lippard, *The Lure of the Local: Senses of Place in a Multicultural Society*, New Press, New York, 1997, p. 8.

2. A description of general Indigenous childbirth practices across Australia can be found in R. and C. Berndt, *The World of the First Australians: Aboriginal Traditional Life: Past and Present*, Aboriginal Studies Press, Canberra, 1999, p. 155; my reconstruction is from Barker, *Journal*, 1 April 1830.

3. Barker, *Journal*, 1 April 1830. I have often also referred to the edited version of Barker's journal, D. J. Mulvaney and N. Green (eds), *Commandant of Solitude: The Journals of Captain Collet Barker 1828–1831*, Melbourne University Press, Carlton, Vic, 1992. Instead of page numbers I will use dates because of the use of both the microfilmed journal and the edited version.

4. Barker recorded the season of *Moken* as being from late April to June, whereas Collie recorded the season of *Mokkar* from late May to July. Collie, 'Anecdotes and Remarks', 5 July 1834, p. 315.

5. Barker, *Journal*, 22 April 1830.

6. Collie, 'Anecdotes and Remarks', 5 July 1834, p. 315.

7. Barker, *Journal*, 1 April 1830.

8. *peep-anger* was recorded by Nind, 'Description of the Natives of King George's Sound', p. 50.

9. Mokaré called these four men his brothers and I re-use this with caution, knowing that in Aboriginal culture the term brother is different from my Western and British nineteenth-century understanding of brother as a birth relation.

10. A. Collie, 'Letter to George Collie, 4 August 1831', in *Letters with Respect to the Early History of Swan River*.

11. Barker, *Journal*, 14 May 1830.

12. Nind, 'Description of the Natives of King George's Sound', pp. 26, 41.

13. ibid., p. 50.

14. Barker, *Journal*, 16 November 1830.

15. de Sainson, in 'Officer's Diaries', J. S. C. D. d'Urville, *An Account in Two Volumes of Two Voyages to the South Seas by Captain (later Rear-Admiral) Jules S.C. Dumont d'Urville, of the French Navy to Australia, New Zealand, Oceania 1826–1829, in the Corvette l'Astrolabe and to the Straits of Chile, Oceania, South East Asia, Australia, Antarctica, New Zealand and Torres Strait 1837–1840, Volume 1: Astrolabe 1826-1829*, Helen Rosenman (ed.), Melbourne University Press, Carlton, Vic, 1987, vol. I, p. 38.

16. Barker, *Journal*, 9 May 1830.

17. Nind, 'Description of the Natives of King George's Sound', p. 44.

18. W. C. Ferguson, 'Mokaré's Domain', in D. J. Mulvaney, and P. J. White (eds), *Australians to 1788*, Fairfax, Broadway, NSW, Syme and Weldon, 1987 p. 121; de Sainson sketched Yallapoli and Patyet – said to be father and son, and I have deduced that Patyet was also Mokaré's father as he was Yallapoli's brother.

19. Barker, *Journal*, 3 February 1831.

20. de Sainson, 'A Night Spent with the Natives', in d'Urville, *Two Voyages to the South Seas*, p. 40.

21. Nind, 'Description of the Natives of King George's Sound', p. 25.

22. Barker, *Journal*, 26 January 1830.

23. Nind, 'Description of the Natives of King George's Sound', p. 25.

24. ibid.

25. Bruner, *Acts of Meaning*, p. 12.

26. ibid., p. 11.

27   See Main Characters p. 217.

28   Nind, 'Description of the Natives of King George's Sound', p. 43.

29   A. Collie, 'Account of an Explorative Excursion to the NW of King George's Sound, in 1832 by A. Collie Surgeon R.N.' in J. Shoobert (ed.), *Western Australian Exploration: vol. 1 1826–1835*, Hesperian Press, Carlisle, WA, 2005, p. 311.

30   Barker, *Journal*, 4 May 1830.

31   I will however, use the term 'Aborigine' as a noun.

32   T. B. Wilson, *Narrative of a voyage round the world : comprehending an account of the wreck of the ship Governor Ready in Torres Straits, a description of the British settlements on the coasts of New Holland, more particularly Raffles Bay, Melville Island, Swan River, and King George's Sound : also, the manners and customs of the Aboriginal tribes : with an appendix containing remarks on transportation, the treatment of convicts during the voyage, and advice to persons intending to emigrate to the Australian colonies*, Dawson of Pall Mall, London, 1968 (1835), p. 242.

33   R. Clint, 'Journal of an Excursion to the Mountain Range to the Northward and Eastward of Porrong-u-rup, 20 Dec 1831, by Raphael Clint, Assistant Surveyor', in Shoobert (ed.), *Western Australian Exploration*, p. 292.

34   J. Browne, 'The Aborigines of Australia', Read before the Canadian Institute, 16 February 1856, *Nautical Magazine and Navy Chronicle*, p. 488.

35   Collie, 'Anecdotes and Remarks', 9 August 1834, p. 335.

36   Wilson, *Narrative of a voyage round the world*, p. 283.

37   Ferguson, 'Mokaré's Domain', p. 128.

38   Ferguson also notes the inland camp sites.

39   Barker, *Journal*, 3 February 1830.

40   King, *Narrative*, vol. II, p. 141.

41   Vancouver, *A Voyage of Discovery*, pp. 338–9.

42   Barker, *Journal*, 4 February 1831.

43   This description of *Tondirrup* comes from Lockyer, 'Fair Copy', 26 December 1826.

44   Barker, *Journal*, 22 July 1830.

45   Ferguson, 'Mokaré's Domain', p. 125.

46   King, *Narrative*, vol. II, p. 138.

47   Wilson, *Narrative of a voyage round the world*, 3 December 1829, p. 238.

48   King's River (now known as King River) was named after Phillip Parker King in 1829 by Wilson. King had examined the lower reaches of the watercourse during his hydrographic survey in 1818. Collie recorded the King Ya-nup crossing point in A. Collie, 'Account of four excursions in the vicinity of King George's Sound between 27 April and 15 June 1831, by Alexander Collie, Surgeon', Shoobert, *Western Australian Explorations*, 17 May 1831, p. 249.

49   Collie recorded the King Ya-nup word for corroboree as *toortunggur* in 'Anecdotes and Remarks', but Barker and other newcomers always referred to these dancing ceremonies with the generic term: corroboree.

50   Barker, *Journal*, 25 November 1830.

51   A. Brearley, *Ernest Hodgkin's Swanland: Estuaries and Coastal Lagoons of South-western Australia*, University of Western Australia Press, Crawley, WA, 2005, p. 406. French's River, or *Riviere des Francais*, was named by Baudin in 1803. In April 1831, Collie recorded the river's native name as *Kal-gan-up*. It was not generally referred to as the Kalgan River until later in 1832.

52   Collie, 'Anecdotes and Remarks', 12 July 1834, p. 319.

53   Nind, 'Description of the Natives of King George's Sound', p. 28.

54   ibid.

55   Barker, *Journal*, 26 January 1830.

56   ibid., 10 May 1830 and 31 January 1831.

57   Nind, 'Description of the Natives of King George's Sound', p. 44.

58   Barker, *Journal*, 1 February 1830. See also Nind who refers to this marriage custom as *Parn Yocker*, p. 38.

59   Barker, *Journal*, 17 June 1830.

60   ibid., 1 February 1830.

61   ibid.

62   I. and P. Crawford, *Contested Country: A History of the Northcliffe Area, Western Australia*, University of Western Australia Press, Nedlands, WA, 2003, p. 9.

63   Barker, *Journal*, 1 December 1830.

64   J. Bruner, 'Narrative Construction of Reality', *Critical Inquiry*, vol. 18, no. 1, Autumn 1991, p. 19.

65   S. J. Hallam, *Fire and Hearth: A Study of Aboriginal Usage and European Usurpation in South-Western Western Australia*, Canberra, Australian Institute of Aboriginal Studies, 1975.

66   King, *Narrative*, 21–31 January 1818, vol. I, p. 16.

67   Nind, 'Description of the Natives of King George's Sound', p. 37.

68   Barker, *Journal*, 1 August 1830.

69   ibid., 19 January 1831.

70   Hallam, *Fire and Hearth*, p. 30. The burning season is recorded by Barker and Collie.

71   Barker, *Journal*, 21 January 1831.

72   ibid.

73   ibid., 16 March 1830. Barker and Collie's lists of King Ya-nup seasons have distinct crossovers too, showing the complexity of seasonal change.

74   ibid., 17–18 November 1830.

75   ibid., 30 January 1830.

76   ibid.

77   Ferguson, 'Mokaré's Domain', p. 455.

78   Browne, 'Aborigines of Australia', p. 488.

79   *Perth Gazette*, 12 July 1834, p. 318.

80   Browne, 'Aborigines of Australia', p. 488.

81   ibid., p. 489.

82   P. Chauncey, 'Notes and Anecdotes of the Aborigines of Australia', Appendix A in R. Brough Smyth, *The Aborigines of Victoria, with notes relating to the Habits of the Natives of other parts of Australia and Tasmania, compiled from various sources for the government of Victoria*, vol. II, John Ferres, Government Printer, Melbourne, Vic., 1878, p. 268.

83   Daisy Bates, quoted in Crawford, *Contested Country*, p. 11.

84   Nind, 'Description of the Natives of King George's Sound', p. 47.

85   Barker, *Journal*, 17 July 1830.

86   M. C. Howard, in R. and C. Berndt (eds), *Aborigines of the West: Their Past and their Present*, University of Western Australia Press, Nedlands, 1979, p. 91.

87   Barker, *Journal*, 18 April 1830.

88   ibid., 25 April 1830.

89   Nind, 'Description of the Natives of King George's Sound', p. 37.

90   ibid., p. 42.

91   ibid., p. 96.

92   ibid., pp. 42–3.

93   ibid., p. 44.

94   Barker, *Journal*, 3 July 1830.

95   Collie, 'Anecdotes and Remarks', 2 August 1834, p. 332.

96   N. Sharp, *Saltwater People: The Waves of Memory*, Allen and Unwin, Crow's Nest, NSW, 2002, p. 6.

97   ibid., pp. 6–7.

98   ibid., p. 10.

99   There is scant evidence of some possible earlier use of shellfish on the south-west coast and on the west coast north of Moore River. See C. E. Dortch, G. W. Kendrick and K. Morse, 'Aboriginal mollusc exploitation in southwestern Australia', *Archaeology in Oceania*, 19, no. 3, October, 1984, pp. 81–104.

100   Nind, 'Description of the Natives of King George's Sound', pp. 33–4.

101   G. Grey, *Journals of Two Expeditions of discovery in north-west and western Australia, during the years 1837, 38 and 39, with observations on the moral and physical condition of the Aboriginal inhabitants, &c. &c.*, vol. II, facsimile edition, Libraries Board of South Australia, Adelaide, 1964 (1841), p. 237.

102   Vancouver, *A Voyage of Discovery*, p. 341.

103   ibid., pp. 341–2.

104   King, *Narrative*, vol. II, 31 December 1821, pp. 137–8.

105   ibid., 20 January 1830.

106   Barker, *Journal*, 20 January 1830.

107   ibid., 20 March 1830.

108   R. M. Lyon, 'A Glance at the Manners and Language of the Aboriginal Inhabitants of Western Australia; with a short vocabulary, 23 March 1833', *Perth Gazette*, 30 March 1830, p. 51.

109   R. Darnton, *The Great Cat Massacre: And Other Episodes in French Cultural History*, New York, Basic Books, 1984, p. 78.

110   ibid.

111   S. Hallam, 'Coastal does not equal Littoral', *Australian Archaeology*, No. 25, December, 1987, p. 15.

112   ibid., p. 11.

113   ibid.

114   ibid., p. 13.

115   ibid., p. 23.

3 Setting Up the Fringe

1   E. Lockyer, 'Report by Major Lockyer on the Newly-formed Settlement at King George's Sound' in *HRA*, series III, vol. VI, p. 488.

2   Lockyer, 'Fair Copy', 21 January 1827.

3   ibid.

4   'Darling to Major Lockyer, 4 November 1826', *HRA*, series I, vol. XII, p. 701.

5   For the discussions about the establishment of a British garrison at King George's Sound see: *HRA* series I, vol. XII, pp. 218, 640, 701.

6   d'Urville, *Two Voyages to the South Seas*, 14 October 1826, p. 32.

7   Lockyer, 'Report', p. 487.

8   A. Macleay, 'Letter from Colonial Secretary Macleay to Major Lockyer', letter marked no. 1, 4 November 1826, *HRA*, series III, vol. VI, p. 454.

9   E. Lockyer, 'Journal of an Excursion up the River Brisbane in the year 1825' in H. R. Stuart, *The Genesis of Queensland: An account of the first exploring*, Sydney, Turner and Henderson, 1888, pp. 589–601.

10   Lockyer, 'Fair Copy', 26 January 1827.

11   ibid., 15 January 1827.

12   ibid., 30 December 1826.

13   The other recorded use of the name *Frederickstown* was by John Kent in his report of his expedition with Thomas Braidwood Wilson and Mokaré to the north-west of the settlement in December 1829: J. Kent, 'An Account of a West Australian Expedition from King George Sound in December 1829, by John Kent of Berkshire', in Shoobert, *Western Australian Exploration*, pp. 122–5; and in the sketch by Nind (see image 17).

14   J. Sweetman, *The Military Establishment and Penal Settlement at King George Sound, Western Australia*, Australian Studies Booklet no. 1, Hesperian Press, Carlisle, WA, 1989, pp. 6–12.

15   Lockyer, 'Fair Copy', 4 March 1827.

16   ibid.

17   Wilson, *Narrative of a voyage round the world*, p. 274.

18   Lockyer, 'Rough Copy', 28 January 1827. A *scourger* was a person who inflicted punishment.

19   ibid., 27 January 1827.

20   Lockyer, 'Fair Copy', 27 January 1827.

21   A 'black hole' would later be created for punishment.

22   Lockyer, 'Rough Copy', 24 January 1827.

23   Lockyer, 'Fair Copy', 6 February 1827 and 11 February 1827.

24   ibid., 24 February 1827.

25   Barker, *Journal*, 3 September 1830.

26   This idea of Sturt's was taken up further by A. Frost and M. Aveling (eds), *Australians to 1838*, Fairfax, Syme and Weldon, Sydney, 1987, p. xvii.

27   The Swan River settlement's port town was located to the south at Fremantle.

28   R. Gibson, 'Ocean Settlement', *Meanjin*, 53 (4), 1994, p. 668.

29   Lockyer, 'Report', p. 490.

30   Lockyer, 'Rough Copy', 27 January 1827 and 'Fair Copy', 28 December 1826.

31   Lockyer, 'Report', p. 506.

32   The gardener John Brown also died on 29 May from inflammation of the liver.

33   J. Wakefield, 'Letter from Joseph Wakefield to Colonial Secretary Macleay, 21 May 1827', *HRA*, series III, vol. VI, p. 507.

34   ibid.

35   Many British settlements included a 'Green Island' or 'Garden Island' where seeds were sown in the early days of settlement. There was a 'Green Island' in Sydney Harbour and near D'Entrecasteaux Channel in Van Diemen's Land and a Garden Island at Swan River.

36   C. Hanson, 'Colonel Hanson's Pamphlet', *Perth Gazette*, 12–26 January 1833.

37   R. Darling, 'Governor Ralph Darling to Lord Viscount Goderich, 24 December 1827', Despatch No. 131, *HRA* series I, vol. XIII, p. 667.

38   R. W. Huskisson, 'Right Hon. R.W. Huskisson to Governor Darling, 30 January 1828', Despatch No. 9, *HRA*, series I, vol. XIII, pp. 741–2.

39   Wilson, *Narrative of a voyage around the world*, p. 232.

40   ibid., p. 234.

41   Sleeman, Enclosure from 16 February 1829 in 'Letter from Lieutenant Sleeman to Colonial Secretary Macleay' 7 September 1829, *HRA*, series III, vol. VI, p. 543.

42   Hoop, 'Letter from Serjeant Hoop to Lieutenant Sleeman', King George's Sound, 5 May 1829, Enclosure No. 14, *HRA*, series III, vol. VI, p. 535.

43   Sleeman, 'Letter from Sleeman to Macleay, King George's Sound, 7 October 1829', *HRA*, series III, vol. VI, p. 544.

44   Barker, *Journal*, 26 November, 1830.

45   ibid., 21 April 1830.

46   ibid., 27 April 1830.

47   ibid., 22 April 1830.

48   Quicksilver was mercury.

49   ibid., 20 January 1830.

50   ibid., 10 January 1831.

51   Mulvaney and Green, *Commandant of Solitude*, pp. 3–4.

52   Barker, *Journal*, 15–16 October 1830.

53   ibid., 6 October 1830.

54   Her name was also written as 'Waterloo' at Raffles Bay and 'Riveral' at King George's Sound.

55   Wilson, *Narrative of a voyage round the world*, p. 282.

56   Barker, *Journal*, 10 June 1830.

57   ibid., 20 January 1830.

58   ibid., 8 January 1831.

59   ibid., 25 January 1831.

60   ibid., 17 June 1830.

61   ibid., 1 September 1830.

62   The instructions from Governor Ralph Darling are in AO NSW (AO reel 4/4551).

63   Collie, 'The Meteorological Journal, by A. Collie Esq., from April 1831 to April 1832', in J. Cross, *Journals of Several Explorations made in Western Australia, during the years 1829, 1830, 1831, and 1832*, London, J. Cross, 1833, pp. 239–62.

64   Collie, 'Letter from Alexander Collie to his brother George, 28 July 1832', *Letters with Respect to the Early History of Swan River*.

65   ibid., 30 October 1831.

66   ibid., 28 July 1832.

67   Collie, 'Letter to Stirling, July 31, 1832', in Cross, pp. 204–5.

68   Collie, 'Report to Governor James Stirling, 1831', *Swan River Papers*, vol. 9, pp. 110–21, SRO WA.

Reflection: Shaking Hands

1   F. F. Armstrong, 'Manners and Habits of the Aborigines of Western Australia, from information collected by Mr. F Armstrong, Interpreter', *Perth Gazette and Western Australian Journal*, 29 October 1836, p. 789; also in G. F. Moore, 'Descriptive Vocabulary', p. 20, in *Diary of Ten Years Eventful Life of an Early Settler in Western Australia and also a Descriptive Vocabulary of the Language of the Aborigines*, M. Walbrook, London, 1884.

2   ibid.; for other Western Australian examples see also Grey, *Journals of Two Expeditions*, vol. I, pp. 301–2.

3   Nind, 'Description of the Natives of King George's Sound', p. 47.

4   ibid., p. 50.

5   Barker, *Journal*, 1 June 1830.

6   I take encounters to mean sightings and soundings of others, and it can be assumed that the Aborigines saw and heard Vancouver even though they never met him. So the *first* encounters between Aborigines and Europeans at King George's Sound, as experienced by the Aborigines, were not recorded.

7   Lockyer, 'Rough Copy', 27 December 1826.

8   Lockyer, 'Fair Copy', 27 December 1826.

9   Barker, *Journal*, throughout March 1830.

10   ibid., 14 May 1830.

11   'Emigration Advertisement for King George's Sound in England', undated 1832, *Swan River Papers*, vol. 9, p. 73, SRO WA.

12   Ferguson, 'Mokaré's Domain', pp. 137–42.

13   N. Green, 'King George Sound: The Friendly Frontier', in Moya Smith (ed.), *Archaeology in ANZAAS*, Western Australian Museum, WA, 1983, pp. 68–74.

14   T. Austen, *A Cry in the Wind: Conflict in Western Australia 1829–1929*, Darlington Publishing Group, Darlington, WA, 1998; N. Green, *Broken Spears: Aborigines and Europeans in the Southwest of Western Australia*, Focus Education Series, Perth, 1983.

15   Green, 'Friendly Frontier', p. 72.

16   R. Baker, 'Coming In? The Yanyuwa as a case study in the geography of contact history', *Aboriginal History*, vol. 14, 1990, p. 25.

17   I. Clendinnen, *Dancing With Strangers*, Text Publishing, 2003, Melbourne, pp. 138, 174.

18   Baker, 'Coming In?', p. 30.

19   ibid., pp. 30–1.

20   A. McGrath, *Born in the Cattle: Aborigines in Cattle Country*, Allen and Unwin, Sydney, 1987, p. 20.

21   Baker, 'Coming In?', p. 31.

22   Collie, 'Letter from Alexander Collie to his brother George, 4 August 1831', *Letters with respect to the early history of the Swan River*.

23   Barker, *Journal*, 27 August 1830.

24   ibid., 24 November 1830; Collie also notes the seasonal presence of the King Ya-nup, in 'Anecdotes and Remarks', 2 August 1834, p. 332.

25   Barker, *Journal*, 1 March 1830.

26   ibid., 22 January 1830.

27   ibid., 18 January 1830.

28   E. Sapir, 'The Emergence of the Concept of Personality in a Study of Cultures, *Journal of Social Psychology*, 5, 1934, quoted in Turner, 'Social Dramas', p. 140.

29   ibid.

30   Berndt, *The World of the First Australians*, p. 23.

31   Lockyer, 'Rough Copy', 22 January 1827.

32   Lockyer, 'Fair Copy', 9 March 1827.

33   The Oyster Bay Tribe was the largest and most well-known group in Van Diemen's Land in the early nineteenth century. Their country was located along the east coast of Van Diemen's Land from St Patrick's Head to the Derwent Estuary, to the mouth of the Jordan River. See L. Ryan, *The Aboriginal Tasmanians*, University of Queensland Press, St Lucia, QLD, 1981, p. 17.

34   Wakefield, 'Letter from Captain Joseph Wakefield to Colonial Secretary Macleay, 21 May 1827'; 'Wakefield Time' is how the King Ya-nup referred to Wakefield's presence at the garrison, similar to Donald Thompson's 'Thompson Time' in northern Australia.

35   ibid.

36   Nind and Wilson explained that Mokaré had been living in the settlement.

37   Wakefield, 'Letter from Captain Wakefield to Colonial Secretary Macleay 21 May 1827'.

38   Barker, *Journal*, 26 January 1830.

39   ibid.

40   Nind, 'Letter from Assistant Surgeon Nind to Lieutenant Sleeman, 15 January 1829, King George's Sound', Enclosure No. 1, *HRA*, series III, vol. VI, p. 528.

41   Wilson, *Narrative of a Voyage Around the World*, p. 274.

42   ibid., p. 282.

43   S. Henty, 'Exploration to the north of King River by Stephen George Henty', December 1831, Shoobert (ed.), *Western Australian Explorations*, p. 292.

44   Collie, 'Anecdotes and Remarks', 5 July 1834, p. 315.

45   This idea of additional Aboriginal languages comes from the work of D. Eades, 'They don't speak an Aboriginal language, or do they?', I. Keen (ed.), *Being Black: Aboriginal Cultures*

in Settled Australia, Aboriginal Studies Press, Canberra, 1988, pp. 97–117; I refer to this language as a pidgin language, rather than Creole, because not everybody spoke the language – Creole languages are usually spoken by a majority.

46   For more on the construction of pidgin contact languages in Australia see, J. Harris, 'North Australian Kriol and the Kriol 'Holi Baibul', in T. Swain and D. Rose (eds), *Aboriginal Australians and Christian Missions*, The Australian Association for the Study of Religions, Bedford Park, SA, 1988, pp. 412–13.

47   Barker, *Journal*, 25 April 1830.

48   Isaac, *The Transformation of Virginia*, p. 324.

49   I have not been able to find out which encyclopaedia Barker consulted, but he was interested enough in Aboriginal religions to bring one with him. It is probable that this encyclopaedia was French as there were several French ethnographic encyclopaedia's published in the late eighteenth and early nineteenth centuries, and Barker spoke French.

50   Barker, *Journal*, 21 January 1830.

51   ibid.

52   ibid., 30 April 1830.

53   ibid., 12 July 1830.

54   Nind, 'Description of the Natives of King George's Sound', p. 47.

55   Wilson, *Narrative of a Voyage Around the World*, p. 241.

56   Barker, *Journal*, 15 April 1830.

4 Violence Performed

1   The journals were those of Vancouver, Flinders and King.

2   Lockyer, 'Rough Copy', 25 December 1826.

3   Lockyer, 'Fair Copy', 25 December 1826.

4   L. Johnson, *Major Edmund Lockyer: Forgotten Australian Pioneer*, Western Australian Museum, Albany, WA, 2002.

5   E. Lockyer, 'Journal of an Excursion up the River Brisbane'.

6   For clarity I will refer to this man as Jack, even though he only later became known as Jack to Lockyer.

7   Lockyer, 'Rough Copy', 26 December 1826.

8   ibid.

9   Lockyer, 'Fair Copy', 26 December 1826.

10   Lockyer, 'Rough Copy', 26 December 1826.

11   Lockyer, 'Fair Copy', 26 December 1826.

12   Lockyer would retrospectively increase their numbers to eight.

13   Lockyer, 'Rough Copy', 27 December.

14   ibid.

15   Lockyer, 'Fair Copy', 26 December 1826.

16   ibid.

17   ibid.

18   Lockyer, 'Rough Copy', 27 December 1826.

19   Nind, 'Description of the Natives of King George's Sound', p. 45.

20   Lockyer, 'Rough Copy', 28 December 1826.

21   Lockyer, 'Fair Copy', 5 January 1827. It seems that after this meeting, Lockyer began to refer to this young man as Jack in his Rough Copy Journal.

22   ibid., 10 January 1827.

23   ibid., 11 January 1827.

24   King, vol. II, p. 130.

25   d'Urville, *Two Voyages to the South Seas*, 8 October 1826, p. 27.

26   Lockyer, 'Rough Copy', 12 January 1827.

27   The 'high hill' was Mt Clarence to the east of the camp.

28   Lockyer, 'Fair Copy', 13 January 1827.

29   ibid.

30   ibid., 14 January 1827.

31   ibid., 10 March 1827.

32   Wakefield, 'Letter from Wakefield to Macleay, King George's Sound, 21 May 1827', pp. 508–9.

33   Lockyer, 'Rough Copy', 7 January 1827.

34   D. J. Mulvaney, *Encounters in Place: Outsiders and Australians 1606–1985*, University of Queensland Press, St Lucia, QLD, 1989, p. 1.

35   Isaac, *Transformation of Virginia*, p. 324.

36   ibid.

37   Hallam, *Fire and Hearth*; See also C. Dortch, *Devil's Lair: A Search for Ancient Man in Western Australia*, Western Australian Museum, Perth, 1976, p. 81.

38   Nind, 'Description of the Natives of King George's Sound', p. 26.

39   Grey, *Journals of Two Expeditions*, pp. 298–9.

40   King, *Narrative*, vol. II, 24 December 1821, p. 124.

41   Barker, *Journal*, 9–11 July 1830.

42   S. J. Hallam, 'A View from the Other Side of the Western Australian Frontier: Or "I Met a Man Who Wasn't There…"', *Aboriginal History*, vol. 7, 1983, p. 149.

43   ibid.

44   Bruner, *Acts of Meaning*, p. 110.

45   Clendinnen, 'Spearing the Governor', p. 169.

46   'Judicious Order of Major Lockyer', in Wilson, *Narrative of a Voyage Around the World*, p. 235.

47   Clendinnen, 'Spearing the Governor', p. 163.

5 Violence Told

1   Barker, *Journal*, 25 January 1830.

2   ibid., 1 February 1830.

3   ibid., 8 March 1830.

4   ibid., 12 March 1830.

5   Nind, 'Description of the Natives of King George's Sound', p. 36.

6   Browne, 'The Aborigines of Australia', p. 488; P. Chauncy, 'Notes and Anecdotes of the Aborigines of Australia', in R. B. Smyth, *The Aborigines of Victoria*, vol. II, p. 268.

7   Nind, 'Description of the Natives of King George's Sound', p. 46.

8   Collie, 'Anecdotes and Remarks', 5 July 1834, p. 315. My emphasis.

9   Green, *Broken Spears*, pp. 226–31. Green has also tabled Aboriginal-non-indigenous conflict.

10   ibid., p. 226.

11   J. Cashmere, 'The social uses of violence in ritual: Charivari or religious persecution?', *European History Quarterly*, no. 21, 1991, p. 291.

12   Barker, *Journal*, 19 June 1830.

13   ibid., 23 April 1830.

14   For other examples around Australia see: Berndt, *The World of the First Australians*, p. 304; A. P. Elkin, *Aboriginal Men of High Degree*, 2nd edn, University of Queensland Press, St Lucia, 1977 ; B. Nance, 'The Level of Violence: Europeans and Aborigines in Port Phillip', *Australian Historical Studies*, vol. 19, no. 77, October 1981, pp. 532–52.

15   Nind, 'Description of the Natives of King George's Sound', p. 45.

16   Barker, *Journal*, 12 March 1830.

17   ibid.

18   ibid., 22 March 1830.

19   ibid., 19 March 1830.

20   Barker explains the term *mialopen* on 15 January 1831.

21   ibid., 8 April 1830.

22   ibid.

23   ibid., 13 March 1830.

24   ibid., 10 April 1830.

25   ibid., 2 April 1830.

26   ibid., 3 April 1830.

27   ibid., 15 April 1830.

28   ibid., 16 April 1830.

29   ibid.

30   ibid., 17 April 1830.

31   ibid., 11 May 1830.

32   ibid.

33   Nind, 'Description of the Natives of King George's Sound', p. 44.

34   Collie, 'Anecdotes and Remarks', 2 August 1834, p. 332.

35   B. Douglas, 'Doing Ethnographic History: The Case of Fighting in New Caledonia', in J. G. Carrier (ed.), *History and Tradition in Melanesian Anthropology*, University of California Press, Berkeley, 1992, p. 98.

36   ibid.

37   C. Von Brandenstein, *Nyungar Anew: Etymological, Text Samples and Etymological and Historical 1500-word Vocabulary of an Artificially Re-created Aboriginal Language in the South-West of Australia*, Pacific Linguistics, Australian National University Printing Service, Canberra, ACT, 1988, p. vi.

38   Browne, 'The Aborigines of Australia', p. 488.

39   M. Fels, *Good Men and True: The Aboriginal Police of the Port Phillip District 1837–1853*, Melbourne University Press, 1988, Carlton, Vic., p. 3.

40   Barker, *Journal*, 9 May 1830.

41   Grey, *Journal of Two Expeditions*, pp. 304–5.

42   Nind, 'Description of the Natives of King George's Sound', p. 45.

43   Barker, *Journal*, 23 April 1830.

44   ibid., 9 May 1830.

45   ibid., 14 April 1830.

46   There is no date attached to this comment, but John Mulvaney and Neville Green have attached it to p. 356 in their edited journal.

47   Wilson, *Narrative of a voyage round the world*, pp. 245–6.

48   Barker, *Journal*, 24 April 1830.

49   It is remarkable that Barker used the term 'business' for King Ya-nup activity that did not include the British, considering the term is so often used today in regards to Indigenous cultural practices.

50   Barker wrote that it was the King's birthday, however, it was St George's Day, the patron saint of England. The King's birthday was 12 August. No holiday was recorded in Barker's journal on 12 August.

51   ibid., 23 April 1830.

52   ibid., 20 May 1830.

53   ibid., 15 November 1830.

54   ibid., 23 April 1830.

55   ibid., 12 May 1830.

56   ibid., 13 July 1830.

57   ibid., 1 January 1831.

58   ibid., 20 January 1831.

59   ibid., 12 June 1830.

60   ibid., 13 July 1830.

61   ibid., 22 November 1830.

62   ibid., 15 April 1830.

63   ibid., 3 January 1831.

64   ibid., 20 December 1830.

65   ibid., 14 July 1830.

66   ibid., 30 November 1830.

67   ibid., 13 February 1831.

68   ibid., 1 February 1830.

69   ibid., 13 February 1831.

70   ibid., 22 November 1830.

71   Collie, 'Anecdotes and Remarks', 16 August 1834, p. 339.

72   ibid., 9 August 1834, p. 335.

73   ibid.

74   R. Metcalfe, 'Who Should Rule at Home?', *Journal of American History*, vol. 61, no. 3, December 1974, p. 652.

75   ibid., p. 653.

76   There are of course good exceptions, for a Victorian example see: Fels, Marie, *Good Men and True*; and for New South Wales see: M. Nugent, *Botany Bay: Where Histories Meet*, Allen and Unwin, Crows Nest, NSW, 2005.

77   Nind, 'Description of the Natives of King George's Sound', p. 38.

78   Barker, *Journal*, 25 January 1830.

79   ibid., 13 July 1830.

Reflection: Contexts of Violence

1   Green, *Broken Spears*, pp. 40–2; Garden, *Albany*, pp. 32–3; Johnson, *Major Edmund Lockyer*, pp. 67–8.

2   J. Backhouse, *Narrative of a Visit to the Australian Colonies*, Hamilton, Adams, London, 1843, p. 525.

3   E. Lockyer, 'Judicious Order', in Wilson, *Narrative of a Voyage around the World*, p. 235.

4   Clendinnen, *Dancing with Strangers*, p. 189.

5   A. Blok, 'The Enigma of Senseless Violence', in G. Ajimer and J. Abbink (eds), *Meanings of Violence: A Cross-Cultural Perspective*, Berg Publishers, Oxford, New York, 2000, p. 24.

6   ibid.

6 *Caibre*: The Ship as Symbol

1   King, *Narrative*, vol. II, 25 December 1821, p. 126.

2   King's vocabulary list was collected during his December 1821 and January 1822 visits and published in vol. II, pp. 144–7.

3   Hordern, *King*, p. 83.

4   ibid.

5   G. Dening, 'Sharks that Walk on the Land', *Meanjin*, issue 41, no. 4, December 1982, pp. 427–37; and M. Sahlins, *Historical Metaphors and Mythical Realities: Structure in the Early History of the Sandwich Islands Kingdom*, University of Michigan Press, Ann Arbor, 1981.

6　G. Moore, 'Descriptive Vocabulary', in *Diary of Ten Years*, pp. 78–9.

7　Wilson, *Narrative of a Voyage Around the World*, p. 323.

8　ibid., p. 236; There are several comments in Barker's journal about the sealers arriving in 'boats, not ships', *Journal*, 25 January 1830.

9　Barker, *Journal*, 13 February 1830.

10　ibid., 13 August 1830. Barker told some of the King Ya-nup the direction to the boat so that they could cross Oyster Harbour on their own to go to the good wallaby ground called *Coranup*.

11　ibid., 5 August 1830.

12　ibid., 14 August 1830.

13　ibid., 3 September 1830.

14　ibid., 6 September 1830.

15　*Hobart Town Courier*, 7/9/1832 and reprinted in *Perth Gazette* 12/1/1833.

16　ibid., also found in I. Berryman, *Swan River Letters*, WA, Swan River Press, Glengarry, 2000, p. 267. 'Waddy' is the term for spear thrower on the east coast.

17　Barker, *Journal*, 20 December 1830.

7　Travelling Knowledge: 'Manyat's Sole Delight'

1　Collie, 'Anecdotes and Remarks', 12 July 1834, p. 319.

2　In 1831 Alexander Collie recorded the name of the Stirling Ranges as *Koi-kyeun-u-ruff*, as told to him by Mokaré. In 1828, Wakefield, commandant at King George's Sound wrote down *Porrengorup*. Nind recorded the ranges as *Borringorrup* and *Cojernurruf* and Barker referred to them as *Porongorrup* and *Cojineruf* throughout his journal. Here I use Collie's recording.

3　Sleeman, 'Letter from Sleeman to Colonial Secretary Macleay, King George's Sound 25 March 1829', *HRA*, series III, vol. VI, p. 525.

4　Sleeman, 'List of Seeds sent by the Lucy Ann, 1829', Enclosure no. 17 , in *HRA*, series III, vol. VI, p. 536.

5　The first box contained soil from around the settlement, the second box was collected on the banks of French's River and Oyster Harbour, the third box was from the Porongurup Range and the fourth was from 'Mt Woolurope, N of the Settlem't and about 8 miles distant', this was *Woollyongup*. 'Letter from Captain Wakefield to Colonial Secretary Macleay, King George's Sound, 14 June, 1828', *HRA*, series III, vol. VI, p. 518.

6　M. L. Pratt, *Imperial Eyes: Travel Writing and Transculturation*, Routledge, London, New York, 1992, p. 15.

7　ibid., p. 24.

8　D. Malouf, *Spirit of Play, The Making of Australian Consciousness*, Boyer Lectures, ABC books for Australian Broadcasting Commission, Sydney, 1988, p. 10.

9　D. Bates, *Native Tribes of Western Australia*, I. White (ed.), National Library of Australia, Canberra, 1985, p. 22; Crawford, *Contested Country*, p. 12; Barker, *Journal*, 22 November 1830.

10　Barker, *Journal*, 10, 11, 12 September and 22 November 1830.

11　ibid., 1 January 1831.

12　ibid.

13　Barker, 26 June 1830.

14　ibid., 7 June 1830.

15　ibid.

16　ibid., 18 April 1830.

17　ibid., 7 June 1830.

18　ibid., 8 June 1830.

19   ibid., 12 August 1830.

20   ibid., 30 January 1830.

21   ibid., 11 May 1830.

22   ibid., 1 March 1830.

23   R. Dale, 'Robert Dale's excursion from King George's Sound to Koi-kyeun-u-ruff Ranges, January 1832', Shoobert (ed.), *Western Australian Explorations*, pp. 298–9.

24   ibid.

25   Nind, 'Description of the Natives of King George's Sound', p. 35.

26   Dale, 'excursion' p. 301.

27   *Perth Gazette*, 24 September 1836, 12 November 1836, 18 February 1837, 25 March 1837; G. F. Moore, *Evidences of an Inland Sea: Collected from the Natives of the Swan River settlement*, William Curry, Dublin, 1837.

28   Hanson, 'Pamphlet', *Perth Gazette*, Saturday 12 January–26 January 1833 (original emphasis).

29   J. S. Roe, 'To the Northward and Westward of King George's Sound in December 1831 by J. S. Roe', Shoobert (ed.), *Western Australian Exploration*, p. 275.

30   Wilson, *Narrative of a voyage round the world*, pp. 236–7.

31   ibid., p. 237.

32   ibid., p. 240.

33   Wilson confused the Will's group for a person called 'Will'.

34   ibid., p. 242.

35   ibid. Sylvia Hallam discusses this encounter with the Wills man and the excursion more generally in her article, 'A View from the Other Side of the Western Australian Frontier', p. 138.

36   ibid.

37   ibid., pp. 252, 253–4.

38   ibid., p. 254.

39   ibid., p. 282.

40   Barker, *Journal*, 6 September 1830.

41   ibid., 7 September 1830.

42   ibid., 25 December 1830.

43   Allan Cunningham, quoted in Hordern, *King*, p. 388.

44   This method of carrying a lit banksia cone was commented on by de Sainson, during d'Urville's visit in October 1826. The lit banksia cone was used for warmth and for keeping a fire alight, in d'Urville, p. 30.

45   Collie created two records of this trip: one is a travel narrative, Collie, 'Account of an Explorative Excursion to the NW of King Georges Sound', and he also reflected on the trip, months afterwards in Collie, 'Anecdotes and Remarks', 16 August 1834, p. 340.

46   Collie, 'Account of an Exploration to the NW of King Georges Sound', p. 311.

47   ibid., pp. 307–8.

48   Collie, 'Anecdotes and Remarks', 16 August 1834, p. 340.

49   Collie, 'Letter to Governor James Stirling', p. 204.

50   ibid.

51   Collie, 'Account of an Exploration to the NW of King Georges Sound', p. 312.

52   Professor Stephen Hopper, Director, Kew Gardens, Kew, United Kingdom, personal communication, 23 November 2006.

53   Barker, *Journal*, 28 July 1830 and 15 August 1830.

54   Collie, 'Account of an Exploration to the NW of King Georges Sound', p. 312.

55   Chessel, G., Alexander Collie: Colonial Surgeon, Naturalist and Explorer, UWA Press, Crawley, WA, 208, p. 61.

56   Collie, 'Letter to N. A. Vigors, 26 January 1830', Secretary of the Zoological Society and editor of the Zoological Journal, published in Zoological Journal, vol. v, pp. 238–41.

57   Collie, 'Letter from Alexander Collie to his brother George Collie, Albany, King George's Sound, 28 July 1832', in *Letters with respect to the Early History of the Swan River*.

58   Collie, 'Anecdotes and Remarks', pp. 52–3.

59   Wilson, *Narrative of a voyage round the world*, pp. 265–6.

60   Collie, 'Anecdotes and Remarks', 16 August 1834, p. 340.

61   ibid.

62   P. Turnbull, 'Learning to Understand Western and Indigenous Sciences', in P. Turnbull (ed.), *Indigenous Knowledge*, Special Issue, *Humanities Research*, 1, 2000, p. 10.

63   ibid., p. 11.

64   Collie, 'Anecdotes and Remarks', 16 August 1834, p. 340.

65   Collie, 'Report to Governor James Stirling'.

66   J. Buzard, 'The Grand Tour and After', in P. Hulme and T. Youngs (eds), *The Cambridge Companion to Travel Writing*, Cambridge University Press, Cambridge, 2002, pp. 37–8.

67   ibid.

68   A. Salmond, 'Their Body is Different, Our Body is Different: European and Tahitian Navigators in the 18th Century', *History and Anthropology*, vol 16, no. 2, June 2005, pp. 167–86.

69   H. Reynolds, *With the White People*, Penguin, Ringwood, Vic., 1990.

70   B. Goodchild, Geographic Names Committee, Department of Land Information, Western Australia, personal communication, 25 November 2005.

8 Aboriginal Voyagers

1   F. C. Irwin, 'Irwin to Lord Viscount Goderich, 26 January 1833', *Report of Select Committee on Aborigines, (British Settlements), Australian Colonies, with the minutes of evidence*, Appendix no. 4, item no. 7, p. 132.

2   Appleyard, *The Beginning*, p. 157; Shoobert, (ed.), *Western Australian Exploration*, p. xvii.

3   J. Morgan, 'Letter from John Morgan to Colonial Secretary Hay, 28 January, and 3 February 1833', *Swan River Papers*, vol. 15, p. 52, SRO WA.

4   ibid.

5   I use the term 'colonist' here only when referring to those people who were part of the colonial authority of the Swan River settlement. Other European arrivals to Swan River will be referred to as 'migrants', which incorporates their more permanent status of living in the new colony compared to the temporary King George's Sound 'newcomers'.

6   The names and descriptions of these Aboriginal territories were written down by the colonists several years after European arrival and I re-use them here with scepticism due to the many discrepancies in the sources.

7   Armstrong, 'Manners and Habits', 29 October 1836, p. 790.

8   As I have mentioned before there were no chiefs in the Aboriginal groups of the south-west, but the colonists and newcomers often attempted to define particular individuals as leaders. These leaders were usually individual personalities who were making their presence known among the newcomers.

9   'Meeting of Executive Council of Western Australia, 4 October 1832, *Swan River Papers*, vol. 18, pp. 54–5.

10   R. M. Lyon, 'Letter from Robert Menli Lyon to Frederick Robinson, 1 January 1833', *Swan River Papers*, vol. 10, pp. 116–17.

11   Crawford, *Contested Country*, pp. 16–17.

12   Barker, *Journal*, 30 March 1830.

13   *Perth Gazette*, 19 January 1833, p. 10.

14   ibid.

15   ibid.

16   'John Henry Monger', P. Stratham, *Dictionary of Western Australians 1829–1914, vol. 1, Early Settlers 1829–1850*, University of Western Australia Press, Nedlands, WA, 1979, p. 86.

17   *Perth Gazette*, 19 January 1833, p. 15.

18   M. Douglas, *Implicit Meanings: Essays in Anthropology*, Routledge and Paul, London, 1975, p. 85.

19   Green, *Broken Spears*, p. 51.

20   Lyon, 'A Glance at the Manners', 20 April 1833, p. 63.

21   N. Green, 'Aborigines and White Settlers in the Nineteenth Century', in C. T. Stannage (ed.), *A New History of Western Australia*, University of Western Australia Press, Nedlands, WA, 1981, p. 81.

22   *Perth Gazette*, 19 January 1833, p. 10.

23   ibid.

24   Irwin, 'Irwin to Goderich, 26 January 1833', p. 132.

25   Lyon, 'A Glance at the Manners', 20 April 1833, p. 64.

26   Armstrong, 'Manners and Habits', 5 November 1836, p. 793.

27   Hallam, 'A View from the Other Side', pp. 135–7.

28   *Perth Gazette*, 19 January 1833, p. 10.

29   Irwin, 'Irwin to Goderich, 26 January 1833', p. 132.

30   *Perth Gazette*, 26 January 1833, p. 15.

31   ibid., 2 March 1833.

32   ibid., 26 January 1833.

33   *Perth Gazette*, 26 January 1833, p. 15.

34   G. F. Moore, *Extracts from the letters and journals of George Fletcher Moore: now filling a judicial office at the Swan River Settlement*, Doyle, Martin, (ed.), Orr and Smith, London, 1834, p. 224.

35   *Perth Gazette*, 26 January 1833, p. 15.

36   Hallam, 'A View from the Other Side', p. 136.

37   *Perth Gazette*, 9 February, 1833, p. 23.

38   G. Bolton and J. Gregory, *Claremont*, p. 5.

39   ibid.

40   G. Spiller, *Micro-breweries to Monopoly and Back: Swan River Colony Breweries 1829-2002*, Perth, Western Australian Museum, 2003, p. 13.

41   Lyon, 'A Glance at the Manners', 20 April 1833, p. 63.

42   W. de Vlamingh, *Voyage to the Great South Land, 1696-1697, by Willem de Vlamingh*, Gunter Schilder (ed.), C. De Heer (tr.), Royal Australian Historical Society, Sydney, 1985, p. 61.

43   H. S. G. Downey, *Mosman Park, Western Australia*, University of Western Australia Press, Nedlands, WA, 1971, pp. 9–11.

44   *Perth Gazette*, Lyon's letter was written on 4 March 1833, but the *Perth Gazette* published it on 9 March 1833.

45   Bolton and Gregory, *Claremont*, p. 7.

46   J. Backhouse, *A Narrative of a Visit to the Australian Colonies*, Hamilton, Adams, London, 1843, p. 549. This term for ship: *kibra*, is similar to the King Ya-nup name for it: *caibre*.

47   ibid.

48   Irwin, 'Letter from Francis Chidley Irwin to Peter Brown, Perth 22 January 1833', WA SRO, CSR 26/75.

49   Irwin, 'Irwin to Goderich, 26 January 1833', p. 132.

50   *Perth Gazette*, 9 February 1833, p. 23.

51   ibid.

52   Morgan, 'Letter from Morgan to Hay, 28 January 1833 &3 February 1833', p. 60.

53   P. Sutton, 'Aboriginal Maps and Plans', in D. Woodward and G. M. Lewis (eds), *The History of Cartography*, vol. 2, book 3, University of Chicago Press, Chicago, 1998, p. 409.

54   Morgan, 'Letter from Morgan to Hay, 28 January 1833 &3 February 1833', p. 60.

55   Moore, 25 January 1833, in J. M. R. Cameron, (ed.), *The Millendon Memoirs: George Fletcher Moore's Western Australian Diaries and Letters, 1830–1841*, Hesperian Press, Carlisle, WA, 2006, p. 197.

56   Moore, *Diary*, pp. 159–60.

57   ibid.

58   S. Hallam and L. Tilbrook, *Aborigines of the Southwest Region 1829–1840, the Bicentennial Dictionary of Western Australians*, vol. VIII, University of Western Australia Press, Nedlands, WA, pp. 387–8.

59   *Perth Gazette*, 16 February 1833, p. 27.

60   Moore, *Diary*, p. 162.

61   ibid.

62   *Perth Gazette*, 9 March 1833, p. 38.

63   Irwin, 'Irwin to Lord Viscount Goderich, 10 April 1833', *Report of the Select Committee on Aborigines* p. 134.

64   *Perth Gazette*, 9 March 1833, p. 38.

65   Moore, *Diary*, p. 162.

66   Moore, 25 February 1833, Cameron, *Millendon Memoirs*, p. 203.

67   ibid., p. 204.

68   ibid.

69   ibid.

70   *Perth Gazette*, 9 March 1833.

71   Moore, Diary, p. 166.

72   *Perth Gazette*, 9 March 1833.

73   ibid.

74   Irwin, 'Irwrin to Goderich, 10 April 1833', p. 134.

75   Bates, *Native Tribes of Western Australia*, p. 22; Crawford, *Contested Country*, p. 12; Barker, *Journal*, 22 November 1830.

76   Moore, *Diary*, p. 166.

77   ibid., pp. 166–7.

78   ibid.

79   Irwin, 'Irwin to Goderich, 10 April 1833', p. 134.

Reflection: Amphibians: Voyaging Across the Fringe

1   Browne, 'The Aborigines of Australia', p. 486.

2   *Perth Gazette*, 5 May 1838.

3   ibid.

4   *Perth Gazette*, 22 July 1837.

5   ibid., 12 May 1838.

6   ibid.

7   *Perth Gazette*, 15 July 1837, p. 937.

8   A. Salmond, *The Trial of the Cannibal Dog: Captain Cook in the South Seas*, Allen Lane for Penguin, London, 2003, pp. 75–6.

9   B. Douglas, 'The Lure of Texts and the Discipline of Praxis: Cross-Cultural History in a
Post Empirical World', in *Humanities Research*, vol. XIV, no. 1, 2007, p. 20, available at:
<www.epress.anu.edu.au/hrj/2007_01/pdf/cho2.pdf> accessed on 2 November 2007.

9 Peter Pindar's Razors

1   King, *Narrative*, vol. II, 31 December 1821, p. 137.

2   ibid., p. 138.

3   ibid.

4   P. Pindar, 'A Country Bumpkin and Razor-seller'; For the context of Pindar's poetry see:
J. Maylon, 'Peter Pindar and his world', in *Paragon Review*, issue 7, October 1998, available at:
<www.hull.ac.uk/oldlib/archives/paragon/1998/cpage.html> accessed 8/10/2007.

5   Cunningham, *Journal*, 27 December 1821.

6   Nind, 'Description of the Natives of King George's Sound', p. 26.

7   ibid.

8   Barker, *Journal*, 23 November 1830.

9   ibid., 1 October 1830.

10   Lockyer, 'Rough Copy', 17 March 1827.

11   ibid. Lockyer's 'Fair Copy' says 'Spears as Presents' and his 'Rough Copy' says 'Spears *and*
Presents'.

12   Lockyer, 'Rough Copy', 17 March 1827.

13   Barker, *Journal*, 29 October 1830. These birds are now referred to as '28's' because their call
resembles someone saying *twenty-eight*.

14   It is hard to know who Barker meant by the 'Colonel', perhaps he was referring to the
Colonial Secretary, or the Governor in Sydney?

15   ibid., 30 October 1830.

16   ibid., 25 November 1830.

17   ibid., 28 November 1830.

18   ibid., 5 December 1830.

19   ibid., 7 December 1830.

20   ibid., 12 December 1830.

21   Collie, 'Anecdotes and Remarks', 16 August 1834, p. 339.

22   J. Purkis, 'Letter from Purkis, 26 June 1832', *Morning Herald*, 13 December 1832, quoted in
Berryman, *Swan River Letters*, p. 259.

23   Ferguson, 'Mokaré's Domain', p. 122.

24   Ransonnet, 'Report to Captain Baudin'.

25   Lockyer, 'Fair Copy', p. 473.

26   Sleeman, 'Enclosure from 16 February', p. 543.

27   Collie, 'Anecdotes and Remarks', 26 July 1834, p. 328.

28   Barker, *Journal*, 13 February 1830.

29   Collie, 'Anecdotes and Remarks', 2 August 1834, p. 331.

30   ibid.

31   Wilson, *Narrative of a Voyage around the World*, p. 243.

32   Lockyer, 'Fair Copy', 13 January 1827.

10 A Delicate Friendship

1   Collie, 'Anecdotes and Remarks', 22 June, 1831.

2   ibid.

3   Collie, 'Letter to George, 4 August 1831', *Letters with Respect to the Early History of Swan
River*.

4   Collie, 'Anecdotes and Remarks', 26 July 1834, p. 327.

5   ibid.

6   ibid.

7   ibid.

8   Barker and Dr Davis were present at Taragon's death, but not his burial in March 1830. See Barker, *Journal*, 8 March 1830.

9   ibid., 4 November 1830.

10   ibid., 22 May 1830.

11   B. Smith, 'The 'History Wars' and Aboriginal Health', *Australian Book Review*, April 2005, no. 270, p. 16.

12   Armstrong, 'Manners and Habits', 5 November 1836, p. 793.

13   Lockyer, 'Rough Copy', 27 March 1827.

14   Nind, 'Description of the Natives of King George's Sound', p. 42.

15   B. Smith, 'Illness in Colonial Australia', Australian Academic Scholarly Publishing, forthcoming 2009, chapter 1, p. 5.

16   J. Campbell, *Invisible Invaders: Smallpox and Other Diseases in Aboriginal Australia 1780–1880*, Melbourne University Press, Melbourne, 2002, p. 2.

17   P. Taylor, *Treatment of Aborigines at King George's Sound and the Swan River*, Letter to Aborigines Protection Society, 1844, BL, PR11344.

18   Campbell, *Invisible Invaders*, p. xi.

19   ibid., p. 17.

20   I do not know what Collie meant by an open winter. In some parts of the northern hemisphere the term referred to a winter in which there had been no fog or frost and therefore, the ports had remained open. The theory was, I believe, that bacteria and viruses better survived the warmer conditions.

21   Collie, 'Letter to George, 9 November 1831'.

22   ibid.

23   Collie, 'Letter to Stirling, 24 January 1832'.

24   Barker, *Journal*, 27 April 1830.

25   ibid., 21 January 1830.

26   ibid., 20 April 1830.

27   ibid., 13 July 1830.

28   ibid., 28 September 1830.

29   ibid., 1 February 1830.

30   ibid., 21 August, 1830 and 1 September 1830.

31   ibid., 15 October 1830.

32   ibid., 16 October 1830.

33   Collie, 'Anecdotes and Remarks', 5 July 1834, p. 315.

34   ibid., 2 August 1834, p. 331.

35   P. Jalland, *Australian Ways of Death: A Social and Cultural History, 1840–1918*, Oxford University Press, Melbourne, New York, 2002, pp. 5 and 85.

36   Barker, *Journal*, 6 May 1830.

37   ibid.

38   ibid., 23 April 1830.

39   Wilson, *Narrative of a voyage round the world*, p. 274.

40   ibid., p. 275.

41   ibid.

42   Barker, *Journal*, 28 February 1830.

43   Collie, 'Anecdotes and Remarks', 2 August 1834, p. 332.

44   Wilson, *Narrative of a Voyage Around the World*, p. 259.

45   ibid.

46   Barker, *Journal*, 16 October 1830.

47   ibid., 22–23 October 1830.

48   ibid.

49   ibid., 26 October 1830.

50   ibid., 29 October 1830.

51   ibid., 19 December 1830.

52   ibid., 5 March 1830.

53   ibid., 6 March 1830.

54   ibid., throughout March 1830.

55   Nind, 'Description of the Natives of King George's Sound', p. 41.

56   Barker, *Journal*, 22 January 1830.

57   ibid., 7 November 1830.

58   Moore, 'Descriptive Vocabulary', p. 46, in *Diary of Ten Years*.

59   Nind, 'Description of the Natives of King George's Sound', p. 42.

60   Barker, *Journal*, 11 July 1830.

61   ibid., 15 July 1830.

62   ibid., 24–27 August 1830.

63   ibid., 27 August 1830.

64   Collie, 'Anecdotes and Remarks', 2 August 1834, p. 331.

65   ibid.

66   Collie, 'Letter to Stirling, 24 January 1832'.

67   Collie, 'Anecdotes and Remarks', 2 August 1834, p. 331.

68   R. Dale, *Descriptive Account of the Panoramic View of King George's Sound, and the Adjacent Country*, Cross and R. Havell, London, 1834, p. 7.

Epilogue

1   Mulvaney and Green, *Commandant of Solitude*, p. 3. Barkers' journals were edited and published in 1992.

2   Governor's Despatches NSW, ML A1267, part 4, no. 1, 4 March 1831.

3   ibid., p. 26.

4   C. Sturt, *Two Expeditions into the Interior of Southern Australia*, vol. II, Doublebay Australia, Lane Cove, NSW, 1982 (1833), p. 240.

5   Nind, 'Description of the Natives of King George's Sound', p. 44; Collie, 'Anecdotes and Remarks', 9 August 1834, p. 336; Flinders, *Voyage to Terra Australis*, January 1802, p. 67; King, *Narrative*, vol. II, 27–28 December 1821, p. 132.

6   Sturt, *Two Expeditions into the Interior*, p. 241.

7   Mulvaney and Green, *Commandant of Solitude*, p. 26; R. M. Davis, 'Letter form Davis to Colonial Secretary, 19 May 1831', in 'Memorial to Captain Collet Barker, at Mount Barker', in *Proceedings of the Royal Geographical Society of Australasia: South Australian Branch*, session 1902–1903, vol. VI, p. 25.

8   Sturt, *Two Expeditions into the Interior*, p. 240.

9   J. Browne, 'Statement Respecting Natives by James Browne for the Aborigines Protection Society', 26 June 1839, ML (AK34), p. 4.

10   Collie, 'Letter to Stirling, 24 Jan 1832'.

11   Browne, 'Statement Respecting Natives', p. 5.

12   R. Sholl, 'Letter from Richard Sholl to George Collie, 25 June 1836', *Alexander Collie Papers 1835–1861*, BL, ACC 393A.

13   Sholl, 'Letter from Richard Sholl to George Collie, 13 June 1836 and 25 June 1836, *Alexander Collie Papers 1835–1861*, BL, ACC 393A.

14   See Jalland, *Australian Ways of Death*.

15   Chessel, *Alexander Collie*, p. 188.

16   J. S. Roe, 'Letter from John Septimus Roe to George and James Collie, 7 October 1840', *Alexander Collie Papers 1835–1861*, BL, ACC 393A; *Western Australian Government Gazette*, Saturday 15 February 1840, p. 4.

17   B. Howard, 'Mokaré had vital role in colony's success', *Albany Advertiser*, Thursday 31 August 1995, p. 19.

18   'Racist motive feared in statue damage', *Albany Advertiser*, 10 June 1997, p. 3.

19   P. Taylor, 'Statue vandalism – local morons at work', *Albany Advertiser*, 17 June 1997, p. 2.

20   C. Fforde, 'Yagan', in Cressida Fforde, J. Hubert and P. Turnbull (eds), *The Dead and Their Possessions: Repatriation in Principle, Policy and Practice*, Routledge, London and New York, 2002, pp. 231–3.

21   Barker, *Journal*, 24 December 1830.

Bibliography

Abbreviations

NLA – National Library of Australia.

HRA – Historical Records of Australia.

BL – Battye Library.

CSO – Colonial Secretary Office Records.

AO NSW – Archives Office of New South Wales.

SRO WA – State Records Office of Western Australia.

ML – Mitchell Library, Sydney.

Contemporary Works

Armstrong, F., 'Manners and Habits of the Aborigines of Western Australia, from information collected by Mr. F. Armstrong, Interpreter', *Perth Gazette*, 29 October – 12 November 1836, pp. 789–7.

Backhouse, J., *Narrative of a Visit to the Australian Colonies*, Hamilton, Adams, London, 1843.

Barker, Captain C. *Journal at King George's Sound*, 18 January 1830 – 26 March 1831, microfilm copy at BL (ACC 2545A). Original journal missing from AO NSW (AO9/2748).

Bell, H. 'Anatomical Measurements by Hugh Bell', in Flinders, M., *Voyage to Terra Australis: Undertaken for the purpose of completing the discovery of that vast country and prosecuted in the years 1801, 1802 and 1803, in His Majesty's ship Investigator and subsequently in the armed vessel Porpoise and Cumberland schooner: with an account of the shipwreck of the Porpoise, arrival of the Cumberland at Mauritius, and imprisonment of the Commander during six years and a half in that island*, Facsimile edition, Libraries Board of South Australia, Adelaide, 1966 (1814).

Bates, D., *Native Tribes of Western Australia*, White, I. (ed.), National Library of Australia, Canberra, 1985.

Brown, R., 'Character and Description of KINGIA, a New Genus of Plants found on the South-West Coast of New Holland: with observations on the structure of its Unimpregnated Ovulum; and on the Female Flower of Cycadea and Conifera', Read before the Linnean society of London, 1 & 15 November 1825, in King, P. P., *Narrative of a Survey of the Intertropical and Western Coasts of Australia. Performed between the Years 1818 and 1822 by Captain Phillip Parker King, RN*, Facsimile edition, Libraries Board of South Australia, Adelaide, 1969, pp. 534–5.

Browne, J., 'Statement Respecting Natives by James Browne for the Aborigines Protection Society', 26 June 1839, pp. 1–19, ML (AK34).

Browne, J., 'The Aborigines of Australia', Read before the Canadian Institute, 16 February 1856, *Nautical Magazine and Navy Chronicle*, 1856, pp. 485–93.

Chauncy, P., 'Notes and Anecdotes of the Aborigines of Australia', Appendix A in R. B. Smyth, *The Aborigines of Victoria: With notes relating to the habits of the Natives of other parts of Australia and Tasmania, compiled from various sources for the Government of Victoria*, vol. II, John Ferres, Government Printer, Melbourne, Vic, 1878, pp. 221–84.

Clark, W. N., 'Journal of a Second Expedition to the Westward of King George's Sound as far as Point d'Entrecasteux, in the months of April, May and June, in 1841', *Inquirer*, 2 March 1842.

Clint, R., 'Journal of an Excursion to the Mountain Range to the Northward and Eastward of Porrong-u-rup, 20 Dec 1831', by Raphael Clint, Assistant Surveyor, in Joanne Shoobert (ed.), *Western Australian Exploration: vol.1 1826-1835*, Hesperian Press, Carlisle, WA, 2005, pp. 292–6.

Collie, A., 'Account of Four Excursions in the vicinity of King George's Sound between 27 April and 15 June 1831, by Alexander Collie, surgeon', in Shoobert, J. (ed.), *Western Australian Exploration: vol. 1 1826–1835*, Hesperian Press, Carlisle, WA, 2005, pp. 242–52.

Collie, A., 'Account of an Explorative Excursion to the NW of King George's Sound, in 1832 by A. Collie Surgeon R.N.' in Joanne Shoobert (ed.), *Western Australian Exploration: vol. 1 1826-1835*, WA, Hesperian Press, Carlisle, WA, 2005, pp. 307–315.

Collie, A., 'Anecdotes and Remarks Relative to the Aborigines of King George's Sound', first published anonymously in *Perth Gazette and Western Australian Journal*, 5, 12, 26 July and 2, 9, 16 August 1834, pp. 315–40.

Collie, A., *Letters with Respect to the Early History of the Swan River Settlement 1828–1835, written by Dr Alexander Collie to his brother George*. BL microfilm (ACC 332A).

Collie, A., 'Letter to Stirling, Albany King George's Sound, Western Australia, July 31, 1832', in Cross, J., *Journals of Several Expeditions made in Western Australia, during the years 1829, 1830, 1831, and 1832*, London, J. Cross, 1833, pp. 204–5.

Collie, A., 'Report to Governor James Stirling, 1831', my copy in *Swan River Papers*, vol. 9, pp. 110–21, SRO WA.

Collie, A., 'The Meteorological Journal, by A. Collie Esq., from April 1831 to April 1832', in Cross, J., *Journals of Several Explorations made in Western Australia, during the years 1829, 1830, 1831, and 1832*, J.Cross, London, 1833, pp. 239–62.

Cunningham, A., 'Appendix to the Account of the Voyages of Captain King', in King, P. P., *Narrative of a Survey of the Intertropical and Western Coasts of Australia. Performed between the Years 1818 and 1822 by Captain Phillip Parker King, RN, in two volumes*, Facsimile edition, Adelaide, Libraries Board of South Australia, 1969 (1827).

Cunningham, Allan, *Journal of the brig Bathurst 1821–1822*, CSO papers 1788–1825 NLA, AO Reel no. 6034, SZ8, pp. 1–248.

Dale, R., *Descriptive Account of the Panoramic View of King George's Sound, and the Adjacent Country*, J. Cross and R. Havell, London, 1834.

Dale, R., 'Robert Dale's Excursion from King George's Sound to Koi-kyeun-u-ruff Ranges, January 1832', in Shoobert, Joanne (ed.), *Western Australian Exploration: vol. 1 1826–1835*, Hesperian Press, Carlisle, WA, 2005, pp. 298–301.

Darling, R., 'Darling to Major Lockyer, 4 November 1826', *HRA* series I, vol. XII, p. 701.

Darling, R., 'Darling to Lord Viscount Goderich', 24 December 1827, Despatch No. 131, *HRA*, series I, vol. XIII, p. 667.

Darling, R., 'Secret Instructions by Governor Darling to Major Lockyer, 4 November 1826', *HRA*, series I, vol. XII, p. 701.

Davis, R. M., 'Letter to Colonial Secretary, 19 May 1831', in 'Memorial to Captain Collet Barker, at

Mount Barker', *Proceedings of the Royal Geographical Society of Australasia: South Australian Branch*, vol. VI, session 1902–1903, pp. 19–29.

de Vlamingh, W., *Voyage to the Great South Land, 1696–1697, by Willem de Vlamingh*, Gunter Schilder (ed.), C. De Heer (tr.), Royal Australian Historical Society, Sydney, 1985.

d'Urville, J. S.C. D., *An Account in Two Volumes of Two Voyages to the South Seas by Captain (later Rear-Admiral) Jules S.C. Dumont d'Urville, of the French Navy to Australia, New Zealand, Oceania 1826–1829, in the Corvette l'Astrolabe and to the Straits of Magellan, Chile, Oceania, South East Asia, Australia, Antarctica, New Zealand and Torres Strait 1837–1840 in the Corvettes l'Astrolabe and Zelee*, Helen Rosenman (tr. and ed.), Melbourne University Press, Carlton, Vic, 1987.

Flinders, M., *Voyage to Terra Australis: Undertaken for the purpose of completing the discovery of that vast country and prosecuted in the years 1801, 1802 and 1803, in His Majesty's ship Investigator and subsequently in the armed vessel Porpoise and Cumberland schooner: with an account of the shipwreck of the Porpoise, arrival of the Cumberland at Mauritius, and imprisonment of the Commander during six years and a half in that island*, Facsimile edition, Libraries Board of South Australia, Adelaide, 1966 (1814).

Grey, G., *Journals of Two expeditions of discovery in north-west and western Australia, during the years 1837, 38, and 39 … with observations on the moral and physical condition of the aboriginal inhabitants, &c. &c.*, vol. II, Facsimile edition, Libraries Board of South Australia, Adelaide, 1964 (1841).

Hanson, 'Colonel Hanson's Pamphlet', *Perth Gazette*, 12 January–26 January 1833.

Henty, S., 'Exploration to the North of King River by Stephen George Henty', December 1831, in Shoobert, J. (ed.), *Western Australian Exploration: vol.1 1826–1835*, Hesperian Press, Carlisle, WA, 2005, pp. 290–2.

Hoop, 'Letter from Serjeant Hoop to Lieutenant Sleeman, King George's Sound, 5 May 1829', Enclosure No. 14, *HRA*, series III, vol. VI, p. 535.

Historical Records of Australia, series III, vol. VI, 'Official Papers Relating to the Settlement of King George's Sound, West Australia, 1826–1829', pp. 453–548.

Huskisson, 'Right Honourable R.W. Huskisson to Governor Darling, 30 January 1828', Despatch No. 9, *HRA* series I, vol. XIII, pp. 741–2.

Irwin, F. C., 'Irwin to Peter Brown, 22 January 1833', CSR 26/75, SRO WA.

Irwin, F. C., 'Irwin to Lord Viscount Goderich, 26 January 1833', *Report of Select Committee on Aborigines, (British Settlements), Australian Colonies, with the minutes of evidence*, Appendix No. 4, item No. 7, p. 132.

Irwin, Francis Chidley, 'Irwin to Lord Viscount Goderich, 10 April 1833', *Report of Select Committee on Aborigines, (British Settlements), Australian Colonies, with the minutes of evidence*, Appendix No. 8, pp. 134–5.

Kent, J., 'An Account of a West Australian Expedition from King George Sound in December 1829, by John Kent of Berkshire', in Shoobert J. (ed.), *Western Australian Exploration: Vol. 1 1826–1835*, Hesperian Press, Carlisle, WA, 2005, pp. 122–5.

King, P. P., *Narrative of a Survey of the Intertropical and Western Coasts of Australia. Performed between the Years 1818 and 1822 by Captain Phillip Parker King, RN, in two volumes*, Facsimile edition, Libraries Board of South Australia, Adelaide, 1969 (1827).

Lockyer, E., *Journal of Major Lockyer*, 8 November 1826-2 April 1827, 'Fair copy', in *HRA* vol. III, series VI, pp. 460–87, original held at AO NSW, 'CSO relating to King George's Sound', (4/2092).

Lockyer, E., *Journal of Major Edmund Lockyer, Commandant of the Expedition sent from Sydney in 1826 to found a settlement at King George's Sound, Western Australia*, 'Rough copy', BL typescript 919.412/ALB, original in Mitchell Library (A 1498).

Lockyer, E., 'Journal of an Excursion up the River Brisbane in the year 1825', Russel, S. H., *The Genesis of Queensland: An Account of the First Exploring*, Turner and Henderson, Sydney, 1888, pp. 589–601.

Lockyer, E., 'Report by Major Lockyer on the Newly-formed Settlement at King George's Sound' in *HRA*, series III, vol. VI, pp. 501–6.

Lyon, R. M., 'A Glance at the Manners and Language of the Aboriginal Inhabitants of Western Australia; with a short vocabulary, 23 March 1833', *Perth Gazette*, 30 March–20 April 1833, pp. 51–64.

Lyon, R. M., 'Letter from Lyon to Frederick Robinson, 1 January 1833', *Swan River Papers*, vol. 10, pp. 110–33, SRO WA.

Macleay, A., 'Letter from Colonial Secretary Macleay to Edmund Lockyer', letter marked No. 1, 4 November 1826, *HRA*, series III, vol. VI, p. 454.

'Meeting of Executive Council, Western Australia', *Swan River Papers*, vol. 18, pp. 54 and 73, SRO WA.

Moore, G. F., *Extracts From the Letters and Journals of George Fletcher Moore: now filling a judicial office at the Swan River Settlement*, Martin Doyle (ed.), Orr and Smith, London, 1834.

Moore, G. F., *Evidences of an Inland Sea: Collected from the Natives of the Swan River Settlement*, William Curry, Dublin, 1837.

Moore, G. F., *Diary of Ten Years Eventful Life of an Early Settler in Western Australia; and also a Descriptive Vocabulary of the Language of the Aborigines*, M. Walbrook, London, 1884.

Morgan, John, 'Letter from John Morgan to Colonial Secretary Hay, 28 January and 3 February 1833', *Swan River Papers*, vol. 15, pp. 50–65, SRO WA.

Nind, I. S., 'Description of the natives of King George's Sound (Swan River Colony) and adjoining country', written by Isaac Scott Nind and communicated by Robert Brown, *Royal Geographical Society*, vol. 1, 1831, 1832, London, pp. 21–51.

Nind, I. S., 'Letter from Assistant Surgeon Nind to Lieutenant Sleeman, 15 January 1829, King George's Sound', Enclosure No. 1, *HRA*, series III, vol. VI, p. 528.

Péron, F., *Voyage of Discovery to the Southern Lands, Second ed., 1824, Book 1–3, comprising chapters I–XXI, by F. Péron, continued by Louis de Freycinet*, Christine Cornell (tr. and ed.), Friends of the State Library of South Australia, Adelaide, 2006.

Purkis, J., 'Letter from James Purkis', 26 June 1832, *Morning Herald*, 13 December 1832, quoted in Berryman, I. (ed.), *Swan River Letters*, Swan River Press, Glengarry, WA, 2002.

Ransonnet, J. J., 'Report written on board the Geographe in 1803 to Captain Baudin from midshipman Ransonnet about Ransonnet's exploration of the King George Sound area, Mt Gardner and Bald Island and his meeting with Aborigines', typescript of translation by P. Bevan, 1975, BL (PR10532).

Roe, J. S., 'Letter from John Septimus Roe to George and James Collie, 7 October 1840', *Alexander Collie Papers 1835–1861*, BL (ACC 393A).

Roe, J. S., 'To the Northward and Westward of King George's Sound in December 1831 by J.S. Roe', in Shoobert, J. (ed.), *Western Australian Exploration: Vol. 1 1826–1835*, Hesperian Press, Carlisle, WA, 2005, pp. 274–89.

Sholl, R., 'Letter from Richard Sholl to George Collie, 13 and 25 June 1836', *Alexander Collie Papers 1835-1861*, BL (ACC393A).

Sleeman, Enclosure from 16 February 1829 in 'Letter from Lieutenant Sleeman to Colonial Secretary Macleay', 7 September 1829, *HRA*, series III, vol. VI, p. 543.

Sleeman, 'Letter from Sleeman to Colonial Secretary Macleay, King George's Sound, 25 March 1829', *HRA*, series III, vol. VI, pp. 525–8.

Sleeman, 'Letter from Sleeman to Macleay, King George's Sound, 7 October 1829', *HRA*, series III, vol. VI, pp. 543–44.

Sleeman, 'List of Seeds sent by Lucy Ann, 1829', Enclosure No. 17, *HRA*, series III, vol. VI, p. 536.

Stirling, Governor J., 'Proclamation by Lieutenant-Governor Stirling of His Majesty's Settlement in Western Australia thus effecting the settlement of the colony, 18 June 1829', SRO WA (WAS1243, CONS 620/1).

Sturt, C., *Two Expeditions into the Interior of Southern Australia*, vol. II, Lane Cove, NSW, 1982 (1833).

Taylor, P., 'Treatment of Aborigines at King George's Sound and the Swan River', Letter to Aborigines Protection Society, 1844, BL (PR11344).

Vancouver, Captain G., *A Voyage of Discovery to the North Pacific Ocean and Round the World 1791–1795*, vol. I., W. Kaye Lamb (ed.), Hakluyt Society, London, 1984 (1798).

Wakefield, Captain J., 'Letter from Wakefield to Colonial Secretary Macleay, King George's Sound, 21 May 1827', *HRA*, series III, vol. VI, pp. 506–9.

Wakefield, Captain J., 'Letter from Wakefield to Colonial Secretary Macleay, King George's Sound, 14 June 1828', *HRA*, series III, vol. VI, p. 518.

Wilson, T. B., *Narrative of a voyage round the world : comprehending an account of the wreck of the ship Governor Ready in Torres Straits, a description of the British settlements on the coasts of New Holland, more particularly Raffles Bay, Melville Island, Swan River, and King George's Sound : also, the manners and customs of the Aboriginal tribes : with an appendix containing remarks on transportation, the treatment of convicts during the voyage, and advice to persons intending to emigrate to the Australian colonies*, Facsimile edition, Dawson of Pall Mall, London, 1968 (1835).

Later Works

Appleyard, R. and Manford, T. (eds), *The Beginning: European Discovery and Early Settlement of Swan River Western Australia*, University of Western Australia Press, Nedlands, WA, 1979.

Austen, T., *A Cry in the Wind: Conflict in Western Australia 1829–1929*, Darlington Publishing Group, Darlington, WA, 1998.

Baker, R., 'Coming In? The Yanyuwa as a case study in the geography of contact history', *Aboriginal History*, vol. 14, 1990, pp. 25–60.

Beer, G., 'Travelling the Other Way', N. Jardine, J.A. Secord and E.C. Spary (eds), *Cultures of Natural History*, Cambridge University Press, Cambridge, 1996, pp. 322–37.

Berndt, R. and Berndt, C., *The World of the First Australians: Aboriginal Traditional Life: Past and Present*, Aboriginal Studies Press, Canberra, 1999.

Berndt, R. and C., *Aborigines of the South-West: Their Past and their Present*, University of Western Australia Press for the Education Committee of the 150th celebrations, Nedlands, WA, 1979.

Berryman, I. (ed.), *Swan River Letters*, Swan River Press, Glengarry, WA, 2002.

Blok, A., 'The Enigma of Senseless Violence', in Ajimer, G. and Jon A. (eds), *Meanings of Violence: A Cross-Cultural Perspective*, Berg Publishers, Oxford, New York, 2000, pp. 23–38.

Bolton, G. and Gregory, J., *Claremont: A History*, University of Western Australia Press, Nedlands, WA, 1999.

Brearley, A., *Ernest Hodgkin's Swanland: Estuaries and Coastal Lagoons of Southwestern Australia*, University of Western Australia Press, Crawley, WA, 2005.

Bruner, J., *Acts of Meaning: Four Lectures on Mind and Culture*, Jerusalem-Harvard Lectures, Harvard University Press, Cambridge, MA, 1990.

Bruner, J., 'Narrative Construction of Reality', *Critical Inquiry*, vol. 18, no. 1, Autumn 1991, pp. 1–21.

Buzard, J., 'The Grand Tour and After', in Hulme, P. and Young, T. (eds), *The Cambridge Companion to Travel Writing*, Cambridge University Press, Cambridge, 2002, pp. 37–52.

Cameron, J. M. R. (ed.), *The Millendon Memoirs: George Fletcher Moore's Western Australian Diaries and Letters, 1830–1841*, Hesperian Press, Carlisle, WA, 2006.

Campbell, J., *Invisible Invaders: Smallpox and Other Diseases in Aboriginal Australia 1780–1880*,

Melbourne University Press, Carlton, Vic, 2002.

Cashmere, J., 'The social uses of violence in ritual: Charivari or religious persecution?', *European History Quarterly*, 21, 1991, pp. 291–319.

Chessel, G., *Alexander Collie: Colonial Surgeon, Naturalist and Explorer*, University of Western Australia Press, Crawley, WA, 2008.

Clendinnen, I., 'Spearing the Governor', Kate Darian-Smith (ed.), *Challenging Histories: Reflections on Australian History*, Special Issue, *Australian Historical Studies*, 2002, pp. 157–74.

Clendinnen, I., *Dancing With Strangers*, Melbourne, Text Publishing, 2003.

Clendinnen, I., 'Response to Correspondence' in Davidson, Robyn, 'No Fixed Address: Nomads and the Fate of the Planet', *Quarterly Essay*, issue 24, 2006, pp. 77–88.

Crawford, I. and Crawford, P., *Contested Country: A History of the Northcliffe Area, Western Australia*, University of Western Australia Press, Nedlands, WA, 2003.

Darnton, R., *The Great Cat Massacre and Other Episodes in French Cultural History*, Basic Books, New York, 1984.

Dening, G., 'Sharks that Walk on the Land', *Meanjin*, issue 41, no. 4, December 1982, pp. 427–37.

Dening, G., *Readings/Writings*, Melbourne University Press, Carlton, Vic., 1998.

Dickson, R. (ed.), *To King George the Third Sound for Whales: A Voyage Aboard the British Whaling Vessel Kingston of London, Captain Thomas Dennis, 1800–1802*, transcribed from the original ship's log by Rod Dickson, Hesperian Press, Carlisle, WA, 2006.

Dortch, C. E., *Devil's Lair: A Search for Ancient Man in Western Australia*, Western Australian Museum, Perth, 1976.

Dortch, C. E., Kendrick, G. W. and Morse, K., 'Aboriginal Mollusc Exploitation in south-western Australia', *Archaeology in Oceania*, 19, no. 3, October 1984, pp. 81–104.

Douglas, B., 'Doing Ethnographic History: The Case of Fighting in New Caledonia', in James G. Carrier (ed.), *History and Tradition in Melanesian Anthropology*, University of California Press, Berkeley, 1992, pp. 86–115.

Douglas, B., *Across the Great Divide: Journeys in History and Anthropology*, Harwood Academic Publishers, Amsterdam, Netherlands, 1998.

Douglas, B., 'Encountering Agency: Islanders, European Voyagers, and the Production of Race in Oceania', in Hermann, E. (ed.), *Changing Contexts – Shifting Meanings: Transformations of Cultural Traditions in Oceania*, forthcoming 2009.

Douglas, M., *Implicit Meanings: Essays in Anthropology*, Routledge and Paul, London, Boston, 1975.

Downey, H. S. G., *Mosman Park, Western Australia*, University of Western Australia Press, Nedlands, WA, 1971.

Eades, D., 'They don't speak an Aboriginal language, or do they', in Keen, I. (ed.), *Being Black: Aboriginal Cultures in Settled Australia*, Aboriginal Studies Press, Canberra, 1988, pp. 97–117.

Elkin, A. P., *Aboriginal Men of High Degree*, 2nd edn., University of Queensland Press, St Lucia, QLD, 1977.

Fels, M., *Good Men and True: The Aboriginal Police of the Port Phillip District, 1837–1853*, Melbourne University Press, Carlton, Vic, 1988.

Ferguson, W. C., 'Mokaré's Domain', Mulvaney, D. J. and White, P. J. (eds), *Australians to 1788*, Fairfax, Syme and Weldon, Broadway, NSW, 1987, pp. 121–45.

Fforde, C., 'Yagan', in Cressida Fforde, Hubert, J. and Turnbull, P. (eds), *The Dead and their Possessions: Repatriation in Principle, Policy and Practice*, Routledge, London, 2002, pp. 229–241.

Frost, A. and Aveling, M. (eds), *Australians to 1838*, Fairfax, Syme and Weldon, Broadway, NSW, 1987.

Garden, D. S., *Albany: A Panorama of the Sound from 1827*, Thomas Nelson, West Melbourne, Vic., 1977.

Geertz, C., *The Interpretation of Cultures: A Selection of Essays*, Basic Books, New York, 1973.

Geertz, C., 'On the Nature of Anthropological Understanding', *American Scientist*, vol. 63, no. 1, January – February 1975, pp. 47–53.

Gibson, R., 'Ocean Settlement', *Meanjin*, 53 (4), 1994, pp. 665–78.

Green, N., 'Aborigines and White Settlers in the Nineteenth Century', in Stannage C. T., *A New History of Western Australia*, University of Western Australia Press, Nedlands, WA, 1981, pp. 72–123.

Green, N., 'King George Sound: The Friendly Frontier', in Smith, M. (ed.), *Archaeology in ANZAAS 1983*, Western Australian Museum, Perth, WA, 1983, pp. 68–74.

Green, N., *Broken Spears: Aborigines and Europeans in the Southwest of Western Australia*, Focus Education Series, Perth, 1984.

Green, N. (ed.), *Nyungar: The People: Aboriginal Customs in the Southwest of Australia*, Creative Research in association with Mt Lawley college, Perth, 1979.

Green, N. (ed.), *Aborigines of the Albany Region 1821–1898, The Bicentennial Dictionary of Western Australians*, vol. VI, University of Western Australia Press, Nedlands, WA, 1989.

Hallam, S. *Fire and Hearth: A Study of Aboriginal Usage and European Usurpation in South-Western Western Australia*, Australian Institute of Aboriginal Studies, Canberra, 1975.

Hallam, S. 'Population and Resource Usage on the Western Littoral', in *Archaeology in ANZAAS 1977*, vol. 2, pp. 16–22.

Hallam, S., 'Coastal Does Not Equal Littoral', *Australian Archaeology*, No. 25, December 1987, pp. 10–29.

Hallam, S. and Tilbrook, L. (eds), *Aborigines of the Southwest Region 1829–1840, The Bicentennial Dictionary of Western Australians*, vol. VIII, University of Western Australia Press, Nedlands, WA, 1990.

Hallam, S. J., 'A View from the Other Side of the Western Australian Frontier: Or "I met a man who wasn't there".' *Aboriginal History*, vol. 7, 1983, pp. 134–56.

Harris, J., 'North Australian Kriol and the Kriol "Holi Baibul"', in Swain, T. and Rose, D. (eds), *Aboriginal Australians and Christian Missions*, The Australian Association for the Study of Religions, 1988, Bedford Park, SA, pp. 412–21.

Hordern, M., *King of the Australian Coast: The Voyages of Phillip Parker King in the Mermaid and Bathurst*, Melbourne University Press, Carlton, Vic., 1997.

Howard, M. C., in Berndt, R. M., and Berndt, C. H. (eds), *Aborigines of the West: Their Past and their Present*, University of Western Australia Press, Nedlands, WA, 1979, pp. 90–99.

Isaac, R., *The Transformation of Virginia, 1740–1790*, University of North Carolina Press, Chapel Hill, Williamsburg, 1982.

Jalland, P., *Australian Ways of Death: A Social and Cultural History, 1840–1918*, Oxford University Press, Melbourne, New York, 2002.

Johnson, L., *Major Edmund Lockyer: Forgotten Australian Pioneer*, Western Australian Museum, Albany, WA, 2002.

Lippard, L. R., *The Lure of the Local: Senses of Place in a Multicultural Society*, New Press, New York, 1997.

Malouf, D., *Spirit of Play: The Making of Australian Consciousness*, Boyer Lectures, ABC Books for the Australian Broadcasting Commission, Sydney, 1988.

McGrath, A., *Born in the Cattle: Aborigines in Cattle Country*, Allen and Unwin, Sydney, 1987.

Merwick, D., *Death of a Notary: Conquest and Change in Colonial New York*, Cornell University Press, Ithica, New York, 1999.

Merwick, D., *The Shame and the Sorrow: Dutch-Amerindian Encounters in New Netherland*, University of Pennsylvania Press, Philadelphia, 2006.

Metcalfe, R., 'Who Should Rule at Home?', *Journal of American History*, vol. 61, no. 3, December 1974, pp. 651–65.

Mulvaney, D. J., *Encounters in Place: Outsiders and Australians 1606–1985*, University of Queensland

Press, St Lucia, QLD, 1989.

Mulvaney, D. J. and Green, N. (eds), *Commandant of Solitude: The Journals of Captain Collet Barker 1828–1831*, Melbourne University Press, Carlton, Vic., 1992.

Nance, B., 'The Level of Violence: Europeans and Aborigines in Port Phillip, *Australian Historical Studies*, vol. 19, no. 77, October 1981, pp. 532–52.

Nugent, M., *Botany Bay: Where Histories Meet*, Allen and Unwin, Crows Nest, NSW, 2005.

Pratt, M. L., *Imperial Eyes: Travel Writing and Transculturation*, London, New York, Routledge, 1992.

Ricouer, P. , *Memory, History, Forgetting*, University of Chicago Press, Chicago, London, 2004.

Reynolds, H., *With the White People*, Penguin, Ringwood, Vic., 1990.

Ryan, Lyndall, *The Aboriginal Tasmanians*, University of Queensland Press, St Lucia, QLD, 1981.

Sahlins, M., *Historical Metaphors and Mythical Realities: Structure in the Early History of the Sandwich Islands Kingdom*, University of Michigan Press, Ann Arbor, 1981.

Salmond, A., *The Trial of the Cannibal Dog: Captain Cook in the South Seas*, Allen Lane for Penguin, London, 2003.

Salmond, A., 'Their Body is Different, Our Body is Different: European and Tahitian Navigators in the Eighteenth Century', *History and Anthropology*, vol. 16, no. 2, June 2005, pp. 167–86.

Sapir, E., 'The Emergence of the Concept of Personality in a Study of Cultures, *Journal of Social Psychology*, no. 5, 1934, pp. 408–15.

Scott, K., *Kayang and Me*, Scott, K. and Brown, H, Fremantle Arts Centre Press, Fremantle, WA, 2005.

Sharp, N., *Saltwater People: The Waves of Memory*, Allen and Unwin, Crows Nest, NSW, 2002.

Smith, B., 'The "History Wars" and Aboriginal Health', *Australian Book Review*, April 2005, no. 270, pp. 16–18.

Smith, B., 'Illness in Colonial Australia', Australian Academic Scholarly Publishing, forthcoming 2009.

Spiller, G., *Micro-breweries to Monopoly and Back: Swan River Colony Breweries 1829–2002*, Western Australian Museum, Perth, 2003.

Stanner, W. E. H., 'Aboriginal Territorial Organisation: Estate, Range, Domain and Regime', *Oceania*, 36, no. 1, September 1965, pp. 1–26.

Stratham, P. (ed.), *Dictionary of Western Australians, 1829–1914*, vol. I, *Early Settlers 1829–1850*, University of Western Australia Press, Nedlands, WA, 1979.

Sweetman, J., *The Military Establishment and Penal Settlement at King George Sound*, Australian Studies Booklet no. 1, Hesperian Press, Carlisle, WA, 1989.

Sutton, P., 'Aboriginal Maps and Plans', in Woodward, D. and Malcolm, G. L. (eds), *The History of Cartography*, vol. II, book III, University of Chicago Press, Chicago, 1998, pp. 387–413.

Thompson, E.P. , 'The Moral Economy of the English Working Class', *Past and Present*, no. 50, February 1971, pp. 76–136.

Turnbull, P., 'Learning to Understand Western and Indigenous Sciences', in Turnbull, P. (ed.), *Indigenous Knowledge*, Special Issue, *Humanities Research*, no. 1, 2000, pp. 7–20.

Turner, V., 'Social Dramas and Stories about them', in Mitchell, W. J. T., (ed.), *On Narrative*, University of Chicago Press, Chicago and London, 1980, pp. 137–64.

Von Brandenstein, C. G., *Nyungar Anew: Etymological, Text Samples and Etymological and Historical 1500-word Vocabulary of an Artificially Re-created Aboriginal Language in the South-West of Australia*, Pacific Linguistics, Australian National University Printing Service, Canberra, ACT, 1988.

Watson, D., *Caledonia Australis: Scottish Highlanders on the Frontier of Australia*, Collins, Sydney, 1984.

Wineburg, S., *Historical Thinking and Other Unnatural Acts: Charting the Future of Teaching the*

Past, Temple University Press, Philadelphia, 2001.

White, H., 'The Value of Narrativity in the Representation of Reality', in Mitchell, W. J. T. (ed.), *On Narrative*, University of Chicago Press, Chicago and London, 1981, pp. 1–23.

White, I. M., 'The Birth and Death of a Ceremony', in *Aboriginal History*, vol. 4, 1980, pp. 33–41.

Newspapers

Perth Gazette and Western Australian Journal, BL microfilm.

Sydney Gazette, 23 April 1829 and 13 June 1829.

Government Gazette, 11 February 1842.

Morning Herald, 13 December 1832.

Western Australian Government Gazette, 15 February 1840.

Howard, B., 'Mokare had vital role in Colony's success,' *Albany Advertiser*, Thursday 31 August 1995, p. 19.

'Racist Motive Feared in Statue Damage', *Albany Advertiser*, 10 June 1997, p. 3.

Taylor, Paige, 'Statue Vandalism – Local Morons at Work,' *Albany Advertiser*, 17 June 1997, p. 2.

Online Resources

Douglas, B., 'The Lure of Texts and the Discipline of Praxis: cross-cultural history in a post-empirical world', in *Humanities Research*, vol. XIV, no. 1, 2007, available at <www.epress.anu.edu.au/hrj/2007_01/pdf./ch02.pdf> accessed 25/07/08.

Maylon, Julie, 'Peter Pindar and his world', in *Paragon Review*, issue 7, October 1998, available at: <www.hull.ac.uk/oldlib/archives/paragon/1998/cpage.html> accessed 8/10/2007

Index

About the Author

Tiffany completed her PhD in history at the History Program, Australian National University in 2007. She is currently a lecturer in Indigenous and Australian colonial history at Deakin University in Melbourne. Tiffany publishes frequently in historical journals.

www.ingramcontent.com/pod-product-compliance
Lightning Source LLC
Chambersburg PA
CBHW060749240726
48664CB00009BA/1663